★ NEW EDITION ★

GRAMMAR
BRIDGE 3

그래머 브릿지

Grammar Bridge NEW EDITION ❸

지은이 넥서스영어교육연구소, 김경태
펴낸이 임상진
펴낸곳 (주)넥서스

출판신고 1992년 4월 3일 제311-2002-2호 35
10880 경기도 파주시 지목로 5
Tel (02)330-5500 Fax (02)330-5555

ISBN 979-11-6683-359-5 54740
　　　979-11-6683-360-1 54740 (SET)

www.nexusbook.com

NEW
EDITION

그래머 브릿지

GRAMMAR BRIDGE

넥서스영어교육연구소 · 김경태 지음

The bridge that takes
your English to the next level

Level

3

NEXUS Edu

Preface

영어하면 떠오르는 말이 무엇입니까?
시험, 성적, 내신일지도 모릅니다.

하지만, 영어 하면 떠오르는 말은 시험, 성적, 내신이 아니어야 합니다. 영어는 우리말과 같은 하나의 언어입니다. 영어는 어렵고 암기해야 할 것이 많은 학습의 대상이 아니라, 자연스럽게 습득하고 이해해야 하는 언어입니다. 영어과 교육과정의 학습 목표가 의사소통에 필요한 언어 형식의 학습인 것을 보아서도 알 수 있듯이 우리는 영어를 의사소통을 위한 도구로 활용할 수 있어야 합니다.

영어의 가장 기본이 되는 것은 단어입니다. 단어가 모여서 문장이 됩니다. 하지만, 단어를 아무렇게나 나열한다고 해서 문장이 되는 것은 아닙니다. 제대로 된 문장을 만들려면 문법을 알아야 합니다. 하지만, 문법을 무조건 암기하는 것은 효과적인 학습법이 아닙니다.

우리는 학교에서 국어를 배웁니다. 영어도 배웁니다. 국어와 영어는 학습적인 측면에서 차이가 없는 것처럼 보일지도 모르지만, 언어 사용적 측면에서는 현격한 차이가 납니다. 우리는 영어보다 국어를 훨씬 많이 사용합니다. 전문가들은 영어를 모국어처럼 사용하고자 한다면 약 4배 더 많이 사용하고 접해야 한다고 말합니다.

더욱 강화된 **GRAMMAR BRIDGE** NEW EDITION!
보너스 유형별 문제와 워크북을 추가하여
영문법 체화 학습의 길을 더욱더 견고히 다졌습니다.

우리가 국어를 많이 사용해서 자연스럽게 그 쓰임을 익히듯이, 영문법 또한 그 쓰임을 자연스럽게 익힐 수 있는 방법이 있다면 적극적으로 활용해야 할 것입니다. 학습자들이 영어를 어려운 외국어로 보지 않고, 자연스럽게 이해하고 체득할 수 있도록 도와드리고자 고민하였습니다. 가능한 한 간단하게 한 번에 한 가지씩 문법 요소를 설명하려 했습니다. 쉽고 간단한 문법 요소에서 시작해서 높은 수준의 문법 요소로 학습이 진행되는 계단식 학습 방식을 고려하였습니다.

기본보다 더 다양하고 많은 문제를 제공할 수 있도록 NEW EDITION 개정을 통해 실제 시험과 유사한 서술형 문제와 수능 대비형 문제를 수록하여 학습 자극을 유도하도록 했습니다. 또한 워크북을 새롭게 추가하여 철저하게 단원 학습을 마무리할 수 있도록 했습니다. 보다 더 강화되고 풍부해진 문제와 간단하고 이해하기 쉬운 설명, 단계적 연습 문제를 통해 영문법을 쉽고 체계적으로 익힐 수 있기를 기대합니다.

이 책의 구성과 특징

Grammar Point

학교 내신 시험에 꼭 나오는 문법 사항을 수록하였습니다. 여러 가지 문법 요소를 나열한 것이 아니라 한 번에 한 가지 문법 요소를 설명하여 이해가 쉽게 했습니다. 헷갈리기 쉬운 부분에 Tips를 달아 다시 한번 개념 정의를 돕도록 구성하였습니다.

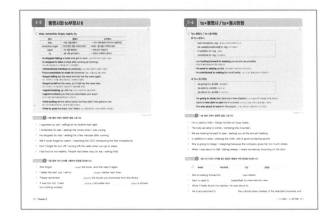

Exercise

문제를 푸는 동안 저절로 문법을 습득할 수 있도록 풍부한 연습문제를 수록하였습니다. 문법 개념을 이해하고 문제를 푸는 학습뿐만 아니라, 문제를 풀면서 스스로 문법 개념을 체계화할 수 있도록 구성하였습니다.

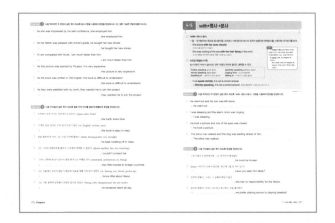

Review Test

실제 내신 기출 문제를 분석하여 수록하였습니다. 객관식, 단답식 유형뿐만 아니라, 점점 증가하는 서술형 문제에도 대비할 수 있도록 다양하고 많은 문제를 수록하였습니다.

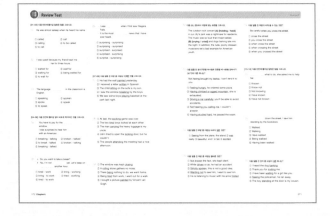

보너스 유형별 문제

각 Chapter를 완벽하게 마무리 지을 수 있도록 실제 시험과 같은 서술형 문제를 수록하여
내신을 대비할 수 있습니다. 또한 고난도의 수능 대비형 문제를 풀어보며 자신의 실력을
점검해 볼 수 있고 그에 따른 학습 동기 부여의 효과를 기대할 수 있습니다.

Workbook

Chapter별로 다양한 유형의 단답형/서술형 연습문제를
수록하여 학습한 내용을 종합적으로 점검할 수 있도록
Workbook을 새롭게 추가하였습니다.

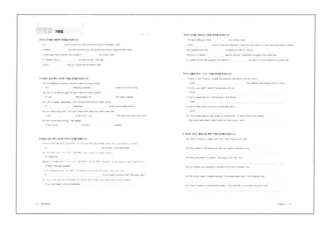

부가자료 무료 제공(www.nexusbook.com)

모바일 단어장
VOCA TEST

모바일 단어장
& VOCA TEST

어휘 리스트
& 어휘 테스트

문장 배열 영작

통문장 영작

기타 활용 자료

1 진단 평가
2 문법 용어 정리
3 불규칙 동사 변화표
4 형용사와 부사의 비교급 리스트

이 책의 차례

Chapter 1

시제

1-1 현재완료

현재완료(have[has]+p.p.)

과거에 일어난 일이 현재까지 영향을 미치거나 현재와 관련이 있을 때 사용한다.

❶ **경험** : 과거에서 현재까지 겪은 경험을 나타내며, once, ever, never, before, often 등과 함께 쓰인다.
- **Have** you ever **seen** a dolphin? 너는 돌고래를 본 적 있니?
- I **have** never **been** to Australia. 나는 한 번도 호주에 가본 적이 없다.

❷ **계속** : 과거에서 현재까지 계속된 상태를 나타내며, for, since 등과 함께 쓰인다.
- She **has lived** in Seoul for five years. 그녀는 5년 동안 서울에 살고 있다.
- He **has been** ill since last Sunday. 그는 지난 일요일 이후로 계속 아프다.

❸ **완료** : 현재 시점에서 동작이 완료됨을 나타내며, just, now, already 등과 함께 쓰인다.
- He **has** already **done** his homework. 그는 이미 숙제를 끝마쳤다.
- She **has** just **arrived** home. 그녀는 집에 막 도착했다.

❹ **결과** : 과거에 행해진 동작의 결과가 현재에도 남아 있음을 나타내며, go, lose, leave 등의 동사가 주로 결과의 의미로 쓰인다.
- She **has gone** to France. 그녀는 프랑스로 가버렸다. (지금 여기 없다.)
- I **have lost** my laptop computer. 나는 노트북 컴퓨터를 잃어버렸다. (아직 찾지 못했다.)

> **TIPs**
> 명백한 과거를 나타내는 표현 (ago, yesterday, last night, 과거 연도, 의문사 when 등)은 완료 시제와 함께 쓰지 않는다.
> - I ~~have lost~~ my wallet <u>yesterday</u>. 나는 어제 지갑을 잃어버렸다.

Answers: p.02

Exercise 1 다음 괄호 안의 단어를 사용하여 현재완료 시제로 문장을 완성하시오.

1 We _____ _____ of Alaska before. (hear)

2 English _____ _____ a world language. (become)

3 _____ you _____ _____ a horse? (ever, ride)

4 She _____ _____ _____ to Japan. (never, be)

5 I _____ _____ the horror movie. (already, see)

6 My parents _____ _____ _____ a letter to my brother. (just, send)

Exercise 2 다음 〈보기〉에서 알맞은 것을 골라 현재완료 시제로 문장을 완성하시오.

🔍 visit	finish	read	be	live

1 How often _____ you _____ Japan?

2 _____ you _____ the newspaper yet?

3 She _____ just _____ her master's degree.

4 Mrs. Fuller _____ in this house since 1990.

5 I _____ _____ to Europe three times on business.

Exercise **3** 다음 짝지어진 두 문장이 같은 뜻이 되도록 문장을 완성하시오.

1 Paul lost his umbrella, so he doesn't have it now.
    ⇨ Paul _____ _____ his umbrella.

2 Amanda went to Busan, so she is not here now.
    ⇨ Amanda _____ _____ to Busan.

3 I moved to Seoul in 2020, and I still live there.
    ⇨ I _____ _____ in Seoul since 2020.

4 He went into the library two hours ago, and he is still in the library.
    ⇨ He _____ _____ in the library for two hours.

5 James started to study English three years ago, and he still studies English.
    ⇨ James _____ _____ English for three years.

Exercise **4** 다음 우리말과 같은 뜻이 되도록 괄호 안의 단어를 알맞게 배열하시오.

1 나는 방금 아침 식사를 끝마쳤다. (just, I, breakfast, have, finished)
    ⇨ _____

2 그 의사는 아직 도착하지 않았다. (has, yet, not, the doctor, arrived)
    ⇨ _____

3 그는 도서관에 안경을 두고 왔다. (his, has, the library, he, glasses, left, in)
    ⇨ _____

4 나는 전에 물고기를 잡아본 적이 없다. (never, I, have, a fish, before, caught)
    ⇨ _____

5 나는 전에 그 축구 선수를 만난 적이 있다. (met, soccer player, I, the, have, before)
    ⇨ _____

6 그녀는 2005년부터 고아를 돌보고 있다. (2005, taken care of, has, the orphans, she, since)
    ⇨ _____

7 Sally는 이십 년 동안 생물학을 가르치고 있다. (taught, twenty, has, years, for, Sally, biology)
    ⇨ _____

8 그는 자신의 아들을 위해 스마트폰을 구입했다. (has, he, son, bought, for, his, a smartphone)
    ⇨ _____

9 그녀는 영어 공부하러 미국에 가 버렸다. (study, has, to the USA, she, gone, to, English)
    ⇨ _____

📑 **현재진행 (am / is / are + -ing)**

현재 시점에서 동작이 계속됨(~하는 중이다)을 나타낸다.

· They **are playing** in the playground now. 그들은 지금 운동장에서 놀고 있다.

· He **is talking** on the phone now. 그는 지금 통화 중이다.

📑 **현재완료진행 (have[has] been + -ing)**

과거부터 현재까지 동작이 계속됨을 나타내며, 현재진행과 완료 시제가 결합된 것이다. 과거에 시작한 동작이 현재에도 계속되고 있음을 강조할 때 쓴다.

· I **have been waiting** for an hour. 나는 한 시간 동안 기다렸다. 〈지금도 기다리는 중〉

= I started to wait an hour ago, and I am still waiting.

· It **has been raining** since last night. 어젯밤 이후로 계속 비가 왔다. 〈지금도 오는 중〉

= It began to rain last night, and it is still raining.

Answers: p.02

Exercise 1 다음 괄호 안에서 가장 알맞은 말을 고르시오.

1 It (has / has been) raining for a week.

2 They (are / have been) having dinner now.

3 How long (did / have) you been learning French?

4 I've (reading / been reading) Romeo and Juliet for two hours.

5 The children (have / have been) playing in the garden since lunch time.

Exercise 2 다음 괄호 안의 단어를 사용하여 현재진행 시제로 문장을 완성하시오.

1 Kelly _____ the radio right now. (listen to)

2 Charles _____ for his piano recital. (practice)

3 She _____ the newspaper while drinking coffee. (read)

4 Len _____ his father's car to get his allowance now. (wash)

5 The boys _____ along the road with their dogs following them. (run)

Exercise 3 다음 괄호 안의 단어를 사용하여 현재완료진행 시제로 문장을 완성하시오.

1 My baby _____ a nap for three hours. (take)

2 He _____ television since this morning. (watch)

3 I _____ you at the station for an hour. (wait for)

4 They _____ books for two hours in the cafeteria. (read)

5 Jeremy and his father _____ since last night at this lake. (fish)

과거완료 (had + p.p.)

과거의 어느 한 시점을 기준으로 그 이전에 일어난 동작이나 상태를 나타내며, 경험, 계속, 완료, 결과 등을 의미한다.

· I **had** never **eaten** raw fish before I came to Korea. 〈경험〉
  나는 한국에 오기 전에는 생선회를 먹어 본 적이 없었다.

· They **had lived** in London before they moved to Paris. 〈계속〉
  그들은 파리로 이사하기 전에 런던에 살았다.

· The game **had** already **started** when we got to the stadium. 〈완료〉
  우리가 운동장에 도착했을 때 경기는 이미 시작했다.

· My brother **had** already **gone** to the library when I got up in the morning. 〈결과〉
  내가 아침에 일어났을 때 내 동생은 이미 도서관에 가고 없었다.

> **TIPs**
> **before**와 **after**와 같이 앞뒤 순서를 분명히 알 수 있는 접속사가 있을 경우 과거완료 시제 대신 과거 시제가 올 수 있다.

과거완료진행 (had been + -ing)

과거의 어느 한 시점 이전부터 그 과거 시점까지 계속되는 동작으로, 과거완료와 진행 시제가 결합된 것이다.

· He **had been looking** out of the window for two hours before he left school.
  그는 학교를 떠나기 전에 두 시간 동안 창밖을 쳐다보고 있었다.

· We **had been learning** Chinese for two years before we lived in Beijing.
  우리는 베이징에 살기 전에 2년 동안 중국어를 배웠다.

Answers: p.02

Exercise 1 다음 괄호 안에서 알맞은 말을 고르시오.

1 He (has lost / had lost) his wallet when I met him.

2 He (has learned / had learned) Taekwondo since last year.

3 He (has lived / had lived) in Seoul for five years before he left there.

4 He (has stayed / had stayed) in the hotel for two days when I met him.

5 The movie was more exciting than we (have expected / had expected).

6 The train (has already left / had already left) when we got to the station.

7 I (have seen / had seen) a lion a few times on TV before I visited the zoo.

8 My father (has been / had been) to Japan three times before I was born.

9 Julie (has learned / had learned) ballet since she was twelve years old.

10 It (has been raining / had been raining) for two days when I arrived in Seattle.

11 I (have left / had left) my wallet at the office, so I borrowed money from James.

12 She (has practiced / had practiced) a lot before she participated in the concert.

13 They (have been walking / had been walking) along the river for an hour when it started raining.

14 He (has been watching / had been watching) movies for sixty-eight hours. I think he'll be the winner of this event.

15 I (have been preparing / had been preparing) for an exam since six o'clock when my mother finally came home at 9 o'clock.

다음 괄호 안의 단어를 사용하여 과거완료 시제 또는 과거완료진행 시제로 문장을 완성하시오.

1 I forgot to bring the book you _____ last week. (ask for)

2 She _____ the piano for an hour when I called her. (play)

3 My friends _____ when I entered the gym. (leave, already)

4 My father _____ in New York for 10 years before I was born. (live)

5 He _____ TV for two hours when his mother came home. (watch)

6 When I got to the library, I found that I _____ my glasses at home. (leave)

7 Cindy _____ the detective novel for an hour when I saw her in the cafeteria. (read)

8 Mr. Kowalski _____ English before he moved from Poland to Canada to find work. (learn)

다음 문장의 밑줄 친 부분을 바르게 고치시오.

1 She had been going through a lot of stress at work lately.

2 Cindy has already gone to the theater when he came home.

3 James had been learning Taekwondo since he moved to Korea.

4 She has worked at the hospital as a nurse before she became a singer.

5 I have been playing computer games for an hour when Mom entered my room.

다음 우리말과 같은 뜻이 되도록 괄호 안의 단어를 알맞게 배열하여 문장을 완성하시오.

1 그는 학교에 도착해서 숙제를 집에 두고 온 것을 알았다. (he, homework, had, at home, left, his)

⇒ He found that _____ when he arrived at school.

2 Peter와 Kelly는 독서 클럽에 가입하기 전에 이미 서로 알고 있었다.
(had already, Peter and Kelly, each other, known)

⇒ _____ before they joined the reading club.

3 기차가 그곳에 도착했을 때쯤 그녀는 세 시간 동안 잡지를 읽고 있었다.
(hours, had, a magazine, been, for, reading, three, she)

⇒ By the time the train arrived there, _____ .

4 내가 아침에 일어났을 때, 이미 나를 위해 아침이 차려져 있었다.
(had already, breakfast, prepared, for, been, me)

⇒ When I woke up in the morning, _____ .

미래완료 (will have + p.p.)

미래의 어느 한 시점까지의 경험, 계속, 완료, 결과를 나타낸다.

- If I watch the movie again, **I'll have watched** it three times. 〈경험〉
  이번에 그 영화를 또 보면 세 번째 보게 될 것이다.
- We**'ll have lived** in Busan for seven years next month. 〈계속〉
  다음 달이면 우리는 부산에서 7년 동안 살게 될 것이다.
- I **will have finished** my homework by nine o'clock. 〈완료〉
  나는 아홉 시까지 숙제를 끝낼 것이다.
- She **will have gone** to Paris by the time you arrive here. 〈결과〉
  당신이 여기에 도착할 때쯤이면 그녀는 파리에 가고 없을 것이다.

Answers: p.02

Exercise 1 다음 괄호 안에서 알맞은 말을 고르시오.

1. By next year, Johnnie and Janet (have seen / will have seen) each other for five years.

2. My sister (has volunteered / will have volunteered) at the orphanage since she was twenty years old.

3. If you don't hurry, the plane (has taken off / will have taken off) by the time we arrive at the airport.

4. Emma (has lived / will have lived) in Seattle alone for 5 years by the time her family moves to Seattle next month.

5. Clinton's book-signing event (has already finished / will have already finished) by the time you get to the bookstore.

Exercise 2 다음 우리말과 같은 뜻이 되도록 괄호 안의 단어를 알맞게 배열하여 문장을 완성하시오.

1. 내년이면 그들은 호주에 산 지 10년이 될 것이다. (Australia, for ten years, have, they, lived, in, will)

   ⇨ By next year _____.

2. 그녀가 항구에 도착할 때쯤에 그 배는 이미 떠났을 것이다. (already left, have, the boat, will)

   ⇨ _____ by the time she gets to the harbor.

3. 일본으로 돌아갈 때쯤에 그녀는 2년 동안 한국어를 공부하게 될 것이다.
   (will, she, Korean, studied, have, for two years)

   ⇨ By the time she comes back to Japan, _____.

4. 다음 달 말이면 직원훈련과정이 끝날 것이다. (completed, the staff training process, have, will, been)

   ⇨ By the end of next month, _____.

Review Test

[01-04] 다음 빈칸에 들어갈 알맞은 말을 고르시오.

01
> Tom can't buy the book because he _____ all his money.

① spends
② had spent
③ was spent
④ has spent
⑤ was spending

02
> Alice missed her train yesterday because of a traffic jam on her way to the station. By the time she got to the station, her train _____.

① has already left
② had already left
③ already was left
④ has been leaving
⑤ will have already left

03
> I lost the watch that my wife _____ for me.

① is going to buy
② has bought
③ had bought
④ was bought
⑤ was buying

04
> He _____ in the army for thirty years when he retires next year.

① is
② was
③ had been
④ have been
⑤ will have been

05 다음 현재완료의 쓰임이 <u>다른</u> 하나는?

① I don't think I've ever seen so many people here.
② I have never met Mr. Johnson.
③ I have known him for ten years.
④ I have read the book three times.
⑤ Have you ever been to New Zealand?

[06-07] 다음 〈보기〉의 현재완료와 쓰임이 같은 것을 고르시오.

06
> I have studied English for two days.

① I <u>have lost</u> my wallet.
② He <u>has</u> never <u>eaten</u> Korean food.
③ My sister <u>has</u> just <u>left</u> for London.
④ She <u>has</u> just <u>finished</u> her homework.
⑤ She <u>has lived</u> in Paris since she was four.

07
> I have already had dinner.

① He <u>has been</u> to China once.
② She <u>has been</u> sick for a week.
③ She <u>has</u> just <u>arrived</u> at the museum.
④ I <u>have</u> never <u>played</u> the piano before.
⑤ My family <u>has lived</u> in Hawaii since 2021.

08 다음 밑줄 친 부분을 고쳐 쓴 것 중 바르지 <u>않은</u> 것은?

① I <u>have see</u> the movie once.
  ⇒ I have seen the movie once.
② He <u>is</u> ill for a week.
  ⇒ He has been ill for a week.
③ I <u>have gone</u> to France twice.
  ⇒ I have been to France twice.
④ When <u>have you gone</u> to Boston?
  ⇒ When have you been to Boston?
⑤ She hasn't finished her homework <u>already</u>.
  ⇒ She hasn't finished her homework yet.

[09-10] 다음 두 문장이 같은 뜻이 되도록 빈칸에 들어갈 말을 고르시오.

09 I began to ride this motorcycle three years ago, and I still ride the motorcycle.
 ⇨ I _____ this motorcycle for three years.

① ride   ② am riding
③ rode   ④ was riding
⑤ have ridden

10 I began to listen to classical music when I was six, and I'm still listening to classical music.
 ⇨ I _____ classical music ever since I was six.

① listen to
② am listening to
③ am listened to
④ have been listened to
⑤ have been listening to

[11-12] 다음 중 어법과 의미상 바른 것을 고르시오.

11 ① He has already seen the movie.
 ② She doesn't told him anything yet.
 ③ I have never talked to him already.
 ④ Have you gone to Switzerland?
 ⑤ She has been a teacher since she graduates from college.

12 ① Did you ever met him before?
 ② Have you being waiting long?
 ③ Judy hasn't done her homework yet.
 ④ Do you have thought about your future?
 ⑤ The game has been played since two hours.

[13-14] 다음 중 어법과 의미상 어색한 것을 고르시오.

13 ① He had left before she came home.
 ② He has tried to get a driver's license since March.
 ③ He has passed the examination last semester.
 ④ She had written a letter to me before I accepted her apology.
 ⑤ She and I had known each other before we went to the same college.

14 ① We haven't eaten anything since last night.
 ② He has watched that program before.
 ③ I haven't seen him ever since he moved out of our town.
 ④ He has been sick for three days, so he looks very tired.
 ⑤ The final game has already finished when we got to the gym.

15 다음 〈보기〉의 의문문에 대한 가장 알맞은 대답은?

 Has he done his homework yet?

 ① No, he did his homework yet.
 ② Yes, he didn't do his homework yet.
 ③ Yes, he has already done his homework.
 ④ No, he has already done his homework.
 ⑤ Yes, he had already done his homework.

16 다음 〈보기〉와 의미가 같은 것은?

 I have lost my key.

 ① I lost my key, and I found it.
 ② I have my key in my pocket.
 ③ I lost my key, but I have it now.
 ④ I lost my key, and I still don't have it.
 ⑤ I didn't have a key from the beginning.

[17-20] 다음 빈칸에 들어갈 말이 바르게 짝지어진 것을 고르시오.

17
A: How long have you been _____ for your company?
B: I _____ for ten years.

① working - was working
② worked - had been working
③ working - had been working
④ worked - have been working
⑤ working - have been working

18
When I _____ Penn Station, the train for Boston had already _____ .

① get to - left
② got to - left
③ got to - leaving
④ have gotten to - left
⑤ am getting to - been leaving

19
· Lucy _____ sick in bed for a week before she was hospitalized.
· I _____ since last Saturday.

① is - hadn't slept
② was - had slept
③ has been - haven't slept
④ has been - was sleeping
⑤ had been - haven't slept

20
· _____ the time he woke up in the morning, the rain had already stopped.
· We will have been married _____ twenty-five years by next year.
· My sister has been talking on the phone _____ she came home.

① In - for - for
② By - for - for
③ By - for - since
④ By - during - for
⑤ In - during - since

21 다음 대화의 질문으로 알맞은 것은?

A: _____
B: Yes, she's been there once.

① Will she go to Alaska?
② Has she been leaving Alaska?
③ Has she ever visited Alaska?
④ How many times has she been to Alaska?
⑤ Had she been to Alaska before she came here?

22 다음 우리말을 영어로 잘못 옮긴 것은?

① 우리는 어제 저녁 레스토랑에서 저녁 식사를 했다.
⇨ We had dinner at the restaurant last night.
② 나는 이틀 후면 여기에 있은 지 1년이 된다.
⇨ I had been here for a year in two days.
③ 버스를 타기 전에 이 약을 먹어라.
⇨ Take this medicine before you get on the bus.
④ 그의 아이들은 세 시부터 그곳에서 놀고 있었다.
⇨ His children have been playing there since three o'clock.
⑤ 전쟁이 발발했을 때 그는 수년 동안 미국에 살고 있었다.
⇨ He had been living in America for many years when the war broke out.

23 다음 중 대화가 <u>어색한</u> 것은?

① A : Have you ever seen a koala?
B : No, I have never seen a koala.
② A : Have you ever been to Los Angeles?
B : No, I haven't.
③ A : Have you ever been to America?
B : Yes, I have once.
④ A : How long have you been here?
B : I came here three weeks ago.
⑤ A : It began to rain this morning, and it is still raining.
B : Right, it will have been raining since this morning.

24 다음 짝지어진 두 문장의 의미가 같지 않은 것은?

① She has been to Jejudo.

= She is on her way to Jejudo.

② I haven't seen Alex since Monday.

= Monday was the last time I saw Alex.

③ It's been raining for an hour.

= It started raining an hour ago, and it is still raining.

④ Amy and Bob have been married for 20 years.

= Amy and Bob married 20 years ago, and they are still married.

⑤ Joe and Ralph have lived together for a year.

= Joe and Ralph started to live together a year ago, and they still live together.

[25-27] 다음 우리말과 같은 뜻이 되도록 〈보기〉에서 알맞은 것을 골라 문장을 완성하시오.

보기 | already   just   yet

25 · 그는 여기에 막 도착했다.

⇒ He has _____ arrived here.

· 나는 학교에서 방금 돌아왔다.

⇒ I have _____ returned from school.

26 · 그는 이미 그 영화를 보았다.

⇒ He has seen that film _____.

· 그 작가는 아직 오지 않았다.

⇒ The writer has not come _____.

27 · Tom이 그곳에 도착했을 때 그녀는 이미 가고 없었다.

⇒ She had _____ gone when Tom arrived there.

· 그녀가 방금 사무실을 떠났으니 서두르면 만날 수 있을 것이다.

⇒ She has _____ left the office, so you can catch her if you hurry.

[28-32] 다음 우리말과 같은 뜻이 되도록 괄호 안의 단어를 사용하여 문장을 완성하시오.

28 우리 선생님은 교장 선생님과 두 시간 동안 얘기하고 계신다.

⇒ My teacher _____ _____ the headmaster for two hours. (talk with)

29 그가 방으로 들어 왔을 때 나는 계속 그 책을 읽고 있었다.

⇒ When he came into the room, I _____ _____ the book. (read)

30 우리 부모님이 나를 데리러 올 때쯤 나는 세 시간 동안 영어 공부를 한 것이 될 것이다.

⇒ I _____ English for three hours when my parents come to pick me up. (study)

31 그는 아들이 대학에 입학하기 전에 아들에게 했던 약속이 생각났다.

⇒ He remembered the promise that he _____ _____ to his son before his son went to college. (make)

32 나는 방금 내 남동생을 배웅하러 공항에 다녀왔다.

⇒ I _____ just _____ to the airport to see off my brother. (be)

33 다음 밑줄 친 부분을 가장 알맞은 시제로 고쳐 쓰시오.

· I knew that I <u>meet</u> the girl somewhere before.

· I know L.A. well because I <u>visit</u> the city many times before.

Answers: p.04

[1-3] 다음 글을 읽고, 물음에 답하시오.

서술형

I got very angry when I got back home from my vacation last week. The house was a total mess. It was obvious that somebody (A) (break) into my house. (B) I was frustrated because the thief has stolen my brand-new bike. I called the police immediately, but they said it would be difficult to get it back. But I've just received a phone call from the police. (C) (arrested, been, the thief, has). I guess I'll be able to get my bike back.

1 밑줄 친 (A)를 어법에 맞게 바꿔 쓰시오.

_____

2 밑줄 친 (B)에서 어법상 어색한 부분을 찾아 고쳐 쓰시오.

_____

3 밑줄 친 (C)의 주어진 단어를 알맞게 배열하시오.

_____

4 다음 글의 밑줄 친 부분 중, 어법상 틀린 것은?

수능 대비형

    Tonight, I went to my younger sister's piano recital. She was very nervous, even though she ① has been practicing every night for several weeks. I knew she ② would do a great job if she would relax and trust herself. When it was her turn to perform, she came up to the stage, took a deep breath, and began ③ to play. She hit every note ④ perfectly. The audience applauded loudly ⑤ when she was finished. She stood up, took a bow, and smiled to the crowd.

* recital: 발표회
** note: 음, 음표

Chapter 2

to부정사

📑 주어, 목적어, 보어 역할을 하는 **to**부정사

· **To play** the piano is very difficult. 〈주어〉

= It is very difficult **to play** the piano. 피아노를 치는 것은 매우 어렵다.

· Brenda likes **to read** novels. 〈목적어〉 Brenda는 소설 읽는 것을 좋아한다.

· My job is **to design** computer programs. 〈보어〉 나의 직업은 컴퓨터 프로그램을 설계하는 것이다.

· Alice doesn't know **how to cook** spaghetti. 〈의문사+to부정사〉

Alice는 스파게티 요리법을 모른다.

· I don't know **what to do**. 〈의문사+to부정사〉 나는 무엇을 해야 할지 모르겠다.

> **TIPs**
> 「의문사+**to**부정사」는 그 자체가 명사구 역할을 한다.

📑 목적어로 **to**부정사를 취하는 동사

> agree, ask, choose, decide, expect, fail, hope, need, offer, plan, pretend, promise, refuse, seem, want, wish 등

· I **hope to pass** the entrance exam. 나는 입학시험에 합격하기를 희망한다.

· They **want to go** to the beach this weekend. 그들은 이번 주말에 해변에 가고 싶어 한다.

· She has **decided to become** a lawyer. 그녀는 변호사가 되기로 결심했다.

Answers: p.04

Exercise 1 다음 〈보기〉에서 알맞은 단어를 골라 to부정사로 바꿔 문장을 완성하시오.

🔍
| give up | go | swim | collect |
| feel | send | read | watch over |

1 I want _____ comic books.

2 _____ stamps is very interesting.

3 He decided _____ buying a new car.

4 My plan is _____ to Spain this summer.

5 _____ alone in the river is very dangerous.

6 She pretended _____ bad about what she said.

7 They agreed _____ more soldiers to that area.

8 My job is _____ these cattle from morning till night.

Exercise 2 다음 〈보기〉에서 알맞은 말을 골라 문장을 완성하시오.

🔍
| how to use | how to drive | where to stay | what to say |

1 She wanted to learn _____ a car.

2 Do you know _____ this new copy machine?

3 I didn't decide _____ during my business trip to Europe.

4 We don't know _____ to him because his application was rejected.

Exercise 3 다음 문장을 「It ~ to …」 문장으로 바꿔 쓰시오.

1 To learn English is very interesting.

⇨ _____

2 To play volleyball on the beach is fun.

⇨ _____

3 To read people's minds is not possible.

⇨ _____

4 To break one's bad habits is very difficult.

⇨ _____

5 To prepare for the annual festival was hard.

⇨ _____

6 To complete the project by myself is impossible.

⇨ _____

Exercise 4 다음 우리말과 같은 뜻이 되도록 괄호 안의 단어를 알맞게 배열하여 문장을 완성하시오.

1 나의 임무는 경찰을 대신해서 범죄자를 잡는 것이다.

(the criminals, on behalf of, the police, catch, to)

⇨ My duty is _____ .

2 장군은 더 많은 병사를 분쟁지역에 보내겠다고 약속했다.

(more, to, troops, to, send, the conflict area)

⇨ The general promised _____ .

3 어릴 때부터 내 소원은 훌륭한 배우가 되는 것이었다.

(to, great, childhood, since, a, become, actor)

⇨ My wish has been _____ .

4 시청에 어떻게 가는지 말씀해 주시겠습니까? (to, get, to, City Hall, how)

⇨ Could you tell me _____ ?

5 3개월 내에 저 다리를 건설하는 것은 불가능하다. (to, within, build, the bridge, months, three)

⇨ It is impossible _____ .

6 그들은 계약을 1년 더 연장하기로 합의했다. (extend, to, the contract, an, for, year, additional)

⇨ They agreed _____ .

☐ **명사 수식**
- Mike has no house **to live in**. Mike는 살 집이 없다.
- It's time **to leave** for the station. 역으로 떠날 시간이다.
- There is nothing **to eat** at home. 집에 먹을 것이 하나도 없다.

☐ **「be+to부정사」**
- They are **to meet** tonight. 〈예정 = be going to〉 그들은 오늘 밤 만날 예정이다.
- You are **to do** your homework. 〈의무 should〉 너는 숙제를 해야만 한다.
- They were **to love** each other. 〈운명 = be destined to〉 그들은 서로 사랑할 운명이었다.
- If you are **to be** a teacher, you have to study hard. 〈의도 = intend to〉 교사가 되려면, 열심히 공부해야 한다.
- No one was **to be seen** in the gym. 〈가능 = can〉 체육관에서 아무도 볼 수 없었다.

☐ **「to부정사+전치사」**
to부정사가 앞에 나오는 명사를 수식할 때, 명사를 직접목적어로 취할 수 없으면 전치사를 꼭 써야 한다.

> **TIPs**
> 전치사의 필요 여부는 to부정사 뒤에 수식받는 명사를 놓아 보면 쉽게 알 수 있다.
> to write with a pen (O)
> to write a pen (X)

- I need a friend **to talk with**. 나는 말할 친구가 필요하다.
- We need a couch **to sit on**. 우리는 앉을 소파가 필요하다.
- I need a pen **to write with**. 나는 쓸 펜이 필요하다.

Answers: p.05

Exercise ① 다음 〈보기〉에서 알맞은 단어를 골라 to부정사를 사용하여 문장을 완성하시오.

🔍 take care of   eat   buy   visit   show

1 Liam didn't have enough money _____ a new car.

2 I need someone _____ my dog during the holidays.

3 He was looking for opportunities _____ his abilities.

4 There are many beautiful places _____ in New York.

5 Today I was too busy, and I had no time _____ lunch.

Exercise ② 다음 밑줄 친 부분을 어법에 맞게 고쳐 문장을 다시 쓰시오.

1 It's to go time to school.

⇨ _____

2 You have to give her paper to write.

⇨ _____

3 I would like to have drink something.

⇨ _____

4 Andrew just transferred to a new school, so he doesn't have many friends to hang out.

⇨ _____

1   All children should respect their parents.
    ⇨ _____

2   The document could not be found again.
    ⇨ _____

3   The World Cup is going to be held next year.
    ⇨ _____

4   Aaron was destined never to see his country again.
    ⇨ _____

5   If you intend to pass the exam, you have to study hard.
    ⇨ _____

Exercise **4** 다음 우리말과 같은 뜻이 되도록 괄호 안의 단어를 사용하여 문장을 완성하시오.

1   나는 내일까지 끝내야 하는 숙제가 있다. (finish)
    ⇨ I have _____ by tomorrow.

2   나는 그 계획에 대해 할 말이 아무것도 없다. (say)
    ⇨ I have _____ about the plan.

3   Natalie는 댄스파티에 입고 갈 예쁜 드레스가 있다. (beautiful, wear)
    ⇨ Natalie has _____ to the dance party.

4   나는 어제 크리스마스 휴가 동안 읽을 책을 한 권 샀다. (read)
    ⇨ Yesterday, I bought _____ over the Christmas holiday.

Exercise **5** 다음 우리말과 같은 뜻이 되도록 괄호 안의 단어를 알맞게 배열하여 문장을 완성하시오.

1   William은 훌륭한 배우가 될 운명이었다. (be, a, was, actor, to, great)
    ⇨ William _____.

2   성공하고 싶다면, 절대로 포기하지 마라. (succeed, you, if, to, are)
    ⇨ _____, never give up.

3   너는 수필 쓰는 것을 내일까지 끝내야 한다. (are, finish, to, writing, your essay)
    ⇨ You _____ by tomorrow.

4   국제회의는 3월 3일 컨벤션 센터에서 개최될 예정이다. (the convention center, take place, to, is, at)
    ⇨ The international conference _____ on March 3rd.

2-3 부사적 쓰임

▢ to부정사는 부사처럼 동사, 형용사, 부사를 수식하고, 목적, 감정의 원인, 판단의 근거, 결과 등을 나타낸다.

· He studied hard **to become** a lawyer. 〈목적〉 그는 변호사가 되기 위해 열심히 공부했다.

= He studied hard **in order to become** a lawyer.

= He studied hard **so that** he **could become** a lawyer.

· She was surprised **to hear** the news. 〈감정의 원인〉 그녀는 그 뉴스를 듣고서 놀랐다.

· He must be a fool **to do** such a thing. 〈판단의 근거〉

그러한 일을 하다니 그는 바보임이 틀림없다.

· He grew up **to be** a pilot. 〈결과〉 그는 자라서 조종사가 되었다.

· This book is difficult **to understand**. 〈형용사 수식〉 이 책은 이해하기 어렵다.

> **TIPs** to부정사가 주로 다음과 같은 형용사를 수식할 때 감정의 원인을 의미한다.
> glad, sad, pleased, sorry, surprised

Answers: p.05

Exercise 1 다음 〈보기〉와 같이 문장을 완성하시오.

🔍 Danny is going to Seoul to attend the annual meeting.

⇨ Danny is going to Seoul ＿＿＿ in order to attend the annual meeting ＿＿＿ .

⇨ Danny is going to Seoul ＿＿＿ so that he can attend the annual meeting ＿＿＿ .

1 My sister is saving money to buy a laptop computer.

⇨ My sister is saving money ＿＿＿＿＿＿＿＿＿ .

⇨ My sister is saving money ＿＿＿＿＿＿＿＿＿ .

2 They went to the stadium to watch the soccer game.

⇨ They went to the stadium ＿＿＿＿＿＿＿＿＿ .

⇨ They went to the stadium ＿＿＿＿＿＿＿＿＿ .

3 He turned on the computer to play computer games.

⇨ He turned on the computer ＿＿＿＿＿＿＿＿＿ .

⇨ He turned on the computer ＿＿＿＿＿＿＿＿＿ .

4 She studied English very hard to become a diplomat.

⇨ She studied English very hard ＿＿＿＿＿＿＿＿＿ .

⇨ She studied English very hard ＿＿＿＿＿＿＿＿＿ .

5 I dropped by his office to tell him the result of his exam.

⇨ I dropped by his office ＿＿＿＿＿＿＿＿＿ .

⇨ I dropped by his office ＿＿＿＿＿＿＿＿＿ .

6 Michael exercised hard to win a gold medal at the Olympic Games.

⇨ Michael exercised hard ＿＿＿＿＿＿＿＿＿ .

⇨ Michael exercised hard ＿＿＿＿＿＿＿＿＿ .

Exercise 2 다음 〈보기〉에서 알맞은 말을 골라 to부정사를 사용하여 문장을 완성하시오.

🔍 go　　　　hear　　　　surf　　　　run across　　　　be

1　I turned on the computer _____ the Internet.
2　She grew up _____ a great singer-songwriter.
3　He must be tired _____ to bed at 9 p.m.!
4　He was pleased _____ an old friend on the street.
5　I was so sad _____ the news that the bridge was destroyed by the flood.

Exercise 3 다음 〈보기〉에서 밑줄 친 to부정사의 쓰임을 고르시오.

🔍 결과　　　　목적　　　　감정의 원인　　　　판단의 근거　　　　형용사 수식

1　We are very happy to meet you again.　　⇨ _____
2　She must be kind to help her younger sister.　　⇨ _____
3　He worked hard, only to fail the entrance exam.　　⇨ _____
4　The independent film is very difficult to understand.　　⇨ _____
5　Tracy went to the Netherlands to study architecture.　　⇨ _____

Exercise 4 다음 우리말과 같은 뜻이 되도록 괄호 안의 단어를 알맞게 배열하여 문장을 완성하시오.

1　이 선반은 조립하기 쉽다. (easy, assemble, is, to)
　⇨ This shelf _____.

2　그녀의 딸은 자라서 유명한 피아니스트가 되었다. (be, pianist, a, grew up, famous, to)
　⇨ Her daughter _____.

3　그는 식료품을 사러 가게에 갈 것이다. (buy, go, the market, to, to)
　⇨ He will _____ some food.

4　우리는 당신을 회의에 초대하게 되어 매우 기쁩니다.
　(invite, are, the meeting, to, to, so, you, pleased)
　⇨ We _____.

5　상대성 이론을 전개하다니 아인슈타인은 천재였음이 틀림없다.
　(to, the theory of relativity, a genius, develop)
　⇨ Einstein must have been _____.

2-4 의미상의 주어

to부정사의 의미상의 주어

❶ 문장의 주어와 일치하는 경우
- **Ally** wants **to see** her grandparents. Ally는 자신의 조부모를 보고 싶어 한다.
- **We** like **to listen** to classical music. 우리는 고전음악 듣는 것을 좋아한다.

❷ 문장의 목적어와 일치하는 경우
allow, ask, advise, expect, get, tell, force, persuade, encourage, enable과 같은 동사는
「동사+목적어+to부정사」 형태로 자주 사용된다.
- I **told him to work** hard. 나는 그에게 열심히 일하라고 말했다.
- She **asked him to come** tomorrow. 그녀는 그에게 내일 오라고 부탁했다.

❸ 「for+목적어+to부정사」로 쓰는 경우
to부정사의 의미상 주어는 일반적으로 「for+목적격」으로 나타낸다.
- It is too difficult **for you to solve** the problem. 네가 그 문제를 푸는 것은 너무 어려운 일이다.
- It is time **for you to go** to bed. 네가 잠자리에 들어야 할 시간이다.

❹ 「of+목적어+to부정사」로 쓰는 경우
사람의 성격을 나타내는 형용사(kind, nice, rude, careless, foolish, wise, clever 등)가 오면
부정사의 의미상의 주어는 「of+목적격」으로 나타낸다.
- It is very nice **of you to help** me. 저를 도와주시다니 당신은 정말 친절하군요.
- It was foolish **of him to do** such a thing. 그러한 행동을 하다니 그는 어리석었어요.

Answers: p.05

Exercise 1 다음 대화를 읽고, 〈보기〉와 같이 문장을 완성하시오.

> Angelina : I think I have a bad cold. I don't feel well.
> Thomas : You had better take a rest.
> ⇨ Thomas told _____Angelina to take a rest_____ .

1 Beth : Could you help me carry the baggage? It's too heavy.
   Tony : Sure, Beth.
   ⇨ Beth asked _____ .

2 Mark : What do you want me to do?
   Diane : I want you to repair my computer.
   ⇨ Diane wants _____ .

3 Mom : Carol, your room is too messy. Clean up your room.
   Carol : Yes, Mom.
   ⇨ Carol's mom ordered _____ .

4 David : Mom, I finished my homework.
   Mom : You may go out and play.
   ⇨ David's mom allowed _____ .

다음 괄호 안에서 알맞은 말을 고르시오.

1 The bag was too heavy (for / of) him to carry.

2 It was very kind (for / of) you to help an old man.

3 It's smart (for / of) her to solve the difficult math questions.

4 It's very careless (for / of) you to make the same mistake again.

5 It was very generous (for / of) you to donate the blankets to a shelter.

6 It is impossible (for / of) me to remember everyone's face and name right now.

Exercise 3 다음 문장의 밑줄 친 부분을 바르게 고치시오.

1 The king ordered him sold the boat.　　　　　⇨ _____

2 My doctor advised me taking a rest.　　　　　⇨ _____

3 I will not allow my son go to the beach.　　　　⇨ _____

4 Do you want me do the homework now?　　　　⇨ _____

5 I didn't expect him understand the theory.　　　⇨ _____

6 The teacher told us doing our best on tests.　　⇨ _____

7 He forced me finished the project within a month.　⇨ _____

8 The Internet enables people to sharing information globally.　⇨ _____

9 The government encouraged us used public transportation.　⇨ _____

10 Please ask Linda calling me as soon as she comes to the office.　⇨ _____

Exercise 4 다음 우리말과 같은 뜻은 되도록 괄호 안의 단어를 알맞게 배열하여 문장을 완성하시오.

1 의사는 그에게 담배를 끊으라고 충고했다. (him, advised, smoking, stop, to)

⇨ The doctor _____.

2 그렇게 얘기하다니 당신은 정말 무례했어요. (you, say, rude, to, of)

⇨ It was so _____ so.

3 내가 너와 함께 도서관에 가 주기를 원하니? (go, want, the library, me, to, to)

⇨ Do you _____ with you?

4 우리 어머니는 내가 오늘 밤에 댄스파티에 가는 것을 허락했다. (go, to, me, allowed)

⇨ My mom _____ to the dance party tonight.

5 우리 선생님은 John이 숙제를 끝내도록 내가 John을 도와주기를 기대한다. (to, me, help, expects)

⇨ My teacher _____ John finish his homework.

부정형 / 가주어 / 가목적어

☐ **to부정사의 부정형**
to부정사 바로 앞에 **not** 또는 **never**를 쓴다.
- He told us **not to waste** money. 그는 우리에게 돈을 낭비하지 말라고 말했다.
- Elderly people have to be careful **not to catch** a cold. 노인들은 감기에 걸리지 않도록 조심해야 한다.

☐ **가주어**
주어가 **to부정사**이면서 긴 경우, 가주어 **it**을 사용한다.
- **It** is not safe **to ride** a motorcycle without a helmet.
  = **To ride** a motorcycle without a helmet is not safe.
    헬멧 없이 오토바이를 타는 것은 안전하지 않다.
- **It** is impossible **to master** a foreign language within six months.
  = **To master** a foreign language within six months is impossible.
    여섯 달 안에 외국어를 통달하는 것은 불가능하다.

☐ **가목적어**
동사 **make, find, think** 등의 목적어가 부정사일 때 가목적어 **it**을 사용한다.
- I found **it** easy **to read** this book. 나는 이 책을 읽는 것이 쉽다는 것을 알았다.
- Bridget makes **it** a rule **to take a walk** every morning. Bridget은 매일 아침 산책하는 것을 규칙으로 삼는다.

Answers: p.06

Exercise ① 다음 〈보기〉에서 알맞은 단어를 골라 to부정사의 부정형을 사용하여 문장을 완성하시오.

🔍 worry	use	meet	be	swim	fail

1   She asked me ＿＿＿＿＿＿＿＿＿＿ Ian again.

2   He studied hard ＿＿＿＿＿＿＿＿＿＿ the exam.

3   My teacher asked me ＿＿＿＿＿＿＿＿＿＿ late again.

4   Alex promised ＿＿＿＿＿＿＿＿＿＿ the copy machine.

5   Jim ordered us ＿＿＿＿＿＿＿＿＿＿ in the river at night.

6   My teacher told me ＿＿＿＿＿＿＿＿＿＿ about the mistakes.

Exercise ② 다음 문장을 읽고, 어법상 어색한 부분을 찾아 바르게 고치시오.

1   I decide to not eat meat until I lose weight.   ⇨ ＿＿＿＿＿＿

2   I think that they did their best to not lose the game.   ⇨ ＿＿＿＿＿＿

3   You have to get up early to not missed the school bus.   ⇨ ＿＿＿＿＿＿

4   You have to be careful to not making noise at midnight.   ⇨ ＿＿＿＿＿＿

5   He decided not to spent money buying new video games anymore.   ⇨ ＿＿＿＿＿＿

6   Mom told me to skip not breakfast, but I don't have time to eat breakfast.   ⇨ ＿＿＿＿＿＿

🔍 **To steal your friend's money is not good.**
⇒ _____ It is not good to steal your friend's money. _____

1 To read many English books is useful.

⇒ _____

2 To do exercise every day is important.

⇒ _____

3 To speak Chinese fluently is not easy for me.

⇒ _____

4 To break the bad habit of nail-biting is hard for me.

⇒ _____

5 To climb up mountains like Everest is difficult for amateurs like us.

⇒ _____

Exercise **4** 다음 우리말과 같은 뜻이 되도록 괄호 안의 단어를 사용하여 문장을 완성하시오.

1 나는 그 책을 이해하는 것이 어렵다는 것을 알았다. (understand)

⇒ I found _____ hard _____ the book.

2 나는 아침에 산책하는 것을 습관으로 삼았다. (take a walk)

⇒ I made _____ a rule _____ in the morning.

3 그곳에서 혼자 수영하는 것은 위험할 수 있다. (swim)

⇒ _____ can be dangerous _____ there alone.

4 우리는 달에 가는 것이 불가능하다고 생각했다. (go)

⇒ We thought _____ impossible _____ to the moon.

5 당신의 건강을 위해 규칙적으로 운동하는 것이 필요하다. (exercise)

⇒ _____ is necessary for your health _____ regularly.

6 나는 같은 일을 반복하는 것은 가치 없는 일이라고 생각했다. (repeat)

⇒ I thought _____ useless _____ the same things over again.

7 뉴욕에서 밤에 지하철로 이동하는 것은 안전하지 않다. (travel)

⇒ _____ is not safe _____ by subway in New York at night.

부정사의 시제

☐ **to부정사의 시제**

❶ to부정사의 시제가 주절과 같은 경우 「to+동사원형」을 쓴다.

· He **seems to be** sick.

= It **seems** that he **is** sick. 그는 아픈 것 같다.

· He **seemed to be** sick.

= It **seemed** that he **was** sick. 그는 아픈 것 같았다.

❷ to부정사의 시제가 주절의 시제보다 앞선 경우 「to+have+p.p.」를 쓴다.

· He **seems to have been** ill.

= It **seems** that he **was[has been]** ill.

그는 아팠던 것 같다.

· He **seemed to have been** ill.

= It **seemed** that he **had been** ill.

그는 아팠던 것 같았다.

> **TIPs**
> want, wish, hope, expect, intend 등의 동사 뒤에 나오는 to부정사는 미래를 의미한다.
> · I expect him **to pass** the exam.
> = I expect that he **will pass** the exam. 나는 그가 시험에 통과할 거라고 예상한다.

Answers: p.06

Exercise ❶ 다음 짝지어진 두 문장이 같은 뜻이 되도록 문장을 완성하시오.

1 It seems that she knows what really happened.

⇨ She seems _____ what really happened.

2 It seems that he is popular among his classmates.

⇨ He seems _____ popular among his classmates.

3 It seems that he devotes all his efforts to studying English.

⇨ He seems _____ all his efforts to studying English.

4 It seems that she has dinner at that restaurant every day.

⇨ She seems _____ dinner at that restaurant every day.

Exercise ❷ 다음 짝지어진 두 문장이 같은 뜻이 되도록 문장을 완성하시오.

1 It seemed that he had stolen the suitcase.

⇨ He seemed _____ the suitcase.

2 It seems that he has broken the Persian-style china.

⇨ He seems _____ the Persian-style china.

3 It seemed that Mary had been a famous dermatologist.

⇨ Mary seemed _____ a famous dermatologist.

4 It seems that Fred worked at the electronics company.

⇨ Fred seems _____ at the electronics company.

다음 짝지어진 두 문장이 같은 뜻이 되도록 문장을 완성하시오.

1 She seemed to be aware of the fact.
   ⇨ It seemed that _____ .

2 It seemed that he had lost his wallet.
   ⇨ He seemed _____ .

3 He expects that he will win the match.
   ⇨ He expects _____ .

4 She seems to have seen a ghost in the restroom.
   ⇨ It seems that _____ .

5 We expect our soccer team to advance to the finals.
   ⇨ We expect that _____ .

6 It seems that he went to the International Film Festival by himself.
   ⇨ He seems _____ .

다음 우리말과 같은 뜻이 되도록 괄호 안의 단어를 알맞게 배열하시오.

1 Helen은 나에게 화가 난 것 같다.
   (to, at, be, angry, Helen, me, seems)

   ⇨ _____

2 그는 유명한 축구 선수였던 것 같았다.
   (a, been, seemed, soccer player, have, he, famous, to)

   ⇨ _____

3 Jessy는 프로젝트를 제시간에 끝마치기를 바란다.
   (to, Jessy, finish, in, the project, time, hopes)

   ⇨ _____

4 그녀는 전에 Tim과 함께 일했던 것 같다.
   (before, has worked, she, it, Tim, seems, that, with)

   ⇨ _____

5 그녀는 꽤 매력적인 여자인 것 같다.
   (is, that, seems, she, woman, quite, an attractive, it)

   ⇨ _____

6 Eric은 전 세계로부터 많은 우표를 수집해온 것처럼 보였다.
   (Eric, have collected, to, stamps, all over the world, from, many, seemed)

   ⇨ _____

원형부정사

원형부정사는 동사원형을 말하고, 지각동사나 사역동사의 목적격보어 자리에 쓴다.

❶ 「지각동사+목적어+동사원형」

지각동사에는 see, hear, watch, feel, listen to 등이 있다.

· I **saw** them **cross** the street. 나는 그들이 길을 건너는 것을 보았다.

· Jasmine **heard** him **sing** a song.
Jasmine은 그가 노래 부르는 것을 들었다.

❷ 「사역동사+목적어+동사원형」

사역동사는 '~에게 …을 시키다'라는 의미를 갖는 동사를 말하며,
사역동사에는 let, have, make가 있다.

· **Let** me **know** what he said. 나에게 그가 말했던 것을 알려 줘.

· My mother **had** me **wash** the dishes. 우리 어머니는 내게 설거지를 하게 시켰다.

· He **made** me **clean** the room. 그는 나에게 방 청소를 시켰다.

❸ 「help+목적어(+to)+동사원형」

help는 목적격보어 자리에 동사원형과 to부정사를 모두 쓸 수 있다.

· Julia **helped** him **(to) finish** the work within this week.
Julia는 그가 이번 주 안으로 그 일을 끝내도록 도왔다.

TIPs
동작이 진행 중임을 강조할 경우,
동작의 일부만 본 경우 동사원형 대신에
현재분사(-ing)를 쓴다.
· I saw him playing soccer.
나는 그가 축구하는 것을 보았다.

TIPs
목적어와 목적격보어가 수동의 관계
이면 목적격보어 자리에 과거분사가 온다.
· She had her hair cut.
그녀는 머리카락을 잘랐다.
(그녀의 머리카락이 잘리는 것)

TIPs
get은 사역동사의 의미로 쓰여도
목적격보어 자리에 to부정사를 쓴다.
· I got him to repair my car.
나는 그에게 내 차를 수리하도록 했다.

Answers: p.06

Exercise ❶ 다음 괄호 안에서 알맞은 것을 <u>모두</u> 고르시오.

1 I heard my name (call / to call / calling / called).

2 Let me (knowing / know / to know / known) what happened there.

3 I saw him (play / to play / playing / played) the piano on the stage.

4 I saw students (enter / to enter / entering / entered) the classroom.

5 Karen had her children (paint / to paint / painting / painted) the fence.

6 My mother let me (clean / cleaning / to clean / cleaned) the bathroom.

7 Christina made her sister (watering / water / to water / watered) the garden.

8 Carol helped me (solve / to solve / solving / solved) difficult math problems.

Exercise ❷ 다음 문장을 읽고, 어법상 <u>어색한</u> 부분을 찾아 바르게 고치시오.

1 I could see the dog to run toward me.

2 Sophie got the children join the English club.

3 I saw him waited for a bus on my way to school.

4 My mom had me to read many books when I was in my teens.

🔍 study	cry	fix	watch	take

1 I heard my baby _____ in her room.

2 My mom didn't let me _____ TV after dinner.

3 Can you let me _____ a look at your ID card?

4 The boss made the repairman _____ the computer.

5 My parents got me _____ English harder when I went to middle school.

Exercise **4** 다음 우리말과 같은 뜻이 되도록 괄호 안의 단어를 알맞게 배열하시오.

1 빨간 셔츠가 그녀를 어려 보이게 했다. (the red shirt, her, made, look, younger)

⇨ _____

2 나는 그 피아니스트가 피아노 연주하는 것을 들었다. (heard, I, play, the pianist, the piano)

⇨ _____

3 나는 그에게 9시까지 숙제를 끝마치게 시켰다. (his homework, finish, him, I, by nine, made)

⇨ _____

4 나는 동굴 안에 있는 아이들이 도움을 요청하는 소리를 들었다.
(I, yelling for, the kids, in, the cave, help, heard)

⇨ _____

5 그들은 Eddie가 자신의 친구들과 야구하는 것을 보았다.
(watched, his, with, they, Eddie, baseball, play, friends)

⇨ _____

6 Mandy는 자신의 머리 위에서 무엇인가가 기어가는 것을 느꼈다.
(Mandy, her, something, on, felt, head, crawling)

⇨ _____

7 지진이 일어났을 때, 나는 집이 흔들리는 것을 느꼈다.
(when, happened, the earthquake, shake, my house, felt, I)

⇨ _____

enough to / too ~ to

📖 「형용사/부사 + **enough to** + 동사원형」= 「**so** + 형용사/부사 + **that** + 주어 + **can** …」 ~할 정도로 충분히 …하다
- Neil is rich **enough to** buy a fantastic car.
  = Neil is **so** rich **that** he **can** buy a fantastic car.
  Neil은 매우 부자여서 멋진 차를 살 수가 있다.
- The firefighters acted quickly **enough to** put out the fire.
  = The firefighters acted **so** quickly **that** they **could** put out the fire.
  그 소방관들은 매우 빠르게 행동을 취해서 화재를 진압할 수 있었다.

📖 「**too** + 형용사/부사 + **to** + 동사원형」= 「**so** + 형용사/부사 + **that** + 주어 + **cannot** …」 너무 ~해서 … 할 수 없다
- He is **too** young **to** work.
  = He is **so** young **that** he **cannot** work.
  그는 너무 어려서 일을 할 수 없다.
- That book was **too** difficult for me **to** understand.
  = That book was **so** difficult **that** I **couldn't** understand it.
  나는 그 책이 너무 어려워서 이해할 수 없었다.

Answers: p.06

Exercise 1 다음 짝지어진 두 문장이 같은 뜻이 되도록 문장을 완성하시오.

1 I was too tired to play basketball anymore.
  ⇨ I was _____ .

2 The picture is small enough to fit into a box.
  ⇨ The picture is _____ .

3 The young boy was so shy that he couldn't talk to her.
  ⇨ The young boy was _____ .

4 Diane was so energetic that she could run a marathon.
  ⇨ Diane was _____ .

Exercise 2 다음 우리말과 같은 뜻이 되도록 괄호 안의 단어를 사용하여 문장을 완성하시오.

1 이 물은 마시기에 너무 뜨겁다. (hot, drink)
  ⇨ This water is _____ .

2 그녀는 학교에 갈 만큼 충분히 나이가 들었다. (old, go)
  ⇨ She is _____ to school.

3 그는 번지점프를 할 만큼 충분히 용감하다. (brave, do)
  ⇨ He is _____ bungee jumping.

4 나는 너무 바빠서 저녁을 먹을 수 없었다. (busy, have)
  ⇨ I was _____ that _____
  dinner.

2-9 독립부정사

독립부정사는 **to**부정사가 포함된 부사구를 말하며, 문장 전체를 수식한다.

to tell the truth 사실을 말하면	to be frank with you 솔직히 말해서
to be sure 확실히	to make matters worse 설상가상으로
so to speak 말하자면	strange to say 이상한 말이지만
needless to say 말할 필요도 없이	not to mention ~은 말할 것도 없이
to sum up 요약하면	to begin with 우선

- **To tell the truth**, I have never been to Paris.
  사실, 나는 한 번도 파리에 가본 적이 없다.

- **To be frank with you**, I told a lie to him.
  솔직히 말해서, 나는 그에게 거짓말을 했다.

- **To sum up**, we need more time to finish this project.
  요약하면, 이 프로젝트를 끝내려면 우리에게 시간이 더 필요하다.

Answers: p.07

Exercise 1 다음 우리말과 같은 뜻이 되도록 괄호 안의 단어를 사용하여 문장을 완성하시오.

1 말할 필요도 없이, 나는 당신을 매우 사랑합니다. (say)

   ⇨ _____, I love you so much.

2 솔직히 말하면, 우리가 결승전에 진출하는 것은 쉽지 않다. (frank)

   ⇨ _____, it is not easy for us to enter the final.

3 말하자면, 내 여동생은 책벌레다. (speak)

   ⇨ My younger sister is, _____, a book worm.

4 이상한 말이지만, 나는 생일파티를 원치 않는다. (strange)

   ⇨ _____, I don't want to hold my birthday party.

5 그는 영어는 말할 것도 없고, 일어도 매우 잘한다. (mention)

   ⇨ He speaks Japanese very well, _____ English.

Exercise 2 다음 문장을 밑줄 친 부분에 유의하여 해석하시오.

1 <u>To make matters worse</u>, he made another mistake.

   ⇨ _____

2 <u>To sum up</u>, you have to exercise every day for your health.

   ⇨ _____

3 <u>To be frank with you</u>, your computer cannot be fixed by tomorrow.

   ⇨ _____

4 <u>Needless to say</u>, we want to go to the beach during the summer holiday.

   ⇨ _____

Review Test

[01-04] 다음 〈보기〉의 밑줄 친 부분과 쓰임이 같은 것을 고르시오.

01 I don't have enough money <u>to buy</u> a car.

① I was glad <u>to see</u> you.
② He wants <u>to travel</u> to Europe.
③ She doesn't have a house <u>to live in</u>.
④ <u>To solve</u> the math problem is too hard.
⑤ I went to a department store <u>to buy</u> a gift.

02 I planned <u>to go</u> to America.

① Tony wants <u>to meet</u> you.
② I have so many things <u>to do</u>.
③ Do you want something <u>to drink</u>?
④ He went to Canada <u>to learn</u> English.
⑤ She grew up <u>to become</u> a famous singer.

03 I went to the library <u>to read</u> books.

① He wants <u>to learn</u> Taekwondo.
② I don't have any books <u>to read</u>.
③ <u>To read</u> storybooks is interesting.
④ His dream is <u>to collect</u> rare sportscars.
⑤ She turned off the radio <u>to go</u> to bed.

04 The meeting <u>is to be</u> held tomorrow.

① You <u>are to do</u> as you are told.
② He <u>is to leave</u> Singapore tonight.
③ No man <u>was to be seen</u> in the street.
④ You <u>are to be</u> home by ten o'clock at the latest.
⑤ You must be honest if you <u>are to remain</u> friends.

05 다음 우리말을 영어로 옮길 때 빈칸에 알맞은 것은?

아이들은 예의 바르게 행동하는 법을 배워야 한다.
⇒ Kids must learn _____ to behave politely.

① who   ② how
③ when   ④ what
⑤ where

[06-09] 다음 빈칸에 들어갈 알맞은 말을 고르시오.

06 I'll have them _____ how to use this new scanner.

① know   ② to know
③ known   ④ knowing
⑤ knew

07 Last night, we saw John _____ baseball with his brother at the playground.

① play   ② to playing
③ to play   ④ was played
⑤ have played

08 My mother ordered me _____ up the room by noon.

① clean   ② to clean
③ cleaning   ④ cleaned
⑤ to be cleaned

09 I asked him _____ us when we moved to the new apartment.

① help   ② to help
③ helping   ④ helped
⑤ to be helped

10 다음 중 to부정사의 쓰임이 <u>다른</u> 하나는?

① He must be a fool <u>to say</u> so.

② This question is hard <u>to answer</u>.

③ They did their best <u>to win</u> the prize.

④ You are <u>to come</u> here by 10 o'clock.

⑤ Tom grew up <u>to be</u> an English teacher.

[11-12] 다음 빈칸에 들어갈 말이 바르게 짝지어진 것을 고르시오.

11 · It's dangerous _____ him to climb the mountain alone.

· It's very kind _____ you to help me.

① of - of   ② of - for

③ for - of   ④ for - for

⑤ to - of

12 · I saw her _____ out of the room.

· We had them _____ some cookies and milk.

① to go - take   ② go - take

③ go - to take   ④ gone - taken

⑤ to go - to take

13 다음 빈칸에 들어갈 말을 <u>모두</u> 고르시오.

The teacher _____ his students clean the classroom.

① got   ② made

③ had   ④ asked

⑤ told

14 다음 빈칸에 들어갈 수 <u>없는</u> 말은?

Christopher _____ her to pick him up at the airport.

① wanted   ② let

③ advised   ④ forced

⑤ told

15 다음 문장에서 not이 들어가기에 알맞은 곳은?

Students ① have ② to ③ be careful ④ to ⑤ catch a cold.

[16-17] 다음 밑줄 친 부분과 바꿔 쓸 수 있는 것을 고르시오.

16 If you <u>are to</u> succeed, you have to work hard.

① intend to   ② be

③ have to   ④ can

⑤ are destined to

17 The meeting <u>was to</u> take place at 3:00 p.m. but it was canceled.

① liked to   ② was able to

③ must   ④ was supposed to

⑤ was sure to

18 다음 괄호 안의 단어를 알맞게 배열한 것은?

She is _____ this book.
(enough, smart, to, read)

① smart enough to read

② read to smart enough

③ to read smart enough

④ smart enough read to

⑤ enough smart to read

19 다음 빈칸에 to를 쓸 수 <u>없는</u> 문장은?

① It's good _____ see you.

② It is easy _____ speak English.

③ We expect you _____ meet him.

④ I saw her _____ dance in the gym.

⑤ She hopes _____ visit her grandparents.

[20-22] 다음 중 어법상 바르지 <u>않은</u> 것을 고르시오.

20　① I told him stop making noise.
　② I heard him playing the guitar.
　③ You are too young to understand it.
　④ This book is too hard for me to read.
　⑤ He works hard so as not to fail the exam.

21　① It is foolish of him to do it.
　② I don't know how to swim.
　③ We had him to come into the room.
　④ Do you have something cold to drink?
　⑤ The box is light enough for him to carry.

22　① I heard him singing songs.
　② I expected her to come here.
　③ We saw him enter the garage.
　④ The kid wanted him to tell the truth.
　⑤ We watched them to play football.

[23-24] 다음 빈칸에 들어갈 수 <u>없는</u> 말을 고르시오.

23　It was ＿＿＿＿＿ of her not to attend the meeting.

　① silly　　　　② clever
　③ rude　　　　④ wise
　⑤ hard

24　It's ＿＿＿＿＿ for us to open the unknown box.

　① hard　　　　② necessary
　③ careless　　　④ important
　⑤ easy

25　다음 빈칸에 들어갈 말이 나머지와 <u>다른</u> 하나는?

　① It's kind ＿＿＿＿＿ you to say so.
　② It is nice ＿＿＿＿＿ you to help me.
　③ It's foolish ＿＿＿＿＿ her to do such a thing.
　④ It's not easy ＿＿＿＿＿ me to answer the question.
　⑤ It was careless ＿＿＿＿＿ him not to lock the gate.

[26-27] 다음 우리말을 영어로 바르게 옮긴 것을 고르시오.

26　의사는 나에게 기름기 있는 음식을 먹지 말라고 조언했다.

　① The doctor advised me not eating fatty food.
　② The doctor advised me to eat not fatty food.
　③ The doctor advised me not to eat fatty food.
　④ The doctor advised me eating not fatty food.
　⑤ The doctor advised me to not eating fatty food.

27　아버지가 내게 자동차를 세차하도록 시켰다.

　① My father had me wash his car.
　② My father had me to wash his car.
　③ My father had washed me his car.
　④ My father had me to washing his car.
　⑤ My father had me washed his car.

28　다음 〈보기〉의 밑줄 친 it과 쓰임이 같은 것은?

Special effects make <u>it</u> possible to create a wonderful world.

　① I can't forget <u>it</u>.
　② How will you send <u>it</u>?
　③ I feel very bad about <u>it</u>.
　④ You will find <u>it</u> hard to study English.
　⑤ Did you really make <u>it</u> all by yourself?

29 다음 대화의 빈칸에 들어갈 말이 바르게 짝지어진 것은?

> A: Let's get the luggage.
> B: Wow! What did you put in these suitcases? Rocks?
> A: Only clothes. Why? Are they heavy?
> B: Yes. They're too heavy _____ me to carry. I'm not strong enough _____ help you.

① from - to   ② for - from
③ for - to   ④ from - for
⑤ buy - from

[30-31] 다음 빈칸에 공통으로 들어갈 말을 쓰시오.

30 · Eating fresh vegetables is necessary _____ us to stay healthy.
· It is very important _____ you to make good friends.

31 · I found _____ dangerous to swim in this river.
· _____ is dangerous to swim in this river.

[32-33] 다음 우리말과 같은 뜻이 되도록 괄호 안의 단어를 알맞게 배열하시오.

32 그의 필체가 너무 나빠서 읽을 수가 없다.

(his, bad, is, handwriting, too, read, to)

⇒

33 Richard는 그 퍼즐을 풀 만큼 충분히 똑똑했다.
(Richard, smart, to, the puzzle, enough, solve, was)

⇒

[34-36] 다음 두 문장이 같은 뜻이 되도록 빈칸에 알맞은 말을 쓰시오.

34 He was so foolish that he couldn't understand the meaning.
⇒ He was too foolish _____ the meaning.

35 It seems that she was an architect.
⇒ She seems _____ an architect.

36 Paul was so full that he could not eat anymore.
⇒ Paul was _____ full _____ eat anymore.

[37-38] 다음 괄호 안의 말을 사용하여 문장을 완성하시오.

37 My sister asked me _____ the volume. (not, turn up)

38 The room was large enough _____ thirty people. (hold)

[39-40] 다음 우리말과 같은 뜻이 되도록 괄호 안의 말을 사용하여 영작하시오.

39 설상가상으로, 나는 학교에 지각했다. (be late for)

⇒

40 이상한 말이지만, 나는 대학에 가고 싶지 않다. (go, university)

⇒

Answers: p.08

[1-2] 다음 대화를 읽고, 물음에 답하시오. 　서술형

A　Hey, Lucas. Are you going to enter the singing contest at the school festival?

B　No. I don't sing (A) (do, enough, to, well) that.

A　Last time I heard you sing, (B) 너는 노래를 매우 잘 하는 것 같았어.

B　Thanks. But instead, Emmett and I signed up for the dance contest. We are practicing very hard so that we can win.

1 밑줄 친 (A)의 주어진 단어를 알맞게 배열하시오.

→ _____

2 밑줄 친 (B)의 우리말과 같은 뜻이 되도록 영작하시오.

→ you _____ _____ _____ very well

3 다음 글의 밑줄 친 부분 중, 어법상 틀린 것은? 　수능 대비형

　　Three high school computer hackers have been arrested and are facing charges of theft. The three 16-year-old boys used a complex Internet scheme ① to steal expensive computer equipment. They broke into a local Internet server, ② stole credit card numbers and then used them to buy things online. They ordered $3,000 worth of computers, which were delivered to vacant homes in the area where it could be picked up after school. The neighbors, ③ who were suspicious of some strange activity, called the police and they responded ④ enough quickly to get there on time. When the boys were asked why they carried out ⑤ such a scheme, they said they wanted to do something exciting.

* face charge of: ~의 혐의를 받다
** scheme: 계획, 책략
*** suspicious of: ~에 대해 수상쩍어 하는

동명사

「동사+-ing」의 형태로 동사의 성질을 가지고 있으면서 명사처럼 쓰여 주어, 목적어, 보어 역할을 한다.

· **Taking** the subway is faster than driving a car. 〈주어〉
지하철을 타는 것이 운전하는 것보다 빠르다.

· My hobby is **riding** a bicycle. 〈보어〉

· I like **going** shopping at the shopping mall. 〈동사의 목적어〉
나는 쇼핑몰에 쇼핑하러 가는 것을 좋아한다.

· They are fond of **swimming** in the river. 〈전치사의 목적어〉
그들은 강에서 수영하는 것을 좋아한다.

· She is good at **managing** her time. 〈전치사의 목적어〉
그녀는 시간 관리를 잘한다.

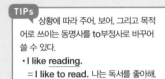

TIPs
상황에 따라 주어, 보어, 그리고 목적어로 쓰이는 동명사를 to부정사로 바꾸어 쓸 수 있다.
· I like reading.
= I like to read. 나는 독서를 좋아해.

Answers: p.09

Exercise 1 다음 〈보기〉에서 알맞은 단어를 골라 동명사를 사용하여 문장을 완성하시오.

| win | become | read | take | say | give |

1 Actually _____ a nap is good for our health.

2 His hobby is _____ novels written in English.

3 Michelle has a dream of _____ a Hollywood movie star.

4 She left the classroom without _____ goodbye to her friends.

5 Maggie is not interested in _____ the prize at the music contest.

6 She is good at _____ a presentation in front of a group of people.

Exercise 2 다음 두 문장의 의미가 같도록 동명사를 이용한 문장으로 바꿔 쓰시오.

1 The most important thing is to enjoy your life.

⇨ _____

2 She loves to read classic novels.

⇨ _____

3 To go shopping is my favorite activity.

⇨ _____

4 The instructor started to practice yoga in 2015 and began to teach in 2021.

⇨ _____

3-2 동명사의 시제

☐ 단순형 동명사 「V-ing」
  문장의 동사와 같은 시제를 나타내거나 미래를 나타낸다.
  · He **is** ashamed of **being** lazy.
    = He **is** ashamed that he **is** lazy. 그는 게으른 것을 부끄럽게 여긴다.
  · He **is** sure of **passing** the test.
    = He **is** sure that he **will pass** the test. 그는 자신이 시험에 통과할 거라고 확신한다.
  · He **was** ashamed of **being** lazy.
    = He **was** ashamed that he **was** lazy. 그는 게으른 것을 부끄럽게 여겼다.

☐ 완료형 동명사 「having+p.p.」
  문장의 동사보다 앞선 시제를 나타낸다.
  · He **is** ashamed of **having been** lazy.
    = He **is** ashamed that he **was** lazy. 그는 게을렀던 것을 부끄럽게 여긴다.
  · He **was** ashamed of **having been** lazy.
    = He **was** ashamed that he **had been** lazy. 그는 게을렀던 것을 부끄럽게 여겼다.

Answers: p.09

Exercise 1 다음 짝지어진 두 문장이 같은 뜻이 되도록 문장을 완성하시오.

1 He is ashamed that he is poor.
   ⇒ He is ashamed of _____.

2 They are proud that they are early adopters.
   ⇒ They are proud of _____.

3 Daniel was proud that he had won the marathon race.
   ⇒ Daniel was proud of _____.

4 Sujin was ashamed that she had done such a foolish thing.
   ⇒ Sujin was ashamed of _____.

Exercise 2 다음 우리말과 같은 뜻이 되도록 괄호 안의 단어를 알맞게 배열하여 문장을 완성하시오.

1 발을 밟아서 죄송해요. (on, stepped, toes, having, your)
   ⇒ I'm sorry for _____.

2 그는 마라톤에서 우승한 것을 자랑스러워했다. (having, the marathon, won)
   ⇒ He was proud of _____.

3 나는 내 여동생과 옷을 함께 입는 것을 꺼리지 않는다. (my little sister, sharing, clothes, with)
   ⇒ I don't mind _____.

4 나는 그 대학으로부터 합격 통지서를 받아서 정말 기뻤다. (having received, letter, acceptance, an)
   ⇒ I was so happy about _____ from the university.

3-3 의미상의 주어 / 부정형

□ **동명사의 의미상의 주어**

❶ 의미상의 주어를 표시하지 않는 경우

- I am afraid of **failing** the test. 〈주어와 일치〉
  나는 시험에 떨어지는 것이 두렵다.

- Thank you for **helping** me. 〈목적어와 일치〉
  나를 도와줘서 고마워요.

- **Walking** is a good way to keep healthy. 〈일반인〉
  걷는 것은 건강을 유지하는 좋은 방법이다.

❷ 의미상의 주어를 표시하는 경우

명사나 대명사의 소유격을 사용하는 것이 원칙이나 목적격을 사용하기도 한다.

- I am afraid of **his[him] being** fired.
  나는 그가 해고되는 것이 두렵다.

- He is proud of **his daughter's[his daughter] having passed** the exam.
  그는 자신의 딸이 시험에 합격한 것을 자랑스러워한다.

□ **동명사의 부정형**

동명사 바로 앞에 **not**을 쓴다.

- I am sorry for **not arriving** on time. 제시간에 도착하지 못해서 죄송합니다.

- Thank you for **not telling** the secret to anyone. 그 비밀을 아무에게도 말하지 않아 줘서 고마워요.

Answers: p.09

Exercise 1 다음 짝지어진 두 문장이 같은 뜻이 되도록 〈보기〉와 같이 문장을 고쳐 쓰시오.

> Would you mind if I open the window?
> ⇒ Would you mind _____my opening the window_____?

1 I am proud that my son is clever.

   ⇒ I am proud of _____.

2 I was sorry that my brother was rude.

   ⇒ I was sorry for _____.

3 They are worried that he is jealous of her.

   ⇒ They are worried about _____.

4 She is afraid that they might be late for the meeting.

   ⇒ She is afraid of _____.

5 He was excited that his cousins visited him last week.

   ⇒ He was excited about _____.

6 We had no doubt that she would win the gold medal this time.

   ⇒ We had no doubt about _____.

1 He insisted on <u>his father's going</u> there.

　⇨ _____

2 I was proud of <u>my son's having been chosen</u> for the national team.

　⇨ _____

3 Wilson is sure of <u>his grandfather's having fought</u> in the Korean War.

　⇨ _____

4 Tom remembered <u>her entering the building</u> when he parked his car.

　⇨ _____

Exercise ③ 다음 우리말과 같은 뜻이 되도록 주어진 단어와 동명사의 부정형을 사용하여 문장을 완성하시오.

1 약속을 지키지 못해서 미안해요. (keeping, the promise)

　⇨ I'm sorry for _____ .

2 그는 그녀가 자신에게 사실을 말해주지 않아서 화가 났다. (telling, him)

　⇨ He was upset about _____ the truth.

3 이 건물 안에서는 금연하여 주시기 바랍니다. (smoking, this building)

　⇨ We thank you for _____ .

4 그녀는 어제 그에게 그 책을 빌려주지 않은 것을 후회했다. (lending, the book)

　⇨ She regretted _____ yesterday.

Exercise ④ 다음 우리말과 같은 뜻이 되도록 괄호 안의 단어를 알맞게 배열하시오.

1 네가 시험에 실패해서 유감이다. (I, sorry, failing, your, the test, am, for)

　⇨ _____

2 그녀는 그가 거짓말을 하는 것을 부끄럽게 여겼다. (his, was, of, ashamed, she, lying)

　⇨ _____

3 우리는 그의 한국 방문을 고대하고 있습니다. (Korea, we, visiting, to, his, looking forward, are)

　⇨ _____

4 나는 아이들이 그 강아지를 괴롭힐까 봐 걱정이다. (I, kids', about, bothering, am, the puppy, worried)

　⇨ _____

3-4 동명사와 to부정사 I

📖 동명사를 목적어로 취하는 동사, to부정사를 목적어로 취하는 동사, 동명사와 to부정사 둘 다를 목적어로 취하는 동사가 있다.

❶ 동명사를 목적어로 취하는 동사

> enjoy, finish, mind, avoid, give up, postpone, put off, consider, stop, suggest, quit, deny, imagine, practice, keep (on) 등

- I **enjoyed reading** the detective novel. 나는 그 추리소설 읽는 것을 즐겼다.
- Tracy **finished doing** her homework. Tracy는 숙제하는 것을 마쳤다.
- Do you **mind opening** the window? 창문 좀 열어 주실래요?
- She **suggested sharing** the password. 그녀는 비밀번호를 공유하자고 제안했다.

❷ to부정사를 목적어로 취하는 동사

> want, hope, expect, decide, manage, refuse, fail, agree 등

- I **hope to see** you again. 나는 너를 다시 보기를 바란다.
- The politician **decided to publish** a book about his life.
  그 정치인은 자신의 삶에 관한 책을 출판하기로 결정했다.
- They **expected to meet** more people in Seoul.
  그들은 서울에서 더 많은 사람을 만날 것을 기대했다.
- He **refused to discuss** the matter with his friends.
  그는 그 문제에 대해 친구들과 토의하기를 거부했다.

❸ 동명사와 to부정사 둘 다를 목적어로 취하면서 의미상의 차이가 거의 없는 동사

> like, love, start, begin, continue, prefer, hate 등

- Tom **began playing** the piano when he was twelve.
  = Tom **began to play** the piano when he was twelve. Tom은 열두 살에 피아노를 치기 시작했다.
- I **love going** to the movies.
  = I **love to go** to the movies. 나는 영화 보러 가는 것을 좋아한다.

Answers: p.09

Exercise ① 다음 괄호 안에서 알맞은 말을 <u>모두</u> 고르시오.

1 I have decided (go / to go / going) to college.

2 Do you mind (open / to open / opening) the window?

3 (Go / To go / Going) to such a dangerous place is a bad idea.

4 I finished (write / to write / writing) a letter before going to bed.

5 I like (listen to / to listen to / listening to) music when I'm alone.

6 I succeeded in (solve / to solve / solving) the mystery by myself.

7 Don't put off (do / to do / doing) the things which you have to do today.

8 Valerie refused (receive / to receive / receiving) money from the government.

Exercise 2 다음 문장을 읽고, 어법상 <u>어색한</u> 부분을 찾아 바르게 고치시오.

1 I gladly agreed accepting their offer.

2 Can you imagine to go to Mars in the future?

3 He expected meeting her parents on Saturday.

4 The city authorities planned renovating the public library.

5 The reporters enjoyed to talk with the gold medalists.

6 The students finished to read the book that their teacher recommended.

Exercise 3 다음 〈보기〉에서 알맞은 단어를 골라 동명사 또는 to부정사로 바꿔 문장을 완성하시오.

| hold | go | take turns | meet | turn off | practice |

1 We agreed _____ doing the daily chores.

2 Would you mind _____ the light when you leave the room?

3 I considered _____ to the exhibition with Scott this weekend.

4 He decided _____ playing the piano much more for the concert.

5 They put off _____ the opening ceremony due to the earthquake.

6 The professor expected _____ colleagues and students at the conference.

Exercise 4 다음 우리말과 같은 뜻이 되도록 괄호 안의 단어를 사용하여 문장을 완성하시오.

1 그는 내게 변호사가 되기 위해 공부하는 것을 포기하지 말라고 말했다. (give up, study, become)

⇒ He told me not to _____ a lawyer.

2 그 정치가는 개인적인 논평을 피하려고 했다. (avoid, make)

⇒ The politician tried to _____ personal comments.

3 그들은 기자회견을 다음 주 월요일까지 연기하는 데 동의했다. (agree, postpone, hold)

⇒ They _____ the press conference until next Monday.

4 내 여동생은 자신이 음악적 감각이 없다는 것을 깨달았을 때 바이올린 배우는 것을 그만두기로 결정했다.
(decide, quit, learn)

⇒ My sister _____ the violin when she realized she didn't have
musical sense.

동명사와 to부정사 II

☐ **stop, remember, forget, regret, try**

동사	동명사	to부정사
stop	~하는 것을 멈추다	~ 하기 위해 멈추다 (부사적 쓰임(목적))
remember, forget	(과거) 했던 것을 기억하다/잊다	(미래) ~할 것을 기억하다/잊다
regret	~한 것을 후회하다	~하게 되어 유감이다
try	~을 시험 삼아 해보다	~하려고 노력하다, 애쓰다

· He **stopped taking** a break and got to work. 그는 휴식은 멈추고 일을 시작했다.
· He **stopped to take** a break after working all morning.
  그는 아침 내내 일하고 나서 휴식을 취하기 위해 멈췄다.
· I **remembered meeting** her yesterday. 나는 어제 그녀를 만난 것을 기억했다.
· Please **remember to meet** her tomorrow. 내일 그녀를 만날 것을 기억해.
· I **forgot telling** her the news and told her the news again.
  나는 그녀에게 그 소식을 전했던 것을 잊고, 그녀에게 또 말했다.
· I **forgot to tell** her the news, so I'll tell her the news later.
  나는 그녀에게 그 소식을 전하는 것을 잊어서 나중에 말할 것이다.
· I **regret breaking** up with her. 나는 그녀와 헤어진 것을 후회한다.
· I **regret to inform** you that you have failed your exam.
  당신이 시험에 떨어졌음을 알리게 되어 유감입니다.
· I **tried putting on** the yellow pants, but they didn't look good on me.
  나는 노란 바지를 입어봤지만, 나에게 잘 어울리지 않았다.
· I **tried to pass** the exam, but I failed. 나는 시험에 통과하기 위해 노력했지만, 떨어졌다.

Answers: p.09

Exercise 1 다음 괄호 안에서 알맞은 말을 고르시오.

1 I regretted (to yell / yelling) at my brother last night.

2 I remember (to see / seeing) the movie when I was young.

3 He stopped (to rest / resting) for a few minutes after running.

4 We'll never forget (to watch / watching) the CEO introducing the first smartphone.

5 Don't forget (to turn off / turning off) the radio when you go to sleep.

6 Fast food is not healthy. People had better stop (to eat / eating) that.

Exercise 2 다음 괄호 안의 단어를 사용하여 문장을 완성하시오.

1 She forgot _____ (read) the book, and she read it again.

2 I failed the test, but I will try _____ (study) harder next time.

3 Please remember _____ (return) the books you borrowed from the library.

4 It was too hot. I tried _____ (drink) cold water and _____ (take) a shower, but nothing worked.

3-6 to+동명사 / to+동사원형

「to+동명사」/「to+동사원형」

❶ 「to+동명사」

- look forward to -ing ~을 학수고대하다[간절히 바라다]
- be used[accustomed] to -ing ~에 익숙하다
- in addition to -ing ~외에도
- contribute to -ing ~에 공헌하다

- I am **looking forward to meeting** you as soon as possible.
  가능한 한 빨리 당신을 만나기를 고대합니다.
- I'm **used to staying** up late. 나는 늦게까지 깨어 있는 것에 익숙하다.
- He **contributed to making** the world better. 그는 더 나은 세상을 만드는 데 공헌했다.

❷ 「to+동사원형」

- be going to+동사원형 ~할 예정이다
- be able to+동사원형 ~할 수 있다
- be about to+동사원형 막 ~하려 하다

- I'm **going to study** dairy farming in New Zealand. 나는 뉴질랜드에서 낙농업을 공부할 예정이다.
- Jasmine **was able to spot** me in a crowd. Jasmine은 군중 속에서 나를 발견할 수 있었다.
- She **was about to leave** for the airport. 그녀는 공항으로 막 출발하려고 하고 있었다.

Answers: p.10

Exercise 1 다음 괄호 안에서 알맞은 말을 고르시오.

1 He is used to (ride / riding) his bike on busy roads.

2 The kids are able to (climb / climbing) the mountain.

3 We are looking forward to (see / seeing) you at the annual meeting.

4 In addition to (play / playing) the violin, she is good at playing sports.

5 She is going to (resign / resigning) because the company gives her too much stress.

6 When I was about to (fall / falling) asleep, I heard somebody knocking on the door.

Exercise 2 다음 〈보기〉에서 단어를 골라 알맞은 형태로 바꿔 문장을 완성하시오.

| wear | receive | cry | play |

1 She is looking forward to _____ your letters.

2 Sam is used to _____ basketball by international rules.

3 When I finally found my nephew, he was about to _____.

4 He is accustomed to _____ the cultural dress instead of the standard business suit.

❶ be busy -ing ～하느라 바쁘다
- I **am busy doing** my homework. 나는 숙제를 하느라 바쁘다.
- She **is busy taking** care of her children. 그녀는 아이들을 돌보느라 바쁘다.

❷ feel like -ing ～하고 싶다
- Today I don't **feel like playing** soccer after school. 나는 오늘 방과 후에 축구를 하고 싶지 않다.

❸ There is no saying ~ = It is impossible to know ~ ～은 알 수 없다, 모르겠다
- **There is no saying** what may happen in the future.
  = **It is impossible to know** what may happen in the future. 미래에 어떤 일이 일어날지 알 수 없다.

❹ It is no use -ing = It is useless to + 동사원형 ～해도 소용없다
- **It is no use crying** over spilt milk.
  = **It is useless to cry** over spilt milk. 엎질러진 물이다. (후회해도 소용없다.)

❺ can't help -ing = cannot but + 동사원형
- I **can't help laughing** at the picture.
  = I **cannot but laugh** at the picture. 나는 그 사진을 보고 웃지 않을 수 없다.

❻ on -ing = as soon as ～하자마자
- **On hearing** the news, she began to cry.
  = **As soon as** she heard the news, she began to cry. 그녀는 그 소식을 듣자마자 울기 시작했다.

❼ cannot[never] ⋯ without -ing = Whenever ~ ～하기만 하면 꼭 ⋯하다, ～하지 않고는 ⋯할 수 없다
- He **cannot** study **without listening to** music.
  = **Whenever** he studies, he listens to music. 그는 공부할 때마다 음악을 듣는다.

❽ be worth -ing ～할 가치가 있다
- The book **is worth reading** many times. 이 책은 여러 번 읽을 가치가 있다.

❾ make a point of -ing = make it a point to + 동사원형 ～하도록 노력하다, 반드시 ～하다
- I **made a point of donating** ten dollars to the orphanage once a month.
  = I **made it a point to donate** ten dollars to the orphanage once a month.
  나는 한 달에 한 번 보육원에 10달러씩 기부하려고 노력했다.

❿ far from -ing ～이기는커녕, ～와 거리가 먼
- He is **far from helping** other people. 그는 다른 사람을 전혀 도와주지 않는다.

⓫ go[come] -ing ～하러 가다[오다]
- They **went swimming** in the river. 그들은 강에 수영하러 갔다.
- My relative **came visiting** my family last month. 지난달에 나의 친척이 우리 가족을 방문하러 왔다.

⓬ have difficulty[problem, trouble, a hard time] (in) -ing ～하는 데 어려움을 겪다
- She **has a hard time getting over** the car accident. 그녀는 자동차 사고를 극복하는 데 어려움을 겪고 있다.
- He **is having trouble checking** his e-mail. 그는 이메일을 확인하는 데 어려움을 겪고 있다.

⓭ how[what] about -ing = let's + 동사원형 ～ 하는 것은 어때?, ～하자
- **How about playing** tennis this afternoon?
  = **What about playing** tennis this afternoon?
  = **Let's play** tennis this afternoon. 오늘 오후에 테니스 치자.

⓮ spend + 시간 · 돈 등 + -ing ～ 하는 데 시간, 돈 등을 쓰다
- She **spends** her leisure time **drawing** pictures. 그녀는 그림을 그리면서 여가를 보낸다.

Exercise 1 다음 〈보기〉에서 단어를 골라 알맞은 형태로 바꿔 문장을 완성하시오.

🔍   adjust   go   smile   watch   arrive   bring

1   I couldn't help _____ when I saw the baby dancing.

2   It was too hot. On _____ home, I took a shower.

3   I don't feel like _____ on a picnic today. I think I have a cold.

4   He has a strange habit. He cannot come home without _____ strange things.

5   We've just moved into this town and had difficulty _____ to the new environment.

6   This movie is more astonishing than any other movie that I've seen. The movie is worth _____ several times.

Exercise 2 다음 짝지어진 두 문장이 같은 뜻이 되도록 문장을 완성하시오.

1   What about eating out tonight?
   ⇨ _____

2   He made it a point to get up at 6 a.m.
   ⇨ He _____ at 6 a.m.

3   I couldn't help laughing at his funny costume.
   ⇨ I _____ .

4   It is useless to regret what you've done already.
   ⇨ _____ what you've done already.

Exercise 3 다음 우리말과 같은 뜻이 되도록 괄호 안의 단어를 알맞게 배열하여 문장을 완성하시오.

1   우리 집을 찾는 데 힘들었습니까? (finding, difficulty, did, you, my house, have)
   ⇨ _____

2   그녀를 설득하려고 노력해도 아무 소용이 없다. (is, persuade, no use, trying, to, her, it)
   ⇨ _____

3   그녀는 매일 산책을 하려고 노력했다. (of, every day, a point, she, a walk, made, taking)
   ⇨ _____

4   나는 Jacob을 볼 때마다 그의 형이 생각난다.
   (couldn't, thinking of, I, look at, his brother, without, Jacob)
   ⇨ _____

 **Review Test**

[01-07] 다음 빈칸에 들어갈 알맞은 말을 고르시오.

01 A : Do you enjoy _____ cards with Anne?
B : Yes. She's a clever girl.

① play ② playing
③ to play ④ played
⑤ being played

02 A : I am feeling cold. Would you mind
_____ the window?
B : No problem.

① open ② close
③ to open ④ closing
⑤ to close

03 She is good at _____ difficult
customers.

① deal with ② being dealt with
③ to deal with ④ dealing with
⑤ to have dealt with

04 We had difficulty _____ our project.

① finish ② finishing
③ to be finishing ④ to finish
⑤ finished

05 Please stop _____ so much noise. I'm
trying _____.

① to make - to sleep ② making - to sleep
③ making - sleep ④ to make - sleeping
⑤ make - sleeping

06 Mary spent a lot of time _____ me
complete the project.

① help ② helps
③ to have helped ④ helping
⑤ to have taken

07 She gave up _____ comic books
because she didn't have enough money.

① to buy ② buying
③ to have bought ④ being bought
⑤ buy

[08-09] 다음 빈칸에 들어갈 수 없는 말을 고르시오.

08 Steven _____ telling about the car
accident he watched yesterday.

① avoided ② started
③ began ④ stopped
⑤ wanted

09 He _____ playing soccer on weekends.

① enjoys ② practices
③ likes ④ keeps
⑤ hopes

10 다음 〈보기〉의 밑줄 친 부분과 쓰임이 같은 것은?

I like traveling very much.

① I heard her singing Chinese songs.
② A dancing doll is my niece's favorite.
③ We enjoyed playing tennis yesterday.
④ Who is the woman talking with Tom?
⑤ He was traveling in China when I called.

11 다음 중 어법상 올바른 문장은?

  ① Would you mind not to smoke here?

  ② I want going to the movies tonight.

  ③ Tom cannot help take exercise hard.

  ④ He felt like to laugh at the good news.

  ⑤ She finished writing the book last night.

12 다음 중 밑줄 친 부분의 쓰임이 <u>다른</u> 것은?

  ① I'm <u>working</u> on a new project.

  ② I often think of <u>going</u> to Spain.

  ③ My father stopped <u>smoking</u> last year.

  ④ I finished <u>writing</u> a letter to my mother.

  ⑤ She enjoyed <u>reading</u> books when she was young.

[13-15] 다음 중에서 어법상 <u>어색한</u> 문장을 고르시오.

13 ① The book is worth reading twice.

  ② I had trouble to concentrate on my work.

  ③ Have you considered becoming a doctor?

  ④ She enjoyed having a wonderful date last night.

  ⑤ Don't forget to pay the money back by tomorrow.

14 ① Do you mind reading it aloud?

  ② How about inviting her to our party?

  ③ My sister is looking forward to see you.

  ④ Sujin went shopping to buy some clothes.

  ⑤ I'm busy packing baggage for the journey.

15 ① Talking is easier than doing.

  ② On leaving school, he got a job.

  ③ They are used to walking to school.

  ④ She is proud of being praised by him.

  ⑤ She denied to know anything about it.

16 다음 〈보기〉의 밑줄 친 부분과 쓰임이 같은 것은?

  In England, <u>making</u> tea is a very serious matter.

  ① He looks like a <u>sleeping</u> baby.

  ② She is proud of <u>winning</u> the gold medal.

  ③ Peter is <u>speaking</u> to my parents right now.

  ④ The boy <u>sleeping</u> in the bed is my cousin.

  ⑤ When I visited her house yesterday, Cindy was <u>studying</u> English.

17 다음 밑줄 친 부분 중 어법상 <u>어색한</u> 것은?

  Grace ① <u>as well as</u> Eddie forgot ② <u>writing</u>

  ③ <u>a thank-you letter</u> ④ <u>to Mr. Johnson</u>

  ⑤ <u>after</u> the party because they were too busy.

[18-19] 다음 주어진 문장과 의미가 같은 문장을 고르시오.

18   I remember deleting the folder.

  ① I remember to delete the folder.

  ② I remember I am deleting the folder.

  ③ I remember that I'll delete the folder.

  ④ I remember that I deleted the folder.

  ⑤ I remember that I should delete the folder.

19   It is no use regretting what happened.

  ① It is useful to regret what happened.

  ② It is worth regretting what happened.

  ③ It is useless to regret what happened.

  ④ It is useful regretting what happened to us.

  ⑤ Regretting what happened is useful for us.

[20-22] 다음 우리말을 바르게 영작한 것을 고르시오.

20 | 그는 젊었을 때 빈둥거리며 논 것이 부끄럽다.

① He is ashamed of being idle in his youth.
② He was ashamed of being idle in his youth.
③ He was ashamed of having been idle in his youth.
④ He had been ashamed of being idle in his youth.
⑤ He is ashamed of having been idle in his youth.

21 | 당신과 사랑에 빠지지 않을 수 없어요.

① I can't help fall in love with you.
② I can't help falling in love with you.
③ I cannot but falling in love with you.
④ I can't help to falling in love with you.
⑤ I cannot but to falling in love with you.

22 | Sally는 그 다음 달에 삼촌을 방문해야 한다는 것을 기억했다.

① Sally remembered to visit her uncle the following month.
② Sally remembered visiting her uncle the following month.
③ Sally remembered to have visited her uncle the following month.
④ Sally remembered having visited her uncle the following month.
⑤ Sally remembered to be visited her uncle the following month.

[23-25] 다음 빈칸에 들어갈 말이 바르게 짝지어진 것을 고르시오.

23 | · You made it worse. It's far _____ helping us.
· They are accustomed _____ dancing on a stage.

① to - to   ② from - to
③ to - from   ④ for - to
⑤ for - for

24 | · Stop _____ and listen to me.
· Tom went out without _____ goodbye.

① talk - says   ② talked - said
③ talking - saying   ④ to talk - to say
⑤ to talk - saying

25 | · The boy kept _____ about his mother.
· I feel like _____ to the music.
· Seoul is worth _____.

① talking - to dance - to visit
② talking - dancing - visiting
③ to talk - dancing - visiting
④ to talk - to dance - to visit
⑤ talking - dancing - to visit

26 다음 빈칸에 공통으로 들어갈 말을 쓰시오.

· I always wanted _____ go to L.A.
· Don't forget _____ visit me tomorrow.
· I am looking forward _____ seeing you.

[27-29] 다음 두 문장이 같은 뜻이 되도록 빈칸에 알맞은 말을 넣어 문장을 완성하시오.

27 Alice made a mistake of telling our secret, and she feels bad that she did that.
→ Alice regrets _____ a mistake of telling our secret.

28 I could not help laughing at his appearance.
→ I could not _____ _____ _____ his appearance.

29 To eat too many sweets is not good for your teeth.
→ _____ too many sweets is not good for your teeth.

30 다음 우리말과 같은 뜻이 되도록 괄호 안의 단어를 사용하여 문장을 완성하시오.

만화책이 너무 재미있어서 읽는 것을 멈출 수가 없다.
→ The comic book is so funny that I can't _____ it. (stop, read)

31 다음 괄호 안의 단어를 사용하여 문장을 완성하시오.

· Woolen clothes are used to _____ warm. (keep)
· I'm used to _____ difficult math problems. (solve)

[32-33] 다음 두 문장이 같은 뜻이 되도록 빈칸에 알맞은 말을 넣어 문장을 완성하시오.

32 As soon as he left school, he went to Europe.
→ _____ school, he went to Europe.

33 I am sure that she will win the race.
→ I am sure of _____ the race.

[34-36] 다음 문장을 읽고, 어법상 <u>어색한</u> 부분을 찾아 바르게 고쳐 쓰시오.

34 My grandmother is ashamed of being not able to read.
_____ → _____

35 On arrive here, they found they weren't able to get enough food and water for two weeks.
_____ → _____

36 They felt like to cry when they heard the news of the outbreak of war.
_____ → _____

[37-38] 다음 우리말과 같은 뜻이 되도록 문장을 완성하시오.

37 나는 기말고사 공부를 하느라 바쁘다.
→ _____ for the finals.

38 그녀는 그 동물원을 방문했던 것을 기억했다.
→ She _____ .

Answers: p.12

[1-2] 다음 대화를 읽고, 물음에 답하시오.   서술형

A Do you want to be a soccer player when you grow up? You always talk about Son Heung-min.

B I'm not sure what I enjoy doing. How about you?

A (A) 나는 요리사가 되려고 생각 중이야.

B I remember when you made that delicious pasta for me.

A Yes. I love cooking. I hope you have a goal, too. (B) 네가 좋아하는 일을 찾도록 노력해 봐.

B I'll try. Thanks. Good luck with your dream.

1 밑줄 친 (A)를 주어진 단어를 이용하여 영작하시오.

→ I'm _____ a chef. (consider, become)

2 밑줄 친 (B)를 주어진 단어를 이용하여 영작하시오.

→ _____ what you _____. (try, find, like, do)

3 다음 글의 밑줄 친 부분 중, 어법상 틀린 것은?   수능 대비형

Monica and her husband created a family calendar ① to keep track of their activities and appointments. With three children, there was a lot going on, and Monica had trouble ② to get everyone to the right place at the right time. Luke had soccer practice, Amanda had cello lessons, and Jessie had choir practice. Monica ③ put the new calendar on the wall in the kitchen, and they reviewed the schedule in a family meeting every Sunday evening. ④ After several weeks, Monica felt she ⑤ could manage everyone's time much more effectively.

* keep track of: ~대해 계속 파악하다
** choir: 합창단, 성가대

Chapter 4

분사

분사의 종류

□ 현재분사 : 「동사원형+ing」의 형태를 취하며, 진행이나 능동의 의미를 담고 있다.
  a **dancing** girl (춤추는 소녀)　　　　　　　a **crying** baby (우는 아기)

□ 과거분사 : 「동사원형+ed」의 형태를 취하며, 수동이나 완료의 의미를 담고 있다.
  fallen leaves (떨어진 나뭇잎: 낙엽)　　　a **wounded** dog (상처 입은 개)

□ **분사의 쓰임**

  ❶ 명사 수식 : 단독으로 쓰인 분사는 명사 앞에서, 수식어와 함께 쓰인 분사는 명사 뒤에서 명사를 수식한다.
    · The **crying** baby is my cousin. 저 울고 있는 아기가 나의 사촌이다.
    · The baby **crying on the sofa** is my cousin. 소파에서 울고 있는 아기가 나의 사촌이다.

  ❷ 보어 역할 : 분사는 주어 또는 목적어의 상태나 동작을 보충 설명하는 보어로 쓰인다.
    · The audience was completely **touched**. 〈주격보어〉
      청중은 완전히 감동을 받았다.
    · The book is very **interesting**. 〈주격보어〉
      그 책은 매우 재미있다.
    · We saw him **taken** to the hospital. 〈목적격보어〉
      우리는 그가 병원으로 실려 가는 것을 보았다.
    · I heard Sarah **singing** in the gym. 〈목적격보어〉
      나는 Sarah가 체육관에서 노래하는 것을 들었다.

> **TIPs**
> 목적어와 목적격보어의 관계가 수동일 경우 목적격보어로 과거분사가 쓰인다.
> · She had **her computer repaired**.
>   그녀는 자신의 컴퓨터가 수리되도록 했다.

  ❸ 감정을 나타내는 분사 : '~한 감정을 느끼게 하는'이라는 의미일 때는 현재분사를, '~한 감정을 느끼는'이라는 의미일 때는 과거분사를 사용한다.
    · The soccer game was **exciting**. 그 축구경기는 매우 흥미 있었다.
    · They are **excited** about the soccer game. 그들은 그 축구 경기에 신이나 있었다.

Answers: p.12

Exercise ❶ 다음 괄호 안에서 알맞은 말을 고르시오.

1 Look at (fallen / falling) leaves on the street.

2 I have a good friend (calling / called) Nicole.

3 I heard my name (calling / called) in the bank.

4 They are looking for the (stealing / stolen) painting.

5 A (used / using) car is cheaper than a new car.

6 Do you know the woman (sit / sitting) next to the tall man?

7 The man (played / playing) the violin in the auditorium is my uncle.

8 Can you see the house (covered / covering) with snow over there?

9 Those students (playing / played) baseball in the park go to the same school as I do.

🔍 **The trip to Disneyland excited the children.**
⇨ **The children were** _____excited_____ **about the trip to Disneyland.**
⇨ **The trip to Disneyland was** _____exciting_____ **for the children.**

1 The lecture on physics bored me.
⇨ I was _____ with the lecture on physics.
⇨ The lecture on physics was _____ to me.

2 The teacher's compliment pleased the new student.
⇨ The teacher's compliment was _____ to the new student.
⇨ The new student was _____ with the teacher's compliment.

3 Her kid's rude behavior embarrassed Sharon.
⇨ Her kid's rude behavior was _____ to Sharon.
⇨ Sharon was _____ by her kid's rude behavior.

4 The bomb explosion frightened all the villagers.
⇨ All the villagers were _____ by the bomb explosion.
⇨ The bomb explosion was _____ for all the villagers.

Exercise **3** 다음 〈보기〉와 같이 문장을 완성하시오.

🔍 **The cat is my sister's. It is lying on the couch.**
⇨ **The cat** _____lying on the couch_____ **is my sister's.**

1 The boy is my cousin. He is standing at the bus stop.
⇨ The boy _____ is my cousin.

2 I'm reading a fantasy novel. It is written by J. K. Rowling.
⇨ I'm reading a fantasy novel _____.

3 My sister and I went to the library. It is located in the center of the city.
⇨ My sister and I went to the library _____.

4 Jake has lived in the house. It was built two years ago by his grandfather.
⇨ Jake has lived in the house _____.

5 Do you know the girls? They are wearing the same school uniform as you.
⇨ Do you know the girls _____?

분사구문

분사구문은 현재분사나 과거분사를 사용하여 부사절(접속사+주어+동사 ~)을 분사가 이끄는 구의 형태로 간단하게
나타낸 것을 말한다.

분사구문 만드는 법

❶ 접속사를 생략한다.
- ~~When~~ I came into my room, I found the TV on.

❷ 부사절의 주어가 주절의 주어와 같을 경우 주어를 생략한다.
- ~~I~~ came into my room, I found the TV on.

❸ 동사를 -ing형태로 바꾼다.
- **Coming** into my room, I found the TV on.
  나는 방에 들어와서 TV가 켜져 있는 것을 발견했다.

분사구문의 의미

❶ 시간 : when, while, as, after
- **When I was walking** along the street, I ran into a friend of mine.
- = **(Being) Walking** along the street, I ran into a friend of mine.
  나는 거리를 따라 걷다가 친구를 만났다.

❷ 이유 : as, because, since
- **As he had** a bad cold, he couldn't go outside.
- = **Having** a bad cold, he couldn't go outside.
  그는 심한 감기에 걸려서 밖에 나갈 수 없었다.

❸ 조건 : if
- **If you turn** to the left, you will find the post office.
- = **Turning** to the left, you will find the post office.
  왼쪽으로 돌면 우체국을 찾을 수 있을 것이다.

❹ 양보 : though, although, even though, even if
- **Though he is** rich, he still works.
- = **Being** rich, he still works.
  그는 부자이지만, 아직도 일한다.

> **TIPs**
> not이나 never와 같은 부정어는
> 분사 앞에 온다.
> - **Not** knowing what happened
>   there, we stayed home all day.
>   → As we didn't know what
>   happened there, we stayed
>   home all day.
>   우리는 그곳에서 어떤 일이 일어났는
>   지 알지 못해서 온종일 집에 있었다.

부대상황 : 동시동작 (~하면서), 연속동작 (그리고 ~하다)

- Mrs. Ward entered the classroom, **as she smiled** at us.
- = Mrs. Ward entered the classroom, **smiling** at us. 〈동시동작〉
  Ward 선생님은 우리에게 미소를 지으며 교실로 들어오셨다.
- The train left at five **and reached** Seoul at ten.
- = The train left at five, **reaching** Seoul at ten. 〈연속동작〉
  그 기차는 다섯 시에 출발해서 열 시에 서울에 도착했다.

분사구문의 뜻을 명확히 하기 위해 접속사를 남겨 두기도 한다.

- **While she was working** in Canada, she met and married Brandon.
- = **While working** in Canada, she met and married Brandon.
  그녀는 캐나다에서 일하는 동안 Brandon을 만나서 결혼했다.

Exercise ① 다음 짝지어진 두 문장이 같은 뜻이 되도록 분사구문을 사용하여 문장을 완성하시오.

1 When he saw me on the street, he ran away.

⇨ _____ , he ran away.

2 Though you hate the project, you should finish it.

⇨ _____ , you should finish it.

3 Because she was sick, she went to see a doctor.

⇨ _____ , she went to see a doctor.

4 If you solve this problem, you will get this prize.

⇨ _____ , you will get this prize.

5 While he was waiting for Susie, he saw a car accident.

⇨ _____ , he saw a car accident.

6 If you turn to the right, you will find the house.

⇨ _____ , you will find the house.

7 As she smiled at them, Sandra said, "I'll be back soon."

⇨ _____ , Sandra said, "I'll be back soon."

Exercise ② 다음 〈보기〉에서 알맞은 접속사를 골라 부사절을 사용하여 문장을 완성하시오.

🔍　　even though　　　　when　　　　because

1 (Being) Walking down the street, I met my teacher.

⇨ _____ , I met my teacher.

2 Hearing the bad news, I was disappointed.

⇨ _____ , I was disappointed.

3 Buying a new car, he gave me the old car.

⇨ _____ , he gave me the old car.

4 Being poor, he couldn't go to school.

⇨ _____ , he couldn't go to school.

5 Living near the school, he is always late for class.

⇨ _____ , he is always late for class.

6 Opening the door, she saw her father watching TV.

⇨ _____ , she saw her father watching TV.

1 Turning to the left,　　　　　　·　　　　· a it looks like a tiger.

2 Feeling very tired,　　　　　　·　　　　· b you will find the park.

3 Walking on the beach,　　　　　·　　　　· c I couldn't send him the document.

4 Being seen from a distance,　·　　　　· d I went to bed earlier than usual.

5 Not knowing his e-mail address, ·　　　· e I saw people swimming in the sea.

Exercise **4** 다음 짝지어진 두 문장이 같은 뜻이 되도록 분사구문을 사용하여 문장을 완성하시오.

1 As he waved his hand, he got in the car.

⇨ _____ his hand, he got in the car.

2 He fired, and he wounded one of the enemies.

⇨ He fired, _____ one of the enemies.

3 She cleaned the bathroom while she was singing happily.

⇨ She cleaned the bathroom, _____ happily.

4 She sometimes read books while she was listening to music.

⇨ She sometimes read books, _____ music.

5 He left New York at 7 and arrived in Los Angeles at 11.

⇨ He left New York at 7, _____ in Los Angeles at 11.

Exercise **5** 다음 우리말과 같은 뜻이 되도록 괄호 안의 단어를 알맞게 배열하여 문장을 완성하시오.

1 그녀는 집에 들어가서 모자를 벗었다. (her, the house, off, entered, taking, hat)

⇨ She _____ , _____ .

2 나는 그림에 관심이 있어서 루브르 박물관에 갔다. (paintings, being, in, interested)

⇨ _____ , I went to the Louvre Museum.

3 길을 걷다가 우연히 나의 옛 친구를 만났다. (across, I, walking, the street, came, along)

⇨ _____ , _____ an old friend of mine.

4 학생들은 생물학 강의를 들으면서 필기를 했다. (lecture, the, took, listening to, notes, biology)

⇨ The students _____ , _____ .

5 그는 현기증이 나서 10분 동안 휴식하기를 원했다. (break, to, he, dizzy, take, a, feeling, wanted)

⇨ _____ , _____ for ten minutes.

단순형 분사구문 (동사원형+**-ing**)

주절의 동사와 같은 시제를 나타낸다.

- **Living** in the countryside, I rarely have visitors.

  = As I **live** in the countryside, I rarely have visitors. 나는 시골에 살기 때문에 방문객이 거의 없다.

- **Living** near the beach, I could enjoy beautiful ocean views.

  = When I **lived** near the beach, I could enjoy beautiful ocean views.

  나는 해변 근처에 살았을 때 아름다운 바다 전망을 즐길 수 있었다.

완료형 분사구문 (**having+p.p.**)

주절의 동사보다 앞선 시제를 나타낸다.

- **Having lived** in America, he is good at speaking English.

  = As he **lived** in America, he is good at speaking English. 그는 미국에 살았기 때문에 영어를 잘한다.

- **Having finished** the task, he watched TV.

  = After he **had finished** the task, he watched TV. 그는 그 일을 마친 후에 TV를 시청했다.

Answers: p.12

Exercise ❶ 다음 짝지어진 두 문장이 같은 뜻이 되도록 분사구문을 사용하여 문장을 완성하시오.

1 While I was looking out of the window, I drank coffee.

⇨ _____ , I drank coffee.

2 After he had fixed his car, he left for Seoul.

⇨ _____ , he left for Seoul.

3 As I completed my project yesterday, I am very happy now.

⇨ _____ , I am very happy now.

4 As Linda had lost her diamond ring, she called the police.

⇨ _____ , Linda called the police.

5 If you save enough money, you can buy the car.

⇨ _____ , you can buy the car.

6 When he arrived home, he opened all the windows.

⇨ _____ , he opened all the windows.

7 Although I took the medicine, I still feel pain in my back.

⇨ _____ , I still feel pain in my back.

8 As she lived in Germany when she was young, she speaks German fluently.

⇨ _____ , she speaks German fluently.

9 After I arrived at the airport, I found out I left my passport at home.

⇨ _____ , I found out I left my passport at home.

1 Having finished the race, we all were exhausted.

⇨ After _____, we all were exhausted.

2 Having read the book, I returned it to the library.

⇨ As _____, I returned it to the library.

3 Not having any money, I can't treat you to lunch today.

⇨ As _____, I can't treat you to lunch today.

4 Having found the lost wallet, he brought it to the police.

⇨ After _____, he brought it to the police.

5 Having finished my homework, I watched my favorite TV program.

⇨ After _____, I watched my favorite TV program.

6 Arriving at home, he knew that he had left his watch in the library.

⇨ After _____, he knew that he had left his watch in the library.

7 Having watched the movie twice, she doesn't want to watch it again.

⇨ As _____, she doesn't want to watch it again.

8 Going straight for two blocks, you'll see the train station on your left.

⇨ If _____, you'll see the train station on your left.

Exercise **3** 다음 괄호 안의 단어와 분사구문을 사용하여 문장을 완성하시오.

1 그는 저녁을 많이 먹었음에도 아직도 배가 고프다. (have, a big dinner)

⇨ _____, he is still hungry.

2 나는 전에 그를 만난 적이 있기 때문에, 그를 알아볼 수 있었다. (meet, before)

⇨ _____, I could recognize him.

3 내 지갑을 집에 두고 와서, 너에게 돈을 빌려줄 수 없다. (leave, wallet)

⇨ _____, I can't lend you any money.

4 나는 내 휴대 전화를 잃어버렸기 때문에, 내 여동생에게 전화할 수 없다. (lose, cell phone)

⇨ _____, I can't make a call to my sister.

5 그는 대학에서 프랑스어를 공부했기 때문에, 프랑스어를 매우 잘한다. (study, at university)

⇨ _____, he can speak French very well.

6 우리는 그곳에서 즐거운 시간을 보냈기 때문에, 그곳에 다시 방문하기를 희망한다. (have, a great time)

⇨ _____, we hope to visit it again.

주의해야 할 분사구문

분사구문의 부정

부정어는 분사 앞에 온다.

Not knowing what to do, he asked for my help.

= **As he didn't know** what to do, he asked for my help. 그는 무엇을 할지 몰라서 나에게 도움을 청했다.

being/having been의 생략

수동 분사구문에서 **being**과 **having been**은 생략할 수 있다.

(Being) Tired, I want to get some rest.

= **As I am tired**, I want to get some rest. 나는 피곤해서 쉬고 싶다.

(Having been) Written by Japanese historians, the book contains a lot of misinformation.

= **As it was written** by Japanese historians, the book contains a lot of misinformation.
그 책은 일본 역사학자들에 의해 쓰여서 잘못된 정보를 많이 담고 있다.

Answers: p.13

Exercise 1 다음 짝지어진 두 문장이 같은 뜻이 되도록 분사구문을 사용하여 문장을 완성하시오.

1 As I didn't know what to say, I remained silent

⇨ _____ , I remained silent.

2 As he didn't have breakfast, he is hungry now.

⇨ _____ , he is hungry now.

3 Because he didn't have any friends, he was lonely.

⇨ _____ , he was lonely.

4 As he hadn't slept well, he felt very tired.

⇨ _____ , he felt very tired.

5 Because he didn't do his homework, he is worried about it.

⇨ _____ , he is worried about it.

6 As I have never read the book, I cannot criticize it.

⇨ _____ , I cannot criticize it.

7 Because he didn't want to stay home, he went out of the house.

⇨ _____ , he went out of the house.

8 As he didn't have enough money, he couldn't buy a new house.

⇨ _____ , he couldn't buy a new house.

9 Though I didn't read the novel, I know what the story is about.

⇨ _____ , I know what the story is about.

10 As she is not tall enough, she is not allowed to ride the roller coaster.

⇨ _____ , she is not allowed to ride the roller coaster.

다음 짝지어진 두 문장이 같은 뜻이 되도록 분사구문을 사용하여 문장을 완성하시오. (단, 생략 가능한 부분에 괄호할 것)

1 As she was impressed by his self-confidence, she employed him.

   ⇨ _____, she employed him.

2 As her father was pleased with Annie's grade, he bought her new shoes.

   ⇨ _____, he bought her new shoes.

3 If I am compared with Scott, I am much faster than him.

   ⇨ _____, I am much faster than him.

4 As this picture was painted by Picasso, it is very expensive.

   ⇨ _____, this picture is very expensive.

5 As the book was written in Old English, the book is difficult to understand.

   ⇨ _____, the book is difficult to understand.

6 As they were satisfied with my work, they wanted me to join the project.

   ⇨ _____, they wanted me to join the project.

Exercise **3** 다음 우리말과 같은 뜻이 되도록 괄호 안의 단어를 알맞게 배열하여 문장을 완성하시오.

1 우주에서 보면 지구는 푸른색으로 보인다. (space, seen, from)

   ⇨ _____, the Earth looks blue.

2 이 책은 쉬운 영어로 쓰여 있어서 읽기 쉽다. (in, English, written, easy)

   ⇨ _____, the book is easy to read.

3 잠을 충분히 못 자서 그는 수업 시간에 졸았다. (sleep, having gotten, not, enough)

   ⇨ _____, he kept nodding off in class.

4 나는 그녀의 전화번호를 몰라서 그녀에게 연락할 수 없었다. (phone number, her, not, knowing)

   ⇨ _____, I couldn't contact her.

5 그녀는 건축에 관심이 있어서 종종 외국으로 여행을 간다. (interested, architecture, in, being)

   ⇨ _____, she often travels to foreign countries.

6 나는 서울에서 자라지 않기 때문에 서울에 대해 거의 알지 못한다. (in, having, not, Seoul, grown up)

   ⇨ _____, I know little about Seoul.

7 그는 시험 결과에 실망해서 온종일 잠자코 있었다. (being, with, disappointed, the test result)

   ⇨ _____, he remained silent all day.

with + 명사 + 분사

◻ 「**with+명사+분사**」

'~을 …한 채로'라는 뜻으로 동시동작을 나타낸다. 이때 명사와 분사의 관계가 능동이면 현재분사를, 수동이면 과거분사를 쓴다.

· She stood **with her eyes closed**.
  그녀는 눈을 감은 채 서 있었다.

· She was looking at the sea **with her hair flying** in the wind.
  그녀는 바람에 머리카락이 날리는 채로 바다를 보고 있었다.

> **TIPs**
> 독립분사구문은 분사구문의 주어와 주절의 주어가 다른 경우로, 분사구문의 주어를 생략하지 않고 그대로 써야 한다.
> · It being cold, we stayed at home.
> → As it was cold, we stayed at home. 우리는 날씨가 추워서 집에 있었다.

◻ 비인칭 독립분사구문

분사구문의 주어가 일반인인 경우 주절의 주어와 달라도 생략할 수 있다.

frankly speaking 솔직히 말해서	generally speaking 일반적으로 말해서
strictly speaking 엄밀히 말해서	judging from ~으로 판단하건대
speaking of ~ 이야기가 나와서 말인데	talking of ~ 이야기가 나와서 말인데

· If we **speak strictly**, it is not a correct answer.
  = **Strictly speaking**, it is not a correct answer. 엄격히 말하자면, 그것은 맞는 답이 아니다.

Answers: p.13

Exercise 1 다음 짝지어진 두 문장이 같은 뜻이 되도록 「with+명사+분사」 구문을 사용하여 문장을 완성하시오.

1 He went out and his son was left alone.
   ⇨ He went out _____ .

2 I was sleeping and the alarm clock was ringing.
   ⇨ I was sleeping _____ .

3 He took a picture and one of his eyes was closed.
   ⇨ He took a picture _____ .

4 The blind man walked and the dog was leading ahead of him.
   ⇨ The blind man walked _____ .

Exercise 2 다음 우리말과 같은 뜻이 되도록 문장을 완성하시오.

1 그의 이름으로 판단하건대, 그는 한국인이 틀림없다.
   ⇨ _____ , he must be Korean.

2 James 이야기가 나와서 말인데, 최근에 그를 본 적이 있니?
   ⇨ _____ , have you seen him lately?

3 엄격히 말해서, 그녀는 그 실패에 책임이 없다.
   ⇨ _____ , she has no responsibility for the failure.

4 솔직히 말해서, 우리는 야구보다 축구하는 것을 좋아한다.
   ⇨ _____ , we prefer playing soccer to playing baseball.

[01-03] 다음 빈칸에 들어갈 알맞은 말을 고르시오.

01
He was almost asleep when he heard his name _____.

① called   ② call
③ calling   ④ to be called
⑤ to call

02
I was upset because my friend kept me _____ her for three hours.

① waited for   ② wait for
③ waiting for   ④ being waited for
⑤ to wait for

03
The language _____ in the classroom is English.

① speaking   ② spoken
③ spoke   ④ speak
⑤ to speak

[04-06] 다음 빈칸에 들어갈 말이 바르게 짝지어진 것을 고르시오.

04
· You have to pay for the _____ window.
· I was surprised to hear him _____ with an American.

① breaking - talking   ② broken - talked
③ to break - talked   ④ broken - talking
⑤ breaking - talked

05
A : Do you want to take a break?
B : No, I'm not _____ yet. Let's keep on _____ another hour.

① tired - work   ② tiring - working
③ tiring - to work   ④ tired - working
⑤ tired - to work

06
· I was _____ when I first saw Niagara Falls.
· It is the most _____ news that I have ever heard.

① surprising - surprising
② surprising - surprised
③ surprised - surprised
④ surprised - surprising
⑤ surprise - surprising

[07-09] 다음 밑줄 친 부분 중 어법상 어색한 것을 고르시오.

07 ① He had the wall <u>painted</u> yesterday.
② I received a letter <u>written</u> in Spanish.
③ The child <u>sitting</u> on the sofa is my son.
④ I saw the window <u>breaking</u> by the boys.
⑤ We saw some boys <u>playing</u> baseball at the park last night.

08 ① At last, the <u>exciting</u> game was over.
② The two <u>tired</u> boys looked at each other.
③ The man <u>carrying</u> the heavy luggage is my uncle.
④ John tried to open the <u>locking</u> door, but he couldn't.
⑤ The people <u>attending</u> the meeting had a nice afternoon.

09 ① The window was kept <u>closing</u>.
② A <u>rolling</u> stone gathers no moss.
③ There <u>being</u> nothing to do, we went home.
④ Being <u>tired</u> from work, I went out for a walk.
⑤ I bought a picture <u>painted</u> by Vincent van Gogh.

10 다음 (A), (B)에서 어법에 맞는 표현을 고르시오.

The outdoor rock concert **(A) [holding / held]** in our city's park was a nightmare for residents. The music was so loud that it kept babies **(B) [crying / cried]** and dogs barking late into the night. In addition, the rude, poorly dressed musicians set a bad example for American youth.

11 다음 밑줄 친 분사구문을 부사절로 전환할 때 사용될 접속사가 〈보기〉와 다른 하나는?

Not having brought my laptop, I can't lend it to you.

① Feeling hungry, he ordered some pizza.
② Having climbed a rugged mountain, she is exhausted.
③ Driving a car carefully, you'll be able to avoid accidents.
④ Not hearing you calling me, I couldn't answer.
⑤ Having studied hard, he passed the exam.

12 다음 밑줄 친 부분 중 어법상 바르지 않은 것은?

① Seeing from the plane, the island ② was really ③ beautiful, and I ④ felt ⑤ excited.

13 다음 밑줄 친 부분 중 어법상 올바른 것은?
① Not known the fact, she kept silent.
② While driven a car, he had an accident.
③ Strictly spoken, this is not a good idea.
④ Wanting not to see him, I went to see him.
⑤ He is listening to music with his arms folded.

14 다음 밑줄 친 부분과 바꿔 쓸 수 있는 것은?

Be careful when you cross the street.

① cross the street
② you cross the street
③ when cross the street
④ when crossing the street
⑤ when you crossed the street

[15-16] 다음 빈칸에 들어갈 알맞은 말을 고르시오.

15 _____ what to do, she asked me to help her.

① Known
② Know not
③ Not knowing
④ Have known
⑤ Have not known

16 _____ down the street, I saw him standing by the bookstore.

① Walked
② Walking
③ Have walked
④ Being walked
⑤ Having been walked

17 다음 밑줄 친 단어 중 쓰임이 다른 하나는?
① I heard the dog barking.
② Thank you for inviting me.
③ I have been waiting for a girl like you.
④ Seeing the policeman, he ran away.
⑤ The boy standing at the door is my cousin.

[18-21] 다음 밑줄 친 부분을 분사구문으로 바르게 바꿔 쓴 것을 고르시오.

18 As the weather was wonderful, we could play soccer on the ground.

① Being wonderful
② Having been wonderful
③ The weather was wonderful
④ Being the weather wonderful
⑤ The weather being wonderful

19 Because she was born in France, she can speak French fluently.

① Born in France
② Was born in France
③ Been born in France
④ Having born in France
⑤ Have been born in France

20 As she traveled a lot, she knows a lot about other countries.

① Travel a lot
② Traveled a lot
③ To travel a lot
④ Being traveled a lot
⑤ Having traveled a lot

21 When she entered the room, she found them scribbling on the wall.

① Entered the room
② Entering the room
③ When entered the room
④ Being entered the room
⑤ Having entered the room

22 다음 빈칸에 들어갈 알맞은 전치사는?

He was walking slowly _____ his eyes closed.

① to
② with
③ in
④ at
⑤ for

[23-25] 다음 빈칸에 들어갈 알맞은 말을 고르시오.

23 As there were no empty seats, we had to keep standing for a while.
⇨ _____ no empty seats, we had to keep standing for a while.

① Being
② Been
③ There being
④ There be
⑤ There been

24 As I didn't finish my homework, I couldn't play soccer.
⇨ _____ my homework, I couldn't play soccer.

① Not finishing
② Finished not
③ Not finished
④ As finished
⑤ Finished never

25 A : Why didn't you go to the concert?
B : _____ , I didn't have enough money for the ticket.

① Generally speaking
② Frankly speaking
③ Judging from the ticket
④ Speaking of money
⑤ Speaking strictly

[26-27] 다음 우리말을 바르게 영작한 것을 고르시오.

26 나는 손가락을 꼰 채(행운을 빌면서) 그에게 말했다.

① I said to him with my fingers crossed.
② I said to him with my fingers be crossed.
③ I said to him with my fingers being crossing.
④ I said to him with my fingers having crossed.
⑤ I said to him with my fingers having been crossed.

27 나는 그의 의견이 마음에 들지 않았기 때문에, 그의 제안을 수락하지 않았다.

① Liked not his idea, I didn't accept his offer.
② Not liked his idea, I didn't accept his offer.
③ Liking not his idea, I didn't accept his offer.
④ Not liking his idea, I didn't accept his offer.
⑤ Have not liking his idea, I didn't accept his offer.

[28-29] 다음 우리말과 같은 뜻이 되도록 괄호 안의 단어를 사용하여 문장을 완성하시오.

28 어제 우리 마을 근처의 거리에서 충격적인 사건이 발생했다. (shock)

⇨ A _____ accident happened on the street near my town yesterday.

29 일반적으로 말해서, 소녀들이 소년들보다 영어를 잘한다. (speak)

⇨ _____, girls speak English better than boys.

30 다음 두 문장이 같은 뜻이 되도록 빈칸에 알맞은 단어를 쓰시오.

The child is my son. He is dancing on the stage.
⇨ The child _____ on the stage is my son.

31 다음 문장을 읽고, 어법상 어색한 부분을 찾아 바르게 고쳐 쓰시오.

I couldn't make myself understanding in English.

[32-33] 다음 두 문장이 같은 뜻이 되도록 문장을 완성하시오.

32 Having dinner at the restaurant, I met a friend of mine.

⇨ _____ at the restaurant, I met a friend of mine.

33 When he was surprised at the news, he turned pale.

⇨ _____ at the news, he turned pale.

[34-35] 다음 우리말과 같은 뜻이 되도록 괄호 안의 단어를 사용하여 분사구문 문장을 완성하시오.

34 숙제를 다 했기 때문에, 나는 컴퓨터 게임을 할 수 있다. (finish)

⇨ _____,
I can play a computer game.

35 나는 그와 말을 하기 싫어서 침묵을 지켰다. (talk to)

⇨ _____,
I remained silent.

36 다음 글을 읽고, 괄호 안의 단어를 적절히 바꿔 쓰시오.

I slept well and got up early. My brother was (A) _____ (water) the plants in the garden. After having breakfast, I read a novel (B) _____ (write) by an American novelist. But it was too difficult for me to understand.

Answers: p.15

[1-2] 다음 글을 읽고, 물음에 답하시오. 서술형

(A) <u>자원봉사를 하는 동안</u> at the children's hospital last summer, I came to know one of the patients, (B) <u>name</u> Kyle. He was the sweetest kid I had ever met. He liked helping other patients and talking with them even though he was a patient himself. Soon we became friends, and I asked him why he was wearing a hat in the summer. Instead of answering my question, he just smiled and took off his hat. To my surprise, he had no hair. He was fighting cancer. I was really (C) <u>shock</u> because he always looked healthy and happy. I was so impressed with his bravery. He is the bravest person I I know.

1 (A)의 우리말을 두 단어의 영어로 옮겨 쓰시오.

→ _____

2 (B)와 (C)의 동사를 알맞은 형태로 바꾸시오.

→ (B) _____

→ (C) _____

3 다음 글의 밑줄 친 부분 중, 어법상 <u>틀린</u> 것은? 수능 대비형

If you haven't found an ① <u>exciting</u> summer vacation destination, here is exactly what you have been looking for! We offer transportation to and from White Valley, ② <u>leave</u> from the Town Park at 9 a.m. ③ <u>Don't</u> worry about the camping and rafting equipment. The price ④ <u>includes</u> all the equipment you need as well as food. In addition, our professional guides will help you ⑤ <u>explore</u> the valley, so you can enjoy the trip with maximum safety and pleasure.

* destination: 목적지
** professional: 전문적인

Chapter 5

조동사

5-1 can / could

can의 의미
- I **can** do it by myself. 〈능력 : ~할 수 있다〉
  = I **am able to** do it by myself. 나는 그것을 혼자 할 수 있다.
- They **can't** play tennis well. 〈능력 : ~할 수 없다〉
  = They **are not able to** play tennis well. 그들은 테니스를 잘 치지 못한다.
- This theater **can** accommodate up to five hundred people. 〈가능성 : ~할 수 있다〉
  이 극장은 5백 명의 사람을 수용할 수 있다.
- He **could** solve the problem. 〈능력 : ~할 수 있었다〈can의 과거〉〉
  = He **was able to** solve the problem. 그는 그 문제를 풀 수 있었다.
- It **cannot** be true. 〈추측 : ~일 리가 없다〉 그것은 사실일 리가 없다.
- **Can I** use your pen? 〈허락 : ~해도 될까?〉 네 펜을 사용해도 될까?
  - Yes. **You can** use my pen. 〈허락 : ~해도 좋다〉 응. 내 펜을 사용해도 돼.
- **Can you** do me a favor? 〈요청 : ~해줄래?〉 부탁 좀 들어줄래?
- **Could you** pass me the salt? 〈정중한 부탁 : ~해 주시겠습니까?〉 소금 좀 건네주시겠습니까?

Answers: p.15

Exercise 1 다음 문장의 밑줄 친 부분에 유의하여 해석하시오.

1 The news <u>cannot</u> be true.
   ⇒ _____

2 <u>Could you</u> say that again?
   ⇒ _____

3 <u>Can I</u> eat some more pizza on the table?
   ⇒ _____

4 I <u>can't clean</u> the whole house by myself.
   ⇒ _____

Exercise 2 다음 짝지어진 두 문장이 같은 뜻이 되도록 be able to를 사용하여 문장을 완성하시오.

1 The boy can take off his jacket by himself.
   ⇒ The boy _____ his jacket by himself.

2 Can you pick up my daughter at school?
   ⇒ _____ my daughter at school?

3 I can't help you with the homework this time.
   ⇒ I _____ you with the homework this time.

4 Can she play Beethoven's *Moonlight Sonata* on the piano?
   ⇒ _____ Beethoven's *Moonlight Sonata* on the piano?

5-2 may / might

📑 **May의 의미**

- **May** I use your phone? 〈허가(=can) : ~해도 된다〉 전화 좀 써도 될까요?
  - Yes, you **may**. 응. 써도 돼.
  - No, you **may not**. 아니, 안 돼. / No, you **must not**. 아니, 안 돼. 〈강한 금지〉
- You **may** go home now. 〈허가〉 지금 집에 가도 좋아.
- My mom said that I **might** go out and play. 〈허가 : may의 과거〉
  우리 엄마가 나에게 나가 놀아도 된다고 하셨다.
- You **may** get this at that store. 〈추측 : ~일 수도 있다〉 너는 저 가게에서 이것을 살 수 있을지도 몰라.
- She **may** not be at home now. 〈추측〉 그녀는 지금 집에 없을지도 몰라.
- She **might** change her mind. 〈추측〉 그녀가 마음을 바꿀지도 몰라.
- **May** God bless you! 〈기원(May+주어+동사원형 ~) : ~하기를〉 신의 축복이 있기를!

Answers: p.15

Exercise **1** 다음 문장의 밑줄 친 부분에 유의하여 해석하시오.

1 May you succeed!

⇨ _____

2 I'm not sure, but he may be in the theater.

⇨ _____

3 I might be ten minutes late for the meeting.

⇨ _____

4 My father told me that I might go camping with my friends.

⇨ _____

Exercise **2** 다음 우리말과 같은 뜻이 되도록 may를 사용하여 문장을 완성하시오.

1 그것은 쉽지 않을 수도 있다.

⇨ It _____ _____ _____ easy.

2 너는 인터넷 카페에 가도 돼.

⇨ You _____ _____ to the Internet Cafe.

3 확실하지는 않지만, 그는 도서관에 있을 거야.

⇨ I'm not sure, but he _____ _____ in the library.

4 이 건물에서 담배를 피우시면 안 됩니다.

⇨ You _____ _____ _____ in this building.

5 너는 내가 출장 중에 내 차를 사용해도 좋다.

⇨ You _____ _____ my car while I'm out of town on a business trip.

5-3 will / would

will/would의 의미

- You **will** be sorry for it later. 〈추측(= be going to) : ~일 것이다〉 너는 나중에 그것을 후회할 것이다.
- I **will** do my best. 〈강한 의지 : ~하겠다〉 최선을 다하겠습니다.
- He **won't[= will not]** do it again. 〈will의 부정〉 그는 다시는 그것을 하지 않을 것이다.
- I thought he **would** come back soon. 〈will의 과거〉 나는 그가 곧 돌아올 거라고 생각했다.
- **Will you** have some more tea? 〈권유 : ~할래?〉 차 좀 더 마실래?
- **Would you** hold this for me for a second? 〈공손한 제안 : ~해 주시겠습니까?〉
  저를 위해서 잠깐 동안 이것을 잡고 있어 주시겠습니까?
- Accidents **will** happen. 〈습성. 경향 : ~하기 마련이다〉 사고는 일어나기 마련이다.
- I **would** take a nap after lunch. 〈과거의 습관 : ~하곤 했다〉 나는 점심식사 후에 낮잠을 자곤 했다.
- **Would** you **like something** to drink? 〈would like+명사 : ~을 원하다〉 마실 것을 원하십니까?
- I **would like to go** to the movies. 〈would like to+동사원형 : ~하고 싶다〉 나는 영화 보러 가고 싶어.

Answers: p.15

Exercise 1 다음 괄호 안에서 알맞은 것을 고르시오.

1 (Must / Will) you bring my bag to me?

2 I (will / would) like to give you a piece of advice.

3 He said he (might / would) be eighteen years old soon.

4 She (will / would) often go skiing when she was in college.

5 (Will / May) you keep an eye on my suitcase for a moment?

Exercise 2 다음 문장의 밑줄 친 부분에 유의하여 해석하시오.

1 A drowning man <u>will catch</u> a straw.
   ⇨ _____

2 He said he <u>would</u> give it back to me.
   ⇨ _____

3 I'<u>d like</u> some coffee before the meeting.
   ⇨ _____

4 She <u>won't attend</u> the meeting because she is sick in bed.
   ⇨ _____

5 I <u>would</u> often take a walk in the morning when I was young.
   ⇨ _____

5-4 must / have to

📖 must/have to의 의미

- You **must** run as fast as you can. 〈의무 : ~해야 한다(= have to)〉
  = You **have to** run as fast as you can.
  너는 가능한 한 빨리 달려야 한다.

- You **have to** study hard to pass the exam. 〈의무 : ~해야 한다(= must)〉
  = You **must** study hard to pass the exam.
  시험에 통과하려면 열심히 공부해야 한다.

- He said he **had to** work late. 〈must의 과거〉 그는 늦게까지 일해야 한다고 말했다.

- He **must** be a liar. 〈강한 추측 : ~임이 틀림없다〉 그는 거짓말쟁이임이 틀림없다.

- There **has to** be a good reason for this. 〈확신 : 틀림없이 ~일 것이다〉 이것에 대한 합당한 이유가 분명히 있을 거야.

> **TIPs** have to를 사용한 의문문
> · Do you have to leave now?
> 너는 지금 떠나야 하니?

📖 must not과 don't have to의 의미 비교

must와 have to는 같은 뜻이지만, 부정형은 의미가 다르다.

- You **must not** tell a lie. 〈금지 : ~해서는 안 된다〉 거짓말을 하면 안 된다.

- You **must not** go to the party. 너는 파티에 가지 말아야 한다.

- He **doesn't have to** go there. 〈불필요 : ~할 필요가 없다〉
  = He **need not** go there. 그는 그곳에 갈 필요가 없다.

- You **don't have to** go to school. 너는 학교에 갈 필요가 없다.

> **TIPs** 조동사는 나란히 쓸 수 없다.
> · You will must learn Japanese during the summer vacation. (X)
> You will have to learn Japanese during the summer vacation. (O)
> 너는 여름 방학 동안 일본어를 공부해야 할 것이다.

Answers: p.15

Exercise 1 다음 짝지어진 두 문장이 같은 뜻이 되도록 have to를 사용하여 문장을 완성하시오.

1 You must repair my car by tomorrow.
  ⇒ _____ my car by tomorrow.

2 Must I go to the hospital now?
  ⇒ _____ to the hospital now?

3 You need not bring it back to me by today.
  ⇒ _____ it back to me by today.

4 She must go abroad on business next week.
  ⇒ _____ abroad on business next week.

Exercise 2 다음 괄호 안에서 알맞은 것을 고르시오.

1 I (must / had) to go see a doctor yesterday.

2 You (must / have) not drive when you are drunk.

3 I think that John (must / has) go home and get some rest.

4 There (can / must) be something wrong with your watch. It can't be nine already!

5 Does he (must / have) to study harder to get better grades?

6 She skipped breakfast, so she (must / cannot) be hungry now.

☐ **shall : 제안의 의미로 쓰인다.**
- **Shall** we dance? 우리 춤출까요?
- **Shall** I close the window? 제가 창문을 닫을까요?

☐ **should**
- Everything **should** be ready by Saturday. 〈의무, 당연 : ~해야 한다(= ought to)〉
  = Everything **ought to** be ready by Saturday. 모든 것이 토요일까지 준비되어야 한다.
- We **ought not to** treat them like that. 〈ought to의 부정〉
  우리는 그들을 그렇게 대하면 안 된다.
- He **ordered** that the work **(should)** be done by tomorrow.
  〈주장, 제안, 명령, 요구 동사+that+주어(+should)+동사원형 ~ : ~하도록 …하다〉
  그는 내일까지 그 일을 해내라고 명령했다.

☐ 「**used to+동사원형**」
- She **used to** play the piano in the afternoon.
  = She **would** play the piano in the afternoon.
  〈과거의 습관(동작) : ~하곤 했다〉
  그녀는 오후에 피아노를 치곤 했다.
- There **used to** be a church here.
  There **would** be a church here. (X)
  〈과거의 상태 : 이전에는 ~였다(would로 바꿔 쓸 수 없다.)〉
  전에는 여기에 교회가 있었다.

☐ **need**
- You **need not** meet her. 〈부정문〉
  = You **don't have to** meet her. 너는 그녀를 만날 필요가 없다.
- **Need** she **go** there? 〈의문문〉 그녀가 그곳에 가야 할 필요가 있니?

> **TIPs**
> be used to+명사(명사구) (~하는 데 익숙하다)
> **vs. be used to+동사원형** (~하는 데 사용되다)
> • We are used to eating Korean food.
>   우리는 한국 음식 먹는 것에 익숙하다.
> • Bricks were used to build the warehouse.
>   벽돌이 창고를 짓는 데 사용되었다.

> **TIPs**
> 조동사 **need**는 일반적으로 의문문과 부정문에서 많이 쓰이고 긍정문에서는 주로 **need** 다음에 to부정사가 온다.
> • You need to live with your parents.
>   너는 부모님과 함께 살아야 한다.

Answers: p.16

 Exercise 1 다음 괄호 안에서 알맞은 말을 고르시오.

1　He used to (walk / walking) to school last year.

2　You (should / ought) to respect and obey your parents.

3　They (used to / are used to) getting up early in the morning.

4　You (need not / don't need) hand in the report by tomorrow.

5　You need not (come / to come) to the office when you are ill.

6　There (used to / is used to) be a building here two years ago.

7　We are used to (use / using) the Internet to search for information.

8　The government (should / ought) take care of the homeless on the street.

9　Jack (used to / is used to) enjoy playing the drums when he was in college.

10　He (has / must) to read the book carefully because it is a little difficult to understand.

1 Where shall we meet?

   ⇒ _____

2 He ordered that we should do it at once.

   ⇒ _____

3 There used to be a big maple tree in the garden.

   ⇒ _____

4 They used to ride bicycles together when they were in elementary school.

   ⇒ _____

Exercise **3** 다음 짝지어진 두 문장이 같은 뜻이 되도록 문장을 완성하시오.

1 There was a big stone here, but not anymore.

   ⇒ There _____ _____ be a big stone here.

2 He came here every Sunday, but he doesn't now.

   ⇒ He _____ _____ come here every Sunday.

3 You don't have to water the flowers in the garden.

   ⇒ You _____ _____ water the flowers in the garden.

4 He should make a phone call before visiting them.

   ⇒ He _____ _____ make a phone call before visiting them.

Exercise **4** 다음 우리말과 같은 뜻이 되도록 괄호 안의 단어를 알맞게 배열하여 문장을 완성하시오.

1 그는 내게 집에 있으라고 권했다. (should, that, stay, I, home)

   ⇒ He suggested _____.

2 시험에서 부정행위를 하면 안 됩니다. (ought, to, cheat, exams, you, on, not)

   ⇒ _____

3 우리 저녁식사 후 같이 산책할까요? (shall, dinner, take, we, a walk, after)

   ⇒ _____

4 너는 네가 하는 모든 일에 최선을 다해야 한다. (should, best, do, your, in, everything)

   ⇒ You _____ you do.

5-6 조동사 + have + p.p.

📑 「조동사 + have + p.p.」

❶ 「should have + p.p.」: ~했어야 하는데 (하지 않았다) 〈유감, 후회〉
· You **should have studied** English harder. 너는 영어공부를 더 열심히 했어야 했는데.

❷ 「must have + p.p.」: ~이었음이 틀림없다 〈단정적 확신〉
· She **must have missed** the bus this morning. 그녀는 오늘 아침에 버스를 놓쳤음이 틀림없다.

❸ 「cannot have + p.p.」: ~했을 리가 없다 〈단정적 부정〉
· He **cannot have been** honest. 그는 정직했을 리가 없다.

❹ 「may have + p.p.」: ~이었을지도 모른다 〈가능성 있는 추측〉
· She **may have been** hurt. 그녀는 다쳤을지도 모른다.

❺ 「could have + p.p.」: ~할 수 있었는데 (하지 못했다) 〈유감〉
· We **could have caught** the first train. 우리는 첫 기차를 탈 수도 있었는데.

Answers: p.16

Exercise 1 다음 짝지어진 두 문장이 같은 뜻이 되도록 「조동사+have+p.p.」 구문을 사용하여 문장을 완성하시오.

1 You had to stay at the hotel, but you didn't.
⇨ You _____ _____ _____ at the hotel.

2 I'm sure that he passed the college entrance exam.
⇨ He _____ _____ _____ the college entrance exam.

3 I'm sure that he didn't sleep in his bed last night. There was no sign of him.
⇨ He _____ _____ in his bed last night.

4 It is possible that she found the perfect solution to all of our problems.
⇨ She _____ _____ _____ the perfect solution to all of our problems.

Exercise 2 다음 우리말과 같은 뜻이 되도록 괄호 안의 단어를 사용하여 문장을 완성하시오.

1 그는 조종사였을 리가 없다. (be)
⇨ He _____ _____ _____ a pilot.

2 그들은 전에 그 음식을 먹어 본 것이 틀림없다. (eat)
⇨ They _____ _____ _____ the food before.

3 그의 이야기는 사실이었을지도 모르지만, 아무도 그것을 믿지 않았다. (be)
⇨ His story _____ _____ _____ true, but nobody believed it.

4 너는 어젯밤에 그 영화를 봤어야 했어. 그 영화는 환상적이었어. (see)
⇨ You _____ _____ _____ the movie last night. It was fantastic.

5 그는 아팠을 리가 없어. 나는 그가 친구들과 축구하는 것을 봤어. (be)
⇨ He _____ _____ _____ sick. I saw him playing soccer with his friends.

조동사의 관용 표현

❶ 「had better+동사원형」: ∼하는 것이 좋겠다
- You **had better stop** complaining about it. 너는 그것에 대해 불평을 그만하는 것이 좋겠다.
- You **had better not make** noise here. 너는 여기서 소란을 피우지 않는 게 좋겠다.

❷ 「cannot but+동사원형」: ∼하지 않을 수 없다
- I **cannot but laugh** at his performance.
- = I **cannot help laughing** at his performance. 나는 그의 연기를 보고 웃지 않을 수 없다.

❸ 「would rather+동사원형」: 차라리 ∼하겠다
- I **would rather stay** home. 나는 차라리 집에 있겠다.

❹ 「would rather A than B」: B하기보다 차라리 A하겠다
- I **would rather** stay home **than** go out. 나는 외출하기보다는 차라리 집에 있겠다.

Answers: p.16

Exercise 1 다음 문장을 읽고, 어법상 <u>어색한</u> 부분을 찾아 바르게 고쳐 쓰시오.

1 You'd not better go fishing in the ocean today.
⇨ _____

2 I cannot but wondering how far we have come.
⇨ _____

3 Whenever I watch this movie, I cannot help cry.
⇨ _____

4 I'd rather to go shopping with you than staying here doing nothing.
⇨ _____

5 You'd better to get up early tomorrow if you don't want to miss the first train.
⇨ _____

Exercise 2 다음 우리말과 같은 뜻이 되도록 괄호 안의 단어를 사용하여 문장을 완성하시오.

1 너는 외출하지 않는 게 좋겠다. 밖은 몹시 춥다. (go out)
⇨ You _____. It's freezing outside.

2 우리는 그녀의 결단력에 감탄하지 않을 수가 없다. (admire)
⇨ We _____ her determination.

3 나는 커피를 마시는 것보다 차라리 낮잠을 자겠다. (take a nap, drink)
⇨ I _____ than _____.

4 너는 지금 출발하는 게 좋겠다. 그러지 않으면 회의에 늦을 것이다. (leave)
⇨ You _____ now, or you'll be late for the meeting.

5 나는 도시 생활에 싫증이 났기 때문에 차라리 시골에 살겠다. (live)
⇨ I _____ in the countryside because I'm tired of city life.

[01-05] 다음 빈칸에 들어갈 알맞은 말을 고르시오.

01 A : There was a lot of fun at yesterday's party.
    You _____.
    B : Sorry, something unexpected happened.

① must come   ② should have come
③ must have come   ④ should come
⑤ may have come

02 The boy is much stronger now than he
    _____.

① would be   ② needs be
③ would like   ④ used to be
⑤ cannot be

03 Don't shout. Jim is sleeping right now. You
    _____ be quiet.

① can   ② may
③ could   ④ should not
⑤ should

04 A : Did you hear the news? Harry got a perfect
    score on the test.
    B : Oh, he _____ be very happy.

① must   ② maybe
③ would rather   ④ cannot
⑤ ought

05 A : Mike doesn't look well.
    B : I think he _____ take a rest.

① better   ② had better
③ must be   ④ must not
⑤ doesn't have to

06 다음 밑줄 친 부분과 바꿔 쓸 수 있는 것은?

Jenny was not able to write with her left hand.

① can't   ② didn't
③ mustn't   ④ shouldn't
⑤ couldn't

07 다음 대화를 읽고, 대답이 될 수 있는 것을 모두 고르시오.

A : Can you come to the surprise birthday party
    for my sister?
B : _____

① No, I don't.
② Yes, I can't.
③ I'm sorry I can't.
④ Yes. I will come to the party.
⑤ Yes. I have to stay at home.

08 다음 대화의 빈칸에 알맞은 말은?

A : Must I take off my shoes inside the house?
B : No, _____.

① you must
② you may
③ you do
④ you have to
⑤ you don't have to

09 다음 대화를 읽고, 허락을 표현하는 대답을 모두 고르시오.

A : May I stay with you for a week?
B : _____

① Sure, why not?
② Yes, you may.
③ No, you may not.
④ Well, I don't think so.
⑤ No, you don't have to.

10 다음 대화 중 <u>어색한</u> 것은?

① A : May I help you?
　B : Yes. Show me some blouses, please.
② A : Would you please help me?
　B : Sure. What can I do for you?
③ A : Shall we play football?
　B : Sorry, but I'd like to play soccer.
④ A : When shall I visit you?
　B : I'm sorry I can't.
⑤ A : Do I have to put this coat on?
　B : No. You don't have to.

[11-12] 다음 〈보기〉의 밑줄 친 단어와 의미가 같은 것을 고르시오.

11　Your father <u>must</u> be proud of you.

① I <u>must</u> leave now.
② She <u>must</u> be very busy.
③ You <u>must</u> wear a safety hat.
④ We <u>must</u> clean up the mess.
⑤ You <u>must</u> look after your little brothers.

12　You <u>may</u> think I'm lonely.

① <u>May</u> I come in and wait?
② <u>May</u> peace be with you!
③ The news <u>may</u> not be true.
④ <u>May</u> I try one of your cookies?
⑤ Children <u>may</u> enter if accompanied by an adult.

13 다음 빈칸에 공통으로 들어갈 말은?

· You ＿＿＿＿＿ look at it, but you must not touch it.
· You ＿＿＿＿＿ go out and play if you'd like to.

① will
② must
③ can
④ have to
⑤ would

14 다음 빈칸에 들어갈 말로 적당하지 <u>않은</u> 것은?

They ＿＿＿＿＿ that he take part in the meeting.

① suggested
② refused
③ insisted
④ demanded
⑤ proposed

15 다음 밑줄 친 부분 중 생략할 수 있는 것은?

I ① <u>suggested</u> that ② <u>he</u> ③ <u>should</u> buy these things ④ <u>next</u> ⑤ <u>week</u>.

[16-17] 다음 중 짝지어진 두 문장의 의미가 같지 <u>않은</u> 것을 고르시오.

16 ① You have to take out the garbage.
　 = You must take out the garbage.
② He was able to find his lost briefcase.
　 = He could find his lost briefcase.
③ You must not meet him anymore.
　 = You don't have to meet him anymore.
④ Can you see the faraway stars?
　 = Are you able to see the faraway stars?
⑤ He broke his leg, and he isn't able to walk for the time being.
　 = He broke his leg, and he cannot walk for the time being.

17 ① Can I use your cell phone?
　 = May I use your cell phone?
② Can you help me to cook dinner, please?
　 = Will you help me to cook dinner, please?
③ You must make your bed.
　 = You have to make your bed.
④ I used to go to the movies.
　 = I'm used to going to the movies.
⑤ The plane will take off at 7 p.m.
　 = The plane is going to take off at 7 p.m.

18 다음 질문에 대한 대답으로 알맞지 <u>않은</u> 것을 <u>모두</u> 고르시오.

> May I use your computer?

① Sure.
② No, you may.
③ Yes, you may.
④ No, I may not.
⑤ No, you must not.

[19-21] 다음 중 어법상 <u>어색한</u> 것을 고르시오.

19 ① He should have taken the subway.
② You had better not accept their offer.
③ I would rather to eat pizza than spaghetti.
④ You will have to bring your lunch tomorrow.
⑤ There used to be a pond at the center of the park.

20 ① You must be happy to hear the news.
② She may have met my brother before.
③ He used to teach English at a high school.
④ James must have eaten the cake on the table.
⑤ You should take the medicine before you went to bed last night.

21 ① I'd like go out for dinner.
② You need not wait for me tonight.
③ You may take a break if you want.
④ You ought not to cross the street on a red light.
⑤ They would go to the park to play baseball after school.

[22-23] 다음 〈보기〉와 같은 의미의 문장을 고르시오.

22 > She is good at expressing her idea.

① She will express her idea well.
② She can express her idea well.
③ She has to express her idea well.
④ She wants to express her idea well.
⑤ She needs to express her idea well.

23 > Would you like to go to the amusement park?

① May I go to the amusement park?
② Shall I go to the amusement park?
③ Did you use to go to the amusement park?
④ Do you want to go to the amusement park?
⑤ Do you have to go to the amusement park?

24 다음 중 밑줄 친 부분의 쓰임이 <u>다른</u> 하나는?

① He can jump as high as I <u>can</u>.
② I <u>can</u> help you answer the question.
③ We <u>can</u> finish the project as scheduled.
④ They <u>could</u> find the boy who stole my watch.
⑤ He <u>can't</u> be a doctor because he studied history at college.

25 다음 빈칸에 들어갈 수 있는 말을 <u>모두</u> 고르시오.

> A: Mary didn't show up yesterday.
> B: She _____ the appointment.
> A: Yes, she looks very busy these days.

① must have forgotten
② should have forgotten
③ cannot have forgotten
④ might have forgotten
⑤ used to have

26 다음 대화의 빈칸에 공통으로 들어갈 말은?

A: Summer vacation is just around the corner. Do you have any special plans?

B: So far I don't have any plans. Maybe I will stay home and study Korean.

A: That sounds good, but you _____ go out, too.

B: How about you?

A: Why don't you go camping with us for a week?

B: I'd like to, but I _____ stay home. My uncle will be here during the summer vacation.

① can   ② will

③ have to   ④ can't

⑤ may

[27-28] 다음 우리말과 같은 뜻이 되도록 괄호 안의 단어를 알맞게 배열하여 문장을 다시 쓰시오.

27 너는 그 보고서를 쓰지 않아도 된다.

You (have, to, don't, write) the report.

⇒ _____

28 나는 식사를 안 하기보다는 운동을 하겠다.

I (exercise, skip, rather, than, a, meal, would).

⇒ _____

[29-30] 다음 두 문장이 같은 뜻이 되도록 문장을 완성하시오.

29 We cannot but love and admire you.

⇒ We _____ loving and admiring you.

30 You must get up early to see the sunrise.

⇒ You _____ get up early to see the sunrise.

[31-34] 다음 우리말과 같은 뜻이 되도록 문장을 완성하시오.

31 그녀는 선생님께 거짓말을 하지 말았어야 했는데.

⇒ She _____

_____ to her teacher.

32 낯선 사람에게서 온 이메일은 열어보지 않는 것이 좋다.

⇒ You _____

_____ open any e-mails from strangers.

33 주민들은 자전거 전용도로가 있어야 한다고 주장했다.

⇒ The residents insisted that there

_____ _____ a bike-only road.

34 그가 그녀의 집을 방문했을 리가 없다. 그때 그는 나와 함께 있었다.

⇒ He _____

_____ her house. He was with me at that time.

35 다음 우리말과 같은 뜻이 되도록 괄호 안의 단어와 공통으로 들어갈 수 있는 조동사를 사용하여 영작하시오.

• 너는 연장자를 공경해야 한다. (respect, older people)

⇒ _____

_____ .

• 그는 그 회의에 참여했어야 했는데 (참여하지 않았다). (join)

⇒ _____

_____ .

Answers: p.18

[1-2] 다음 글을 읽고, 물음에 답하시오.　　　　　　　　　　　　　　　　　서술형

Chloe borrowed my wireless earbuds last Monday. While she ⓐ using them, she dropped one and broke it. She gave it back to me without an apology. I ⓑ musted take it to the service center and spent $100 to fix it. I told her about this, but she said that it wasn't her fault. I ⓒ been very angry with her since then. I don't want to talk to her ever again. (A) 우리는 좋은 친구였지만, 지금은 아니다. I ⓓ never will forgive her.

1 윗글의 ⓐ~ⓓ를 어법에 맞게 고쳐 쓰시오.

ⓐ _____　　　ⓑ _____

ⓒ _____　　　ⓓ _____

2 주어진 말을 이용하여 밑줄 친 (A)를 우리말로 옮기시오.

→ _____, but not anymore. (good friends)

3 다음 글의 밑줄 친 부분 중, 어법상 틀린 것은?　　　　　　　　　　　　수능 대비형

Last week, I ① was trying to finish my science project about volcanic eruptions. I only needed ② completing the visual part of the project, but as I was getting ready ③ to start, I realized I couldn't find my markers and pens. I was almost certain I left them on my desk the day ④ before, but they weren't there. I looked in the kitchen, the bedroom, even the bathroom, and I ⑤ couldn't find them anywhere. I have no idea where they are!

* volcanic eruption: 화산 폭발
** visual: 시각적인

Chapter 6

수동태

수동태의 전환

수동태

❶ 의미 : 주어가 동작을 당하는 대상이 되는 것을 수동태라고 한다.

❷ 형태 : 「주어+be동사+과거분사+by+행위자(목적격)」

· She took that picture.

⇨ That picture **was taken** by her. 그녀가 저 사진을 찍었다.

> **TIPs**
> 수동태로 사용하지 않는 동사
> appear, become, happen, cost, resemble, have 등
> · She resembles her father.
>   그녀는 아버지를 닮았다.
>   She is resembled by her father. (X)

수동태의 시제

❶ 현재 (is/am/are+p.p.)

· Many people in Switzerland speak French.

⇨ French **is spoken** by many people in Switzerland. 스위스에서는 많은 사람들이 불어를 한다.

❷ 과거 (was/were+p.p.)

· I painted the kitchen wall.

⇨ The kitchen wall **was painted** by me. 나는 부엌 벽을 칠했다.

❸ 미래 (will be+p.p.)

· My father **will build** a house for my family.

⇨ A house for my family **will be built** by my father.

우리 아버지가 우리 가족을 위한 집을 지을 것이다.

> **TIPs**
> 「조동사+be+p.p.」: 조동사가 있는 문장의 수동태
> · We must finish the project by tomorrow.
> → The project <u>must be finished</u> (by us) by tomorrow. 우리는 그 프로젝트를 내일까지 끝내야만 한다.

「by+목적격」의 생략 : 행위자가 일반인이거나 추측할 수 있는 경우에 생략한다.

· Biden was elected the 46th president of the United States in 2020.

바이든은 2020년에 제46대 미국 대통령으로 선출되었다.

Answers: p.18

Exercise 1 다음 괄호 안에서 알맞은 말을 고르시오.

1 This hall (cleans / is cleaned) by the janitors every day.

2 Many accidents (cause / are caused) by careless drivers.

3 The lost child (found / was found) in the forest last night.

4 The telephone (isn't using / isn't being used), so you can use it now.

5 Americans (elected / were elected) J. F. Kennedy as president in 1961.

6 The police (didn't catch / weren't caught) the man who robbed the bank.

Exercise 2 다음 〈보기〉에서 단어를 골라 알맞은 형태로 바꿔 문장을 완성하시오.

🔍 fix	paint	make	translate	invent

1 The bible _____ into Korean in 1882.

2 Do you know that cheese _____ from milk?

3 *The Starry Night* _____ by Vincent van Gogh in 1889.

4 The telephone _____ by Alexander Bell in 1876.

5 The water pipes _____ by the plumber yesterday.

1 She didn't write the letter.
⇨ _____

2 King Sejong invented Hangeul.
⇨ _____

3 I bought a fancy car for my wife.
⇨ _____

4 They must recycle plastic bottles.
⇨ _____

5 My friend lost my watch yesterday.
⇨ _____

6 We should save money for a rainy day.
⇨ _____

7 Some kids drew the pictures on the wall.
⇨ _____

8 A lot of famous singers remade this song.
⇨ _____

9 My mom made those cookies and cakes.
⇨ _____

10 My brother cleans the room every Sunday.
⇨ _____

11 Johnson gave some candies to the children.
⇨ _____

12 They took my mother to the hospital yesterday.
⇨ _____

13 They will perform their summer concert in June.
⇨ _____

14 The electric vehicle manufacturer employed 200 people last year.
⇨ _____

15 The soccer player will wear the new uniform in the next game.
⇨ _____

🔖 **진행형의 수동태 :** 「be+being+p.p.」
- Sarah was knitting Brian's sweater. Sarah는 Brian의 스웨터를 짜고 있었다.
  ⇒ Brian's sweater **was being knitted** by Sarah.

🔖 **완료형의 수동태 :** 「have+been+p.p.」
- *The New York Times* has offered her the editorship. 「뉴욕타임즈」가 그녀에게 편집장 직을 제의했다.
  ⇒ She **has been offered** the editorship by *the New York Times*.

🔖 **의문문의 수동태**
❶ 의문사가 없는 의문문의 수동태 : be동사나 조동사가 문두로 온다.
- Does she love him? 그녀는 그를 사랑하니?
  ⇒ She loves him. 〈평서문으로 전환〉
  ⇒ He is loved by her 〈수동태 문장으로 전환〉
  ⇒ **Is** he **loved** by her? 〈의문문으로 전환〉
❷ 의문사가 있는 의문문의 수동태 : 「의문사+be동사+주어+p.p.~?」
- Who painted that picture? 누가 저 그림을 그렸니?
  ⇒ That picture was painted by whom. 〈수동태 문장으로 전환〉
  ⇒ **By whom was** the picture **painted**? 〈의문문으로 전환〉

🔖 **명령문의 수동태**
❶ 긍정명령문 : 「let+목적어+be+p.p.」
- Do it now. 지금 그것을 해라
  ⇒ **Let it be done** now.
❷ 부정명령문 : 「let+목적어+not+be+p.p./don't let+목적어+be+p.p.」
- Don't do it now. 지금 그것을 하지 마라!
  ⇒ **Let it not be done** now.
  ⇒ **Don't let it be done** now.

Answers: p.18

Exercise ❶ 다음 괄호 안에서 알맞은 말을 고르시오.

1   By whom was the graffiti (drawing / drawn)?

2   Nobody (noticed / was noticed) she entered the hall.

3   This washing machine (has used / has been used) since 2020.

4   The blue pick-up truck (hit / was hit) the roadside tree this morning.

5   The vacuum cleaner (will deliver / will be delivered) by this Saturday.

6   Coffee (has imported / has been imported) into Korea over the past century.

7   The parents (have invited / have been invited) to a play by the children.

8   Please wait! Right after the ceremony, dinner (will serve / will be served).

9   I didn't realize that our conversation (had been recording / had been recorded).

10   (Does your boss respect / Is your boss respected) by the employees?

Exercise 2 다음 능동태 문장을 수동태 문장으로 바꿔 쓰시오.

1 Who founded your school?
   ⇨ _____

2 Do people speak English in India?
   ⇨ _____

3 Did someone water the plants on my desk?
   ⇨ _____

4 My boss hasn't informed me of the event.
   ⇨ _____

5 Exhaust fumes are polluting the air seriously.
   ⇨ _____

6 People have built this building for three years.
   ⇨ _____

7 When I got home, my father was renovating the old couch.
   ⇨ _____

8 People are carrying out many studies on the environment around the world.
   ⇨ _____

Exercise 3 다음 우리말과 같은 뜻이 되도록 괄호 안의 단어를 알맞게 배열하여 능동태 문장을 만들고,
그 능동태 문장을 수동태 문장으로 바꿔 쓰시오.

1 정부가 댐을 건설하는 중이다. (building, the government, a dam, is)
   ⇨ _____
   ⇨ _____

2 그녀는 지난 4년에 걸쳐 다섯 편의 소설을 썼다. (written, she, five, over the last four years, novels, has)
   ⇨ _____
   ⇨ _____

3 누가 미대륙을 발견했습니까? (discovered, the American, who, continent)
   ⇨ _____
   ⇨ _____

4 많은 십대 소년소녀가 그 추리 소설을 읽었다. (a lot of, have, novel, teenagers, read, the detective)
   ⇨ _____
   ⇨ _____

4형식 / 5형식의 수동태

📑 **4형식의 수동태**

❶ 4형식은 간접목적어와 직접목적어를 각각의 주어로 하여 수동태 문장으로 전환할 수 있다.

- She gave **me the book**. 그녀가 나에게 그 책을 주었다.
  - ⇒ **I was given** the book by her. 〈간접목적어를 주어로〉
  - ⇒ **The book was given** (to) me by her. 〈직접목적어를 주어로〉

❷ 직접목적어를 주어로 하여 수동태를 만들 때는 간접목적어 앞에 전치사(to, for, of)를 써 준다.

- to를 쓰는 동사 – give, show, send, tell, teach, bring, pay, offer 등
- for를 쓰는 동사 – make, buy, cook, find, get, build 등
- of를 쓰는 동사 – ask 등
- She gave me an invitation to her party. 그녀가 내게 파티 초대장을 주었다.
  - ⇒ An invitation to her party **was given to me** by her.
- He bought me a computer for my birthday. 그는 내게 선물로 컴퓨터를 사줬다.
  - ⇒ A computer **was bought for me** for my birthday by him.

📑 **5형식의 수동태**

- He made **his daughter** a teacher. 그는 자신의 딸을 교사로 만들었다.
  - ⇒ **His daughter was made** a teacher by him.
- I painted **the wall** red. 나는 벽을 빨간색으로 칠했다.
  - ⇒ **The wall was painted** red by me.
- She asked **me** to clean the house. 그녀는 나에게 집 청소를 해 달라고 요청했다.
  - ⇒ **I was asked** to clean the house by her.

> **TIPs**
> buy, make, cook 등의 동사는 간접목적어를 주어로 사용하여 수동태 문장을 만들지 않는다.
> - I was bought a computer for my birthday by him. (X)

📑 **지각동사, 사역동사가 있는 문장의 수동태**

목적보어가 분사인 경우는 그대로 쓰지만, 목적보어가 원형부정사인 경우는 to부정사로 바꿔 준다.

- I **heard** her **singing** a song. 나는 그녀가 노래 부르는 소리를 들었다.
  - ⇒ She **was heard singing** a song by me.
- She **made** him **sing** a song. 그녀는 그에게 노래하도록 시켰다.
  - ⇒ He **was made to sing** a song by her.

Answers: p.19

Exercise 1 다음 문장을 수동태 문장으로 바꿔 쓰시오.

1 My husband bought me a fancy car.

⇒ A fancy car _____ .

2 My sister cooked me a great dinner.

⇒ A great dinner _____ .

3 My mother made my baby sister a cute doll.

⇒ A cute doll _____ .

4 My grandmother brought me an umbrella after school.

⇒ An umbrella _____ .

1 Elise taught us American history.

   ⇨ _____

   ⇨ _____

2 She paid him five dollars for parking.

   ⇨ _____

   ⇨ _____

3 Tom gave Susan a bunch of flowers.

   ⇨ _____

   ⇨ _____

4 The company offered me a new position.

   ⇨ _____

   ⇨ _____

5 My teacher told us the theory about the origin of life.

   ⇨ _____

   ⇨ _____

6 The students asked him many questions during class.

   ⇨ _____

   ⇨ _____

1 He (calls / is called) Little Giant by us.

2 We (made / were made) to work hard by them.

3 She was seen (enter / entering) the house by us.

4 The new computer was given (to / for) me by my uncle.

5 We are not allowed (to participate / participate) in the event.

6 She (asked / was asked) to attend the meeting by her boss.

7 Henry (heard / was heard) his son playing the piano in the hall.

8 Andrew was seen (get off / to get off) the train in the morning by us.

9 This watch was bought (for / to) him by me when he turned sixteen.

10 I (told / was told) to stop playing computer games after dinner by my mother.

Exercise **4** 다음 문장을 수동태 문장으로 바꿔 쓰시오.

1 She made me come here.
  ⇨ _____

2 Americans elected him president.
  ⇨ _____

3 They saw him leaving the classroom.
  ⇨ _____

4 Her friends call my daughter Cathy.
  ⇨ _____

5 My mom allowed us to eat some more cake.
  ⇨ _____

6 We heard Jenny singing a song in the cafeteria.
  ⇨ _____

7 The teacher told us not to run in the classroom.
  ⇨ _____

8 My father asked me to walk the dog in the morning.
  ⇨ _____

9 They have named her as the new head of department.
  ⇨ _____

Exercise **5** 다음 우리말과 같은 뜻이 되도록 괄호 안의 단어를 사용하여 수동태 문장을 완성하시오.
　　　　　　(단, 한 칸에 한 단어씩 쓰시오.)

1 그녀가 길을 건너는 모습이 목격되었다. (be seen, crossing)
  ⇨ She _____ _____ _____ the road.

2 나는 밖으로 나가 달라고 요구받았다. (be asked, go out)
  ⇨ I _____ _____ _____ _____ _____ .

3 수족관에서 펭귄이 수영하는 것이 과학자들에 의해 관찰되었다. (be observed, swimming)
  ⇨ Penguins _____ _____ _____ in the aquarium by scientists.

4 학생들에게 영어로 일기를 쓰도록 했다. (be made, keep a diary)
  ⇨ The students _____ _____ _____ _____
  _____ in English.

📑 **동사구의 수동태 : 동사구는 하나의 동사로 취급하므로 분리하지 않는다.**

bring up ~을 기르다	call off ~을 취소하다	run over ~을 치다
laugh at ~을 비웃다	look after ~을 돌보다	turn on ~을 켜다
put off ~을 연기하다	carry out ~을 실행하다	take off ~을 벗다

- A car **ran over** the kangaroo. 자동차가 캥거루를 치었다.
  - ⇒ The kangaroo **was run over by** a car.
- My mother **took care of** five children. 우리 어머니는 다섯 명의 아이들을 돌봤다.
  - ⇒ Five children **were taken care of by** my mother.
- His grandparents **brought up** Sam. 조부모님이 Sam을 길렀다.
  - ⇒ Sam **was brought up by** his grandparents.

📑 **by 이외의 전치사를 쓰는 수동태**

be surprised at[by] ~에 놀라다	be satisfied with ~에 만족하다
be interested in ~에 관심이 있다	be pleased with[by] ~에 기뻐하다
be known to ~에게 알려져 있다	be known for ~으로 유명하다
be known by ~으로 알 수 있다	be known as ~으로 알려져 있다
be made of ~으로 만들어지다 (물리적 변화)	be made from ~으로 만들어지다 (화학적 변화)
be filled with ~으로 가득 차다	be covered with[by, in] ~으로 덮여 있다
be married to ~와 결혼하다	be frightened at ~에 겁나다

- This book **is filled with** funny stories.
  이 책은 재미있는 이야기로 가득 차 있다.
- I **was surprised at** the earthquake.
  나는 지진에 놀랐다.
- He **was satisfied with** his exam result.
  그는 자신의 시험 결과에 만족했다.

Answers: p.19

Exercise ❶ 다음 문장의 빈칸에 알맞은 전치사를 쓰시오. (단, by는 제외)

1 I'm satisfied _____ my final result.

2 Her baggage is filled _____ her clothes.

3 He was surprised _____ the shocking news.

4 Everything around us is made _____ atoms.

5 Chloe is married _____ a Korean engineer and teaches English in Suwon.

6 I am interested _____ making model planes.

7 The top of the mountain is covered _____ snow.

8 Kathy was frightened _____ the sight of her blood.

9 He was pleased _____ their performance at the event.

10 Madagascar is known _____ the world for its natural wonders.

1   The dog was run over by a drunk driver.

⇨ _____

2   The judge will make use of the evidence.

⇨ _____

3   The teacher was looked up to by my sister.

⇨ _____

4   The new student is made fun of by the children.

⇨ _____

5   Christina will take care of our cat during the holiday.

⇨ _____

6   She will look after my dog while I'm on a business trip.

⇨ _____

Exercise **3** 다음 밑줄 친 부분을 바르게 고쳐 쓰시오.

1   He was laughed at her so hard.   ⇨ _____

2   She is known to her beautiful appearance.   ⇨ _____

3   The wounded soldiers were looked after the nurses.   ⇨ _____

4   His children will be taken care of me while they are eating out.   ⇨ _____

Exercise **4** 다음 우리말과 같은 뜻이 되도록 괄호 안의 단어를 사용하여 문장을 완성하시오.

1   그녀는 시인으로 알려져 있다. (know)

⇨ She is _____ a poet.

2   우리는 경기 결과에 기뻐했다. (please)

⇨ We were _____ the result of the match.

3   그 산꼭대기는 눈으로 덮여 있었다. (cover)

⇨ The top of the mountain was _____ snow.

4   그들은 나의 여름휴가 계획에 만족했다. (satisfy)

⇨ They were _____ my plan for the summer vacation.

6-5 목적어가 절인 문장의 수동태

목적어가 절인 문장의 수동태

문장의 동사가 say, think, believe, report, consider 등인 경우 「It+be동사+p.p.+that …」 형태의 수동태 문장이나, that절의 주어를 문장 전체의 주어로 사용한 「주어+be동사+p.p.+to+동사원형 ~」 형태의 수동태 문장으로 바꿔 쓸 수 있다.

· They **say that** she is honest.
  ⇒ **It is said that** she is honest.
  ⇒ **She is said to be** honest (by them). 그들은 그녀가 정직하다고 말한다.

· They **believe that** she is a great artist.
  ⇒ **It is believed that** she is a great artist.
  ⇒ **She is believed to be** a great artist. 그들은 그녀가 훌륭한 예술가라고 믿는다.

Answers: p.19

Exercise 1 다음 문장을 두 가지 형태의 수동태 문장으로 바꿔 쓰시오.

1 People believed that the Earth was flat.
   ⇒ _____
   ⇒ _____

2 They reported that the actor had lung cancer.
   ⇒ _____
   ⇒ _____

3 They consider that Andy Warhol is the Father of Pop Art.
   ⇒ _____
   ⇒ _____

4 People say that he is one of the best singers in the world.
   ⇒ _____
   ⇒ _____

5 They say that Mt. Everest is the highest mountain in the world.
   ⇒ _____
   ⇒ _____

6 They said that Daniel was the best player of the final game.
   ⇒ _____
   ⇒ _____

7 People think that taking a walk every day is good for your health.
   ⇒ _____
   ⇒ _____

[01-05] 다음 빈칸에 들어갈 알맞은 말을 고르시오.

01 A new bridge _____ over the river now.

① is being built   ② is having built
③ builds   ④ is building
⑤ is been built

02 The 2002 World Cup _____ in Korea and Japan.

① was held   ② held
③ was been held   ④ will be held
⑤ has held

03 I taught you how to use the microscope, so now use your microscope as you _____ .

① tell   ② to tell
③ told   ④ were told
⑤ were being told

04 Nelson Mandela _____ as the first black president in South Africa.

① elected   ② was electing
③ have elected   ④ elects
⑤ was elected

05 When I was young, I _____ my grandparents.

① took care of by
② was taken care of
③ was taken care of by
④ was looking after
⑤ was looked after

[06-07] 다음 빈칸에 들어갈 말이 바르게 짝지어진 것을 고르시오.

06 · This company _____ in 1724.
· Yesterday, two men _____ in the car accident.

① found - were injured
② founded - injured
③ was found - were injured
④ was founded - have injured
⑤ was founded - were injured

07 · She was satisfied _____ her wonderful performance.
· He is known _____ us as a writer.

① with - for   ② of - from
③ to - to   ④ with - of
⑤ with - to

[08-09] 다음 빈칸에 공통으로 들어갈 말을 고르시오.

08 · Her eyes were filled _____ tears.
· My mom was pleased _____ the gift.

① to   ② with
③ for   ④ by
⑤ of

09 · 이 도시에 국립 박물관이 건설 중이다.
⇨ A National Museum _____ _____ built in this city.
· 파리에서 국제 예술제가 개최되고 있는 중이다.
⇨ The International Arts Festival _____ _____ held in Paris.

① is being   ② has
③ have been   ④ are being
⑤ was being

[10-11] 다음 문장을 수동태 문장으로 바꾼 것 중 <u>어색한</u> 것을 고르시오.

10 ① We found the door open.
　　⇒ The door was found open.
② What did he discover?
　　⇒ What was discovered by him?
③ Did the result satisfy you?
　　⇒ Were you satisfied with the result?
④ We made her go into the room.
　　⇒ She was made go into the room.
⑤ My mother gave me a doll.
　　⇒ A doll was given to me by my mother.

11 ① Open the door.
　　⇒ Let the door be opened.
② They laughed at me.
　　⇒ I was laughed at by them.
③ He paid me fifty dollars.
　　⇒ Fifty dollars was paid to me by him.
④ Who broke the window?
　　⇒ By whom was the window broken?
⑤ They introduced me to their teacher.
　　⇒ Their teacher was introduced to me by them.

12 다음 〈보기〉와 같은 의미의 문장은?

　It was believed that she kept the secret.

① She was believed to keep the secret.
② She believed that she kept the secret.
③ She is believed to be kept the secret.
④ She believes that she keeps the secret.
⑤ She was believed for her to keep the secret.

[13-15] 다음 〈보기〉의 문장을 수동태 문장으로 바르게 고친 것을 고르시오.

13 　Critics found the book interesting.

① The book was founded to be interesting.
② The book is found to interesting.
③ The book was founded interesting.
④ The book was found interesting.
⑤ The book is founded interesting.

14 　The police officer heard a baby crying in the bathroom.

① A baby was heard cry in the bathroom by the police officer.
② A baby was heard crying in the bathroom by the police officer.
③ A baby is heard crying in the bathroom by the police officer.
④ A baby is heard to cry in the bathroom by the police officer.
⑤ A baby was heard cried in the bathroom by the police officer.

15 　They say that he is a very famous writer in Korea.

① They are said that he is a very famous writer in Korea.
② It says that he is a very famous writer in Korea.
③ He says to be a very famous writer in Korea.
④ He is said to be a very famous writer in Korea.
⑤ It is saying that he is a very famous writer in Korea.

103

[16-18] 다음 중 어법상 <u>어색한</u> 문장을 고르시오.

16 ① He is resembled by his father.
② I was made to wash the car by him.
③ A wild raccoon was run over by a car.
④ The car was bought for me by my father.
⑤ The poor old man was found dead in the snow.

17 ① Was Windows invented by Bill Gates?
② The car is being fixed by the mechanic.
③ The two boxes are connected by lines.
④ The computer has been repaired by her.
⑤ Our lives will change by the technological development.

18 ① Butter is made from milk.
② She is interested in ballet.
③ The e-mail was sent to me by Mr. Thomson.
④ A scholarship was offered to her by the college.
⑤ This toy plane was bought to me by my father yesterday.

19 다음 빈칸에 들어갈 말이 바르게 짝지어진 것은?

Trees _____ to make paper. They say that nearly four billion trees worldwide _____ each year for paper. We can reduce the number of trees used for paper by recycling paper.

① are using – cut down
② are used – are cutting down
③ are used – are cut down
④ are being used – cut down
⑤ use – are cut down

[20-21] 다음 빈칸에 알맞은 말을 고르시오.

20 They are taking care of sick people.
⇨ Sick people _____.

① are taken care by them
② are taken care of them
③ are being taken care of them
④ are being taken care by them
⑤ are being taken care of by them

21 They think that she is a famous movie star in France.
⇨ _____.

① She thinks that she is a famous movie star in France.
② She is thought to be a famous movie star in France.
③ They are thought to be a famous movie star in France.
④ It thinks that she is a famous movie star in France.
⑤ It is thought her to be a famous movie star in France.

[22-23] 다음 중 어법상 바른 문장을 고르시오.

22 ① A little boy was run over a truck.
② The room was filled of many books.
③ The shirt was bought my brother by me.
④ The servants have been treated kindly.
⑤ Catherine was watched play the piano.

23 ① She said to be a popular singer.
② They were surprised at the news.
③ He was made clean the classroom.
④ His grandfather is being looked after the nurse.
⑤ I was not allowed watch TV after 11 p.m.

24 다음 빈칸에 들어갈 알맞은 말은?

> Everyone told me that when I turned fifteen, a great internal change would occur. I truly expected it to occur, but nothing happened. When _____ my grandmother, however, I replied, "Yes, I do feel a great change has taken place."

① asking　　　　② I asked to
③ I was asked　　④ I was asked by
⑤ being asked

[25-26] 다음 우리말과 같은 뜻이 되도록 괄호 안의 단어를 알맞게 배열하시오.

25　멕시코에서 스페인어가 사용된다.

(Mexico, Spanish, spoken, is, in)

⇒ _____

26　홍콩은 아름다운 스카이라인으로 유명하다.

(beautiful, Hong Kong, for, is, known, its, skyline)

⇒ _____

_____

[27-28] 다음 괄호 안의 단어를 사용하여 문장을 완성하시오.

27　The 2022 World Cup _____ in the winter. (hold)

28　A lot of trees have _____ to build roads. (cut down)

29 다음 (A), (B), (C)의 괄호 안에서 어법에 맞는 표현으로 가장 적절한 것은?

> We **(A) [sing / are sung]** the old songs. These songs **(B) [have passed down / have been passed down]** from person to person for many generations. My mother told me how these songs **(C) [sang / were sung]** by her grandmother.

[30-35] 다음 능동태 문장을 수동태 문장으로 바꿔 쓰시오.

30　He has told us an amusing story.
　⇒ An amusing story _____
　　by him.

31　We saw him walking in the park.
　⇒ He _____ in the park
　　by us.

32　Many companies have recycled empty bottles.
　⇒ Empty bottles _____
　　by many companies.

33　We heard Mary singing a song on the stage.
　⇒ Mary _____
　　on the stage by us.

34　Susan is using my tablet PC.
　⇒ My tablet PC _____ by
　　Susan.

35　They say that she is a good singer.
　⇒ It _____ that she is a good singer.
　⇒ She _____ a good singer.

Answers: p.21

[1-2] 다음 글을 읽고, 물음에 답하시오.

서술형

Hi, Thanh.

Merry Christmas!

It is a white Christmas here in Korea. (A) 밖은 모든 것이 눈으로 덮여 있어. I dreamed of it, and my wish ⓐ has come true. Even though the snow ⓑ keeps me inside, I'm so happy.

What is Christmas like in Vietnam? ⓒ Do Christmas celebrated in Vietnam? We celebrate Christmas because Jesus ⓓ was born on December 25th. We decorate Christmas trees and sing carols. We also go to church and have special events.

Please tell me about Christmas in Vietnam.

Sooji

1 윗글의 ⓐ ～ ⓓ 중 어법상 어색한 것을 찾아 바르게 고치시오.

→ _____

2 밑줄 (A)의 우리말을 주어진 말을 이용하여 영어로 옮기시오. (everything, cover, snow)

→ _____ outside.

3 다음 글의 밑줄 친 부분 중, 어법상 틀린 것은?

수능 대비형

Register early. Enrollment is on a first-registered, first-enrolled basis. ① When the class is full, students will ② put on a waiting list. Applications ③ must be mailed or delivered in person. We do not accept telephone, email, fax applications. There is a $30 administrative fee per course. Please attach checks to the application. Applications without payment will not be ④ accepted. Applicants are to assume ⑤ that they are scheduled for the program unless told otherwise. Confirmation notifications will not be sent.

* enrollment: 등록
** application: 지원서
*** administrative fee: 행정 수수료
**** notification: 통지

Chapter 7

가정법

가정법 과거

📑 **가정법 과거**

현재의 사실에 반대되는 것이나 실현 불가능한 일을 가정하며, '만일 ∼라면 …할 텐데'라고 해석한다.

조건절	주절
If+주어+동사의 과거형	주어+조동사의 과거형+동사원형

· If I **were** rich, I **could buy** a car.
  만약 내가 부자라면, 차를 살 수 있을 텐데.

  = As I **am not** rich, I **cannot buy** a car.
  나는 부자가 아니기 때문에, 차를 살 수 없다.

· If I **had** enough money, I **could buy** the house on the hill.
  만약 내가 돈이 충분하다면, 언덕 위에 있는 집을 살 수 있을 텐데.

  = As I **don't have** enough money, I **cannot buy** the house on the hill.
  나는 돈이 충분하지 않기 때문에, 언덕 위에 있는 집을 살 수 없다.

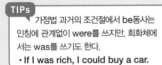

TIPs 가정법 과거의 조건절에서 be동사는 인칭에 관계없이 were를 쓰지만, 회화체에서는 was를 쓰기도 한다.
· If I <u>was</u> rich, I could buy a car.

Answers: p.22

Exercise ① 다음 괄호 안에서 알맞은 말을 고르시오.

1 If we (go / went) by car, we will save time.

2 If I had the book, I (can lend / could lend) it to you.

3 If Tom (is / were) at home, he would answer the phone.

4 If she told me about the matter, I (will help / would help) her.

5 If he were more humorous, many girls (will like / would like) him.

Exercise ② 다음 문장을 〈보기〉와 같이 고쳐 쓰시오.

🔍 **As I am poor, I can't buy the car.**
  ⇒ _____ If I were not poor, I could buy the car. _____

1 As I have a class, I can't go to the concert.
  ⇒ _____

2 As I am not a poet, I can't write a beautiful poem.
  ⇒ _____

3 As I don't have an extra blanket, I can't give it to you.
  ⇒ _____

4 As my teacher isn't here, I can't get advice on this topic.
  ⇒ _____

5 As my children make noise, I can't concentrate on my work.
  ⇒ _____

가정법 과거완료

과거 사실과 반대되는 것을 가정하며, '만일 ~했더라면 …했을 텐데'라고 해석한다.

조건절	주절
If+주어+had+p.p.	주어+조동사의 과거형+have+p.p.

- If he **had worked** hard, he **could have succeeded**.
  그가 만약 열심히 일했더라면, 성공할 수 있었을 텐데.

  = As he **didn't work** hard, he **could not succeed**.
  그는 열심히 일하지 않았기 때문에, 성공하지 못했다.

- If the weather **had been** fine, we **would have gone** on a picnic.
  날씨가 좋았더라면, 우리는 소풍을 갔었을 텐데.

  = As the weather **was not** fine, we **didn't go** on a picnic.
  날씨가 좋지 않았기 때문에, 우리는 소풍을 가지 않았다.

Answers: p.22

Exercise ❶ 다음 괄호 안의 단어를 사용하여 문장을 완성하시오.

1 If we _____ by train, we could have saved time. (go)

2 If the doctor _____ earlier, she wouldn't have died. (come)

3 If I _____ early, I would have been able to work out. (get up)

4 If I had had enough money, I could _____ you some. (lend)

5 If he hadn't gone to the party, he would _____ the report already. (finish)

Exercise ❷ 다음 문장을 〈보기〉와 같이 고쳐 쓰시오.

🔍 **As you weren't honest, I couldn't trust you.**
⇨ _____ If you had been honest, I could have trusted you. _____

1 As this book wasn't published in Korea, I couldn't buy it.
⇨ _____

2 As we didn't make a reservation, we couldn't get good seats.
⇨ _____

3 As I had a lecture in the evening, I couldn't go to the movies.
⇨ _____

4 As they didn't agree with my idea, we couldn't work together.
⇨ _____

5 As she took the subway, she could arrive at home before midnight.
⇨ _____

7-3 I wish 가정법

I wish 가정법

	I wish+가정법 과거	I wish+가정법 과거완료
형태	I wish + 주어+동사의 과거형	I wish + 주어+had+p.p.
	I wish + 주어+조동사의 과거형+동사원형	I wish + 주어 + 조동사의 과거형+have+p.p.
의미	~하면 좋을 텐데	~했다면 좋을 텐데
직설법	I'm sorry (that)+주어+현재 시제	I'm sorry (that)+주어+과거 시제

- I wish it **were** true. 그것이 사실이라면 좋을 텐데.

  = I am sorry it **is not** true. 그것이 사실이 아니라 유감이다.
- I wish I **knew** how to drive. 내가 운전할 줄 알면 좋을 텐데.

  = I am sorry that I **don't know** how to drive. 내가 운전할 줄 몰라서 유감이다.
- I wish I **had bought** the book. 그 책을 샀다면 좋을 텐데.

  = I am sorry I **didn't buy** the book. 그 책을 사지 않아서 유감이다.
- I wish I **hadn't been** late for school. 지각하지 않았다면 좋을 텐데.

  = I am sorry I **was** late for school. 지각해서 유감이다.

Answers: p.22

Exercise 1 다음 괄호 안의 단어를 사용하여 문장을 완성하시오.

1 I wish I _____ (go out) on a date with her yesterday.

2 I wish I _____ (have) a movie ticket now.

3 I wish I _____ (study) harder when I was young.

4 I wish I _____ (can, speak) French well, but I can't.

5 I missed the first train. I wish I _____ (get up) earlier.

6 I wish I _____ (save) some money. I don't have any money now.

7 I wish they _____ (pass) the exam. They failed to enter college.

8 He is leaving tonight. I wish he _____ (can, stay) with me a little longer.

Exercise 2 다음 우리말과 같은 뜻이 되도록 괄호 안의 단어를 사용하여 문장을 완성하시오.

1 나에게 노트북 컴퓨터가 있으면 좋을 텐데. (have, a laptop computer)

   ⇒ I wish _____.

2 내가 수영하는 법을 배웠더라면 좋을 텐데. (learn, how to swim)

   ⇒ I wish _____.

3 내가 여기에서 그를 만날 수 있으면 좋을 텐데. (can, meet, him)

   ⇒ I wish _____.

4 내가 그 여름캠프에 참가했었다면 좋을 텐데. (participate in, the summer camp)

   ⇒ I wish _____.

🔍 **I am sorry that I don't know how to play the guitar.**
⇒ _____ I wish I knew how to play the guitar. _____

1   I am sorry I live far from school.

⇒ _____

2   I am sorry I can't go hiking with you.

⇒ _____

3   I am sorry he doesn't like Italian food.

⇒ _____

4   I am sorry I have to go to school today.

⇒ _____

5   I am sorry I don't speak Korean fluently enough to travel alone.

⇒ _____

Exercise **4** 다음 〈보기〉와 같이 문장을 바꿔 쓰시오.

🔍 **I am sorry I didn't know how to play the guitar.**
⇒ _____ I wish I had known how to play the guitar. _____

1   I am sorry she didn't see my memo earlier.

⇒ _____

2   I am sorry my team didn't win the final game.

⇒ _____

3   I am sorry you couldn't clean your room before noon.

⇒ _____

4   I am sorry you couldn't come to the housewarming party.

⇒ _____

5   I am sorry I didn't inform you about my traveling to Europe.

⇒ _____

혼합가정법

혼합가정법

혼합가정법은 과거에 실현되지 못한 일이 현재에 영향을 줄 때 사용한다. 이때 if절에는 과거완료를, 주절에는 과거를 쓰며, '만일 ~했다면, …할 텐데'라고 해석한다.

조건절	주절
If+주어+had+p.p.	주어+조동사의 과거형+동사원형

· If it **had not snowed** last night, we **could play** baseball now.
어젯밤에 눈이 오지 않았다면, 우리는 지금 야구를 할 수 있을 텐데.
⇒ As it **snowed** last night, we **can't play** baseball now.

· If I **had saved** enough money, I **could buy** a bicycle now.
돈을 충분히 저금했다면, 나는 지금 자전거를 살 수 있을 텐데.
⇒ As I **didn't save** enough money, I **can't buy** a bicycle now.

Answers: p.22

Exercise 1 다음 우리말과 같은 뜻이 되도록 괄호 안의 단어를 사용하여 문장을 완성하시오.

1 네가 저녁을 먹었다면, 지금 배고프지 않을 텐데. (eat, will, be)

⇒ If you ＿＿＿＿＿＿＿＿＿ dinner, you ＿＿＿＿＿＿＿＿＿ hungry now.

2 어젯밤에 눈이 오지 않았다면, 도로가 미끄럽지 않을 텐데. (snow, will, be)

⇒ If it ＿＿＿＿＿＿＿＿＿ last night, the road ＿＿＿＿＿＿＿＿＿ slippery.

3 우리가 버스를 놓치지 않았다면, 지금 공항에 있을 텐데. (miss, will, be)

⇒ If we ＿＿＿＿＿＿＿＿＿ the bus, we ＿＿＿＿＿＿＿＿＿ at the airport now.

4 그가 지난 주말에 열심히 공부했다면, 지금 이 문제에 답할 수 있을 텐데. (study, can, answer)

⇒ If he ＿＿＿＿＿＿＿＿＿ hard last weekend, he ＿＿＿＿＿＿＿＿＿ this question.

Exercise 2 다음 짝지어진 두 문장이 같은 뜻이 되도록 가정법 문장을 완성하시오.

1 As I stayed up all night, I'm very tired now.

⇒ If I ＿＿＿＿＿＿＿＿＿ all night, I ＿＿＿＿＿＿＿＿＿ now.

2 As I lost my umbrella, I can't lend it to you.

⇒ If I ＿＿＿＿＿＿＿＿＿ my umbrella, I ＿＿＿＿＿＿＿＿＿ it to you.

3 As Jeff took my cellular phone, I can't make a call to my mom now.

⇒ If Jeff ＿＿＿＿＿＿＿＿＿ my cellular phone, I ＿＿＿＿＿＿＿＿＿ to my mom now.

4 As Tommy bought a luxury car, he doesn't have enough money now.

⇒ If Tommy ＿＿＿＿＿＿＿＿＿ a luxury car, he ＿＿＿＿＿＿＿＿＿ enough money now.

7-5 as if [as though] 가정법

as if [as though] 가정법

	as if [as though]+가정법 과거	as if [as though]+가정법 과거완료
형태	주절+as if[as though]+주어+동사의 과거형	주절+as if[as though]+주어+had+p.p.
의미	(현재 사실에 반대되는 일) 마치 ~인 것처럼	(과거 사실에 반대되는 일) 마치 ~였던 것처럼

· He talks as if he **knew** the fact. 그는 마치 그 사실을 아는 것처럼 말한다.

= In fact, he **doesn't know** the fact. 사실, 그는 그 사실을 모른다.

· She looks as if she **were** angry. 그녀는 화가 난 것처럼 보인다.

= In fact, she **isn't** angry. 사실, 그녀는 화나지 않았다.

· He talks as if he **had been** ill. 그는 마치 아팠던 것처럼 말한다.

= In fact, he **wasn't** ill. 사실, 그는 아프지 않았다.

· She acts as if she **had visited** Europe. 그녀는 유럽에 가본 것처럼 행동한다.

= In fact, she **didn't visit[hasn't visited]** Europe. 사실, 그녀는 유럽에 가본 적이 없다.

Answers: p.22

Exercise 1 다음 〈보기〉와 같이 문장을 바꿔 쓰시오.

 In fact, he isn't American.

⇒ He talks _____ as if he were American _____.

1 In fact, Mark didn't see a ghost.

⇒ Mark looks _____.

2 In fact, she didn't stay home all day.

⇒ She talks _____.

3 In fact, he didn't witness the accident.

⇒ He talks _____.

4 In fact, he didn't meet her mother before.

⇒ He acts _____.

5 In fact, he isn't an expert on marine mammals.

⇒ He talks _____.

6 In fact, he hasn't used this lawn mower before.

⇒ He acts _____.

7 In fact, Sandra isn't a professional opera singer.

⇒ Sandra talks _____.

8 In fact, he doesn't know the truth behind the accident.

⇒ He talks _____.

> 🔍 **He talks as if he were a university student.**
> ⇒ **In fact,** <u>he isn't a university student</u> .

1 He acts as if he had climbed Mt. Everest.

⇒ In fact, _____ .

2 He talks as if his major were computer science.

⇒ In fact, _____ .

3 Jenny talks as if she worked out at the gym every day.

⇒ In fact, _____ .

4 She talks as if she had made a mistake in the document.

⇒ In fact, _____ .

5 She behaves as if she had cooked all the food for the party by herself.

⇒ In fact, _____ .

6 The reporter talks as if he had interviewed the actress about the new movie.

⇒ In fact, _____ .

1 그는 나에게 거짓말을 하지 않았던 것처럼 행동한다. (lie)

⇒ He acts _____ to me.

2 그는 마치 어린아이처럼 행동한다. (be)

⇒ He behaves _____ a child.

3 그녀는 자신의 실수에 당황하지 않은 것처럼 행동한다. (be embarrassed about)

⇒ She acts _____ her mistake.

4 그녀는 답을 아는 것처럼 보인다. (know)

⇒ She looks _____ the answer.

5 그녀는 홍콩에 살았던 것처럼 말한다. (live)

⇒ She talks _____ in Hong Kong.

6 그의 남동생은 영화배우였던 것처럼 말한다. (be)

⇒ His brother talks _____ a movie star.

7-6 if 생략

if의 생략

if절에 **were**, **should**, **had** 등이 오면 **if**를 생략하고 주어와 동사를 도치시킨다.

· **If I were** strong enough, I could help you carry those heavy boxes.

= **Were I** strong enough, I could help you carry those heavy boxes.

내가 충분히 튼튼하다면, 네가 그 무거운 상자들을 옮기는 것을 도울 수 있을 텐데.

· **If he had** passed the exam, he would have been happy.

= **Had he** passed the exam, he would have been happy.

그가 시험에 합격했다면, 기뻤을 텐데.

· **If you should** change your mind, call me at this number.

= **Should you** change your mind, call me at this number.

마음이 바뀐다면, 이 번호로 전화하세요.

Answers: p.23

Exercise 1 다음 〈보기〉와 같이 문장을 바꿔 쓰시오.

🔍 If you should have any questions, feel free to contact me.

⇨ ___Should you have any questions___ , feel free to contact me.

1 If I were in your position, I would not say so.

⇨ _____ , I would not say so.

2 If I had had a car, I could have come earlier.

⇨ _____ , I could have come earlier.

3 If you should need my help, do not hesitate to ask me.

⇨ _____ , do not hesitate to ask me.

4 If he had told the truth, I would have given him one more chance.

⇨ _____ , I would have given him one more chance.

Exercise 2 다음 우리말과 같은 뜻이 되도록 괄호 안의 단어를 알맞게 배열하여 문장을 완성하시오.

1 그가 정직하다면 그것을 하지 않을 텐데. (he, were, honest)

⇨ _____ , he would not do it.

2 내가 그녀의 주소를 알았다면 소포를 보낼 수 있었을 텐데. (I, had, her, address, known)

⇨ _____ , I would have sent the package to her.

3 내가 돈을 충분히 가지고 있었다면 저 아름다운 성을 살 수 있었을 텐데. (had, money, had, enough, I)

⇨ _____ , I would have bought the beautiful castle.

4 그가 의사의 충고를 들었다면 그의 상태는 더 나아졌을 텐데. (taken, he, the doctor's, advice, had)

⇨ _____ , his condition would have been better.

7-7 without / but for

📂 without / but for

가정법 과거 : ~가 없다면	가정법 과거완료 : ~가 없었다면
If it were not for ~	If it had not been for ~
= Were it not for ~	= Had it not been for~

· **Without [But for]** air, we couldn't breathe.

= **If it were not for** air, we couldn't breathe.

= **Were it not for** air, we couldn't breathe.

공기가 없다면, 우리는 숨 쉴 수 없다.

· **Without [But for]** her help, I wouldn't have been able to conduct the experiment.

= **If it had not been for** her help, I wouldn't have been able to conduct the experiment.

= **Had it not been for** her help, I wouldn't have been able to conduct the experiment.

그녀의 도움이 없었다면, 나는 그 실험을 하지 못했을 것이다.

Answers: p.23

Exercise 1 다음 〈보기〉와 같이 문장을 바꿔 쓰시오.

🔍 If it were not for your help, they couldn't finish the project.

⇨ _____Without your help_____, they couldn't finish the project.

⇨ _____But for your help_____, they couldn't finish the project.

⇨ ___Were it not for your help___, they couldn't finish the project.

1 If it were not for the computer, I couldn't finish my report.

⇨ _____, I couldn't finish my report.

⇨ _____, I couldn't finish my report.

⇨ _____, I couldn't finish my report.

2 If it had not been for his advice, we would have fallen apart.

⇨ _____, we would have fallen apart.

⇨ _____, we would have fallen apart.

⇨ _____, we would have fallen apart.

3 If it were not for the homework, I could visit my grandparents.

⇨ _____, I could visit my grandparents.

⇨ _____, I could visit my grandparents.

⇨ _____, I could visit my grandparents.

4 If it had not been for the rescue workers, the kids would have been frozen to death.

⇨ _____, the kids would have been frozen to death.

⇨ _____, the kids would have been frozen to death.

⇨ _____, the kids would have been frozen to death.

1 그녀의 도움이 없었다면, 나는 은행을 찾을 수 없었을 것이다.

(found, without, the bank, her, couldn't, I, help, have)

⇒ _____

2 물이 없다면, 지구 상의 모든 동물은 존재할 수 없을 것이다.

(exist, without, not, would, on Earth, all animals, water)

⇒ _____

3 이메일이 없었다면, 우리는 세계적인 설문 조사를 할 수 없었을 것이다.

(a worldwide survey, conducted, e-mail, couldn't, without, have, we)

⇒ _____

4 지하철이 없다면, 교통 체증이 지금보다 훨씬 심할 것이다.

(much worse than, but for, be, the traffic, the subway, would, it is now)

⇒ _____

5 그의 차가 없었다면, 우리는 학교에 지각했을 것이다.

(late for, his car, it, been for, been, would, have, if, school, we, had not)

⇒ _____

🔍 **Without his support, we could not succeed.**
⇒ _____ If it were not for his support, we could not succeed. _____

1 Without the map, I would be lost in the middle of the forest.

⇒ _____

2 Without the Internet, we could not collect information easily.

⇒ _____

3 But for the rainy season, we would have had a great vacation.

⇒ _____

4 Without your advice, I could not have started my own business.

⇒ _____

5 But for his leadership, they could not have survived the shipwreck.

⇒ _____

Review Test

[01-06] 다음 빈칸에 알맞은 것을 고르시오.

01　If I were you, I _____ not go there alone.

① can　　　　　② will
③ may　　　　　④ would
⑤ shall

02　If you _____ more exercise, you would be healthier now.

① does　　　　　② do
③ didn't do　　　④ had done
⑤ doesn't do

03　If I _____ my gloves yesterday, I could lend them to you now.

① lost　　　　　② had lost
③ didn't lose　　④ have not lost
⑤ had not lost

04　If I _____ the test was canceled, I wouldn't have stayed up all night.

① know　　　　　② had known
③ knew　　　　　④ will know
⑤ have known

05　I wish I _____ a cute puppy. I was so lonely when I was young.

① have　　　　　② had
③ had had　　　　④ will have
⑤ have had

06　He talks as if he _____ me before.

① have met　　　② met
③ had met　　　④ will meet
⑤ would meet

[07-08] 다음 우리말과 같은 뜻이 되도록 빈칸에 알맞은 말을 고르시오.

07　할아버지께서 아직 살아 계신다면 좋을 텐데.
　⇒ I wish my grandfather _____ still alive.

① be　　　　　② were
③ will be　　　④ is
⑤ has been

08　그녀가 어디 사는지 안다면, 그녀를 방문할 텐데.
　⇒ If I _____ where she lives, I could visit her.

① know　　　　　② had known
③ knew　　　　　④ will know
⑤ have know

09　다음 문장 중 의미가 <u>다른</u> 하나는?

① But for books, we could hardly acquire knowledge.
② Without books, we could hardly acquire knowledge.
③ If it were not for books, we could hardly acquire knowledge.
④ Were it not for books, we could hardly acquire knowledge.
⑤ If it had not been for books, we could hardly have acquired knowledge.

[10-13] 다음 직설법 문장을 가정법 문장으로 전환할 때 빈칸에 알맞은 말을 고르시오.

10 I am sorry I didn't visit you yesterday.
⇒ I wish I _____ you yesterday.

① visited   ② didn't visit
③ have visited   ④ had visited
⑤ hadn't visited

11 As it is not fine, we will not go outside.
⇒ If it _____ fine, we _____ go outside.

① is – will   ② were – would
③ was – will   ④ were – will
⑤ is – would

12 As he didn't have a car, he didn't come here.
⇒ If he _____ a car, he _____ here.

① had had – have come
② has had – would have come
③ had had – would have come
④ were having – have come
⑤ is having – have come

13 As you ate bad food, you have a stomachache now.
⇒ If you _____ bad food, you would not have a stomachache now.

① had eaten   ② have eaten
③ were eaten   ④ have not eaten
⑤ had not eaten

[14-16] 다음 우리말을 바르게 영작한 것을 고르시오.

14 그녀가 거기 있었다면 당신을 도와줬을 텐데.

① If she is there, she will help you.
② If she were there, she would help you.
③ If she had been there, she would help you.
④ If she were there, she would have helped you.
⑤ If she had been there, she would have helped you.

15 그가 용돈을 절약했다면 지금 햄버거를 살 수 있을 텐데.

① If he saves his allowance, he can buy a hamburger now.
② If he saved his allowance, he could buy a hamburger now.
③ If he had saved his allowance, he could buy a hamburger now.
④ If he had saved his allowance, he could have bought a hamburger now.
⑤ If he saved his allowance, he could have bought a hamburger now.

16 내가 네가 병원에 입원한 걸 알았더라면 너를 방문했을 텐데.

① If I know you were in the hospital, I will visit you.
② If I knew you were in the hospital, I would visit you.
③ If I had known you were in the hospital, I would visit you now.
④ If I had known you were in the hospital, I would have visited you.
⑤ If I have known you were in the hospital, I would have visited you.

[17-19] 다음 밑줄 친 부분 중 어법상 어색한 것을 고르시오.

17 ① I wish I <u>could</u> see the movie with her.
② He looks as if he <u>doubted</u> something.
③ They <u>would have reached</u> the top if it had not rained.
④ He <u>might have been successful</u> now if he had not been so lazy.
⑤ If I <u>had made</u> a lot of money in my twenties, I would be happy now.

18 ① You <u>would have caught</u> the train if you had hurried.
② We <u>might have lost</u> the way if he had not helped us.
③ If I were not poor in health, I <u>would carry out</u> my plan.
④ I wouldn't have finished if I <u>didn't work</u> yesterday.
⑤ If the students had started earlier, they <u>would be</u> here now.

19 ① She talks as if I <u>were</u> not here.
② I wish I <u>had met</u> my professor yesterday.
③ Were I you, I <u>would not</u> go there with her.
④ I would visit my grandparents if I <u>had</u> enough time.
⑤ If John <u>played</u> the piano for me, I would have been much happier.

[20-21] 다음 〈보기〉와 의미가 같은 문장을 고르시오.

20
> If you had left earlier, you could have attended the meeting.

① As you left earlier, you could attend the meeting.
② As you leave earlier, you can attend the meeting.
③ As you didn't leave earlier, you could not attend the meeting.
④ As you don't leave earlier, you could not attend the meeting.
⑤ As you have left earlier, you could have attended the meeting.

21
> I wish I had worn the blue shirt yesterday.

① I wear the blue shirt now.
② I'm sorry I wear the blue shirt.
③ I wore the blue shirt yesterday.
④ I'm sorry I don't wear the blue shirt now.
⑤ I'm sorry I didn't wear the blue shirt yesterday.

[22-24] 다음 짝지어진 두 문장의 의미가 같지 않은 것을 고르시오.

22 ① Were I rich, I could buy the apartment.
= As I'm not rich, I can't buy the apartment.
② If he had worked hard, he would not have failed.
= As he didn't work hard, he failed.
③ If you had arrived earlier, you could have met him.
= As you didn't arrive earlier, you couldn't meet him.
④ I'm sorry you have too much work.
= I wish you hadn't had too much work.
⑤ If I had enough time, I could go to India.
= As I don't have enough time, I can't go to India.

23 ① As I am poor, I cannot buy a car.
= If I were not poor, I could buy a car.
② As I were ill, I didn't go there.
= If I hadn't been ill, I would have gone there.
③ I am sorry I can't help you.
= I wish I could help you.
④ In fact, he doesn't know the true story.
= He talks as if he knew the true story.
⑤ As I didn't have enough money, I couldn't buy the house.
= If I had had enough money, I could buy the house.

24 ① If I were a bird, I could fly to you.
= Were I a bird, I could fly to you.

② I wish I had learned English in my youth.
= I'm sorry I didn't learn English in my youth.

③ Without my poverty, I would not have dropped out of college.
= But for my poverty, I would not have dropped out of college.

④ Without the snow, the flea market would have opened as scheduled.
= If it were not for the snow, the flea market would have opened as scheduled.

⑤ If it had not been for her parents' disapproval, she would have gone abroad.
= But for her parents' disapproval, she would have gone abroad.

[25-26] 다음 밑줄 친 부분을 바르게 고쳐 쓰시오.

25 If the Sun disappears, all living things on Earth would die.

⇨ _____

26 If I lived in the Stone Age, I would have been a hunter.

⇨ _____

[27-29] 다음 우리말과 같은 뜻이 되도록 문장을 완성하시오.

27 너의 도움이 없었더라면, 나는 실패했을 것이다.

⇨ If _____

_____ your help, I would have failed in it.

28 그 소식이 사실이라면 좋을 텐데.

⇨ I _____ the news _____ true.

29 그녀는 마치 아픈 것처럼 보인다.

⇨ She looks _____ she were sick.

[30-34] 다음은 직설법 문장을 가정법 문장으로 전환한 것이다. 빈칸에 알맞은 말을 써넣으시오.

30 As you didn't look for the keys carefully, you couldn't find them.

⇨ If you _____ the keys carefully, you could have found them.

31 In fact, he doesn't have a lot of money.

⇨ He speaks as if he _____ a lot of money.

32 I am sorry I didn't know her well.

⇨ I wish I _____ her well.

33 As I didn't finish doing the chores that my mother asked me to do, I cannot go see a movie with you now.

⇨ If I _____ doing the chores that my mother asked me to do, I _____ see a movie with you now.

34 As the economic situation was bad, the opening ceremony was canceled.

⇨ If the economic situation _____ bad, the opening ceremony would _____ canceled.

Answers: p.25

[1-2] 다음 대화를 읽고, 물음에 답하시오.   서술형

Last Saturday, a wildfire broke out in the mountains of Gangwon Province. ⓐ <u>As it was very dry that day, the fire spread quickly.</u> The firefighters tried very hard to put it out, but nothing remained after the fire. The news says that the fire was caused by a cigarette butt. Before the fire, the forests had been always green. I wish I could see the beautiful forests again.

1 밑줄 친 ⓐ와 같은 뜻의 문장을 if를 이용해서 다시 쓰시오.

→ _____

2 윗글을 읽고 괄호에 주어진 단어를 이용하여 본문의 내용과 일치하도록 문장을 완성하시오. (단, 가정법 과거완료로 쓸 것)

If it _____ _____ for the smoker, the forests _____ _____

_____ _____. (destroy)

3 다음 글의 밑줄 친 부분 중, 어법상 틀린 것은?   수능 대비형

My friend Lisa and her husband are considering some changes to their home. Lisa is thinking of adding a second bathroom. Now that their two children are growing bigger and bigger, she thinks they ① <u>need to</u> have their own bathroom. She also wants to have the kitchen expanded. She prepares meals with the kids whenever there is a chance, but the kitchen feels somewhat small for three of them. Her husband, however, has a different idea. He wants ② <u>to install</u> a fireplace. He believes if they had a fireplace, the family ③ <u>will</u> get together more often. He'd also like ④ <u>to have</u> a bigger garage. There are so many things in the garage that he can't work ⑤ <u>comfortably</u> there.

* expand: 확장하다
** fireplace: 벽난로

Chapter
8

비교급, 최상급

비교급과 최상급

📑 **비교급과 최상급 만드는 방법**

❶ tall – taller – tallest 〈대부분의 경우 : 형용사/부사 뒤에 er/est를 붙인다.〉

❷ wise – wiser – wisest 〈-e로 끝나는 경우 : 형용사/부사 뒤에 r/st를 붙인다.〉

❸ big – bigger – biggest 〈「단모음+단자음」으로 끝나는 경우 : 단자음을 한 번 더 써 주고, er/est를 붙인다.〉

❹ happy – happier – happiest 〈-y로 끝나는 경우 : y를 i로 고치고, er/est를 붙인다.〉

❺ difficult – more difficult – most difficult

〈-ful, -less, -ive, - ous, -ing로 끝나는 2음절 단어나, 3음절 이상 단어의 경우 : 형용사/부사 앞에 more/most를 붙인다.〉

❻ 주의해야 할 비교급

형용사 / 부사(원급)		비교급	최상급
good 좋은		better	best
well 잘			
bad 나쁜		worse	worst
ill 아픈			
much 많은, 많이 (양)		more	most
many 많은, 많이 (수)			
little 거의 없는 (양)		less	least
few 거의 없는 (수)		fewer	fewest
late	늦은, 늦게 (시간)	later	latest
	늦은, 늦게, 나중인 (순서)	latter	last
far	먼 (거리)	farther	farthest
	심한, 나아가 (정도)	further	furthest
old	오래된	older	oldest
	나이 든		
	손위의	elder	eldest

Answers: p.25

Exercise 1 다음 우리말과 같은 뜻이 되도록 괄호 안의 단어를 사용하여 문장을 완성하시오.

1 그는 나보다 수학을 더 잘한다. (good)

⇨ He is ＿＿＿＿＿＿＿＿＿ at math than I am.

2 나는 내 친구보다 공을 멀리 던졌다. (far)

⇨ I threw the ball ＿＿＿＿＿＿＿＿＿ than my friends did.

3 나는 이집트의 마지막 왕이 누구였는지 모른다. (late)

⇨ I don't know who the ＿＿＿＿＿＿＿＿＿ king of Egypt was.

4 가장 좋아하는 한국 음식이 무엇입니까? (much)

⇨ What kind of Korean food do you like ＿＿＿＿＿＿＿＿＿?

5 전시된 컴퓨터는 최신 모델이다. (late)

⇨ The computer on display is the ＿＿＿＿＿＿＿＿＿ model.

6 더 이상의 질문이 있으시면 주저 마시고 저에게 연락하세요. (far)

⇨ If you have any ＿＿＿＿＿＿＿＿＿ questions, please don't hesitate to contact me.

1	long		2	hot
3	useful		4	early
5	much		6	old(손위의)
7	far(정도)		8	late(시간)
9	little		10	good
11	wide		12	famous
13	easy		14	funny
15	wise		16	careful
17	ugly		18	short
19	noisy		20	huge
21	important		22	sunny
23	popular		24	interesting
25	ill		26	late(순서)
27	large		28	far(거리)
29	big		30	old(오래된)

Exercise **3** 다음 문장의 밑줄 친 부분을 바르게 고치시오.

1 Kathy is the elder of our four daughters. ⇨ _____

2 She is the more intelligent student in her school. ⇨ _____

3 I think Michael is the little suitable for the position. ⇨ _____

4 His health condition becomes worse, as he gets elder. ⇨ _____

5 Your laptop computer is the more expensive among ours. ⇨ _____

6 I hope that you'll get good scores on the test than others. ⇨ _____

7 It is said that Richard was the later person to see her alive. ⇨ _____

8 We need little water than we expected because it rained last night. ⇨ _____

9 The department store sells the better home appliances made in Korea. ⇨ _____

10 With the coming of winter, the cost of energy becomes high than the fall. ⇨ _____

원급 / 비교급 / 최상급

📑 원급 비교

❶ 「A as+원급+as B」: A는 B만큼 ~하다
- He is **as tall as** his brother. 그는 형만큼 키가 크다.
- Bears are **as dangerous as** alligators. 곰은 악어만큼 위험하다.

❷ 「A not as(so)+원급+as B」: A는 B만큼 ~하지 않다
- My watch is **not as expensive as** yours. 내 시계는 네 것만큼 비싸지 않다.
  = Your watch is **more expensive than** mine. 네 시계가 내 것보다 비싸다.
  = My watch is **less expensive than** yours. 내 시계는 네 것보다 덜 비싸다.

📑 비교급

❶ 「A 비교급+than B」: A가 B보다 더 ~하다
- London is **bigger than** Paris. 런던은 파리보다 더 크다.
- Iron is **more useful than** gold. 철은 금보다 더 유용하다.

❷ 「A less+원급+than B」: A가 B보다 덜 ~하다
- That car is **less expensive than** this one. 저 자동차는 이 자동차보다 덜 비싸다.
- That book is **less thick than** this one. 저 책은 이 책보다 덜 두껍다.

📑 최상급

「the+최상급」: 가장 ~하다
- Gold is **the most precious** of all metals. 〈형용사의 최상급〉
  금은 모든 금속 중에서 가장 귀중하다.
- She works **hardest** in the office. 〈부사의 최상급, the 생략 가능〉
  그녀는 사무실에서 가장 열심히 일한다.

> **TIPs**
> · 「the+최상급+in+장소나 범위의 단수명사」
> · 「the+최상급+of+비교의 대상이 되는 복수명사」

Answers: p.26

Exercise 1 다음 괄호 안에서 알맞은 말을 고르시오.

1 Kyle likes English better (as / to / than) math.

2 He is the cleverest (in / of / by) all his brothers.

3 The diamond is the (hard / harder / hardest) material on Earth.

4 Burj Khalifa in Dubai is the tallest building (in / of / by) the world.

5 Your book is as (interesting / more interesting / most interesting) as mine.

Exercise 2 다음 〈보기〉에 제시된 네 사람의 몸무게를 보고, 괄호 안의 단어를 사용하여 문장을 완성하시오.

🔍 Jack : 50kg   Jenny : 45kg   Michael : 53kg   Joe : 67kg

1 Jenny is ＿＿＿＿＿＿＿ (heavy) than Jack.

2 Jack is not as ＿＿＿＿＿＿＿ (heavy) as Michael.

3 Joe is the ＿＿＿＿＿＿＿ (heavy) of all four students.

4 Michael is ＿＿＿＿＿＿＿ (heavy) than Jack, but ＿＿＿＿＿＿＿ (light) than Joe.

다음 짝지어진 두 문장이 같은 뜻이 되도록 괄호 안의 단어를 사용하여 문장을 완성하시오.

1 James is not as brave as Peter. (brave)

⇨ Peter is _____ than James.

2 Busan is not as populous as Seoul. (populous)

⇨ Busan is _____ than Seoul.

3 This bed isn't as comfortable as that bed. (comfortable)

⇨ That bed is _____ than this bed.

4 Your report was not as impressive as hers. (impressive)

⇨ Her report was _____ than yours.

5 The new policy is not as effective as the old one. (effective)

⇨ The new policy is _____ than the old one.

6 Their new car is not as popular as their rival's car. (popular)

⇨ Their new car is _____ than their rival's car.

다음 〈보기〉에서 단어를 골라 우리말과 같은 뜻이 되도록 문장을 완성하시오.

🔍 old   smart   expensive   crowded   fluently   tall

1 그의 차는 내 차만큼 비싸다.

⇨ His car is _____ .

2 지하철이 버스보다 덜 붐빈다.

⇨ The subway is _____ .

3 그는 자기의 형만큼 키가 크지 않다.

⇨ He is not _____ his elder brother.

4 나는 Jacob만큼 일어를 유창하게 하지 못한다.

⇨ I don't speak Japanese _____ Jacob does.

5 Catherine은 자신의 반에서 제일 똑똑한 학생이다.

⇨ Catherine is _____ in her class.

6 그 교회가 마을에서 가장 오래된 건물이다.

⇨ The church is _____ .

8-3 비교급 강조

📑 **much, still, far, even, a lot** 등은 비교급을 강조해서 '훨씬'이라는 뜻으로 쓰인다.

- This hat is **much bigger than** that hat.
  이 모자가 저 모자보다 훨씬 더 크다.
- The movie was **even worse than** we expected.
  그 영화는 우리가 기대했던 것보다 훨씬 나빴다.
- Learning Japanese is **far easier than** learning Chinese.
  일본어를 배우는 것이 중국어를 배우는 것보다 훨씬 쉽다.
- The cold weather made my job **still more difficult**.
  추운 날씨가 나의 일을 훨씬 더 어렵게 만들었다.
- The meeting has become **a lot longer than** we had planned.
  그 회의는 우리가 계획했던 것보다 훨씬 더 길어졌다.

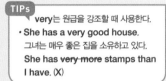

TIPs
very는 원급을 강조할 때 사용한다.
- She has a very good house.
  그녀는 매우 좋은 집을 소유하고 있다.
  She has ~~very more~~ stamps than I have. (X)

Answers: p.26

Exercise 1 다음 괄호 안에서 알맞은 말을 고르시오.

1 He ran (much / more) faster than his brother did.

2 He made his homepage look (very / a lot) better than it really was.

3 The novel I bought yesterday is (more / very) interesting than I thought.

4 We really liked her, but she was (very / much) quiet and didn't speak much.

5 Scott walked (very / much) faster than I did, so I couldn't keep up with him.

6 The traffic was (much / very) heavy, so we were late for the wedding ceremony.

Exercise 2 다음 괄호 안의 단어를 사용하여 문장을 완성하시오.

1 그는 보기보다 훨씬 무겁다. (a lot, heavy)

　⇨ He is ＿＿＿＿＿ ＿＿＿＿＿ ＿＿＿＿＿ he looks.

2 그녀는 자기 오빠보다 훨씬 더 똑똑하다. (even, intelligent)

　⇨ She is ＿＿＿＿＿ ＿＿＿＿＿ ＿＿＿＿＿ her brother.

3 나는 우유가 커피보다 훨씬 더 영양가가 있다고 생각한다. (much, nutritious)

　⇨ I think that milk is ＿＿＿＿＿ ＿＿＿＿＿ ＿＿＿＿＿ coffee.

4 공원은 우리가 예측한 것보다 훨씬 더 붐볐다. (much, crowded)

　⇨ The park was ＿＿＿＿＿ ＿＿＿＿＿ ＿＿＿＿＿ we predicted.

5 그 콘서트는 내가 기대했던 것보다 훨씬 더 환상적이었다. (far, fantastic)

　⇨ The concert was ＿＿＿＿＿ ＿＿＿＿＿ ＿＿＿＿＿ I expected.

6 상황은 그가 우리에게 설명했던 것보다 훨씬 더 나빴다. (a lot, bad)

　⇨ The situation was ＿＿＿＿＿ ＿＿＿＿＿ ＿＿＿＿＿ he explained to us.

8-4 다양한 원급 표현

다양한 원급 표현

❶ 「~ times as … as」 : ~ 배만큼 …한

· This building is **twice as** big **as** that one.
이 건물은 저 건물보다 두 배 더 크다.

· Mr. Smith is **three times as** old **as** his son.
= Mr. Smith is **three times** older **than** his son.
Smith 씨는 자신의 아들보다 나이가 세 배 더 많다.

❷ 「as ~ as possible (= as ~ as one can)」 : 가능한 한 ~하게

· He walked **as** fast **as possible**.
= He walked **as** fast **as he could**.
그는 가능한 한 빨리 걸었다.

Answers: p.26

Exercise 1 다음 우리말과 같은 뜻이 되도록 괄호 안의 단어를 사용하여 문장을 완성하시오.

1 그는 가능한 한 분명하게 말했다. (clearly)

⇨ He spoke _____ _____ _____ he _____ .

2 그녀는 가능한 한 효율적으로 일하려고 애썼다. (efficiently)

⇨ She tried to work _____ .

3 이 휴대 전화가 저 휴대 전화보다 다섯 배 더 비싸다. (expensive, as)

⇨ This cellular phone is _____
_____ that one.

4 태양은 목성보다 약 열 배 크다. (large, than)

⇨ The Sun is almost _____ Jupiter.

Exercise 2 다음 짝지어진 두 문장이 같은 뜻이 되도록 문장을 완성하시오.

1 This wooden table is three times as large as that plastic one.

⇨ This wooden table is _____ .

2 My uncle is four times older than I am.

⇨ My uncle is _____ .

3 He tried to drink water as much as possible.

⇨ He tried to drink water _____ .

4 Thomson always helped people in need as much as he could.

⇨ Thomson always helped _____ .

비교급을 이용한 다양한 표현

❶ 「비교급 and 비교급」: 점점 더 ~한
- The daytime is getting **longer and longer.** 낮이 점점 더 길어지고 있다.
- Michelle becomes **more and more famous.** Michelle은 점점 더 유명해지고 있다.

❷ 「the+비교급 ~, the+비교급 ~」: ~하면 할수록 더욱더 …하다
- **The more** you eat, **the fatter** you will become. 많이 먹으면 먹을수록 더 뚱뚱해질 것이다.
- **The more** he has, **the more** he wants. 그는 가지면 가질수록 더 많이 원한다.

❸ 「the 비교급+of the two」: 둘 중에서 더 ~한
- Gary is **the more intelligent of the two.** 둘 중에서 Gary가 더 똑똑하다.
- My sister's camera is **the more expensive of the two.** 내 여동생의 카메라가 둘 중 더 비싸다.

❹ 「would rather A than B」: B하기보다는 차라리 A하는 게 낫다
- I **would rather** die **than** live in dishonor. 불명예스럽게 사느니 차라리 죽는 게 낫다.
- I **would rather** sleep **than** watch TV. 텔레비전을 보느니 차라리 잠을 자겠다.

Answers: p.26

Exercise 1 다음 우리말과 같은 뜻이 되도록 괄호 안의 단어를 사용하여 문장을 완성하시오.

1 눈이 온 후 점점 더 추워지고 있다. (cold)
⇨ After the snow, it is getting _____ .

2 우리의 근무환경이 점점 더 나빠지고 있다. (bad)
⇨ Our working environment becomes _____ .

3 청중들은 점점 더 지루함을 느꼈고 쉬기를 원했다. (bored)
⇨ The audience felt _____ , and they wanted to take a break.

4 대학 진학 후 그녀의 영어 실력이 점점 더 좋아졌다. (good)
⇨ Her English skills became _____ after she entered college.

5 학생들이 그에게 집중하지 않아서 그의 목소리가 점점 더 커졌다. (loud)
⇨ His voice was getting _____ because the students weren't paying attention to him.

Exercise 2 다음 밑줄 친 부분을 바르게 고쳐 쓰시오.

1 Sienna was smartest of the two girls. ⇨ _____

2 This work is becoming least and least interesting. ⇨ _____

3 I could rather sing a song than play the guitar. ⇨ _____

4 As time goes by, he is getting the stronger and stronger. ⇨ _____

5 The longer you stay here, the much you will be satisfied with our services. ⇨ _____

🔍 **If you eat more, you will become fatter.**

⇒ <u>The more you eat, the fatter you will become.</u>

1 As Richard gets older, he becomes wiser.

⇒ _____

2 As it gets colder, people drink hot coffee more.

⇒ _____

3 As the situation becomes worse, I become calmer.

⇒ _____

4 If you study harder, you'll get better scores.

⇒ _____

5 As the car is more luxurious, it is more expensive.

⇒ _____

6 If you throw the ball further, you will get more points.

⇒ _____

7 If we climb the mountain higher, the air will get thinner.

⇒ _____

8 As he becomes older, he is interested in science more.

⇒ _____

9 As it snows more heavily, the road condition becomes worse.

⇒ _____

10 If you finish the homework sooner, you can watch TV sooner.

⇒ _____

11 As it rains more severely, the cars on the highway move slower.

⇒ _____

12 As she stays abroad longer, her native language skills will become poorer.

⇒ _____

🔍 cold	interested	well	leave
pretty	popular	tall	large
long	little	diligent	healthy

1 우리 집이 둘 중에서 더 크다.

⇨ My house is _____ _____ of the two.

2 두 사람 중 누가 키가 더 큽니까?

⇨ Who is _____ _____ of the two of you?

3 그 두 소년 중 그가 더욱 부지런하다.

⇨ He is _____ _____ _____ of the two boys.

4 나는 여기에 머무르느니 차라리 떠나는 게 낫겠다.

⇨ I _____ _____ _____ _____ stay here.

5 물을 많이 마시면 마실수록, 건강이 더욱더 좋아질 것이다.

⇨ The more you drink water, _____ _____ you will get.

6 날씨가 날마다 점점 더 추워지고 있다.

⇨ The weather is getting _____ _____ _____ day by day.

7 나이가 들면서 그녀는 점점 더 예뻐지고 있다.

⇨ She is becoming _____ _____ _____ as she grows up.

8 그녀가 이사를 한 후, 우리는 점점 덜 보게 되었다.

⇨ After she moved out, we saw _____ _____ _____ of each other.

9 그는 나이를 먹으면서 점점 더 자연에 관심을 갖게 되었다.

⇨ As he got older, he became _____ _____ _____ _____ in nature.

10 우리가 지난주에 본 영화는 점점 더 인기를 얻고 있다.

⇨ The movie we saw last week is getting _____ _____ _____ _____.

11 한국에 오래 살면 살수록, 우리 문화를 더 잘 이해하게 될 것이다.

⇨ _____ _____ you live in Korea, _____ _____ you'll understand our culture.

기타 비교급

❶ 「prefer A to B」: B보다 A를 선호하다
  · Goats **prefer** weeds **to** grass. 염소는 잔디보다 잡초를 더 좋아한다.
❷ 「senior to」: (지위가) 높은, 상위의
  · The young man was bullied by soldiers **senior to** him. 그 청년은 군대 선임에 의해 괴롭힘을 당했다.
❸ 「junior to」: (지위가) 낮은, 부하의
  · Kate is young, but there are many employees **junior to** her at the office.
    Kate은 어리지만 사무실에는 부하 직원이 많이 있다.
❹ 「inferior to」: ~보다 낮은, 떨어지는
  · He feels **inferior to** others. 그는 타인에게 열등감을 느낀다.
❺ 「superior to」: ~보다 우수한
  · This computer is **superior to** that computer. 이 컴퓨터가 저 컴퓨터보다 우수하다.
❻ 「prior to」: ~보다 앞서
  · The accident happened **prior to** his arrival. 그 사고는 그가 도착하기 전에 발생했다.

Answers: p.27

Exercise 1 다음 우리말과 같은 뜻이 되도록 문장을 완성하시오.

1 나는 나보다 직위가 낮은 사람과 일할 때 편하게 느낀다.
  ⇒ I feel comfortable when I work with someone _____ _____ me.

2 그는 고등학교 2년 선배이다.
  ⇒ He is two years _____ _____ me in high school.

3 그는 자신의 친구들에게 열등감을 느낀다고 내게 말했다.
  ⇒ He told me that he felt _____ _____ his friends.

4 스페인어를 말하는 데 있어서 Jessica가 나보다 낫다.
  ⇒ Jessica is _____ _____ come in speaking Spanish.

5 나는 영화를 보는 것보다 책 읽는 것을 더 좋아한다.
  ⇒ I _____ reading books _____ watching movies.

6 이 음식은 어제 우리가 먹은 것보다 못하다.
  ⇒ This food is _____ _____ the one we had yesterday.

7 리그에서 우리 팀이 다른 모든 팀보다 우수하다.
  ⇒ Our team is _____ _____ every other team in the league.

8 James는 우리 회사에 들어오기 전에 자동차 판매원이었다.
  ⇒ James was a car dealer _____ _____ joining our company.

9 직장에서 나보다 직급이 높은 사람은 없다.
  ⇒ There is no one _____ _____ me at work.

최상급 표현 I

□ 원급과 비교급을 이용한 최상급 표현

· Seoul is **the largest city** in Korea.

= **No other** city in Korea is **larger than** Seoul.

= **No other** city in Korea is **so[as] large as** Seoul.

= Seoul is **larger than any other** city in Korea. 서울은 한국에서 가장 큰 도시이다.

· This is **the smallest computer** in the store.

= **No other** computer in the store is **smaller than** this computer.

= **No other** computer in the store is **as small as** this computer.

= This computer is **smaller than any other computer** in the store. 이것이 이 상점에서 가장 작은 컴퓨터이다.

Answers: p.27

Exercise **1** 다음 문장을 〈보기〉와 같이 바꿔 쓰시오.

🔍 Cindy is the tallest girl in her company.

⇨ _____No other girl in her company is taller than Cindy._____

⇨ _____No other girl in her company is as tall as Cindy._____

⇨ _____Cindy is taller than any other girl in her company._____

1 This is the most expensive ring in the shop.

⇨ _____

⇨ _____

⇨ _____

2 Jonathan is the smartest boy in his school.

⇨ _____

⇨ _____

⇨ _____

3 Mt. Everest is the highest mountain in the world.

⇨ _____

⇨ _____

⇨ _____

4 Dennis is the most handsome actor in Canada.

⇨ _____

⇨ _____

⇨ _____

최상급 표현 II

□ 「**one of the**+최상급+복수명사」: 가장 ~한 것 중 하나

· Sam is **one of the greatest soccer players** in the world.
  Sam은 전 세계에서 가장 위대한 축구 선수 중 한 명이다.

· Yuri is **one of the most famous actresses** in Japan.
  Yuri는 일본에서 가장 유명한 여배우 중 한 명이다.

· The Guggenheim Museum is **one of the most popular museums** in the world.
  구겐하임 박물관은 세계에서 가장 인기 있는 박물관 중 하나이다.

□ 「**the**+최상급(+**that**)+주어+**have ever p.p.**」: 지금까지 ~한 것 중에서 가장 …하다

· She is **the most beautiful woman that I've ever seen.**
  그녀는 내가 지금까지 보아온 여자 중에서 가장 예쁘다.

· This is **the most touching movie that I've ever seen.**
  이 영화는 내가 지금까지 본 영화 중에서 가장 감동적이다.

· This is **the saddest book that I've ever read.**
  이 책은 내가 지금까지 읽은 책 중에서 가장 슬프다.

Answers: p.27

Exercise 1 다음 우리말과 같은 뜻이 되도록 괄호 안의 단어를 사용하여 문장을 완성하시오.

1 그는 세계에서 가장 유명한 과학자 중 한 명이다. (famous)

   ⇨ He is _____ in the world.

2 서울은 세계에서 가장 큰 도시 중 하나이다. (large)

   ⇨ Seoul is _____ in the world.

3 Mike는 내가 지금까지 가르친 학생 중에서 가장 영리하다. (smart, teach)

   ⇨ Mike is _____ that _____.

4 이 책은 내가 읽은 책 중에서 가장 두꺼운 책이다. (thick, read)

   ⇨ This book is _____ that _____.

Exercise 2 다음 우리말과 같은 뜻이 되도록 괄호 안의 단어를 사용하여 영작하시오.

1 Roxy Theater는 내가 본 극장 중에서 가장 크다. (big)

   ⇨ _____

2 나일 강은 아프리카에서 가장 긴 강 중 하나이다. (the Nile, long)

   ⇨ _____

3 이것은 내가 먹어 본 것 중에서 가장 맛있는 팬케이크이다. (delicious, pancake, try)

   ⇨ _____

4 Jerry는 세상에서 가장 재능 있는 음악가 중 한 사람이다. (talented, musician)

   ⇨ _____

[01-05] 다음 빈칸에 알맞은 말을 고르시오.

01 They are walking as _____ as they can.

① fast   ② faster
③ fastest   ④ the most fast
⑤ the fastest

02 The new gymnasium is much _____ than the old one.

① good   ② best
③ well   ④ better
⑤ worst

03 We want to help the homeless _____ we can.

① as more as   ② as much as
③ as most as   ④ as good as
⑤ as great as

04 The more you practice, _____ your technique will be.

① the good   ② the great
③ the better   ④ the best
⑤ the well

05 My sister is the tallest _____ her class.

① in   ② of
③ to   ④ at
⑤ as

06 다음 중 최상급이 바르게 연결되지 않은 것은?

① little - least   ② good - best
③ far - most far   ④ old - eldest
⑤ bad - worst

[07-08] 다음 빈칸에 들어갈 수 없는 말을 고르시오.

07 This vase is _____ cheaper than that vase.

① still   ② far
③ even   ④ much
⑤ very

08 Cathy is more _____ than Julie.

① famous   ② beautiful
③ patient   ④ fast
⑤ special

[09-10] 다음 빈칸에 공통으로 들어갈 수 있는 말을 고르시오.

09 · For _____ information, please call 123-456-7890.
· The _____ you study, the more you'll know.

① less   ② higher
③ heavier   ④ further
⑤ weaker

10 · Try to exercise as _____ as you can to be a good athlete.
· His new computer is _____ better than mine.

① still   ② much
③ good   ④ far
⑤ very

11 다음 빈칸에 들어갈 수 없는 말은?

> Mark : To me, _____.
> What about you, Jenny?
> Jenny : I agree with you, Mark. I really love music.

① music is the most important
② nothing is as important as music
③ nothing is more important than music
④ music is not so important as anything else
⑤ music is more important than anything else

12 다음 우리말을 바르게 영작한 것은?

① 파르테논 신전은 콜로세움보다 오래됐다.
  ⇨ The Parthenon is elder than the Colosseum.
② 기린은 코끼리보다 키가 더 크다.
  ⇨ A giraffe is the taller than an elephant.
③ 금성이 화성보다 지구와 더 가깝다.
  ⇨ Venus is close to the Earth than Mars.
④ 몽블랑과 에베레스트 산 중 어느 것이 더 높습니까?
  ⇨ Which is higher, Mont Blanc or Mt. Everest?
⑤ 태평양은 대서양보다 더 크다.
  ⇨ The Pacific Ocean is more large than the Atlantic Ocean.

13 다음 〈보기〉의 밑줄 친 even과 의미가 같은 것은?

> The rumor about the murderer went <u>even</u> stronger.

① He even said that his wife was crazy.
② Mary can read books even in the dark.
③ Sunny walks even faster than her father.
④ Murder was a big social problem even in ancient times.
⑤ Even though she earned two million dollars last month, she didn't spend much money on us.

[14-16] 다음 두 문장이 같은 뜻이 되도록 빈칸에 들어갈 알맞은 말을 고르시오.

14 The policeman ran as fast as possible to catch the thief.
  ⇨ The policeman ran as fast as _____ to catch the thief.

① he can   ② he will
③ he could   ④ he felt
⑤ he was

15 This air conditioner is not as cheap as that one.
  ⇨ That air conditioner is _____ this one.

① not cheaper than   ② cheaper than
③ as cheaper as   ④ less cheaper
⑤ cheapest

16 As the prices get lower, people will buy more.
  ⇨ The _____ the prices get, the _____ people will buy.

① lowest – most   ② low – most
③ lower – more   ④ most – lowest
⑤ more – lower

17 다음 중 뜻이 다른 하나는?

① Mozart is the greatest musician in history.
② No other musician in history is as great as Mozart.
③ No other musician in history is greater than Mozart.
④ Mozart is as great as other musicians in history.
⑤ Mozart is greater than any other musician in history.

137

[18-19] 다음 중 어법상 바른 문장을 고르시오.

18 ① He tried to read as much as he can.
② He is the taller man that I've ever seen.
③ My house is three times as bigger as yours.
④ No other school in my hometown is as big as my school.
⑤ He is smarter than any other students in the science club.

19 ① My mom is more taller than my sister.
② Which skirt is longer, this one or that one?
③ He is doing even well than ever before in science.
④ I run many faster than any other student in my class.
⑤ More money you make, more money you can spend on buying books.

[20-22] 다음 중 어법상 어색한 것을 고르시오.

20 ① The work is getting harder and harder.
② His bag is three times as heavy as hers.
③ He is one of the greatest painter in Canada.
④ I prefer playing outside to watching the movie.
⑤ She is the fastest swimmer that I've ever seen.

21 ① Who is taller of the two pitchers?
② This book is less interesting than that book.
③ Tom runs faster than anybody else in his school.
④ The department store is more crowded than yesterday.
⑤ The more you practice, the more perfect you will become.

22 ① Jejudo is the largest island in Korea.
② This is the cheapest bed in our shop.
③ This is taller than any other trees in my garden.
④ Diana is superior to Linda in playing the piano.
⑤ The harder you practice, the stronger you'll be.

23 다음 짝지어진 두 문장의 뜻이 같지 않은 것은?
① I prefer pink to yellow.
= I like pink more than yellow.
② My daughter is not so smart as Jenny.
= Jenny is not smarter than my daughter.
③ Everyone's senior to me on my team.
= There's no one junior to me on my team.
④ Tokyo is the largest city in Japan.
= No other city in Japan is larger than Tokyo.
⑤ As you study more, you'll get better scores.
= The more you study, the better scores you'll get.

[24-25] 다음 중 우리말을 바르게 영작한 것을 고르시오.

24 그 컴퓨터 게임은 내가 생각했던 것만큼 흥미롭지 않았다.

① The computer game was as exciting as I thought.
② The computer game was not so exciting as I thought.
③ The computer game was much more exciting than I thought.
④ I thought the computer game was more exciting than anything else.
⑤ I thought the computer game was much more exciting than anything else.

25 건강만큼 더 중요한 것은 없다.

① Health is not so important a thing.
② Nothing is as important as health.
③ Health is the least important thing.
④ Health is not as important as anything else.
⑤ Health is less important than anything else.

[26-30] 다음 두 문장이 같은 뜻이 되도록 문장을 완성하시오.

26 I am stronger than you are.
⇨ You're not _____ _____ _____
I am.

27 As we climbed higher, it became colder.
⇨ _____ we climbed,
_____ it became.

28 No other guitar in the world is more expensive
than my guitar.
⇨ No other guitar in the world is _____
_____ my guitar.

29 Baseball is the most important thing in my life.
⇨ Nothing in my life is _____
_____ than baseball.
⇨ Baseball is more important _____
_____ else in my life.

30 Playing baseball was not as difficult as I
thought.
⇨ Playing baseball was _____ difficult
_____ I thought.

[31-32] 다음 우리말과 같은 뜻이 되도록 문장을 완성하시오.

31 이 세탁기가 저 세탁기보다 세 배 더 비싸다.
⇨ This washing machine is _____

than that washing machine.

32 과학 덕택으로, 세계는 점점 더 작아지고 있다.
⇨ Thanks to science, the world is getting
_____ and _____.

33 다음 도표는 여러 도시에서 잃어버린 지갑의 회수율을 기록한 것
이다. 표의 내용과 일치하도록 괄호 안의 단어를 사용하여 글을
완성하시오.

City	Returned	Kept	Return Rate
New York	9	1	90%
Seoul	8	2	80%
Tokyo	5	5	50%
Bangkok	5	5	50%
Hong Kong	3	7	30%

The chart above shows the return rate of the lost wallets among five cities. Seoul showed the second (A) _____ (high) return rate of all the cities. New York showed a (B) _____ (high) return rate than any other city. The return rate of wallets in Tokyo was the same as that in Bangkok. The return rate in Hong Kong was three times as (C) _____ (low) as that in New York. Hong Kong showed the (D) _____ (low) return rate of all the cities.

139

Answers: p.29

[1-3] 다음 글을 읽고, 물음에 답하시오. 서술형

What is the ⓐ (fast) animal on land? If you came up with cheetahs, that's right! (A) No other animal on land is faster than cheetahs. They can run 70 miles per hour. Can you imagine how fast that is? You can imagine a car going 70 miles per hour on the highway. How about other animals? A lion can run 50 miles per hour, and a hyena can run 35 miles per hour. A cheetah can run ⓑ (fast) than a lion, and (B) 하이에나의 두 배만큼 빨리.

1 밑줄 친 ⓐ와 ⓑ를 어법에 맞게 바꿔 쓰시오.

ⓐ _____   ⓑ _____

2 밑줄 친 (A)와 의미가 통하도록 문장을 완성하시오.

→ Cheetahs are _____ on land.

→ Cheetahs are _____ on land.

3 밑줄 친 (B)와 의미가 통하도록 문장을 완성하시오.

→ _____ a hyena (twice)

4 다음 글의 밑줄 친 부분 중, 어법상 틀린 것은? 수능 대비형

I hope you are all doing ① <u>well</u> in your classes as we head into this finals period. It can be an ② <u>especially</u> stressful time, but let's see ③ <u>if</u> we can finish up the cycling season in grand style. This Saturday will be our last Cycling Club meeting for the year. Our destination will be Union Square. Please remember ④ <u>to bring</u> your lunches and water bottles. Hope to see as many of you there as ⑤ <u>possibly</u>!

* cycling: 사이클링, 자전거 타기
** destination: 목적지

Chapter 9

일치, 화법

단수동사를 쓰는 경우

❶ 「every/each+단수명사」 / -thing / -one / -body

· Every boy **was** invited to the party. 모든 소년이 그 파티에 초대되었다.

· Each ticket **costs** ten dollars. 표는 한 장에 10달러입니다.

· Something **is** wrong with this photocopier. 이 복사기에 뭔가 이상이 있다.

· If anyone **calls** me while I'm out, please take a message. 내가 외출한 동안 전화가 오면, 메모를 남겨주세요.

❷ 구나 절

· Collecting coins **is** my hobby. 동전 수집이 내 취미이다.

· To live alone **means** to die alone. 혼자 산다는 것은 혼자 죽는다는 것을 의미한다.

· That he said so **is** true. 그가 그렇게 말한 것은 사실이다.

❸ 「the number of+복수명사」

· The number of patients **is** increasing. 환자의 수가 늘고 있다.

· The number of students **is** decreasing. 학생의 수가 줄고 있다.

❹ 시간, 거리, 가격, 무게 등의 단위

· Twenty years **is** a long time. 이십 년은 긴 시간이다.

· Three hundred dollars **is** enough money to buy a bike. 삼백 달러는 자전거를 사기에 충분한 돈이다.

❺ 학문명, 국가명, 질병명

· Mathematics **is** his favorite subject. 수학은 그가 좋아하는 과목이다.

· The Netherlands **is** famous for windmills. 네덜란드는 풍차로 유명하다.

❻ and로 연결되었지만 하나를 지칭하는 경우와 단일 개념인 경우

· The singer and actor **is** going to attend the ceremony of awarding prizes.
가수이자 배우인 그 사람은 시상식에 참석할 것이다.

· Steady and slow **wins** the race. 천천히 꾸준히 하는 사람이 이긴다.

> **TIPs**
> 주어와 동사가 수식어구의 삽입으로 멀어진 경우, 주어와 동사의 수 일치에 주의한다.
> · The boy (who is holding the books) **is** my brother. 그 책들을 들고 있는 소년은 내 남동생이다.

복수동사를 쓰는 경우

❶ 복수명사이거나 「A and B」 형식일 때

· There **are** only ten students in each class. 각 학급에는 고작 열 명의 학생이 있다.

· A black and a white dog **were** running toward me.
검은 개 한 마리와 흰 개 한 마리가 나를 향해 달려오고 있었다.

❷ 「the+형용사」 : ∼한 사람들 (= 「형용사+people」)

· The young **are** interested in playing computer games. 젊은 사람들은 컴퓨터 게임을 하는 것에 흥미가 있다.

· The injured **were** taken to the hospital. 부상자들이 병원으로 실려 갔다.

❸ 「A number of+복수명사」 : 많은 ∼

· A number of people **are** taking the bus. 많은 사람이 버스를 타고 있다.

· A number of students **were** coming toward the town square.
많은 학생이 마을 광장으로 몰려오고 있었다.

Exercise 1 다음 괄호 안에서 알맞은 말을 고르시오.

1   Diabetes (require / requires) careful medical supervision.

2   Twenty dollars (is / are) not enough money to buy this item.

3   A number of people (was / were) very excited at his performance.

4   The world-famous pianist and poet (was / were) injured yesterday.

5   A pianist and a poet (was / were) injured in a car accident last night.

6   A number of students who had a bad cold (was / were) absent today.

7   This is a guide book for students who (want / wants) to enter our college.

8   A year and half (have passed / has passed) since he departed for America.

9   There are three books on the table. Each book (is / are) in a different color.

10   Every boy and girl (have to / has to) follow the dress code beginning next month.

11   Doing many things in different fields (help / helps) you have various experiences.

12   Improving your English skills (is / are) not simple because you need a lot of time and effort.

Exercise 2 다음 괄호 안의 동사를 사용하여 문장을 완성하시오. (단, 모두 현재 시제로 쓸 것)

1   Every student _____ (know) the answer.

2   The United States _____ (consist of) fifty states.

3   Thirty dollars _____ (be) enough to buy this book.

4   James and Tom _____ (be) in the same tennis club.

5   Bread and butter _____ (be) served before the meal.

6   To answer accurately _____ (be) much more important.

7   The young _____ (be) able to learn a foreign language quickly.

8   My brother, Tim _____ (have) learned economics for four years.

9   Physics _____ (be) not a popular subject among undergraduates.

10   Each member of the club _____ (be) responsible for his or her own safety.

11   The Philippines _____ (be) known for its people's hospitality and joyfulness.

12   The number of tourists visiting Korea _____ (have) increased in the last decade.

1 I don't like men who is late for a date. ⇒ _____

2 All work and no play make Jack a dull boy. ⇒ _____

3 Both cars you want to buy is very expensive. ⇒ _____

4 A black and a white cat is sleeping on the couch. ⇒ _____

5 Twenty miles are a long way to walk in rainy weather. ⇒ _____

6 Every student in the classroom wear a school uniform. ⇒ _____

7 Getting up early in the morning are good for our health. ⇒ _____

8 The number of patients have been increasing since 2022. ⇒ _____

Exercise **4** 다음 우리말과 같은 뜻이 되도록 괄호 안의 단어를 사용하여 문장을 완성하시오.

1 각 나라는 고유의 전통과 문화를 가지고 있다. (country, have)

⇒ _____ _____ _____ its own traditions and cultures.

2 부자가 항상 가난한 사람보다 행복한 것은 아니다. (be)

⇒ _____ rich _____ not always happier than _____ poor.

3 5킬로미터는 어린이가 걷기에 먼 거리이다. (kilometer, be)

⇒ _____ _____ _____ a long distance for children to walk.

4 우표 수집은 모든 연령층에서 매우 인기가 있다. (collect, be)

⇒ _____ _____ _____ very popular with everyone of all ages.

5 도시의 노숙자 수가 증가했다. (number, have)

⇒ _____ _____ of homeless people in the city _____ increased.

6 의사이자 작가인 그는 새로운 소설을 출간할 것이다. (doctor, writer, be)

⇒ _____ _____ _____ _____ going to publish a new novel.

7 기업의 리더가 되고 싶은 학생들에게 경제학은 좋은 전공이다. (economics, be, want)

⇒ _____ _____ a good major for _____ who _____ to be business leaders.

8 많은 사람이 안개로 인한 사고로 부상을 당했다. (number, be)

⇒ _____ _____ of _____ _____ injured in the accidents caused by fog.

9-2 수의 일치 II

📂 부분이나 전체를 나타내는 수식어구 뒤에 오는 명사에 동사의 수를 일치시킨다.

> [분수, most, half, the rest]+of+단수/복수명사 → 단수/복수동사
>
> [all, any, some]+단수/복수 명사 → 단수/복수동사

- Two-thirds of the children **are** from Korea.
  아이들의 3분의 2가 한국에서 왔다.
- Three-quarters of the earth's surface **is** water.
  지구 표면의 4분의 3은 물이다.
- Most of my time **is** spent on reading. 나는 대부분의 시간을 독서하면서 보낸다.
- Most of my books **are** novels. 내 책 대부분은 소설이다.

Answers: p.29

Exercise 1 다음 괄호 안에서 알맞은 말을 고르시오.

1 The rest of the bread (was / were) rotten.

2 All of the money (was / were) stolen in the hotel.

3 Most of the polar bears (has / have) been disappearing.

4 Most of the information which I got from him (was / were) wrong.

5 About half of the inhabitants (is / are) satisfied with their housing.

Exercise 2 다음 괄호 안의 동사를 사용하여 문장을 완성하시오. (단, 모두 현재 시제로 쓸 것)

1 Two-thirds of the building _____ (have) been completed.

2 Most of the employees attending the seminar _____ (look) bored.

3 Some of the vegetables prepared for dinner _____ (be) not that fresh.

4 The rest of the boys _____ (have) been waiting for their lunch for an hour.

5 Half of the money _____ (have) been distributed to five different charities.

Exercise 3 다음 문장을 읽고, 어법상 어색한 부분을 찾아 바르게 고치시오.

1 Half of the sky are dark with black clouds. ⇨ _____

2 Half of the apples in the plastic basket has gone. ⇨ _____

3 Two-thirds of Americans doesn't agree with the policies. ⇨ _____

4 Most of the furniture displayed in the store were made in China. ⇨ _____

5 One-third of the trees in the mountain was cut down last summer. ⇨ _____

6 All of the water in the lake were polluted due to industrial sewage. ⇨ _____

7 The rest of the oil are used to make products such as jet fuel and asphalt. ⇨ _____

수의 일치 III

☐ 상관접속사의 수 일치

접속사	의미	일치
both A and B	A와 B 둘 다	항상 복수
either A or B	A와 B 둘 중 하나	B에 일치
neither A nor B	A와 B 둘 다 아닌	B에 일치
not only A but also B	A뿐만 아니라 B도	B에 일치
B as well as A	A뿐만 아니라 B도	B에 일치

· Both my mother and father **want** me to be a doctor.
  우리 어머니와 아버지 둘 다 내가 의사가 되기를 원한다.

· Either you or he **has** to stay at home.
  너와 그 둘 중 한 명은 집에 있어야 한다.

· Neither her son nor her daughters **were** in the house when she arrived at home.
  그녀가 집에 도착했을 때 아들과 딸들 모두 집에 없었다.

· Not only his brothers but also he **is** able to swim.
  = He as well as his brothers **is** able to swim.
  그의 형제들뿐만 아니라 그도 수영할 수 있다.

Answers: p.29

Exercise 1 다음 괄호 안에서 알맞은 말을 고르시오.

1 Neither you nor I (was / were) unfriendly to the kids.

2 Either you or your younger sister (get / gets) big money.

3 He as well as his twin cousins (is / are) good at playing tennis.

4 Not only you but also she (need / needs) a medical examination.

5 Neither James nor his friends (is / are) invited to Leo's wedding party.

6 Either my sister or I (am / is) going to call you tonight to confirm a meeting arrangement.

Exercise 2 다음 괄호 안에 주어진 동사를 사용하여 문장을 완성하시오. (단, 모두 현재 시제로 쓸 것)

1 Neither he nor I _____ (be) the right person for the position.

2 James as well as his parents _____ (be) going to visit his grandparents.

3 Both Charles and I _____ (be) invited to Fred's birthday party every year.

4 Not only you but also I _____ (be) so busy that we cannot play soccer.

5 Not only you but also he _____ (have to) take responsibility for the financial crisis.

6 Either your co-worker or you _____ (have to) make a presentation at the start of the meeting.

시제의 일치

주절의 시제에 따라 종속절의 시제가 달라진다. 주절의 시제가 현재이면 종속절에 거의 모든 시제가 올 수 있지만, 주절의 시제가 과거이면 주로 과거나 과거완료가 온다.

주절	종속절
현재	모든 시제 사용 가능
과거	과거 또는 과거완료를 사용

> **TIPs**
> 불변의 진리, 현재의 습관이나 반복적 행동, 현재의 일반적인 사실은 시제의 일치 예외로 항상 현재시제를 쓴다.
> • She said that she always wakes up early in the mornig. 그녀는 항상 아침 일찍 일어난다고 말했다.

- He **says** that he **likes** driving. 그는 운전하는 것을 좋아한다고 말한다.
- I **believe** that he **will** get over his illness soon.
  나는 그가 자신의 병을 곧 이겨낼 거라고 믿는다.
- She **says** that she **used to** read a book before going to bed. 그녀는 잠을 자기 전에 책을 읽곤 했다고 말한다.
- I **thought** that he **was** honest. 나는 그가 정직하다고 생각했다.
- He **said** that he **had seen** the treasure map. 그는 보물지도를 본 적이 있다고 말했다.

Answers: p.30

Exercise 1 다음 괄호 안의 동사를 사용하여 문장을 완성하시오.

1 I didn't understand why she _____ (go) to Canada.

2 She knew that he _____ (want) to be a soccer player.

3 I think that my father _____ (read) the newspaper every day.

4 My son said that he _____ (take) Biology 101 last semester.

5 We were very proud that we _____ (win) first prize in the competition.

6 I wondered how long she _____ (have) been sleeping before I woke her up.

Exercise 2 다음 문장의 시제를 과거 시제로 하여 다시 쓰시오.

1 She can't find the place where the book is.

⇒ _____

2 She thinks that Sally will marry Mr. Kim.

⇒ _____

3 Do you see the lion which escaped from the zoo?

⇒ _____

4 I ask my son where he has been all day.

⇒ _____

5 I believe that you will get a perfect score on the test.

⇒ _____

시제 일치의 예외

시제 일치의 예외

❶ 일반적 진리, 격언 : 현재 시제

- We learned that the Earth **moves** around the Sun.
  우리는 지구가 태양 주위를 돈다는 것을 배웠다.
- Did you know the meaning of the old saying "Heaven **helps** those who **help** themselves?"
  너는 "하늘은 스스로 돕는 자를 돕는다."라는 속담의 뜻을 알았니?

❷ 현재의 사실, 습관 : 현재 시제

- He said that he **takes** a walk in the park every Sunday.
  그는 매주 일요일에 공원에서 산책을 한다고 말했다.
- She told me she **goes** hiking with her family every weekend.
  그녀는 나에게 가족과 주말마다 하이킹을 간다고 말했다.

❸ 역사적 사실 : 과거 시제

- I **know** that the Korean War **broke out** in 1950.
  나는 한국전쟁이 1950년에 발발했다는 것을 안다.
- **Do** you know that Michelangelo **painted** *the Creation of Adam*?
  너는 미켈란젤로가 「천지창조」를 그렸다는 것을 아니?

❹ 시간/조건의 부사절 : 시간이나 조건 부사절에서는 현재 시제가 미래 시제를 대신하지만, 주절에서는 미래 시제를 사용한다.

- When he **comes** back, I **will** visit his place.
  그가 돌아올 때, 나는 그의 집을 방문할 것이다.
- If you **don't** stop eating, you **will** gain more weight.   만약 네가 먹는 것을 멈추지 않는다면, 살이 더 찌게 될 것이다.

Answers: p.30

Exercise 1 다음 괄호 안에서 알맞은 말을 고르시오.

1 I didn't know that salmon (migrate / migrated) to lay eggs.

2 She told me that she (doesn't / didn't) watch the program these days.

3 My brother said that the Moon (moves / moved) around the Earth.

4 I know the fact that Columbus (discovers / discovered) America in 1492.

5 The history teacher said that World War II (breaks out / broke out) in 1939.

6 He taught his students that the air (contains / contained) 74 percent nitrogen.

Exercise 2 다음 문장의 밑줄 친 부분을 바르게 고치시오.

1 He learned that the Sun <u>was</u> a star, not a planet.   ⇨ _____

2 Tommy knew that the Earth <u>was</u> round like a ball.   ⇨ _____

3 The boy said that he <u>play</u> baseball after school every day.   ⇨ _____

4 The students know that the Japanese troops <u>invade</u> Korea in 1592.   ⇨ _____

5 If it <u>will be</u> fine tomorrow, we will have a barbecue party in the backyard.   ⇨ _____

6 I know that the U.S. <u>declares</u> independence on the fourth of July in 1776.   ⇨ _____

☐ **직접 화법과 간접 화법**

❶ 직접 화법 : 다른 사람의 말을 인용부호를 사용하여 그대로 전달하는 방식

❷ 간접 화법 : 다른 사람의 말을 접속사를 사용하여 전달자의 입장에서 바꿔 말하는 방식

- She **said to** me, "**I am** very tired." 〈직접 화법〉

  그녀는 나에게 "나는 정말 피곤해."라고 말했다.

- She **told** me **that she was** very tired. 〈간접 화법〉

  그녀는 나에게 정말 피곤하다고 말했다.

☐ **평서문의 화법 전환**

❶ 전달동사를 say → say / say to → tell로 바꾼다.

❷ 쉼표(,)와 인용부호(" ")를 없애고 접속사 that으로 연결한다. 이 때 접속사 that은 생략 가능하다.

❸ 인칭대명사를 전달자의 입장에서 알맞게 바꾼다.

❹ that절의 시제를 바꾼다. 전달동사의 시제가 현재이면 그대로, 과거이면 과거나 과거완료로 쓴다.

- He **said**, "Rachel **is** in the library."

  ⇨ He **said** (that) Rachel **was** in the library. 그는 Rachel이 도서관에 있다고 말했다.

- She **said to** him, "I **met** your uncle."

  ⇨ She **told** him (that) she **had met** his uncle. 그녀는 그에게 그의 삼촌을 만났다고 말했다.

- He **said**, "I **will** leave Korea."

  ⇨ He **said** (that) he **would** leave Korea. 그는 자신이 한국을 떠날 거라고 말했다.

> **TIPs**
> 전달동사의 시제가 과거일 때 과거완료 대신 과거를 쓸 수 있다.
> - She told him that she met[had met] his uncle.

❺ 장소나 때를 나타내는 부사구를 알맞게 바꾼다.

here		there
now		then
ago		before
this		that
these	→	those
today		that day
yesterday		the day before[the previous day]
tomorrow		the next day[the following day]
last week[year, Monday...]		the previous week[year, Monday...]
next week[year, Monday...]		the following week[year, Monday...]

- Jenny said, "I am going to school **now**."

  ⇨ Jenny said that she was going to school **then**.

  Jenny는 그때 학교에 가는 중이라고 말했다.

- Sam said to me, "I have a dental appointment **tomorrow**."

  ⇨ Sam told me that he had a dental appointment **the next day**.

  Sam은 나에게 다음날 치과예약이 있다고 말했다.

- She said to me, "You have to practice playing the guitar **today**."

  ⇨ She told me that I had to practice playing the guitar **that day**.

  그녀가 나에게 그날 기타 연습을 해야 한다고 말했다.

Exercise 1 다음 직접 화법 문장을 간접 화법 문장으로 바꿔 쓰시오.

1 He said to me, "I agree with you."

    ⇨ _____

2 My brother said, "I lost my book yesterday."

    ⇨ _____

3 She said to me, "I have written this report today."

    ⇨ _____

4 Brooke said, "I will study in the library this Saturday."

    ⇨ _____

5 My boss said to me, "You have to come here on time."

    ⇨ _____

6 Edward said, "My family will move to the urban area."

    ⇨ _____

7 She said, "I will go to Japan to study Japanese next week."

    ⇨ _____

Exercise 2 다음 간접 화법 문장을 직접 화법 문장으로 바꿔 쓰시오.

1 My mom said that it might rain that day.

    ⇨ _____

2 Mr. Kim told us that he would join the club.

    ⇨ _____

3 She said that she wanted to go out for dinner.

    ⇨ _____

4 She said that she was excited about going to university.

    ⇨ _____

5 Emma told us that she would go to the beach the following week.

    ⇨ _____

6 Tina said that her sister had gone to China to meet her friend the day before.

    ⇨ _____

의문문의 화법 전환

❶ 의문사가 있는 의문문 : 전달동사를 ask로 바꾸고, 의문문을 「의문사+주어+동사」의 순서로 쓰면서 주어, 동사, 부사를 알맞게 바꿔 준다.

· I **said to** the girl, "**What are you** looking for?"

⇨ I **asked** the girl **what she was** looking for.
나는 그 소녀에게 무엇을 찾고 있냐고 물었다.

· He **said to** her, "**Who did you go** shopping with?"

⇨ He **asked** her **who she went[had gone]** shopping with.
그는 그녀에게 누구와 쇼핑을 갔냐고 물었다.

❷ 의문사가 없는 의문문 : 전달동사를 ask로 바꾸고, 의문문을 「if/whether+주어+동사」의 순서로 쓰면서 주어, 동사, 부사를 알맞게 바꿔 준다.

· He **said to** me, "**Are you** taking your dog for a walk?"

⇨ He **asked** me **if[whether] I was** taking my dog for a walk.
그가 나에게 개를 산책시키는 중이냐고 물었다.

· I **said to** her, "**Have you** ever seen a lion?"

⇨ I **asked** her **if[whether] she had** ever seen a lion.
나는 그녀에게 사자를 본 적이 있는지 물었다.

Answers: p.30

Exercise ❶ 다음 직접 화법 문장을 간접 화법 문장으로 바꿔 쓰시오.

1 He said to me, "How long will you stay here?

⇨ _____

2 She said to me, "Why do you look so sad?"

⇨ _____

3 The man said to me, "Where is the nearest bank?"

⇨ _____

4 Bella said to him "What are you going to do this weekend?

⇨ _____

5 He said to me, "Why didn't you come to the party last Friday?

⇨ _____

6 She said to me, "What conclusion did you draw from the report?"

⇨ _____

7 My mother said to my father, "What do you want to eat for dinner?"

⇨ _____

8 Jessica said to me, "What did you do with your brother yesterday?"

⇨ _____

1 She said to me, "Do you know his full name?"
   ⇒ _____

2 Jack said to me, "Can you lend me some money?"
   ⇒ _____

3 Janet said to me, "Can I borrow your cell phone?"
   ⇒ _____

4 James said to me, "Have you been to Switzerland?"
   ⇒ _____

5 Mom said to me, "Did you go anywhere interesting?"
   ⇒ _____

6 My teacher said to me, "Were you in the class yesterday?"
   ⇒ _____

7 Mary said to me, "Did you talk over your problems with your teacher?"
   ⇒ _____

Exercise **3** 다음은 직접 화법 문장을 간접 화법 문장으로 전환한 것이다. 어법상 <u>어색한</u> 부분을 찾아 바르게 고치시오.

1 He said to me, "Do you like classical music?"
   ⇒ He asked me that I liked classical music.

2 He said to me, "Can you introduce me to her?"
   ⇒ He asked me whether could I introduce him to her.

3 I said to Michael, "Who did you talk with on the phone?"
   ⇒ I asked Michael who I talked with on the phone.

4 She said to me, "When will you come home tonight?"
   ⇒ She asked me whether when I would come home that night.

5 Tom said to me, "Can you go to the movies tomorrow?"
   ⇒ Tom asked me if he could go to the movies the following day.

6 Sarah said to me, "What did you see in the museum yesterday?"
   ⇒ Sarah asked me what did I see in the museum the day before.

7 Steven said to me, "Should we attend the annual meeting next Friday?"
   ⇒ Steven asked me if they should attend the annual meeting the following Friday.

화법 전환 III

📑 **명령문의 화법 전환** : 전달동사를 tell, ask, order, advise 등으로 알맞게 바꿔 주고, 명령문의 동사 앞에 to를 붙여 준다. 부정명령문은 not to를 붙여 준다.

· The teacher **said to** us, "**Be** quiet in the classroom."
  ⇨ The teacher **told** us **to be** quiet in the classroom. 선생님이 우리에게 교실에서 조용히 하라고 말했다.
· My sister **said to** me, "**Go** shopping with me."
  ⇨ My sister **asked** me **to go** shopping with her. 내 여동생이 자신과 함께 쇼핑을 가자고 부탁했다.
· Fredy **said to** me, "**Don't be** late."
  ⇨ Fredy **told** me **not to be** late. Fredy가 나에게 늦지 말라고 말했다.
· The officer **said to** them, "**Don't go** out."
  ⇨ The officer **ordered** them **not to go** out. 그 경관이 그들에게 나가지 말라고 명령했다.

Answers: p.31

Exercise 1 다음 짝지어진 두 문장이 같은 뜻이 되도록 간접 화법 문장을 완성하시오.

1 He said to me, "Organize the stuff on your desk."
  ⇨ He told me _____ .

2 She said to me, "Keep quiet during the test."
  ⇨ She asked me _____ .

3 My mother said to me, "Don't be mean to your little brother."
  ⇨ My mother told me _____ .

4 My teacher said to me, "Don't play soccer in the classroom."
  ⇨ My teacher told me _____ .

Exercise 2 다음 우리말과 같은 뜻이 되도록 괄호 안의 말을 배열하여 문장을 완성하시오.

1 선생님은 그들에게 수업에 다시는 늦지 말라고 말했다.
  (told, to, not, them, be, for, late, the class)
  ⇨ The teacher _____ again.

2 그는 나에게 빨간 신호일 때 길을 건너지 말라고 충고했다.
  (cross, advised, the street, to, me, not)
  ⇨ He _____ when the red light is on.

3 우리 어머니께서 내게 음식물을 입에 물고 얘기하지 말라고 하셨다.
  (full, with, mouth, to, my, talk, not)
  ⇨ My mother told me _____ .

4 우리 아버지가 나에게 자신의 서류가방을 가져다 달라고 부탁했다.
  (bring, briefcase, to, father, asked, his, my, me)
  ⇨ _____

[01-03] 다음 빈칸에 들어갈 알맞은 말을 고르시오.

01　He asked us _____ we had seen her the night before.

　　① what　　　　　② that
　　③ which　　　　④ if
　　⑤ as

02　He thought that the teacher and poet _____ the party.

　　① attend　　　　② would attend
　　③ attends　　　　④ was attended
　　⑤ will attend

03　A student asked his history teacher when Columbus _____ America.

　　① discover
　　② discovers
　　③ discovered
　　④ has discovered
　　⑤ would discover

[04-08] 다음 직접 화법 문장을 간접 화법 문장으로 바꿀 때 빈칸에 들어갈 알맞은 말을 고르시오.

04　The teacher said to me, "Did you read chapter two?"
　　⇒ The teacher asked me _____ chapter two.

　　① if did I read
　　② that I had read
　　③ if you had read
　　④ whether I had read
　　⑤ whether you have read

05　He said to her, "How was your trip to Tokyo?"
　　⇒ He asked her _____.

　　① how was your trip to Tokyo
　　② how is your trip to Tokyo
　　③ how her trip to Tokyo was
　　④ whether how her trip to Tokyo was
　　⑤ whether her trip to Tokyo was

06　She said to me, "Don't be afraid of hard work."
　　⇒ She told me _____ afraid of hard work.

　　① to not be
　　② not to be
　　③ do not be
　　④ not to was
　　⑤ do not was

07　She said to me, "Are you taking a driving test today?"
　　⇒ She asked me _____ taking a driving test that day.

　　① if you are
　　② if you were
　　③ if I was
　　④ whether was I
　　⑤ whether she was

08　Father said to me, "I will leave for London tomorrow."
　　⇒ Father told me that _____.

　　① I will leave for London the previous day
　　② he will leave for London the day before
　　③ I would leave for London the next day
　　④ he would leave for London that day
　　⑤ he would leave for London the following day

[09-12] 다음 빈칸에 들어갈 말이 바르게 짝지어진 것을 고르시오.

09 · The number of new-born babies
_____ on the decrease.
· A number of people _____ enjoying
their meals.
· The old _____ more patient than the
young.

① is – are – are
② is – is – are
③ is – are – is
④ are – is – is
⑤ are – are – is

10 · Everyone _____ his or her own way
of working chores.
· Taking care of babies _____ not an
easy job to do.
· The rest of the students _____
participate in discussion.

① have – are – has to
② has – is – has to
③ have – are – has to
④ has – is – have to
⑤ has – are – have to

11 · Three-fifths of the passengers _____
injured in the accident.
· The half of the story _____ not true.
· Neither smoking nor drinking _____
permitted in the building.

① were – are – are
② was – is – are
③ were – is – is
④ were – is – are
⑤ was - are – is

12 · Physics _____ one of the most
difficult subjects for me.
· Not only she but also you _____ good
at cooking.
· One hundred dollars _____ too
expensive for a pair of gloves.

① is – are – are
② is – is – are
③ is – are – is
④ are – is – is
⑤ are – is – are

[13-14] 다음 중 어법상 바른 문장을 고르시오.

13 ① Every dog have his day.
② All the dog have their names.
③ Three quarters of the world is covered with
water.
④ A number of students is studying in the
library.
⑤ The chestnut trees which are in my garden is
the same age as me.

14 ① If it will rain tomorrow, we'll stay home.
② He thought that she will come back soon.
③ We learned at school that two and two was
four.
④ It is said that Newton discovered the law of
gravitation.
⑤ The number of elephants have decreased for
the last ten years.

15 다음 밑줄 친 부분 중 어법상 어색한 것은?

I am ① <u>the only</u> one in ② <u>this group</u> ③ <u>who</u> ④
<u>are</u> ⑤ <u>invited</u> to play in the All-Star Game.

[16-19] 다음 중 어법상 <u>어색한</u> 문장을 고르시오.

16 ① Three-fourths of the subjects are male.
② Where is the rest of the gold in the box?
③ Taking pictures is one of my favorite hobbies.
④ All of the tables in the restaurant was occupied already.
⑤ A hundred dollars is too much for her to pay for the pants.

17 ① Everyone likes to read books.
② I thought that he was honest.
③ I told you that no one would try to cross the river.
④ We all learned at school that the earth was round.
⑤ I suggested that he should visit the museum tomorrow.

18 ① Slow and steady wins the race.
② Two-thirds of the potato is rotten.
③ Politics are an interesting field of study.
④ Bread and butter was what we ate for breakfast.
⑤ The majority of time was spent on playing computer games.

19 ① Neither she nor I am right.
② Each student has five books.
③ Mathematics is my favorite subject.
④ All the students in my class was there.
⑤ Look at the girls who are singing in the movie.

20 다음 문장의 화법 전환이 바른 것은?

① She said to me, "Go at once."
⇨ She ordered me that I go at once.
② He said to her, "Did you feed your cat?"
⇨ He asked her if she had fed her cat.
③ I said to them, "Don't be late."
⇨ I told them do not late.
④ She said, "I wanted to meet him."
⇨ She said that I had wanted to meet him.
⑤ He said to me, "Did you write the letter?"
⇨ He asked me if you wrote the letter.

[21-23] 다음 문장의 화법 전환이 <u>잘못된</u> 것을 고르시오.

21 ① She said to us, "Don't make noise."
⇨ She told us not to make noise.
② She said to me, "Do you like reading?"
⇨ She asked me that I liked reading.
③ He said to me, "What are you doing?"
⇨ He asked me what I was doing.
④ She said to me, "I'll leave here tomorrow."
⇨ She told me that she would leave there the next day.
⑤ My mom said to me, "Clean the room."
⇨ My mom told me to clean the room.

22 ① She said, "I will go shopping with you."
⇨ She said I would go shopping with you.
② She said to me, "where are you going?"
⇨ She asked me where I was going.
③ The doctor said to me, "Take the medicine three times a day."
⇨ The doctor advised me to take the medicine three times a day.
④ He said to me, "Can you come to the office tomorrow?"
⇨ He asked me if I could come to the office the following day.
⑤ The teacher said to me, "Why are you late for school?"
⇨ The teacher asked me why I was late for school.

23 ① She told him to stop smoking.
⇨ She said to him, "Stop smoking."
② They told us that they would watch the musical that day.
⇨ They said to us, "We will watch the musical today."
③ The man asked me if I could help him move the chair.
⇨The man said to me, "Can you help me move the chair?"
④ Mom ordered me not to play computer games after dinner.
⇨ Mom said to me, "Don't play computer games after dinner."
⑤ John asked me if he could join the band.
⇨ John said to me, "Can you join the band?"

[24-26] 다음 우리말과 같은 뜻이 되도록 괄호 안의 동사를 알맞은 형태로 바꿔 문장을 완성하시오.

24 10월 이후로 선생님뿐만 아니라 학생들도 교실에서 영어를 사용하고 있다.
⇨ The students as well as the teacher _____ used English in the classroom since October. (have)

25 동물원의 모든 동물이 내일 대중에게 선을 보이게 될 것이다.
⇨ Every animal in the zoo _____ going to be shown to the public tomorrow. (be)

26 클럽 회원의 3분의 2가 행사에 참여할 것이다.
⇨ Two-thirds of the club members _____ going to participate in the event. (be)

[27-31] 다음 두 문장이 같은 뜻이 되도록 간접 화법 문장을 완성하시오.

27 My mom said to me, "You have to get up now."
⇨ My mom told me that _____.

28 I said to him, "Why do you look so depressed?"
⇨ I asked him _____.

29 The doctor said to me, "Drink a lot of water."
⇨ The doctor told me _____.

30 His mom said to me, "Have you ever been to France?"
⇨ His mom asked me _____.

31 She said to me, "Whom did you lend your notebooks?"
⇨ She asked me _____.

[32-33] 다음 우리말과 같은 뜻이 되도록 괄호 안의 단어를 사용하여 문장을 완성하시오.

32 공기는 기체라고 선생님이 말했다. (be, air, a gas)
⇨ The teacher said that _____.

33 유권자의 3분의 1이 마음의 결정을 하지 않았다.
(have, make up one's mind)
⇨ One third of the voters _____.

Answers: p.32

[1-3] 글을 읽고, 물음에 답하시오.　　　　　　　　　　　　　　　서술형

The exam results came out yesterday. (A) Most of the results was not bad. But (B) mathematics were awful. I was very disappointed because I had put extra efforts in math. While we were having dinner today, (C) my dad said to me, "Why do you look so sad?" I said, "I studied hard, but I got a C in math." (D) My dad told me not to get depressed. And he said to me, "At least you didn't get an F this time."

1 밑줄 친 (A), (B)에서 어법상 어색한 부분을 찾아 바르게 고쳐 쓰시오.

(A) _____ → _____

(B) _____ → _____

2 밑줄 친 (C)를 간접화법 문장으로 바꿔 쓰시오.

→ my dad _____.

3 밑줄 친 (D)를 직접화법 문장으로 바꿔 쓰시오.

→ My dad _____."

4 다음 글의 밑줄 친 부분 중, 어법상 틀린 것은?　　　　　　　　수능 대비형

Determined to cut back on cakes and cookies, I had been ① looking for some fruit desert. I ② was invited to one of my friends' dinner party and she served us an amazing fruit crisp. After the dinner, I asked her what ③ was it and how to make it. She gave me her recipe and told me ④ to try it at home. I'm not sure it ⑤ is going to taste like hers, but I will keep trying.

* determine: ~하기로 결정하다, 마음먹다
** cut back on: ~을 줄이다

Chapter 10

관계사

who / which / that

📑 관계대명사 : 관계대명사는 문장에서 「접속사+대명사」의 역할을 하며, 관계대명사가 이끄는 절은 앞에 있는 명사를 수식한다. 관계대명사절의 수식을 받는 명사를 선행사라고 한다.

선행사	주격	소유격	목적격
사람	who	whose	whom
사물, 동물	which	of which, whose	which
사람, 사물, 동물	that	—	that

❶ 주격 관계대명사 : 주격 관계대명사는 관계대명사절 안에서 주어 역할을 한다. who는 사람, which는 사물, that은 둘 다를 선행사로 받는다.

· This is **the woman. She** lives next door.
⇒ This is **the woman who[that]** lives next door.
이 사람은 옆집에 사는 여자이다.

· I have **a storybook. It** is very interesting.
⇒ I have **a storybook which[that]** is very interesting.
나는 매우 재미있는 이야기책을 가지고 있다.

❷ 목적격 관계대명사 : 목적격 관계대명사는 관계대명사절 안에서 목적어 역할을 한다. who(m)는 사람, which는 사물, that은 둘 다를 선행사로 받는다.

· This is **the boy. I met him** yesterday.
⇒ This is **the boy who(m)[that]** I met yesterday.   이 사람은 내가 어제 만난 소년이다.

· This is **the dictionary. I bought it** last year.
⇒ This is **the dictionary which[that]** I bought last year.   이것은 내가 작년에 산 사전이다.

❸ 소유격 관계대명사 : 소유격 관계대명사는 관계대명사절 안에서 소유격 역할을 한다. whose는 사람과 사물 모두를 선행사로 받는다.

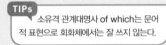

TIPs
소유격 관계대명사 of which는 문어적 표현으로 회화체에서는 잘 쓰지 않는다.

· He met **a lady. Her** job was a teacher.
⇒ He met **a lady whose** job was a teacher.
그는 직업이 교사인 한 여자를 만났다.

· This is **the word. Its** meaning is not clear.
⇒ This is **the word whose** meaning is not clear.   이것은 의미가 불분명한 단어이다.

Answers: p.33

Exercise 1 다음 괄호 안에서 알맞은 말을 고르시오.

1 The man (whom / whose) I met yesterday has short hair.

2 Here are the books (who / which) I bought at the garage sale.

3 What's the name of the man (who / whose) car you borrowed?

4 The woman (which / whom) I wanted to see is my grandmother.

5 Did you see the packages (who / which) were delivered this morning?

6 She loved the man (who / which) went to the same elementary school.

7 I watched many movies (who / which) were made by Steven Spielberg.

다음 빈칸에 알맞은 관계대명사를 넣어 문장을 완성하시오.

1 The doctor _____ Peter knows is my aunt.

2 He wrote a book _____ told us useful things.

3 That's the girl _____ I like most in my school.

4 The book _____ you're reading is very difficult.

5 I have an American friend _____ name is Mike.

6 I don't like movies _____ are full of special effects.

7 That's the woman _____ husband won the award.

8 The man _____ we met in the park is a famous poet.

9 The smartphone _____ my father bought me has two screens.

다음 괄호 안에서 알맞은 말을 고르시오.

1 A thief is someone (which / that) steals things.

2 Those books which are on the table (is / are) mine.

3 Some cars which have poor brakes (is / are) dangerous.

4 A child (who / whose) parents are dead is called an orphan.

5 The pyramids which were built for the Pharaohs of Egypt (is / are) tombs.

다음 문장의 밑줄 친 부분을 알맞게 고쳐 쓰시오.

1 They lived in a house <u>who gate</u> was red. ⇨ _____

2 There are many toys <u>whom</u> I gave to her. ⇨ _____

3 He is the boy <u>whose</u> I wanted to see most. ⇨ _____

4 My sister likes the bag <u>who</u> I bought in London. ⇨ _____

5 He is one of the scientists <u>which</u> we all respect. ⇨ _____

6 The book whose cover is blue <u>belong to</u> Michelle. ⇨ _____

7 Do you know the boys <u>whom are</u> talking with Bill? ⇨ _____

8 She fixed the windows <u>which was</u> broken by her child. ⇨ _____

9 Show me the pictures <u>whom</u> you took at the exhibition. ⇨ _____

10 The tall man that is wearing black jeans <u>are</u> on the basketball team. ⇨ _____

1 The waiter was very polite. He was serving us.

⇨ The waiter _____ was very polite.

2 The bus runs every half hour. It goes to City Hall.

⇨ The bus _____ runs every half hour.

3 The woman is away on holiday. I want to meet her.

⇨ The woman _____ is away on holiday.

4 The girl was injured in the accident. She is in the hospital.

⇨ The girl _____ was injured in the accident.

5 Gaudi was an architect. He designed many beautiful houses and churches.

⇨ Gaudi was an architect _____.

6 I saw my classmate. She was eating lunch on a bench.

⇨ I saw my classmate _____ on a bench.

1 나는 털이 하얀 고양이 한 마리를 샀다. (is, whose, white, hair)

⇨ I bought a cat _____.

2 Mark Smith는 많은 사람들이 좋아하는 수영선수이다. (people, whom, many, like)

⇨ Mark Smith is a swimmer _____.

3 나는 아버지가 의사인 친구가 한 명 있다. (whose, father, a friend, is, a doctor)

⇨ I have _____.

4 우리 언니가 내가 가지고 싶어 했던 컴퓨터를 사주었다. (I, to, wanted, have, which)

⇨ My sister bought me the computer _____.

5 그가 나에게 빨간 드레스를 입은 소녀를 소개했다. (wearing, red, who, a, dress, was)

⇨ He introduced to me a girl _____.

6 이 YouTube 채널은 항상 내 기분을 좋게 해주는 노래들이 많다. (feel, always make, better, me, which)

⇨ This YouTube channel has many songs _____.

📑 관계대명사 **that**

❶ 관계대명사 **that**은 소유격을 제외한 모든 관계대명사를 대신해 쓸 수 있다.

· He is playing with the boy **that[who]** lives next door. 〈주격 관계대명사〉
  그는 옆집에 사는 소년과 놀고 있다.

· He is the teacher **that[whom]** I like. 〈목적격 관계대명사〉
  그는 내가 좋아하는 선생님이다.

❷ 선행사가 다음과 같이 특별한 경우에는 주로 관계대명사 **that**을 쓴다.

① 선행사가 –thing으로 끝나는 경우

· Is there anything **that** we can drink? 우리가 마실 것이 있나요?

② 선행사가 「사람+사물」 또는 「사람+동물」인 경우

· This movie is about a man and his dog **that** are shipwrecked on a desert island.
  이 영화는 무인도에 조난된 남자와 그의 개에 관한 이야기이다.

③ 선행사가 최상급, 서수, the only, the very, the same, every, all 등의 수식을 받는 경우

· He is the greatest poet **that** Korea has ever produced. 그는 한국이 배출한 가장 위대한 시인이다.

· He is the first man **that** reached the North Pole. 그는 북극에 도달한 최초의 인간이다.

· The only problem **that** we have is money. 우리가 가진 유일한 문제는 돈이다.

Answers: p.33

Exercise 1 다음 괄호 안에서 알맞은 것을 고르시오.

1 Jeff is the fastest boy (that / which) I've ever seen.

2 This is the same wallet (that / whom) I lost last weekend.

3 If there is something (that / whom) you want, please let me know.

4 She was the second person (that / whom) crossed the finish line.

Exercise 2 다음 우리말과 같은 뜻이 되도록 괄호 안의 단어를 알맞게 배열하여 문장을 완성하시오.

1 제가 두통을 완화하기 위해 할 수 있는 어떤 방법이 있나요? (my, I, can do, anything, headache, to ease, that)

⇨ Is there _____ ?

2 그 영화는 내가 봤던 영화 중 가장 긴 영화다. (seen, the, movie, have, I, that, longest)

⇨ The movie is _____ .

3 도서관에 첫 번째로 온 학생은 Jason이다. (came, the library, the first student, who, to)

⇨ _____ is Jason.

4 이것이 우리 냉장고에 있는 유일한 음식이다. (the only, in, that, we have, the refrigerator, food)

⇨ This is _____ .

10-3 what

関계대명사 **what** : 선행사를 포함하는 관계대명사로 the thing(s) which[that]으로 바꿔 쓸 수 있으며, '~ 하는 것'으로 해석한다.

· **What** she said makes me happy.
  ⇒ **The thing which** she said makes me happy. 그녀가 말한 것이 나를 행복하게 만든다.
· This is **what** I bought yesterday.
  ⇒ This is **the thing that** I bought yesterday. 이것이 내가 어제 산 것이다.
· Do you understand **what** I mean?
  ⇒ Do you understand **the thing that** I mean? 내가 무슨 말을 하는지 이해하니?

> **TIPs**
> 관계대명사 **what**이 다른 관계대명사(who, which, that)와 다른 점은 선행사가 없다는 것이다.

Answers: p.33

Exercise 1 다음 괄호 안에서 알맞은 말을 고르시오.

1 That's not (that / what) I meant to say.

2 Nobody knows (that / what) will happen next.

3 What he says is different from (that / what) he does.

4 Please tell me (that / what) you want for your birthday.

5 Everything (that / what) happened was captured on his camera.

Exercise 2 다음 우리말과 같은 뜻이 되도록 괄호 안의 단어를 알맞게 배열하여 문장을 완성하시오.

1 그가 한 일은 완전히 잘못된 것이다. (did, he, what)

   ⇒ _____ is totally wrong.

2 그는 내가 요청한 것을 아직 나에게 주지 않았다. (asked for, I, what)

   ⇒ He hasn't given me _____ ?

3 나는 네가 지난여름에 한 일을 알고 있다. (you, what, last, did, summer)

   ⇒ I know _____ .

4 나를 행복하게 한 것은 그녀의 친절한 태도였다. (what, me, made, happy)

   ⇒ _____ was her kind attitude.

5 내가 정말로 하고 싶은 것은 그저 잠을 자는 것이다. (what, do, I, to, want, really)

   ⇒ _____ is just sleep.

6 너 어제 우리가 저녁으로 무엇을 먹었는지 맞춰 볼래? (night, had, we, last, for dinner, what)

   ⇒ Can you guess _____ ?

7 이것은 내가 남동생과 하려고 했던 것이 아니다. (brother, with, what, was supposed to, I, my, do)

   ⇒ This is not _____ .

10-4 관계대명사의 생략

📑 관계대명사의 생략

❶ 목적격 관계대명사는 생략할 수 있다.
- He is the teacher **(who(m))** I met yesterday. 그는 내가 어제 만난 선생님이다.
- The luggage **(which)** I am carrying is very heavy. 내가 들고 있는 이 가방은 매우 무겁다.
- The book **(that)** I am fond of is a comic book. 내가 좋아하는 책은 만화책이다.

❷ 「주격 관계대명사+**be**동사」는 생략할 수 있다.
- The girl **(who is)** playing the piano is my cousin. 피아노를 연주하고 있는 그 소녀는 내 사촌이다.
- It is a tower **(which is)** made of marble. 그것은 대리석으로 만들어진 탑이다.

Answers: p.33

Exercise 1 다음 밑줄 친 부분을 생략할 수 있으면 ○표, 없으면 X표 하시오.

1 A koala is an animal <u>which</u> lives in Australia. ⇨ _____

2 What is the language <u>which is</u> spoken in Brazil? ⇨ _____

3 Do you know the woman <u>whom</u> Joe is talking to? ⇨ _____

4 The people <u>who</u> work in the office are very friendly. ⇨ _____

5 My mother found the keys <u>that</u> I lost the other day. ⇨ _____

6 The person <u>who is</u> delivering some boxes is my brother. ⇨ _____

7 The dress <u>that</u> my sister bought doesn't fit her very well. ⇨ _____

8 The girls <u>that</u> we met at the library were doing their homework. ⇨ _____

Exercise 2 다음 문장에서 생략 가능한 부분을 생략하여 다시 쓰시오.

1 The wallet which Jeff lost was not found.

⇨ _____

2 English is the subject which I'm most interested in.

⇨ _____

3 The man who is looking for his lost dog is my friend.

⇨ _____

4 The woman whom I wanted to see was staying in Seoul.

⇨ _____

5 Do you know the girl who is talking to Charles by the window?

⇨ _____

10-5 관계대명사의 용법

□ **관계대명사의 용법**

❶ 제한적 용법 : 제한적 용법의 관계대명사절은 선행사를 뒤에서 수식하여 선행사의 의미를 제한한다.

· I bought a printer **which** was just released into the market.
나는 이제 막 시장에 출시된 인쇄기를 샀다.

❷ 계속적 용법 : 계속적 용법의 관계대명사절은 선행사에 추가적인 정보를 제공하거나 보충 설명하는 역할을 한다. 계속적 용법으로 쓰이는 관계대명사 앞에는 쉼표(,)가 온다.

· She has two sons, **who** became doctors. 〈계속적 용법〉
그녀는 아들이 두 명 있는데, 둘 다 의사가 되었다. (아들이 두 명 있다.)

· She has two sons **who** became doctors. 〈제한적 용법〉
그녀는 의사가 된 아들 두 명이 있다. (의사가 아닌 아들이 더 있을 수 있다.)

① 계속적 용법의 관계대명사는 의미에 따라 「접속사 (and, or, but, for)+대명사」로 바꿔 쓸 수 있다.

· I played tennis, **which** is my favorite sport.

= I played tennis, **and it** is my favorite sport. 나는 테니스를 쳤는데, 테니스는 내가 제일 좋아하는 운동이다.

② 선행사가 고유명사이거나 특정 인물인 경우, 관계대명사절은 추가적인 정보를 제공하므로 계속적 용법을 사용한다.

· Mozart, **who** was born in Salzburg, lived from 1756 to 1791.
잘츠부르크에서 태어난 모차르트는 1756년부터 1791년까지 살았다.

③ 관계대명사 that은 계속적 용법으로 쓸 수 없다.

· I met Leo, **who** is my classmate.(O) 나는 Leo를 만났는데 그는 우리 반 친구이다.

· I met Leo, ~~that~~ is my classmate.(X)

④ 계속적 용법의 관계대명사 which는 절을 선행사로 받기도 한다.

· She won first prize, **which** made her parents happy. 〈선행사 : She won first prize〉
그녀는 일등을 했고, 이것이 그녀의 부모님을 기쁘게 했다.

Answers: p.33

Exercise 1 다음 빈칸에 알맞은 관계대명사를 써넣으시오.

1 This morning I saw Mark, _____ is from Germany.

2 I will go shopping with Jina, _____ is my best friend.

3 The 63 Building, _____ is in Yeouido, is a 60-story building.

4 Shinzo Abe, _____ is one of the most famous Japanese politicians, died in 2022.

5 The Eiffel Tower, _____ is the tallest building in Paris, was designed by Eiffel.

Exercise 2 다음 괄호 안에서 알맞은 것을 모두 고르시오.

1 The woman (that / who) I helped was Julian's mother.

2 Show me the clothes (that / which) you bought yesterday.

3 My uncle, (that / who) I loved so much, passed away last year.

4 I miss Korean food, (that / which) I have not eaten in a long time.

5 The cook added some sauce in the soup, (that / which) made it tasty.

Exercise 3 다음 문장의 밑줄 친 계속적 용법의 관계대명사를 「접속사+대명사」로 바꿔 쓰시오.

1 I borrowed *Harry Potter*, <u>which</u> was very interesting.
   ⇨ I borrowed *Harry Potter*, _____ _____ was very interesting.

2 I watched the French movie, <u>which</u> was very fantastic.
   ⇨ I watched the French movie, _____ _____ was very fantastic.

3 She read many books, <u>which</u> have influenced her a lot.
   ⇨ She read many books, _____ _____ have influenced her a lot.

4 I met Sarah, <u>who</u> is my English teacher from the U.S.A.
   ⇨ I met Sarah, _____ _____ is my English teacher from the U.S.A.

Exercise 4 다음 두 문장을 계속적 용법의 관계대명사를 사용하여 한 문장으로 바꿔 쓰시오.

1 Jimmy went to the flower shop. It was closed.
   ⇨ _____

2 We stayed at the Hilton Hotel. A taxi driver recommended it to us.
   ⇨ _____

3 Seoul is one of the biggest cities in the world. It is the capital of Korea.
   ⇨ _____

4 Tom Cruise starred in the film *Top Gun: Maverick*. It was released in 2022.
   ⇨ _____

Exercise 5 다음 우리말과 같은 뜻이 되도록 괄호 안의 단어를 알맞게 배열하여 문장을 완성하시오.

1 우리는 공원에 갔는데, 공원은 많은 사람으로 북적이었다. (crowded, people, was, a lot of, which, with)
   ⇨ We went to the park, _____.

2 James는 세 명의 사촌이 있는데, 그들은 모두 변호사가 되었다. (lawyers, became, who)
   ⇨ James has three cousins, _____.

3 Edison은 축음기를 발명했고, 그것이 그를 유명하게 만들었다. (him, made, which, famous)
   ⇨ Edison invented a phonograph, _____.

4 그녀는 어제 학교에 지각했고, 그것이 선생님을 화나게 했다. (her teacher, which, upset, made)
   ⇨ She was late for school yesterday, _____.

전치사 + 관계대명사

□ 「전치사+관계대명사」: 관계대명사가 전치사의 목적어로 쓰인 경우, 전치사는 관계대명사 앞이나 관계대명사절 뒤에 온다. 전치사가 관계대명사절 뒤에 온 경우, 관계대명사는 생략이 가능하다.

Do you know <u>the woman</u>? + Nicole is talking to <u>her</u>.

⇒ Do you know <u>the woman</u> **(who(m))** Nicole is talking **to**?

= Do you know <u>the woman</u> **to whom** Nicole is talking? 〈전치사+관계대명사〉

= Do you know <u>the woman</u> **to** Nicole is talking? (X) 〈전치사 뒤의 관계대명사(whom)는 생략 불가〉

= Do you know <u>the woman</u> ~~**to that**~~ Nicole is talking? (X) 〈관계대명사 that은 전치사의 목적어로 쓸 수 없음〉

너는 Nicole과 이야기하고 있는 여자를 아니?

TIPs who는 전치사의 목적어로 쓸 수 없고, whom만 전치사의 목적어로 쓸 수 있다.

Answers: p.34

Exercise 1 다음 〈보기〉와 같이 바꿔 쓰시오.

🔍 **Did you see the girl? I spoke to her a moment ago.**

⇒ Did you see the girl who(m) I spoke to a moment ago?

⇒ Did you see the girl I spoke to a moment ago?

⇒ Did you see the girl to whom I spoke a moment ago?

1 George didn't get the job. He applied for the job.

⇒ _____

⇒ _____

⇒ _____

2 We could go to the wedding. We were invited to the wedding.

⇒ _____

⇒ _____

⇒ _____

3 This is the house. My grandparents have lived in the house for 50 years.

⇒ _____

⇒ _____

⇒ _____

4 This is the tunnel. About thirty thousand cars a day go through it to reach the beach.

⇒ _____

⇒ _____

⇒ _____

10-7 관계부사

관계부사의 종류

구분	선행사	관계부사	전치사+관계대명사
시간	시간을 나타내는 명사 time, day, year 등	when	in/at/on+which
장소	장소를 나타내는 명사 place, house 등	where	in/at/on+which
이유	이유를 나타내는 명사 the reason	why	for+which
방법	방법을 나타내는 명사 the way	how	in+which

❶ 시간 when

· Could you tell me the date **when[on which]** you were born?
  당신이 태어난 날을 저에게 말해 주시겠어요?

· January is the month **when[in which]** it is the coldest in Korea.
  1월은 한국에서 가장 추운 달이다.

❷ 장소 where

· This is the place **where[in which]** I lived. 이곳이 내가 살았던 곳이다.

· Do you remember the cafe **where[at which]** we first met?
  너는 우리가 처음 만났던 카페를 기억하니?

❸ 이유 why

· Do you know the reason **why[for which]** I came here?
  너는 내가 이곳에 온 이유를 아니?

· Tell me the reason **why[for which]** she is very pleased.
  그녀가 매우 기쁜 이유를 나에게 말해 줘요.

❹ 방법 how

· This is **how** I solve the problem.
  = This is the way **in which** I solve the problem.
  = This is the way I solve the problem.
  = This is the way how I solve the problem. (X) 〈선행사 the way와 관계부사 how는 함께 쓸 수 없음〉
    이것이 내가 문제를 해결하는 방식이다.

> **TIPs** 관계부사 뒤에는 완전한 절이 오고, 관계대명사 뒤에는 불완전한 절이 온다.
> · This is the park **where I often ride the bike**. 〈관계부사+주어+동사+목적어〉 이곳은 내가 종종 자전거를 타는 공원이다.
> · This is the bike **which I often ride in the park**. 〈관계대명사+주어+동사〉 이것은 내가 공원에서 종종 타는 자전거이다.

> **TIPs** 관계부사는 that으로 바꿔 쓸 수 있다.

Answers: p.34

Exercise ❶ 다음 괄호 안에서 알맞은 말을 고르시오.

1 I like the way (in which / which) she writes a book.

2 I live in the house (where / which) stands on the hill.

3 There is another reason (how / that) you don't know.

4 That was the way (in which / how) we met each other.

5 I live in the house (where / which) my friends used to live.

6 I remember the day (which / when) he came to my house.

7 Is there any reason (which / why) many audiences were fascinated?

8 The park (where / which) I take a walk in the morning is near my house.

9 We stayed home the day before yesterday (when / which) you left for Tokyo.

10 I didn't know the reason (why / which) many people were standing on the street.

Exercise **2** 다음 빈칸에 알맞은 관계부사를 써넣으시오.

1 The hotel _____ we stayed was not clean.

2 The reason _____ I called you is to meet you.

3 She went back to the city _____ she was born.

4 This is the place _____ the World War I started.

5 I'll always remember the day _____ I first met you.

6 2021 is the year _____ he married his wife, Christine.

7 I don't know the reason _____ he doesn't like his father.

8 I go to school by school bus. This is _____ I go to school.

9 I would like to travel in a country _____ there is plenty of sunshine.

10 Do you know a cafe _____ many young people meet their friends?

Exercise **3** 다음 문장의 밑줄 친 부분을 바르게 고치시오. (단, that으로 고치지 말 것)

1 Tell me the way which you met each other. ⇨ _____

2 Do you know the day which she will be back? ⇨ _____

3 That's the way how I learned how to play the piano. ⇨ _____

4 Do you know the reason which they can't work together? ⇨ _____

5 There is a shop near here which I can buy some goods. ⇨ _____

6 This is the hotel which we are going to stay for the conference. ⇨ _____

Exercise **4** 다음 우리말과 같은 뜻이 되도록 괄호 안의 단어를 사용하여 문장을 완성하시오. (단, 한 칸에 한 단어씩 쓸 것)

1 네가 내 컴퓨터를 어떻게 고쳤는지 말해 줄래? (fix)

⇨ Can you tell me _____ _____ _____ my computer?

2 이곳이 그의 작품이 전시되어 있는 미술관이다. (exhibit)

⇨ This is the art museum _____ his works _____ _____.

3 하늘이 파랗게 보이는 이유를 아니? (be)

⇨ Do you know _____ _____ _____ the sky _____ blue?

4 너는 제2차 세계대전이 일어난 연도를 기억하니? (break out)

⇨ Do you remember _____ _____ _____ the Second World War _____ _____ ?

다음 두 문장을 관계부사를 사용하여 한 문장으로 만드시오. (단, 관계부사와 선행사를 생략하지 말 것)

1   This is the village. I was born there.

   ⇨ _____

2   We went to the city. My grandparents used to live there.

   ⇨ _____

3   This is the hospital. My father works there as a janitor.

   ⇨ _____

4   October 15th is the day. World War Ⅱ ended on the day.

   ⇨ _____

5   He showed me the basement. He had lived there during the war.

   ⇨ _____

6   I know the reason. Joanna broke up with her boyfriend for that reason.

   ⇨ _____

다음 짝지어진 두 문장이 같은 뜻이 되도록 관계부사를 사용하여 문장을 완성하시오.

1   Please tell me the way I can make the best cookies.

   ⇨ Please tell me _____ .

2   This is the restaurant in which we had dinner last night.

   ⇨ This is the restaurant _____ .

3   She told me the way in which she could gather the information.

   ⇨ She told me _____ .

4   We remember the day on which Cathy first came to our school.

   ⇨ We remember the day _____ .

5   Jennifer told us the reason for which she couldn't catch the first train.

   ⇨ Jennifer told us the reason _____ .

6   I don't know the hotel in which they are going to stay during the vacation.

   ⇨ I don't know the hotel _____ .

10-8 복합관계사

Answers: p.34

☐ 복합관계사 : 복합관계사는 선행사를 포함하며 「관계사+**ever**」의 형태로 부사절과 명사절을 이끈다.

복합관계사	양보의 부사절	명사절
whoever	no matter who 누가 ~해도	anyone who ~하는 사람은 누구든지
whomever	no matter whom 누구를 ~해도	anyone whom ~하는 사람은 누구든지
whatever	no matter what 무엇을 ~해도	anything that ~하는 것은 무엇이든지
whichever	no matter which 어느 것을 ~해도	anything which ~하는 어느 것이나

· **Whoever** asks me the question, I will not answer it. 누가 그 질문을 하든 나는 대답하지 않을 것이다.

= **No matter who** asks the question, I will not answer it.

· Give the book to **whoever** comes first. 먼저 오는 사람은 누구에게라도 그 책을 주어라.

= Give the book to **anyone who** comes first.

· **Whatever** she says, I will believe it. 그녀가 무슨 얘기를 하더라도 나는 그것을 믿을 것이다.

= **No matter what** she says, I will believe it.

· I will do **whatever** I can do for you. 나는 당신을 위해 할 수 있는 일은 무엇이든지 할 것이다.

= I will do **anything that** I can do for you.

Exercise 1 다음 짝지어진 두 문장이 같은 뜻이 되도록 빈칸에 알맞은 복합관계사를 써넣으시오.

1 You may take anything that you want.

⇒ You may take _____ you want.

2 No matter what you say, they'll believe you.

⇒ _____ you say, they'll believe you.

3 No matter which team we face, we will win the championship.

⇒ _____ we face, we will win the championship.

4 Anyone who comes first will be first served.

⇒ _____ comes first will be first served.

Exercise 2 다음 우리말과 같은 뜻이 되도록 복합관계사를 사용하여 문장을 완성하시오.

1 너는 무엇을 사더라도 만족하지 못할 것이다.

⇒ _____ you buy, you won't be satisfied.

2 우리는 당신이 선택한 사람이 누구든지 그 사람에게 투표할 것이다.

⇒ We will vote for _____ you choose.

3 나는 당신이 무슨 말을 하더라도 나의 꿈을 포기하지 않을 것이다.

⇒ _____ you say, I'll never give up my dream.

4 콘서트에 가고 싶어 하는 사람 누구에게라도 그 콘서트 표를 주어라.

⇒ Give the concert ticket to _____ wants to go there.

복합관계부사 : 복합관계부사는 선행사를 포함하며 「관계부사+**ever**」의 형태로 부사절을 이끈다.

복합관계부사	양보의 부사절	시간, 장소의 부사절
whenever	no matter when 언제 ~해도	at any time when[that] ~할 때면 언제든지
wherever	no matter where 어디서 ~해도	at any place where[that] ~하는 곳은 어디든지
however	no matter how 아무리 ~해도	

· I will follow you **wherever** you go.

= I will follow you **no matter where** you go.

　당신이 어디에 가더라도 나는 당신을 따라갈 것이다.

· **Whenever** you visit him, you will see him playing the piano.

= **No matter when** you visit him, you will see him playing the piano.

　그를 언제 방문한다 하더라도, 너는 그가 피아노 연주를 하고 있는 것을 보게 될 것이다.

· **However** strong he is, he can't carry the box.

= **No matter how** strong he is, he can't carry the box.

　그가 아무리 강하다 하더라도, 그 상자를 운반할 수는 없다.

Answers: p.35

Exercise 1 다음 우리말과 같은 뜻이 되도록 빈칸에 알맞은 복합관계부사를 써넣으시오.

1 당신이 어디를 가든 나는 당신과 함께할 거예요.

⇨ _____ you go, I'll be with you.

2 우리는 당신이 가길 원하는 곳은 어디든지 데려다 줄 것이다.

⇨ We will take you _____ you want to go.

3 그 노래를 들을 때마다 내 어린시절이 떠오른다.

⇨ _____ I hear the song, it brings back memories of my childhood.

4 아무리 노력을 한다 해도 너는 내일까지 그 일을 마무리하지 못할 것이다.

⇨ _____ hard you try, you can't finish the work by tomorrow.

Exercise 2 다음 짝지어진 두 문장이 같은 뜻이 되도록 복합관계부사를 사용하여 문장을 다시 쓰시오.

1 He went to the beach at any time that he felt lonely.

⇨ _____

2 No matter when you visit the zoo, you can see the lions.

⇨ _____

3 No matter where you go, you can buy our books online.

⇨ _____

4 No matter how difficult the project is, we'll finish it as scheduled.

⇨ _____

[01-05] 다음 빈칸에 들어갈 알맞은 말을 고르시오.

01 This is the boy _____ showed me the way to the post office.

① whom   ② what
③ whose   ④ who
⑤ which

02 Tokyo is the city _____ the 2020 Olympics were held.

① when   ② which
③ where   ④ how
⑤ whose

03 You can invite _____ you want to the party.

① whatever   ② whenever
③ wherever   ④ whomever
⑤ however

04 Can you tell me _____ the machine works?

① where   ② when
③ how   ④ which
⑤ who

05 _____ I need most now is your love.

① Where   ② What
③ Who   ④ Why
⑤ How

06 다음 빈칸에 들어갈 말이 순서대로 짝지어진 것은?

· This is the person _____ has been living in New York for five years.
· I saw the house _____ Tom built.
· Everything _____ the witness told us is true.

① that – that – who
② that – whom – which
③ who – that – that
④ who – which – whose
⑤ which – that – that

[07-11] 다음 두 문장이 같은 뜻이 되도록 빈칸에 알맞은 말을 고르시오.

07 I added some sugar, which made the coffee sweet.
⇒ I added some sugar, _____ made the coffee sweet.

① and it   ② but it
③ for that   ④ because which
⑤ though the coffee

08 This is the thing which I've been looking for.
⇒ This is _____ I've been looking for.

① which   ② what
③ of which   ④ whom
⑤ whose

09 Do you remember the place at which we first met?
⇒ Do you remember the place _____ we first met?

① which   ② when
③ where   ④ who
⑤ what

10 Wherever you go, you can study through online courses.

⇒ _____ you go, you can study through online courses.

① At where ② No matter what
③ No matter where ④ No matter when
⑤ No matter how

11 You can wear whatever you want.
⇒ You can wear _____ you want.

① anything that ② anyone who
③ no matter which ④ at any time when
⑤ no matter where

[12-13] 다음 빈칸에 공통으로 들어갈 말을 고르시오.

12 · We bought some books, _____ were very interesting.
· All of us went out to the beach _____ was covered with sand.
· This is the hotel at _____ they stayed during the holiday.

① who ② which
③ that ④ whose
⑤ where

13 · This is the very book _____ I have been looking for.
· This is the most beautiful river _____ I have ever seen.
· Where is the person _____ asked you about me?

① that ② which
③ what ④ whose
⑤ of which

[14-15] 다음 밑줄 친 부분 중 생략할 수 없는 것을 고르시오.

14 ① He is holding the bag that I gave him.
② Tom likes the girl who is singing now.
③ I know the village in which Mary was born.
④ She gave me the dress which she made last month.
⑤ The man who we saw yesterday was Tiger Woods.

15 ① He is the boy whom everybody likes.
② The scarf which was made in France is hers.
③ This is the picture which was painted by Sam.
④ Look at the students who are studying in the classroom.
⑤ The book that is on the table is very interesting.

16 다음 빈칸에 that을 쓸 수 없는 것은?

① Humans are the only animal _____ can speak.
② I have two sons, _____ are doctors.
③ She is the prettiest girl _____ I have ever seen.
④ Look at the boy and his dog _____ are running there.
⑤ There were few passengers _____ escaped without injury.

17 다음 중 어법상 올바른 문장은?

① What's the name of the pool in I swam?
② The hotel which we stayed was very small.
③ I know a place in you can find many old books.
④ That is the chair on that my cat and dog like to sleep.
⑤ I have a friend whose mother is a famous singer in Korea.

[18-20] 다음 중 어법상 <u>어색한</u> 문장을 고르시오.

18 ① There is something that I forgot.
② This is the house where we live in.
③ Minsu is wearing a jacket I bought.
④ It's the only price that makes them happy.
⑤ He is looking at some photos that Joe took.

19 ① This is not that I'm looking for.
② We checked everything that we needed.
③ He was the first man that got to the South Pole.
④ I have a friend whose father is a lawyer.
⑤ The apples which you bought for me were all rotten.

20 ① What I really want is your help.
② You can choose whatever you want.
③ The jacket you wore last night was nice.
④ This is the picture was painted by Gogh.
⑤ He works for a company located in Tokyo.

[21-22] 다음 빈칸에 들어갈 말이 나머지 넷과 <u>다른</u> 것을 고르시오.

21 ① That is the town _____ I was born.
② That's the Thames, _____ used to be polluted.
③ The city _____ we lived was very large and clean.
④ I know a good place _____ we can set up a tent.
⑤ I want to live in a country _____ there's fresh air.

22 ① I saw Cindy, _____ is my classmate.
② Yesterday I met a boy _____ was impolite.
③ I'll meet Ms. Jones, _____ son is my student.
④ Junho, _____ always arrives on time, hasn't come yet.
⑤ My grandfather, _____ is 70 years old, goes climbing every week.

23 다음 중 밑줄 친 부분을 생략할 수 있는 것은?

① I have a friend <u>whose</u> father is a writer.
② The cup <u>which is</u> on the cupboard is mine.
③ They came into the office in <u>which</u> he worked.
④ That is an elephant <u>which</u> came from Thailand.
⑤ We saw a mountain <u>that</u> was covered with snow.

[24-25] 다음 우리말을 바르게 영작한 것을 고르시오.

24 우리 축구팀이 우승했으며, 그로 인해 많은 사람이 신이 났다.

① Our soccer team won the championship, that made a lot of people excited.
② Our soccer team won the championship, what made a lot of people excited.
③ Our soccer team won the championship, it made a lot of people excited.
④ Our soccer team won the championship, which made a lot of people excited.
⑤ Our soccer team won the championship, in which made a lot of people excited.

25 그 일이 아무리 어려워도 너는 이겨내야 한다.

① Despite difficult the task is, you have to get over it.
② What a difficult the task is, you have to get over it.
③ However difficult the task is, you have to get over it.
④ No matter what difficult the task is, you have to get over it.
⑤ Whatever difficult the task is, you have to get over it.

26 다음 〈보기〉의 밑줄 친 부분과 쓰임이 같은 것은?

> I don't trust doctors <u>that</u> have made many mistakes.

① It is true <u>that</u> the Earth is round.
② He is the man <u>that</u> truly loves me.
③ <u>That</u> boy is the tallest in the class.
④ Of the two books, I like this better than <u>that</u>.
⑤ Mr. Kim was so busy <u>that</u> he didn't go fishing last night.

27 다음 〈보기〉의 밑줄 친 부분과 의미가 같은 것은?

> That's just <u>what</u> I was thinking of.

① <u>What</u>'s your favorite song?
② <u>What</u> time shall we make it?
③ I didn't understand <u>what</u> he said.
④ He really doesn't know <u>what</u> to do.
⑤ Tell me <u>what</u> books you bought then.

28 다음 (A), (B), (C)에서 어법에 맞는 표현을 골라 짝지은 것을 고르시오.

> My father and I were walking on the street **(A) [which / where]** was not busy. We saw a few dogs **(B) [who / which]** were running after a black cat. I asked my father the reason **(C) [why / when]** the dogs were chasing the black cat, but he continued to walk without saying a word.

① where - who - why
② which - which - why
③ where - which - why
④ which - who - when
⑤ where - which - when

[29-30] 다음 두 문장이 같은 뜻이 되도록 문장을 완성하시오.

29 He will help anyone who needs his support.
⇒ He will help _____ needs his support.

30 No matter what you do, you will not succeed.
⇒ _____ you do, you will not succeed.

[31-32] 다음 우리말과 같은 뜻이 되도록 괄호 안의 단어를 알맞게 배열하여 문장을 완성하시오.

31 나는 네가 말한 것을 듣지 못했다. (said, you, what)
⇒ I didn't hear _____ .

32 그는 산책할 때마다, 선글라스를 쓴다.
(he, takes, a, whenever, walk)
⇒ _____ ,
he wears sunglasses.

[33-34] 다음 두 문장을 한 문장으로 바꿔 쓰시오.

33 I have two daughters. They are journalists.
⇒ _____

34 She is the girl. I asked her the way to the hotel this morning.
⇒ _____
_____

[35-36] 다음 우리말과 같은 뜻이 되도록 괄호 안의 단어를 사용하여 문장을 완성하시오.

35 당신이 무엇을 하든, 우리는 항상 당신을 사랑할 것입니다. (do)
⇒ _____ ,
we'll always love you.

36 그가 아무리 똑똑하다 하더라도 그 문제를 풀 수는 없다.
(smart)
⇒ _____
_____ , he can't solve the problem.

Answers: p.37

[1-2] 다음 글을 읽고, 물음에 답하시오. 서술형

Rafael is an artist. He draws and paints very well. People love the pictures (A) _____ he makes. But there's something unusual about Rafael and his art. The thing is that he draws and creates pictures without using paint or a brush. In fact, he draws in the dust on cars. Rafael uses his fingers and moves them around in the dust on a car. His fingers make lines in the dust, and beautiful buildings and birds appear on the car. The pictures look so cool. People leave their dusty cars at (B) _____. They want Rafael to draw on them. For the small price of a parking fee, they get a wonderful work of art.

1 밑줄 친 (A)에 들어갈 단어를 글에서 찾아 쓰시오.

→ _____

2 (B)에 들어갈 말을 괄호에 주어진 단어로 알맞게 배열하시오.

→ _____ (Rafael, where, the parking lot, works)

3 다음 글의 밑줄 친 부분 중, 어법상 틀린 것은? 수능 대비형

Recently I've learned ① to ride a bicycle and decided to ride one to work. The way to work has some nice scenery. First, I ride along the small park ② where I usually spend time with my friends on weekends. ③ On weekdays, I see an old man reading a newspaper on a green bench. After I pass the park, I ④ have to cross a little bridge to get to the street where my office is located. Then, I see a fruit store ⑤ when I often buy fruit after work. Two blocks further is my favorite record store. After a long and busy day at work, I stop by the store and enjoy listening to all kinds of music.

* scenery: 경치
** locate: 두다, 설치하다

Chapter

11

접속사, 전치사

🔖 **both A and B** : A와 B 모두 다
- **Both** animals **and** plants need water. 동물과 식물 모두 물이 필요하다.
- Johnson can speak **both** English **and** French. Johnson은 영어와 프랑스어를 모두 할 수 있다.

🔖 **not only A but (also) B** : A뿐만 아니라 B도 (= B as well as A)
- **Not only** she **but (also)** I am afraid of the dark.
  = I **as well as** she am afraid of the dark.
  그녀뿐만 아니라 나도 어둠을 무서워한다.
- The movie is **not only** interesting **but (also)** fantastic.
  = The movie is fantastic **as well as** interesting.
  그 영화는 재미있을 뿐 아니라 환상적이다.

> **TIPs** 상관접속사가 포함된 주어는 B에 동사의 수를 일치시킨다. 단, both A and B는 복수동사로 받는다.
> - **Either you or he has to go there.** 너와 그 둘 중 한 명이 그곳에 가야 한다.
> - **Both you and he have to go there.** 너와 그 둘 다 그곳에 가야 한다.

🔖 **either A or B** : A 또는 B 둘 중 하나
- **Either** he **or** I am to blame. 그와 나 둘 중 한 명 탓이다.
- You can take **either** this one **or** that one. 당신은 이것과 저것 중 하나를 가져갈 수 있다.

🔖 **neither A nor B** : A와 B 둘 다 아닌
- I met **neither** him **nor** her. 나는 그와 그녀 둘 다 만나지 않았다.
- **Neither** he **nor** I am going to the festival. 그와 나 둘 다 축제에 가지 않을 것이다.

🔖 **not A but B** : A가 아니라 B
- He is **not** a soldier **but** a police officer. 그는 군인이 아니라 경찰관이다.
- Her father is **not** an attorney **but** a judge. 그녀의 아버지는 변호사가 아니라 판사이다.

Answers: p.37

Exercise 1 다음 괄호 안에서 알맞은 것을 고르시오.

1 Sally is not a teacher (and / but) a student.

2 I can (either / neither) confirm nor deny his claim.

3 The exam tested both listening (or / and) reading.

4 Not only you (and / but) he must do the spring-cleaning.

5 In my school, we can choose (either / both) French or German as a second foreign language.

Exercise 2 다음 괄호 안에서 알맞은 것을 고르시오.

1 Either my father or my brother (help / helps) him.

2 Not only she but her parents (is / are) famous writers.

3 Both Rachel and her sister (like / likes) summer sports.

4 Neither we nor he (is / are) going to do your homework.

5 She not only (sing / sings) songs very well but also (write / writes) songs.

다음 우리말과 같은 뜻이 되도록 문장을 완성하시오.

1 나뿐만 아니라 Erin도 스페인에 가게 될 것이다.
   ⇨ Erin _____ I is going to go to Spain.

2 너와 나 둘 중 한 명은 회의에 가야 한다.
   ⇨ _____ you _____ I must attend the meeting.

3 그와 그의 부인 둘 다 아직 도착하지 않았다.
   ⇨ _____ he _____ his wife has arrived yet.

4 Peter와 Jake 둘 다 축구를 잘한다.
   ⇨ _____ Peter _____ Jake play soccer well.

5 그 결과는 우연한 것이 아니라 계획된 것이었다.
   ⇨ The result was _____ by accident _____ by design.

Exercise 4 다음 문장을 읽고, 어법상 어색한 부분을 찾아 바르게 고치시오.

1 Neither his mother nor his sister are at home now.   ⇨ _____
2 You as well as your brother has to go for a regular check-up.   ⇨ _____
3 Both his novel and his essay was published at the same time.   ⇨ _____
4 Not only she but also I is very interested in ancient mythologies. ⇨ _____
5 Either my sister or my brother are going to join me to buy a new car. ⇨ _____

Exercise 5 다음 괄호 안의 어구를 사용하여 두 문장을 한 문장으로 바꿔 쓰시오.

1 He is selfish. He is irresponsible, too. (as well as)
   ⇨ _____

2 I do not have a pen. I do not have a pencil, either. (neither … nor)
   ⇨ _____

3 This book is useful. This book is amusing, too. (not only … but also)
   ⇨ _____

4 He speaks English fluently. She speaks English fluently, too. (both … and)
   ⇨ _____

5 Amanda didn't come to the party. Her best friend didn't come to the party, either. (neither … nor)
   ⇨ _____

종속접속사 I

☐ 명사절을 이끄는 접속사

❶ that : 접속사 that이 이끄는 절은 문장에서 주어, 목적어, 보어 역할을 한다.

· **That** the team won the championship is unbelievable. 〈주어〉

= It is unbelievable **that** the team won the championship. 그 팀이 우승했다는 것은 믿기 어렵다.

· I thought **that** the man standing by the tree was your father. 〈목적어〉
나는 나무 옆에 서 있는 남자가 너의 아버지라고 생각했어.

· What I mean is **that** we failed to rescue the hostages. 〈보어〉
내 말은 우리가 인질을 구하는 데 실패했다는 뜻이다.

❷ whether/if : 접속사 whether/if는 '~인지 아닌지'라는 뜻이며, 명사절을 이끈다.

· **Whether** he will win the award (or not) is not clear. 〈주어〉
그가 상을 받을지 아닐지는 확실하지 않다.

· We don't know **whether** he will come to the party or not. 〈목적어〉

= We don't know **if** he will come to the party or not.
우리는 그가 파티에 올지 안 올지 모른다.

· Our concern is **whether** the traffic is heavy or not. 〈보어〉
우리가 우려하는 것은 교통이 혼잡한지 아닌지이다.

> **TIPs**
> whether or not으로는 쓰지만
> if or not으로는 쓰지 않는다.
> · I don't know whether or not she likes Keith. 나는 그녀가 Keith를 좋아하는지 아닌지 모른다.
> · I don't know if or not she likes Smith. (X)

Answers: p.37

Exercise ❶ 다음 괄호 안에서 가장 알맞은 것을 고르시오.

1 I wonder (if / that) he ever loved me or not.

2 Are you sure (if / that) Mrs. Brown lives on Main Street?

3 It is certain (whether / that) I left my key in my car.

4 (Whether / That) you lost your laptop computer is unfortunate.

5 If she said (whether / that) she would do it, she will do it.

6 We can't predict (whether / if) or not it will be fine tomorrow.

7 I can't believe the fact (whether / that) he refused to help me.

8 We are not sure (whether / that) he will participate in the discussion or not.

Exercise ❷ 다음 빈칸에 whether와 that 중 가장 알맞은 것을 써넣으시오.

1 I want to know _____ he loves me or not.

2 I'm not sure _____ I can get there on time or not.

3 She told me _____ I should accept their apology.

4 It is uncertain _____ England will win the match or not.

5 The rumor _____ he was a famous actor made us surprised.

6 This graph shows _____ the number of the tourists is increasing.

🔍 **That you passed the exam was lucky.**
⇨ _____ It was lucky that you passed the exam. _____

1 That he had a car accident is sad.

⇨ _____

2 That she was still at home was strange.

⇨ _____

3 That she has no knowledge of American history is natural.

⇨ _____

4 That you gather information about the company is important.

⇨ _____

5 That he didn't get a wink of sleep for seventy-two hours is impossible.

⇨ _____

Exercise **4** 다음 우리말과 같은 뜻이 되도록 괄호 안의 단어를 사용하여 문장을 완성하시오. (단, 부정문은 축약형으로 쓸 것)

1 나는 그녀가 가버렸다는 사실을 믿을 수가 없다. (not, can, believe)

⇨ I _____ the fact _____ she's gone.

2 너는 콘서트가 취소되었다는 소식을 들었니? (cancel)

⇨ Did you hear the news _____ the concert was _____?

3 나는 그가 좋은 대통령이 될 수 있을지 없을지 궁금했다. (wonder)

⇨ I _____ he could be a good president.

4 나는 그녀가 내 생각에 동의할지 안 할지 모르겠다. (not, know)

⇨ I _____ she will agree to my idea _____

_____ .

5 그는 바이러스가 완전히 자신의 몸에서 사라졌는지 아닌지 확신하지 못한다. (not, be, sure)

⇨ He _____ _____ the virus is
completely gone from his body.

6 의사는 그에게 사고 후에 자신의 이름을 기억할 수 있었는지 아닌지 물었다. (ask)

⇨ The doctor _____ _____ _____ he could remember
his name after the accident.

📑 부사절을 이끄는 접속사 **as**, **while**, **if**

❶ **as**는 '～할 때', '～ 때문에', '～함에 따라', '～처럼', '～대로'라는 의미를 가진다.

· **As** he entered the room, he felt dizzy. 그는 방에 들어갈 때, 어지러움을 느꼈다.

· **As** it was rainy season, it rained pretty hard. 장마철이라 비가 꽤 많이 내렸다.

· **As** she grew older, she became more and more beautiful. 그녀는 나이를 먹으면서, 점점 더 예뻐졌다.

· Just do **as** he said. 그가 말한 대로 해라.

❷ **while**은 '～하는 동안', '～하는 사이에'라는 의미를 가진다.

· He ate dinner **while** he was watching TV. 그는 TV를 보면서 저녁식사를 했다.

· **While** I was vacuuming the carpet, my sister took out the garbage.
내가 진공청소기로 카펫을 청소하는 동안, 내 여동생은 쓰레기를 내다 놓았다.

❸ **if**는 '～한다면'이라는 의미를 가진다.

> **TIPs**
> 「if ~ not」은 unless로 바꿔 표현 할 수 있다.

· **If** you take a short cut, you'll get there in time.
지름길로 가면 제시간에 그곳에 도착할 거야.

· **If** you don't study hard, you can't pass the exam.
= **Unless** you study hard, you can't pass the exam. 열심히 공부하지 않으면, 시험에 떨어질 거야.

Answers: p.38

Exercise ① 다음 괄호 안에서 알맞은 것을 고르시오.

1 (If / While) I was waiting for a bus, it started to rain.

2 (If / While) it rains tomorrow, we will reschedule our field trip.

3 He read the newspaper (if / while) he was listening to the radio.

4 (As / Unless) time goes by, our friendship will get deeper and deeper.

5 (If / Unless) you stop smoking, your health condition will become worse.

6 She happened to meet her friend (as / unless) she walked down the street.

Exercise ② 다음 우리말과 같은 뜻이 되도록 문장을 완성하시오.

1 날이 점점 추워져서, 나는 불을 지폈다.
⇨ _____ it was getting cold, I made a fire.

2 나는 서울에 머무르는 동안, 한국어를 배웠다.
⇨ _____ I stayed in Seoul, I learned Korean.

3 시간이 지남에 따라, 그는 점점 약해지는 것을 느꼈다.
⇨ _____ time passed, he felt weaker and weaker.

4 우리의 규칙을 따르지 않으면, 당신은 회원자격을 잃게 될 것입니다.
⇨ _____ you follow our rules, you will lose your membership.

□ **부사절을 이끄는 접속사 since, until**

❶ since는 접속사로 '~한 이래로', '~ 때문에' 등의 의미를 가지고, '~한 이래로'라는 뜻으로 쓰일 때는 주로 현재완료 문장과 함께 쓴다.

· She has been working at the bank **since** she was twenty.
그녀는 20세부터 은행에서 근무하고 있다.

· He can't come **since** he is very busy these days.
그는 요즘 매우 바빠서 올 수 없다.

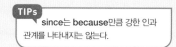

TIPs
since는 because만큼 강한 인과 관계를 나타내지는 않는다.

❷ until은 시간의 계속을 나타내어 '~할 때까지'라는 의미를 가진다.

· I'll wait here **until** the game is over. 경기가 끝날 때까지 여기서 기다릴게.

· You can't go out and play **until** you finish your homework. 너는 숙제를 끝마칠 때까지 나가 놀 수 없어.

Answers: p.38

Exercise ❶ 다음 괄호 안에서 알맞은 것을 고르시오.

1 You have to wait here (until / since) the road is clear.

2 He kept on eating all the food from the fridge (until / since) he no longer felt hungry.

3 The church has been standing on the hill (until / since) 2002.

4 She had never given up her dream (until / since) she succeeded.

5 I usually take the subway to work (until / since) it is faster than the bus.

6 She has been listening to the radio (until / since) she came back home.

Exercise ❷ 다음 우리말과 같은 뜻이 되도록 괄호 안의 단어를 알맞게 배열하여 문장을 완성하시오.

1 군인들은 전쟁이 끝날 때까지 집에 돌아가지 못한다. (over, until, is, the war)

⇨ The soldiers can't come back home _____ .

2 나는 열 살 이후로 아파트에 살고 있다. (have, the apartment, I, since, in, lived)

⇨ _____ I was ten.

3 그는 모든 사람이 방을 떠날 때까지 의자에 앉아 있었다. (the, everyone, until, room, left)

⇨ He had been sitting on the chair _____ .

4 그는 고등학교를 졸업한 이후로 뉴욕에 머무르고 있다. (New York, since, staying, he, been, has, in)

⇨ _____ he graduated from high school.

5 그 경기입장권이 다 팔려서, 우리는 TV로 경기를 시청해야 한다.
(sold out, to, since, been, the tickets, the match, have)

⇨ _____ , we have to watch it on TV.

11-5 종속접속사 Ⅳ

📑 부사절을 이끄는 접속사 even though, although, though, even if

❶ 접속사 even though, although, though는 '비록 ~일지라도', '~라고 할지라도'라는 의미를 가진다.

· **Though** she was young, she was very smart. 그녀는 어리지만, 매우 영리했다.
· **Even though** I love her, I can't marry her. 나는 그녀를 사랑하지만, 그녀와 결혼할 수 없다.

❷ 접속사 even if는 '(비록) ~이라고 할지라도'라는 의미로 어떤 한 가지 일이 발생하더라도 다른 일에는 변함이 없다는 것을 강조할 때 사용한다.

· **Even if** it rains tomorrow, we will play soccer.
내일 비가 온다 하더라도 우리는 축구를 할 것이다.
· **Even if** I invite her, she will not come to the party.
내가 그녀를 초대하더라도 그녀는 파티에 오지 않을 것이다.

> **TIPs**
> despite, in spite of는 전치사로 '~에도 불구하고'라는 의미를 가진다.
> · **Despite heavy rain, they went fishing.** 그들은 폭우에도 불구하고 낚시를 갔다.

Answers: p.38

Exercise 1 다음 괄호 안에서 알맞은 것을 고르시오.

1 He kept going on a diet (even if / despite) a doctor's warning.

2 All the trains arrived on time (although / in spite of) heavy snow.

3 (Even if / In spite of) it rains tomorrow, the concert will not be canceled.

4 (Although / Despite) there was a traffic jam, we could arrive there in time.

5 (Though / Despite) she is in her twenties now, she still looks like a teenager.

6 (Even though / Despite) he is a basketball player, he is shorter than average height.

Exercise 2 다음 우리말과 같은 뜻이 되도록 괄호 안의 말의 사용하여 문장을 완성하시오. (단, 한 칸에 한 단어씩 쓸 것)

1 비록 그는 가난하지만, 나는 그를 사랑한다. (be, poor)

⇨ _____ _____ _____ _____, I love him.

2 나는 비록 밤을 꼬박 새웠지만, 졸리지 않다. (stay up)

⇨ _____ _____ _____ _____ the whole night, I'm not sleepy.

3 그녀의 모든 노력에도, 그들은 프로젝트를 시간 내에 끝낼 수 없었다. (all one's efforts)

⇨ _____ _____ _____ _____, they couldn't finish the project in time.

4 내일 경기에서 우리가 이길 수 없을지라도, 우리는 최선을 다 할 것이다. (win)

⇨ _____ _____ _____ can't _____ the game tomorrow, we'll do our best.

5 나쁜 날씨에도 불구하고, 축구 경기는 계속될 것이다. (weather)

⇨ The soccer game will go on _____ _____ _____ the _____ _____.

11-6 기타 주요 접속사

📑 기타 주요 접속사

❶ so ~ that : 매우 (너무) ~해서 …하다
- The book is **so** difficult **that** I can't read it.
  = The book is **too** difficult for me **to** read. 그 책은 내가 읽기에는 너무 어렵다.

❷ so that : ~하기 위해, ~하도록
- Read the book clearly and loudly **so that** everybody can hear you.
  모두가 들을 수 있도록 그 책을 분명하고 큰 소리로 읽어라.

❸ no sooner ~ than : ~하자마자 …했다
- Tim had **no sooner** sent the e-mail **than** he regretted it.
  = **No sooner** had Tim sent the e-mail **than** he regretted it.
  Tim은 이메일을 보내자마자, 후회했다.

> **TIPs**
> no sooner ~ than은 as soon as로 바꿔 쓸 수 있다.
> - As soon as Tim sent the e-mail, he regretted it.

❹ not A until B : ~가 되어서야 …하다
- I did**n't** realize the value of the book **until** I was thirty.
  = **Not until** I was thirty **did I realize** the value of the book. 나는 서른 살이 되어서야 그 책의 가치를 깨달았다.

❺ by the time : ~할 때쯤
- I'll have finished the work **by the time** you get back. 네가 돌아올 때쯤에는 나는 그 일을 끝마쳤을 것이다.

Answers: p.38

Exercise 1 다음 우리말과 같은 뜻이 되도록 문장을 완성하시오.

1 경기가 시작되자마자, 비가 오기 시작했다.
⇨ The game had _____ started than it began to rain.

2 우리는 그가 돌아올 때쯤이면 청소를 끝마쳤을 것이다.
⇨ We will have finished cleaning _____ he comes back.

3 그는 시험에 합격하기 위해서 열심히 공부한다.
⇨ He studies hard _____ he may pass the examination.

4 우리는 건강을 잃고 나서야 건강의 가치를 안다.
⇨ We _____ its value _____ we lose our health.

5 우리는 그가 매우 친절해 보여서 머물기로 결정했다.
⇨ He looked _____ kind _____ we decided to stay.

6 그는 너무 어려서 혼자 지하철을 탈 수 없었다.
⇨ He was _____ young _____ take the subway by himself.

7 나는 잠자리에 들자마자 누군가 방문을 두드리는 소리를 들었다.
⇨ _____ had I gone to bed _____ I heard someone knocking on the door.

1 He walked too fast to follow.

⇨ He walked _____ fast _____ I couldn't follow him.

2 He exercises not to gain weight.

⇨ He exercises _____ _____ he may not gain weight.

3 Not until I told him the story did he know the truth.

⇨ He _____ _____ the truth _____ I told him the story.

4 Because he was so tired, he couldn't get up early in the morning.

⇨ He was _____ tired _____ he couldn't get up early in the morning.

5 As soon as they went out, the phone started to ring.

⇨ _____ _____ had they gone out _____ the phone started to ring.

6 The students climbed to the top of the mountain to see the sunrise.

⇨ The students climbed to the top of the mountain _____ _____ they _____ see the sunrise.

1 우리가 그 그림을 볼 수 있도록 불을 켜라.(that, we, the picture, can, so, see)

⇨ Turn on the light _____.

2 그 소년은 나를 보자마자 도망쳤다. (had, me, no sooner, seen, the boy, than)

⇨ _____ he ran away.

3 어젯밤에 너무 더워서 나는 잠을 잘 수가 없었다. (couldn't, that, hot, was, sleep, so, I, it)

⇨ _____ last night.

4 그녀는 업무로 너무 바빠서 휴가를 갈 수 없었다. (she, busy, her businesses, with, was, so)

⇨ _____ that she couldn't take a vacation.

5 그는 내 의견을 듣고 나서야 자기 의견을 나에게 말해 줬다. (tell, he, did, not until, my, heard, idea, he)

⇨ _____ me his idea.

6 그 지원자는 면접에 늦지 않으려고 지하철을 탔다. (would, so, she, not, be, that, the interview, late for)

⇨ The applicant took the subway _____.

7 그들은 너무 가난해서 서로에게 크리스마스 선물을 사 줄 수 없었다. (buy, so, they, poor, that, were, couldn't, they)

⇨ _____ Christmas gifts for each other.

전치사 I

쓰임	전치사	예문
원인/이유	from (~ 때문에) of (~로 인해)	Everyone suffered **from** the floods. 모든 사람이 그 홍수 때문에 고통 받았다. The elderly man died **of** lung cancer. 그 노인은 폐암으로 죽었다.
수단/도구/착용	by (~을 타고) in (~으로) in (~을 입은)	I often travel **by** train. 나는 종종 기차를 타고 여행한다. He explained the problem **in** English. 그는 그 문제를 영어로 설명했다. I met a pretty woman **in** red. 나는 빨간 옷을 입은 예쁜 여자를 만났다.
관련/언급	on (~에 관해)	I have to write a paper **on** crime. 나는 범죄에 관한 논문을 써야 한다.
찬성/반대	for (~에 찬성하는) against (~에 반대하는)	I voted **for** the candidate. 나는 그 후보자에게 (찬성) 투표를 했다. I am **against** his idea. 나는 그의 의견에 반대한다.
역할/자격/기능	as (~으로서) (~이라고)	He is famous **as** a singer. 그는 가수로 유명하다. We regard him **as** a genius. 우리는 그를 천재라고 생각한다.

Answers: p.38

Exercise 1 다음 〈보기〉에서 알맞은 것을 골라 문장을 완성하시오. (중복 사용 가능)

🔍　　**as**　　　　　**for**　　　　　**against**　　　　　**on**

1 I am looking for a book ＿＿＿＿＿＿ the Korean War.

2 They don't seem to take my remark ＿＿＿＿＿ a compliment.

3 They refused to fight ＿＿＿＿＿＿ the enemy, which was much stronger.

4 The gym was used ＿＿＿＿＿＿ a temporary classroom during the renovation.

5 Most of the lawmakers voted ＿＿＿＿＿＿ health care reform.

Exercise 2 다음 〈보기〉에서 알맞은 것을 골라 문장을 완성하시오. (중복 사용 가능)

🔍　　**by**　　　　　**in**　　　　　**from**　　　　　**of**

1 His nose was red ＿＿＿＿＿＿ the cold of the midnight air.

2 The girl ＿＿＿＿＿＿ red is the one who will guide sightseers.

3 His mother died ＿＿＿＿＿＿ a heart attack in her sleep last night.

4 We had an encounter with a strange woman dressed ＿＿＿＿＿＿ white.

5 Traveling ＿＿＿＿＿＿ air is much more expensive than traveling ＿＿＿＿＿＿ train.

1 나는 영문법에 관한 논문을 쓰고 있어. (on, a thesis, grammar, English, writing, I'm)

⇨ _____

2 그녀는 스트레스로 심각하게 고통 받고 있다. (has, stress, from, seriously suffering, she, been)

⇨ _____

3 그는 관리자로서 충분한 지도력을 보여주고 있지 않다. (isn't, a manager, showing, leadership, enough, as, he)

⇨ _____

4 우리가 그를 뽑아야 하는 이유가 뭐라고 생각해? (why, him, vote for, have to, we, the reason)

⇨ What do you think of _____ ?

5 제복을 입은 내 남동생은 매우 늠름해 보였다. (manly, uniform, his, very, in, looked)

⇨ My younger brother _____ .

6 나는 그 책이 프랑스어로 쓰여 있어서 읽을 수가 없다. (French, is, since, in, the book, written)

⇨ I can't read that book _____ .

7 그는 항상 나의 의견에 반대하고, 내 말은 한마디도 듣지 않는다. (opinion, always, against, he, my, is)

⇨ _____ , and he never listens to me.

8 매일 거의 만 육천 명의 아이들이 굶어 죽는다. (of, almost, children, die, sixteen-thousand, hunger)

⇨ Every day, _____ .

9 그는 대개 학교에 걸어가지만, 오늘은 자전거를 타고 갔다. (by, he, to, bike, went, school)

⇨ He usually goes to school on foot, but today _____ .

10 레오나르도 다빈치는 예술가로 알려져 있지만, 그는 또한 과학자이자 발명가였다. (as, artist, known, an, is)

⇨ Leonardo da Vinci _____ , but he was also a scientist and inventor.

11-8 전치사 II

thanks to ~ 덕분에	**Thanks to** her, I finished the work. 나는 그녀 덕분에 그 일을 끝마쳤다.
despite/in spite of ~에도 불구하고	**Despite** the high price, I bought the dress. 가격이 고가임에도 불구하고 나는 그 드레스를 샀다. **In spite of** his success, he doesn't look happy. 그는 성공에도 불구하고, 행복해 보이지 않는다.
according to ~에 따르면	**According to** the survey, the number of tourists has increased. 조사에 따르면, 관광객의 수가 증가했다.
instead of ~ 대신에, ~하지 않고	**Instead of** going to the beach, we went to the swimming pool. 우리는 해변에 가는 대신 수영장에 갔다.
in addition to ~뿐만 아니라, ~에 더하여	**In addition to** his help, I got her help. 나는 그의 도움뿐만 아니라 그녀의 도움도 받았다.

Answers: p.39

Exercise 1 다음 〈보기〉에서 알맞은 것을 골라 문장을 완성하시오.

🔍 **thanks to** **instead of** **despite** **according to** **in addition to**

1 _____ her help, I passed the exam.

2 _____ the pay raise, he got promoted.

3 The airport is functioning normally _____ the tornado.

4 _____ the research, the number of newborn babies has decreased.

5 Since it's raining outside, we will stay home and play board games _____ going to the movies.

Exercise 2 다음 우리말과 같은 뜻이 되도록 문장을 완성하시오.

1 나는 할 일이 많았음에도 일하러 가지 않았다.
   ⇨ _____ the fact that I had many things to do, I didn't go to work.

2 온종일 텔레비전만 보지 말고, 우리 나가서 산책하는 게 어때?
   ⇨ _____ watching TV all day, why don't we go out for a walk?

3 네 덕분에 나는 드디어 그림을 다시 시작하기로 결심했다.
   ⇨ _____ you, I have finally decided to take up drawing again.

4 Tom은 컴퓨터에 대한 열정도 있고, 생물학에도 관심이 있다.
   ⇨ _____ his passion for computers, Tom is interested in biology.

5 뉴스 기사에 따르면 세계 인구가 매우 빠르게 증가하고 있다.
   ⇨ _____ a news report, the world population is rising very fast.

11-9 동사, 형용사와 함께 쓰는 전치사

📑 동사와 함께 쓰는 전치사

consist of (~으로 이루어져 있다)	concentrate on (~에 집중하다)
laugh at (~을 비웃다)	participate in (~에 참여하다)
belong to (~에 속하다)	break into (~에 침입하다)
think of A as B (A를 B로 간주하다)	result from (~에서 기인하다)
look after (~을 돌보다)	look for (~을 찾다)
deal with (~을 다루다)	wait for (~을 기다리다)

· Water **consists of** hydrogen and oxygen. 물은 수소와 산소로 이루어져 있다.
· Police are still **looking for** the thief. 경찰은 여전히 그 도둑을 찾고 있다.

📑 형용사와 함께 쓰는 전치사

be afraid of (~을 두려워하다)	be used to (~에 익숙하다)
be poor at (~을 잘 못하다)	be good at (~에 능숙하다)
be proud of (~을 자랑스러워하다)	be tired of (~에 싫증이 나다)
be fond of (~을 좋아하다)	be famous for (~으로 유명하다)
be based on (~에 기반을 두다)	be composed of (~으로 이루어져 있다)

· We **were used to** working together. 우리는 함께 일하는 데 익숙했다.
· I'm **tired of** his long speech. 나는 그의 긴 연설에 싫증이 난다.
· The movie **is based on** a true story. 그 영화는 실화에 근거하고 있다.
· The longest word in English **is composed of** 45 letters. 영어의 가장 긴 단어는 45개의 글자로 이루어져 있다.

Answers: p.39

Exercise 1 다음 괄호 안에서 알맞은 것을 고르시오.

1 She is good (by / at) making things.

2 I think (of / about) him as a good friend.

3 He is proud (of / to) the success of his son.

4 The audience consisted mainly (in / of) teenagers.

5 I do the dishes every day, and I am used (for / to) it.

6 Don't worry, I'll look (to / after) the kids tomorrow.

7 Do you want to participate (out / in) the beauty contest?

8 The southern part of the island doesn't belong (to / in) us.

9 Someone broke (into / out) my car and stole the navigation.

10 They are used (to / as) what they are doing for the homeless.

11 This hotel is famous (as / for) its long history and the antique furniture.

12 The problems resulted (from / in) errors which were made in the past.

주의해야 할 접속사 / 전치사

📖 접속사+절(주어+동사 ~.) vs. 전치사+명사(상당어구)

의미	접속사	전치사
~ 때문에	because	because of
~에도 불구하고	though (although, even though)	despite
~하는 동안	while	during

- I can't go to school **because** I have a bad cold. 〈접속사〉
- I can't go to school **because of** a bad cold. 〈전치사〉 나는 독감 때문에 학교에 갈 수 없다.
- **Though** he is poor, he is happy. 〈접속사〉
- **Despite** his poverty, he is happy. 〈전치사〉 그는 가난할지라도 행복하다.

Answers: p.39

Exercise 1 다음 괄호 안에서 알맞은 것을 고르시오.

1   A burglar broke into his house (during / while) he was sleeping.

2   I took a taxi to work (because / because of) it was raining heavily.

3   Three lions died (while / during) a winter storm due to the cold weather.

4   We can't take a shower (because / because of) the short supply of water.

5   (Despite / Though) his poor health, Michael worked hard and succeeded.

Exercise 2 다음 우리말과 같은 뜻이 되도록 문장을 완성하시오.

1   봄이지만 아직도 춥다.

⇨ _____ it is spring, it is still cold.

2   그는 자신의 질병에도 불구하고 희망을 잃지 않았다.

⇨ He never lost his hope _____ his illness.

3   내가 샤워를 하는 동안 그가 전화했다.

⇨ _____ I was taking a shower, he called me.

4   Eugene은 초과 근무를 해야 했기 때문에 올 수 없었다.

⇨ Eugene couldn't come _____ he had to work overtime.

5   사냥철에 사냥꾼들은 밝은 옷을 입어야 한다.

⇨ Hunters must wear bright clothing _____ hunting season.

6   아이슬란드의 화산재 때문에, 영국 전역에 걸쳐 모든 비행편이 취소되었다.

⇨ _____ Icelandic volcanic ash, all flights over the UK were canceled.

[01-05] 다음 빈칸에 들어갈 알맞은 말을 고르시오.

01 _____ you or she has to clean the room.

① Both   ② Neither
③ And   ④ Either
⑤ Not only

02 I have been learning Korean history _____ I came here.

① so   ② so that
③ though   ④ when
⑤ since

03 They need _____ public and private investment.

① both   ② neither
③ so   ④ either
⑤ not only

04 _____ he is young, he can solve complicated problems.

① If   ② Despite
③ In spite of   ④ Because of
⑤ Even though

05 They are tired _____ wearing the same design and color.

① off   ② of
③ as   ④ at
⑤ like

[06-09] 다음 빈칸에 들어갈 말이 바르게 짝지어진 것을 고르시오.

06 · He invited _____ Eric and Tony to his birthday party.
· _____ she nor I liked the movie.
· I want to learn either Chinese _____ Japanese.

① both - Either - and
② either - Neither - or
③ neither - Both - and
④ either - Both - or
⑤ both - Neither - or

07 · The movie was so boring _____ I fell asleep.
· Make hay _____ the Sun shines.

① as - when   ② that - until
③ unless - while   ④ that - while
⑤ that - if

08 · It's natural that you're interested _____ girls.
· I can't concentrate _____ my studies.

① with - to   ② to - of
③ in - on   ④ on - of
⑤ of - on

09 · The book written _____ Chinese is too difficult to understand.
· For your health, you should drink juice _____ Coke.

① with - instead of   ② in - instead of
③ in - because of   ④ on - instead of
⑤ of - because

[10-11] 다음 우리말을 영어로 바르게 옮긴 것을 고르시오.

10 나뿐만 아니라 그도 학생이다.

① Either I or he is a student.
② Both I and he is a student.
③ He as well as I am a student.
④ Neither he nor I am a student.
⑤ Not only I but he is a student.

11 그들은 궂은 날씨에도 멋진 주말을 보냈다.

① They had a wonderful weekend since the bad weather.
② They had a wonderful weekend due to the bad weather.
③ They had a wonderful weekend despite the bad weather.
④ They had a wonderful weekend though the bad weather.
⑤ They had a wonderful weekend thanks to the bad weather.

[12-13] 다음 밑줄 친 부분과 바꿔 쓸 수 있는 것을 고르시오.

12 <u>Since</u> it was dark, no one could see me from the street.

① If ② Unless
③ Although ④ As
⑤ How

13 We are not sure <u>whether</u> she will be back or not.

① if ② unless
③ although ④ as
⑤ while

[14-15] 다음 〈보기〉의 밑줄 친 단어와 의미와 쓰임이 같은 것을 고르시오.

14 The traffic was very heavy <u>as</u> it rained a lot.

① I have the same bag <u>as</u> you have.
② We will pay three times <u>as</u> much.
③ She is very famous <u>as</u> a singer in Korea.
④ <u>As</u> they wanted to watch TV, they went to the living room.
⑤ <u>As</u> I entered the room, I saw my mom cleaning the room.

15 I have not seen her <u>since</u> I moved to New York.

① I have learned French <u>since</u> kindergarten.
② I have known him <u>since</u> I came here.
③ <u>Since</u> I don't have his address, I can't write a letter to him.
④ They haven't eaten anything <u>since</u> last weekend.
⑤ <u>Since</u> he was hungry, he wanted to eat something.

16 다음 〈보기〉의 밑줄 친 단어와 쓰임이 같은 것은?

It is unbelievable <u>that</u> he is alive.

① Which would you prefer, this or <u>that</u>?
② <u>That</u>'s the reason she came to see me.
③ It is embarrassing <u>that</u> my room is so messy.
④ This is the same camera <u>that</u> I bought yesterday.
⑤ I heard the news <u>that</u> the volcano erupted last night.

[17-19] 다음 우리말과 같은 뜻이 되도록 빈칸에 알맞은 말을 고르시오.

17 그의 도움 덕분에 나는 덴마크에서 직업을 구할 수 있었다.

⇒ _____ his help, I could find a job in Denmark.

① According to　② Despite
③ In spite of　④ Instead of
⑤ Thanks to

18 일기예보에 따르면 밤늦게 눈이 올 것이다.

⇒ _____ the weather forecast, it'll snow late at night.

① According to　② Despite
③ In spite of　④ Instead of
⑤ Thanks to

19 날씨가 좋지 않았음에도 개회식이 계획대로 열렸다.

⇒ _____ the bad weather, the opening ceremony was held as scheduled.

① Owing to　② In addition to
③ In spite of　④ Instead of
⑤ Thanks to

[20-22] 다음 두 문장이 같은 뜻이 되도록 문장을 완성하시오.

20 The boy was too short to reach the top shelf.
⇒ The boy was _____
short _____ he _____
_____ the top shelf.

21 As soon as she came home, she started to cook.
⇒ She had _____ _____ come home than she started to cook.

22 We sent them not only some money but also some food.
⇒ We sent them some food _____
_____ some money.

[23-24] 다음 빈칸에 공통으로 들어갈 알맞은 말을 고르시오.

23
· The movie was based _____ his novel.
· The book _____ foreign affairs is very useful.

① in　② on
③ of　④ off
⑤ at

24
· We are proud _____ our traditional clothes.
· They are afraid _____ being laughed at.

① in　② on
③ of　④ off
⑤ at

[25-26] 다음 두 문장이 같은 뜻이 되도록 빈칸에 들어갈 알맞은 말을 고르시오.

25 If you're not a student, you can't get a discount.
⇒ _____ you're a student, you can't get a discount.

① Since　② Unless
③ If　④ As
⑤ Though

26 Despite her many faults, all of my classmates like her a lot.

⇒ _____ her many faults, all of my classmates like her a lot.

① Even though   ② Since
③ In spite of   ④ Because of
⑤ As

[27-29] 다음 중 어색한 문장을 고르시오.

27 ① If you hurry up, you'll catch the bus.
② While I was cooking, he talked on the phone.
③ He has been living in London since last year.
④ Though he was thirsty, he wanted to drink something.
⑤ She practiced so hard that she could pass the audition.

28 ① We are used to eat raw fish.
② She's better at English than me.
③ Burglars broke into a jewelry shop last night.
④ Thanks to him, I could avoid the accident.
⑤ Many students are against the new school policy.

29 ① The novel was not only interesting but also moving.
② It is certain that she will attend the wedding ceremony.
③ I don't know if she is the girl we are looking for or not.
④ If you are busy tomorrow, let's go to the beach.
⑤ My brother woke up so late that he was late for school.

[30-33] 다음 〈보기〉에서 알맞은 것을 골라 문장을 완성하시오.

보기 | after   for   of   while   as   to

30 Who does this laptop computer belong _____?

31 I have been waiting _____ you here for almost two hours.

32 James is very fond _____ fishing, so he goes fishing once a week.

33 She needs someone to look _____ her baby _____ she is working at the hospital _____ a nurse.

[34-36] 다음 괄호 안의 말을 사용하여 문장을 완성하시오.

34 그는 그 집을 살 수 있는 충분한 돈이 있었음에도 불구하고, 그 집을 사지 않았다. (have)

⇒ _____ _____ _____ _____ _____ _____ to buy that house, he didn't buy it.

35 그가 집을 나서자마자, 눈이 내리기 시작했다. (sooner)

⇒ _____ _____ he left his house than it started to snow.

36 이 영어 책은 열 개의 장으로 구성되어 있다. (consist, chapter)

⇒ This English book _____ _____ _____.

Answers: p.40

[1-3] 다음 대화를 읽고, 물음에 답하시오. `서술형`

> A I texted you an hour ago. Didn't you get it?
>
> B Really? ⓐ아마도 내가 요리하고 있을 때 네가 문자를 했나 봐. What's up?
>
> A I have two tickets to the K-pop Mega Concert. I wonder ① _____ you'd like to join me.
>
> B Great! When is it?
>
> A It's tomorrow at 8 p.m. It is held at the Olympic Stadium.
>
> B We'd better have dinner before the show. When shall we meet?
>
> A We should get into the stadium ② _____ 7:30, so let's meet at 6 at the burger place.

1 위에 밑줄 친 ⓐ와 일치하도록 주어진 단어를 배열하여 문장을 완성하시오.

> was, you, while, maybe, me, texted, I, cooking

→ _____

2 위에 빈칸 ①에 들어갈 알맞은 접속사를 쓰시오.

→ _____

3 위에 빈칸 ②에 들어갈 알맞은 전치사를 쓰시오

→ _____

4 다음 글의 밑줄 친 부분 중, 어법상 틀린 것은? `수능 대비형`

 Five or ten years ago, college graduates ① could finish school feeling confident they would find a job and begin a good career. But these days the situation is very different. With a troubled economy, very few college graduates are able to find work immediately ② after graduation. Fewer companies are hiring new workers ③ because of they simply can't afford to do so. ④ Instead, many graduates are moving in with their parents to save money and accepting unpaid internships ⑤ to gain experience on the job.

* graduate: 졸업생
** confident: 자신감 있는
*** unpaid: 무보수의, 무급의

Chapter
12

특수 구문

12-1 병렬구조

📑 **병렬구조**

문장 안에서 두 어구 이상이 접속사로 연결되어 나란히 쓰이는 형태를 병렬구조라고 한다. 병렬구조에 쓰인 어구는 대체로 서로 동일한 성분으로 이루어진다.

- **Both** <u>listening</u> **and** <u>reading</u> are important. 〈동명사+동명사〉 듣기와 읽기는 둘 다 중요하다.
- You should **either** <u>see a doctor</u> **or** <u>get some rest at home</u>. 〈구+구〉 너는 진찰을 받든지 집에서 좀 쉬든지 해야겠다.

📑 **병렬구조를 이끄는 접속사**

등위접속사	상관접속사
and, or, but 등	both A and B (A와 B 모두) not A but B (A가 아니라 B) not only A but also B (A뿐만 아니라 B도) either A or B (A와 B 중 하나) neither A nor B (A와 B 둘 다 아닌)

- He enjoys writing <u>songs</u> **and** <u>poems</u>. 그는 노래와 시를 쓰는 것을 즐긴다.
- Flies are **not only** <u>annoying</u> **but also** <u>harmful</u>. 파리는 귀찮을 뿐만 아니라 해롭다.
- **Either** <u>he</u> **or** <u>I</u> have to clean up the mess. 그와 나 둘 중 한 명이 어질러진 것을 치워야 한다.

Answers: p.41

Exercise 1 다음 괄호 안에서 알맞은 것을 고르시오.

1 Both you and (I / me) have to stay here.

2 I love both watching and (play / playing) sports.

3 I can speak neither German nor (French / speak French).

4 The key must be either in my bag or (the table / on the table).

5 He went into the bank and (withdrew / to withdraw) some money.

Exercise 2 다음 우리말과 같은 뜻이 되도록 괄호 안의 단어를 알맞게 배열하여 문장을 완성하시오.

1 그는 가수가 아니라 댄서이다. (dancer, singer, a, a, not, but)

    ⇨ He is _____ .

2 나는 식료품점에 가서 수박 하나를 샀다. (watermelon, and, a, bought)

    ⇨ I went to the grocery store _____ .

3 너는 그에게 전화를 하든지 이메일을 쓰든지 해야 한다. (e-mail, call, either, him, or)

    ⇨ You have to _____ .

4 나는 그 책을 너의 가방 안에서도 너의 책상 위에서도 찾을 수 없었다. (bag, desk, nor, neither, in, on, your, your)

    ⇨ I could find the book _____ .

5 Bella는 노래하는 것뿐만 아니라 춤추는 것에도 소질이 있다. (but also, singing, not only, is talented in, dancing)

    ⇨ Bella _____ .

□ **병렬구조의 형태**

❶ 명사(대명사)
- Both **you** and **I** are fond of music. 너와 나 모두 음악을 좋아한다.
- He is not **a doctor** but **a nurse**. 그는 의사가 아니라 간호사이다.

❷ 형용사
- Kate is **pretty**, **smart**, and **attractive**. Kate는 예쁘고 똑똑하고 매력적이다.
- She is not only **smart** but **attractive**. 그녀는 똑똑할 뿐만 아니라 매력적이다.

❸ 부사
- I did my job **well** and **quickly**. 나는 일을 잘 그리고 빨리 처리했다.
- Study English both **hard** and **steadily**. 열심히 그리고 꾸준히 영어를 공부해라.

❹ 전치사구
- He was neither **at school** nor **at home**. 그는 학교에도 집에도 없었다.

❺ 동사
- I neither **drink** nor **smoke**. 나는 술도 안 먹고 담배도 피우지 않는다.
- Josh not only **speaks**, but also **writes** Japanese. Josh는 일본어로 말을 할 줄 뿐만 아니라 쓸 줄도 안다.

❻ 부정사/동명사
- **To be** or **not to be**, that is a question. 사느냐 죽느냐, 그것이 문제로다.
- Neither **lying** nor **sitting** helps. 누워 있거나 앉아 있는 것은 도움이 안 된다.

❼ 구 : How do you go to school, **by bus** or **on foot**? 너는 학교에 버스로 가니 아니면 걸어서 가니?

❽ 절 : **He worked hard**, but **he failed**. 그는 열심히 일했으나 실패했다.

Answers: p.41

Exercise 1 다음 괄호 안에서 알맞은 것을 고르시오.

1 He is not only honest but (kind / kindness).

2 My dad both designed and (build / built) our house.

3 She was neither in the room nor (in / was in) the garden.

4 Jimmy studies hard not for himself but (his mother / for his mother).

Exercise 2 다음 〈보기〉와 같이 병렬 관계에 있는 부분에 밑줄을 그으시오.

🔍 **Nicky can play not only the piano but also the cello.**

1 I have done this not for me but for you.

2 Neither Eric nor his wife is interested in home decoration.

3 You should either tell him the whole thing or keep it to yourself.

4 Both collecting old coins and making miniatures are my hobbies.

5 I was home yesterday not because I had nothing to do, but because I was sick.

동격

☐ **동격**

동격은 명사나 대명사의 의미를 보충하거나, 동일한 사물이나 사람을 다른 말로 표현할 때 사용한다.

동격은 주로 명사나 대명사 뒤에 또 다른 명사[명사구, 명사절]가 오는 구조로 이루어진다.

❶ 쉼표 (,)

· Harry, Mindy's husband, is a surgeon. Mindy의 남편인 Harry는 외과의사이다.
· I visited Madrid, the capital of Spain, during the summer break.
  나는 여름방학 동안에 스페인의 수도인 마드리드를 방문했다.

❷ 동격의 of

· I don't like the idea of borrowing money from the bank. 나는 은행에서 돈을 빌린다는 생각을 좋아하지 않는다.
· My bad habit of biting my nails is not easy to get rid of. 손톱을 물어뜯는 나의 나쁜 습관은 고치기 쉽지 않다.

❸ 동격의 접속사 that

· The detective found the evidence that she killed the politician.
  그 형사는 그녀가 그 정치인을 죽였다는 증거를 발견하였다.

· The rumor that James would leave the company turned out to be true.
  James가 회사를 떠난다는 소문은 사실로 밝혀졌다.

Answers: p.41

Exercise 1 다음 밑줄 친 부분과 동격을 이루는 부분에 밑줄을 그으시오.

1 The fact that Jerry left Bonnie doesn't surprise me.

2 Tommy, one of my classmates, helped me find the key.

3 The idea of living in the countryside sounds appealing to me.

4 I can't believe the news that the Raiders won the championship.

5 My plan of losing weight and getting into better shape in three months has failed.

Exercise 2 다음 우리말과 같은 뜻이 되도록 괄호 안의 단어를 사용하여 문장을 완성하시오.

1 동물의 뼈를 수집하는 너의 취미는 상당히 별나다. (of, collect)

   ⇨ _____ animal bones is quite unusual.

2 내가 손님 목록에 없었다는 사실이 나를 화나게 했다. (the fact, on the guest list)

   ⇨ _____ made me upset.

3 너의 절친한 친구 Timothy가 방금 전화해서 메시지를 남겼다. (Timothy, best friend)

   ⇨ _____, _____, just called and left a message.

4 베이컨을 미끼로 쓰겠다는 너의 아이디어는 완벽했다. (of, use, bacon as bait)

   ⇨ _____ was perfect.

5 일본의 수도인 도쿄는 세계에서 가장 물가가 비싼 도시 중 하나다. (Tokyo, the capital, of)

   ⇨ _____, _____, is one of the most expensive cities
   in the world.

동사의 강조

do/does/did를 일반동사의 원형 앞에 놓아 동사의 의미를 강조한다. '정말 ∼하다'로 해석한다.

- You **do** look great today! 너는 오늘 정말 멋져 보인다!
- I **did** tell him everything, but he didn't believe what I said.
  나는 정말로 그에게 모든 것을 말했지만, 그는 나의 말을 믿지 않았어.

명사(대명사)의 강조

❶ 「the very+명사」 : '바로 그 ∼'
  - This is **the very** book that I want to read. 이것이 내가 읽고 싶은 바로 그 책이다.
❷ 「(대)명사+oneself」 : '∼가 직접'
  - I **myself** finished my homework. 나는 나 스스로 숙제를 끝마쳤다.

비교급 · 최상급의 강조

❶ 비교급 강조 : much, still, even, far, a lot
  - This problem is **much** more difficult than that one. 이 문제는 저것보다 훨씬 더 어렵다.
❷ 최상급 강조 : much, by far, the very
  - He is **by far** the smartest student in this school. 그는 이 학교에서 단연 가장 똑똑한 학생이다.

부정문 강조 : at all '전혀'

- He cannot speak English **at all**. 그는 전혀 영어를 말할 줄 모른다.

의문문 강조: on earth, in the world '도대체'

- Why **on earth** are you waiting for him? 도대체 왜 너는 그를 기다리고 있는 거니?

Answers: p.41

Exercise 1 다음 문장에서 강조를 위해 사용된 말에 밑줄을 그으시오.

1 My dad repaired his car himself.

2 What on earth did you do there?

3 I did have a good time with them.

4 Who in the world told you to do that?

5 You are the very woman I want to see.

6 Dogs can run much faster than humans.

7 This is the very ring that I was looking for.

8 My daughter herself solved the difficult problem.

9 You should have been more careful. I did warn you.

10 This sofa is even more comfortable than I expected.

11 Emily does look pale. I think she should go see a doctor.

12 Ms. Charlton did drop by his office, but she couldn't meet him.

🔍 does	by far	the very	myself	at all	on earth

1 내가 직접 그 멋진 모래성을 지었다.

⇒ I _____ built the wonderful sandcastle.

2 그는 정말로 우리가 자신의 파티에 오기를 바란다.

⇒ He _____ want us to come to his party.

3 그는 프랑스에서 단연 가장 재능 있는 디자이너이다.

⇒ He is _____ the most talented designer in France.

4 너는 도대체 어떻게 굴뚝에 들어간 거니?

⇒ How _____ did you get into the chimney?

5 그가 내가 찾던 바로 그 사람이다.

⇒ He is _____ man that I've been looking for.

6 Lauren은 다른 사람들의 말을 전혀 신경 쓰지 않는다.

⇒ Lauren doesn't care what other people say _____ .

1 우리 형이 직접 그 울타리 모두를 페인트칠했다. (paint)

⇒ My big brother _____ _____ all the fences.

2 오늘 Jones 씨가 정말 피곤해 보이네요. (exhausted)

⇒ Mr. Jones _____ _____ _____ today.

3 너의 새로운 아이디어가 이전 것보다 훨씬 더 좋다. (far)

⇒ Your new idea is _____ _____ _____ the previous one.

4 그가 준 안내서는 나에게 전혀 도움이 되지 않는다. (help)

⇒ The guidebook that he gave me _____ _____ me

_____ .

5 그가 내가 길을 잃었을 때 나를 도와준 바로 그 사람이다. (man)

⇒ He is _____ _____ _____ _____ helped me when

I was lost.

6 그는 도대체 왜 너를 그렇게 괴롭히는 거니? (bother)

⇒ _____ _____ _____ _____ _____

you so much?

「It is[was] ~ that …」 강조 구문

□ 「It is[was] ~ that …」 강조 구문

주어, 목적어, 부사구 등을 강조할 때 「It ~ that …」 구문을 이용한다. 강조하고자 하는 말을 that 앞에 놓고, '…한 것은 (바로) ~이다'라고 해석한다.

· Tiffany met Evan at Kevin's party.

⇒ It was Tiffany **that[who]** met Evan at Kevin's party. 〈주어 강조〉
Kevin의 파티에서 Evan을 만난 사람은 Tiffany였다.

⇒ It was Evan **that[whom]** Tiffany met at Kevin's party. 〈목적어 강조〉
Tiffany가 Kevin의 파티에서 만난 사람은 Evan이었다.

⇒ It was at Kevin's party **that[where]** Tiffany met Evan. 〈부사구 강조〉
Tiffany가 Evan을 만난 곳은 Kevin의 파티였다.

> **TIPs**
> 강조하는 대상이 무엇인지에 따라
> **that**은 관계사 who[whom](사람),
> **which**(물건), **where**(장소), **when**(때)으
> 로 바꿔 쓸 수 있다.

Answers: p.42

Exercise 1 다음 〈보기〉에서 알맞은 것을 골라 문장을 완성하시오.

🔍   when   where   which   who

1   It is Mr. Murphy _____ teaches us Spanish.

2   It was in New York _____ he spent his remaining years.

3   It was the day before yesterday _____ Carol visited me.

4   It was just a bottle of soda _____ I bought from the grocery store.

Exercise 2 다음 밑줄 친 부분을 강조하는 문장으로 바꿔 쓰시오.

1   I found the necklace on the bed.

⇒ _____

2   I graduated from Yale three years ago.

⇒ _____

3   Columbus discovered America in 1492.

⇒ _____

4   I ran into Gary on my way from school.

⇒ _____

5   I borrowed five dollars from Mary yesterday.

⇒ _____

6   Rachel majored in English Literature at Oxford University.

⇒ _____

12-6 도치

📑 **도치**

문장의 어순이 뒤바뀌는 것을 도치라 하는데, 주로 부정어, 보어, 부사를 강조하기 위해 문장의 첫머리로 보내는 경우를 일컫는다.

❶ 부사(구)의 도치 : 「부사(구)+동사+주어 ~」
- **Under the couch** were the socks that I was looking for.
  소파 밑에 내가 찾던 양말이 있었다.
- **There** goes my mother! 저기 저의 어머니가 가고 있어요!

❷ 부정어의 도치 : 「부정어+동사+주어 ~」
- **Never** did I see him again. 나는 다시는 그를 만나지 않았다.
- **Not only** was he brave, but he was wise.
  그는 용감했을 뿐만 아니라 현명하였다.
- **Hardly** can I focus on study. 나는 도저히 공부에 집중할 수가 없다.

❸ **so, neither**의 도치문 : 「**so/neither**+동사+주어」
- A: I'm so tired. 나는 매우 피곤하다.
  B: **So am I**. (= I am tired, too.) 나도 그렇다.
- A: I don't drive a car. 나는 운전하지 않는다.
  B: **Neither do I**. (= I don't drive a car, either.) 나도 그렇다.

> **TIPs**
> 부사 **there, here**가 도치될 때 주어가 인칭대명사이면 주어와 동사는 도치되지 않는다.
> • **Here I go.** (O) / **Here go I.** (X)
> 자, 한다.

> **TIPs**
> 일반동사가 자동사일 경우 자동사 자체가 주어 앞에 오기도 한다.
> • **Along the street** stand lots of shops.
> 거리를 따라 가게가 즐비하게 서 있었다.

> **TIPs**
> **hardly, rarely, little** 등과 같은 표현은 부정의 의미가 포함되어 있으므로 **not**과 함께 쓰지 않는다.

Answers: p.42

Exercise 1 다음 밑줄 친 부사(구)를 강조하는 문장으로 바꿔 쓰시오.

1 The rain came down.
⇨ _____

2 Your wristwatch was in the restroom.
⇨ _____

3 The document was right on his desk.
⇨ _____

4 Steps leading downstairs are behind the door.
⇨ _____

5 The books written by Hemingway were on the desk.
⇨ _____

6 The statue of Don Quixote is in front of the building.
⇨ _____

7 A children's hospital stands at the corner of James and Victoria Streets.
⇨ _____

Exercise 2 다음 밑줄 친 부정어를 강조하는 문장으로 바꿔 쓰시오.

1 I know little about him.

   ⇨ _____

2 It rarely snows in Busan.

   ⇨ _____

3 I can hardly believe what he said.

   ⇨ _____

4 I've never seen such a beautiful sight.

   ⇨ _____

Exercise 3 다음 〈보기〉와 같이 so 또는 neither를 사용하여 A의 말에 맞장구치는 대화를 완성하시오.

🔍 **A: I don't really enjoy watching violent movies.**
   B: _____ Neither do I. _____

1 A: I am so tired and hungry.
   B: _____

2 A: I couldn't sleep at all last night.
   B: _____

3 A: It's raining. I don't want to go out.
   B: _____

4 A: I really had a good time yesterday.
   B: _____

Exercise 4 다음 우리말과 같은 뜻이 되도록 괄호 안의 단어를 알맞게 배열하시오. (단, 밑줄 친 부분을 강조할 것)

1 언덕 위에 큰 나무가 서 있다. (a, tree, on the top of the hill, tall, stands)

   ⇨ _____

2 마룻바닥에 깨진 유리 조각이 있었다. (were, on the floor, pieces of, broken glass)

   ⇨ _____

3 나는 결코 그 이론에 대하여 들은 적이 없다. (heard of, I, have, the theory, never)

   ⇨ _____

4 나는 그 순간 거의 숨을 쉴 수가 없었다. (breathe, hardly, at the moment, I, could)

   ⇨ _____

생략

📑 중복을 피하기 위한 생략

- I went shopping for food and **(I)** came back home.
  나는 식료품을 사러 갔다가 집으로 돌아왔다.
- James went to Greece and his friend **(went)** to Spain.
  James는 그리스에 갔고 그의 친구는 스페인에 갔다.
- Rachel likes reptiles but I don't **(like reptiles)**.
  Rachel은 파충류를 좋아하지만 나는 그렇지 않다.
- He is much younger than **you (are)**. 그는 너보다 훨씬 어리다.

> **TIPs** 목적격 관계대명사와 목적어절을 이끄는 접속사 that은 생략 가능하다.
> - The people (that/whom) I met at the party were nice.
>   내가 파티에서 만난 사람들은 친절했다.
> - I think (that) I can do it by myself.
>   나는 그것을 나 혼자 할 수 있다고 생각한다.

📑 접속사 if, when, while 등이 이끄는 부사절의 「주어+be동사」 생략

- I will give you the money, if **(it is)** necessary.
  만약 필요하다면, 내가 너에게 그 돈을 줄게.
- When **(they are)** sleeping, babies look like an angel. 아기들은 자고 있을 때 천사처럼 보인다.

📑 「관계대명사+be동사」의 생략

관계대명사와 be동사 뒤에 분사가 뒤따를 때 관계대명사와 be동사는 생략될 수 있다.

- The girl **(who is)** singing a song is my cousin. 노래를 부르고 있는 소녀는 나의 사촌이다.
- Have you read a book **(which is)** written by Jane Austen? 너는 Jane Austen이 쓴 책을 읽어 본 적 있니?

📑 감탄문의 「주어+동사」 생략

감탄문에서 「주어+동사」를 생략해도 의미 파악에 문제가 없으면 생략 가능하다.

- What a beautiful girl **(she is)**! 그녀는 정말 아름다운 소녀구나!
- How smart **(you are)**! 너는 정말 똑똑하구나!

Answers: p.42

Exercise ① 다음 문장에서 생략해도 되는 부분에 밑줄을 그으시오.

1 What an awful day it is!

2 He said that he would be back by seven.

3 The Sun rises in the east and it sets in the west.

4 Have you read the book that I recommended to you?

5 She had a simple breakfast and she ran to school.

6 Do you know the old man who is sitting over there?

7 I could finish the work, but he couldn't finish the work.

8 Have you ever seen the woman who was standing in front of the bank?

9 When he was working as a part-time waiter, he saved some money.

10 The novels which were written by Rowling are very popular all around the world.

11 He wanted to play soccer after school, but I didn't want to play soccer after school.

Exercise **2** 다음 문장의 빈칸에 생략된 말을 써넣어 문장을 완성하시오.

1 They were poor, but _____ happy.

2 She didn't know _____ there's no class today.

3 The girl _____ wearing a red skirt is my friend.

4 My brother has a lot of homework, but I don't _____ .

5 What is the name of that restaurant _____ you told me about?

6 The food will be served from six, and the drinks _____ from seven.

7 While _____ having lunch, we had a lot of interesting discussions.

Exercise **3** 다음 문장에서 생략된 부분을 찾아 문장을 다시 쓰시오.

1 Look at the tree. What a tall tree!

   ⇒ _____

2 I tried to talk to her, but I couldn't.

   ⇒ _____

3 Do you know the girl talking to Sam?

   ⇒ _____

4 My younger brother is even taller than Paul.

   ⇒ _____

5 Ted got up and went to the gym right away.

   ⇒ _____

6 Some went there by subway, and others by bus.

   ⇒ _____

7 These are the books you were looking for yesterday.

   ⇒ _____

8 Lisa asked me to stand in for her, but I didn't want to.

   ⇒ _____

9 Everyone knows Jeff is the smartest boy in our school.

   ⇒ _____

10 When in elementary school, we used to play hide-and-seek.

   ⇒ _____

Review Test

[01-04] 다음 빈칸에 알맞은 것을 고르시오.

01 I can't believe the fact _____ we lost the game.

① which   ② who
③ that   ④ when
⑤ where

02 Who _____ can believe such a strange story?

① on earth   ② the very
③ the   ④ does
⑤ oneself

03 He doesn't understand me _____.

① on earth   ② the very
③ at all   ④ does
⑤ oneself

04 He was _____ the fastest runner.

① very   ② a lot
③ by far   ④ little
⑤ many

05 다음 밑줄 친 부분을 강조할 때 빈칸에 알맞은 말은?

My boss wanted me to go to New York with her.
⇒ My hoss _____ me to go to New York with her.

① did wanted   ② do want
③ does want   ④ did want
⑤ do wants

06 다음 〈보기〉의 밑줄 친 부분과 쓰임이 같은 것은?

They do hope you will pass the exam.

① Do you have a pencil?
② I will always do my best.
③ What did you do yesterday?
④ I do believe in the existence of ghosts.
⑤ He speaks English more fluently than I do.

07 다음 중 밑줄 친 부분을 강조하는 문장으로 바르게 바꿔 쓴 것은?

I little dreamed that my son would win the competition.

① Little I dreamed that my son would win the competition.
② Little dreamed I that my son would win the competition.
③ Little did I dream that my son would win the competition.
④ I myself little dreamed that my son would win the competition.
⑤ It was little that I dreamed my son would win the competition.

[08-09] 다음 중 어법상 어색한 문장을 고르시오.

08 ① My mom does enjoy baking cakes.
    ② Never did I see such a beautiful girl.
    ③ Mr. Kim did taught English three years ago.
    ④ Hardly could I understand what was going on.
    ⑤ It was Susan whom I bumped into on the street.

09 ① Here he comes.
    ② When in college, he was diligent.
    ③ Emily did do the dishes by herself.
    ④ It is the book that I bought yesterday.
    ⑤ These trees are the very taller than those.

10 다음 밑줄 친 부분 중 생략할 수 없는 것은?

① I do not like your new hair.
② What a beautiful flower it is!
③ The shirt which is hanging on the wall is mine.
④ He takes a walk in the evening, whenever it is possible.
⑤ When I was in middle school, I would play soccer with friends after school.

11 다음 밑줄 친 부분 중 생략할 수 있는 것은?

① I met an old lady whose husband is a professor.
② The shoes that you were looking for are on the porch.
③ The man who is standing next to Sue is my cousin.
④ The boy who lives next door is one of my classmates.
⑤ The TV which broke down yesterday is working again now.

12 다음 밑줄 친 that의 쓰임이 나머지 넷과 다른 하나는?

① It was your mom that I met on the street.
② It was in the mall that I lost my wallet.
③ It was yesterday that John sent me some presents.
④ It was a Korean musician that performed at the Carnegie Hall.
⑤ It was a fact that the company had fired many foreign workers.

13 다음 문장의 빈칸에 들어갈 수 없는 것은?

The scarf is _____ more expensive than I expected.

① very   ② still
③ much   ④ a lot
⑤ even

14 다음 〈보기〉의 우리말을 바르게 영작한 것은?

그는 우리 동네에 자전거 길을 만들자는 계획을 제안했다.

① He came up with the plan, making a biking trail in our neighborhood.
② He came up with the plan and made a biking trail in our neighborhood.
③ He came up with the plan by making a biking trail in our neighborhood.
④ He came up with the plan of making a biking trail in our neighborhood.
⑤ He came up with the plan that making a biking trail in our neighborhood.

[15-17] 다음 밑줄 친 부분 중 생략 가능한 것을 고르시오.

15 ① What a wonderful ② view ③ it is. I've never seen ④ such a beautiful ⑤ night view.

16 Chris ① wants me ② to help him ③ with his work, but I don't ④ want to ⑤ help him.

17 No one thought ① that we ② would win the championship, ③ but we ④ did do our best and achieved ⑤ what we really wanted.

18 다음 대화의 밑줄 친 부분을 바르게 영작한 것은?

A: Did you meet Tony yesterday or this morning?
B: 내가 Tony를 만난 건 바로 어제였다.

① I met Tony yesterday.
② I did meet Tony yesterday.
③ It was Tony that I met yesterday.
④ It was yesterday that I met Tony.
⑤ It was I that met Tony yesterday.

[19-20] 다음 빈칸에 알맞은 것을 모두 고르시오.

19　It was on my birthday _____ my mom made me some delicious pizza.

① which　　　② who
③ that　　　④ when
⑤ where

20　It was Jeff _____ gave me this beautiful postcard.

① which　　　② who
③ that　　　④ when
⑤ where

[21-23] 다음 〈보기〉에서 알맞은 것을 골라 문장을 완성하시오.

보기 |	at all	so		in the world
	most	neither	the very	much

21　This is _____ present that I want to receive.

22　What _____ are you going to do with your friend?

23　He is _____ taller than everyone else in his class.

24　다음 밑줄 친 very의 의미가 나머지 넷과 다른 하나는?

① I loved it <u>very</u> much.
② Ms. Jones is a <u>very</u> nice lady.
③ The movie was <u>very</u> interesting.
④ I'm <u>very</u> pleased that you can come.
⑤ He is the <u>very</u> man I met at the party.

25　다음 밑줄 친 that의 쓰임이 나머지 넷과 다른 하나는?

① It was Tom <u>that</u> fixed my computer.
② It is the book <u>that</u> I really want to read.
③ It was certain <u>that</u> she would pass the exam.
④ It was yesterday <u>that</u> we played badminton together.
⑤ It was in the Italian restaurant <u>that</u> I met Sally yesterday.

[26-28] 다음 밑줄 친 부분 중 어법상 어색한 것을 고르시오.

26　① <u>Hardly</u> ② <u>I have</u> ③ <u>thought</u> ④ <u>that</u> he would get ⑤ <u>such</u> a good job.

27　I ① <u>broke</u> ② <u>my</u> leg. I didn't ③ <u>go</u> fishing but ④ <u>staying</u> ⑤ <u>at home</u>.

28　① <u>Neither Saturday</u> ② <u>nor</u> ③ <u>on Sunday</u> will be OK. I ④ <u>won't be</u> free ⑤ <u>on</u> these two days.

[29-30] 다음 두 문장이 같은 의미가 되도록 문장을 완성하시오.

29　She doesn't like taking a risk, and I don't like taking a risk, either.
⇒ She doesn't like taking a risk, and
_____ _____ _____.

30　Joe can't play the piano, and Jimmy can't play the piano, either.
⇒ Joe can't play the piano, and _____
_____.

[31-34] 다음 괄호 안에서 알맞은 것을 고르시오.

31 This is the (very / much) film I really want to see.

32 Tony (myself / himself) fixed the broken radio.

33 A: He is interested in volunteering, particularly in helping elderly people.
B: So (am I / I am).

34 A: I couldn't see him coming.
B: (So / Neither) could I.

[35-38] 다음 문장을 주어진 단어로 시작하는 문장으로 다시 쓰시오.

35 I've never heard of such an amazing story.
⇒ Never _____
_____ .

36 She little knew how much I loved her.
⇒ Little _____ .

37 The doctor comes here.
⇒ Here _____ .

38 I've rarely been sick since I became a vegetarian.
⇒ Rarely _____
_____ .

[39-40] 다음 중 어법상 어색한 부분을 찾아 알맞게 고쳐 쓰시오.

39 Ava is bright and diligence.
⇒ _____

40 He can sing and plays the piano at the same time.
⇒ _____

[41-44] 다음 밑줄 친 부분을 강조하는 문장으로 다시 쓰시오.

41 We had a good time.
⇒ _____

42 John lost his dog at the park yesterday.
⇒ It _____
_____ .

43 How did you know this is the thing I wanted to have?
⇒ _____
_____

44 I helped him overcome the difficulties he was facing.
⇒ I _____
_____ .

45 다음 문장의 생략 가능한 부분을 생략하고 문장을 다시 쓰시오.

I am examining a sculpture which was discovered at the ancient historic site.
⇒ _____
_____

Answers: p.44

[1-3] 다음 글을 읽고, 물음에 답하시오. 서술형

I really love table tennis. I enjoy not only watching but also ① _____ (play) it. My school has a table tennis club, so I wanted to join it. But the club doesn't accept everyone that wants to join it. They have to pass a test to join the club. Unfortunately, I failed the test because there were many other students who were ② by far better than me. I had never thought I would fail, and (A) 나의 부모님도 그랬다.

1 윗글의 괄호에 주어진 말을 적절히 변형하여 빈칸 ①을 완성하시오.

→ _____

2 윗글의 밑줄 친 ②를 어법에 맞게 고치시오.

by far → _____

3 윗글의 밑줄 친 (A)를 괄호에 주어진 단어를 활용하여 바르게 영작하시오.

_____ (neither, my parents)

4 다음 글의 밑줄 친 부분 중, 어법상 틀린 것은? 수능 대비형

With the growing popularity of smartphones and computers, ① most people now play games on their machines. But just 20 years ② ago, America's favorite games came in a box with a colorful board and pieces you moved ③ myself. These games — like Monopoly, RISK, and Sorry! — are now fading into history. Toy stores ④ no longer carry many board games, and ⑤ fewer children know what it's like to sit around a table and play a game with friends.

* popularity: 인기, 대중성
** piece: (체스 등의) 말
*** device: 장치, 기구

★ NEW EDITION ★

GRAMMAR BRIDGE

Level

3

Workbook

Chapter 1 시제

A 두 문장의 의미가 통하도록 문장을 완성하시오.

1 My dad lost his driver's license, and he still doesn't have it.

⇨ My dad _____ his driver's license.

2 She started teaching American history last semester, and she still teaches it.

⇨ She _____ American history since last semester.

3 The instructor went out, and he didn't come back.

⇨ The instructor _____ out.

4 I started working as the store manager three years ago, and I am still the store manager.

⇨ I _____ as the store manager for three years.

5 Daniel adopted his cats five years ago, and he still has them.

⇨ Daniel _____ his cats for five years.

6 The law was not changed 40 years ago, and it still remains unchanged today.

⇨ The law _____ unchanged for 40 years.

B 밑줄 친 부분을 바르게 고쳐 문장을 다시 쓰시오.

1 I have gone to France once.

⇨ _____

2 Jeremy doesn't read my text messages yet.

⇨ _____

3 The janitor has mopped the floor yesterday.

⇨ _____

4 We have known each other since ten years.

⇨ _____

C 우리말과 같은 뜻이 되도록 주어진 단어를 배열하시오.

1 우리 아이들이 지난주부터 줄곧 아프네요. (sick, last week, have, since, been)

⇨ My children _____.

2 네가 한국을 떠난 지 3년이 지났어. (passed, you, Korea, has, since, left)

⇨ Three years _____.

3 나는 지금까지 그것 같은 것을 본 적이 없어. (anything, never, like, have, it, seen)

⇨ I _____.

4 Samuel은 두 달간 이 행사를 준비해오고 있다. (for, has, this event, been, two months, preparing)

⇨ Samuel _____.

5 나는 이렇게 행복했던 적이 없어요. (been, have, never, happier)

⇨ I _____.

D 주어진 상황을 읽고, 현재완료 또는 현재완료진행 중 가장 적절한 것 하나를 이용하여 문장을 완성하시오.

1 I got accepted to Oxford University last year, and I am still a student there.

⇒ I _____ a student at Oxford University since last year. (be)

2 I changed my WiFi password yesterday. The guy next door can't get online anymore.

⇒ I _____ my WiFi password, so the guy next door can't access the Internet for free. (change)

3 She started waiting for you 30 minutes ago, and she's still waiting for you.

⇒ She _____ for you for 30 minutes. (wait)

4 I put my mechanical pencil on the desk, but now it's gone.

⇒ Somebody _____ my mechanical pencil! (steal)

5 Alex started to play mobile games this morning, and he's still playing in the evening.

⇒ Alex _____ mobile games all day. (play)

E 우리말과 같은 뜻이 되도록 주어진 단어를 이용하여 문장을 완성하시오.

1 Penelope는 지난주 이후로 그 문제에 시달리고 있어요. (deal)

⇒ Penelope _____ with the problem since last week.

2 그들은 그들의 자녀가 사라졌다는 것을 언제 발견했나요? (discover)

⇒ _____ that their child was missing?

3 지금까지 얼마나 많은 나라를 여행했니? (travel)

⇒ How many countries _____ ?

4 제가 얼마나 바닥에 누워있었나요? (lie)

⇒ How long _____ on the floor?

5 누가 우리 대신에 상자를 다 옮겼네요. 이제 우리 좀 쉬어요. (move)

⇒ Somebody _____ all the boxes for us. Now let's get some rest.

F 밑줄 친 부분을 어법에 맞게 고쳐 쓰시오.

1 The bus has already left when we arrived.   ⇒ _____

2 He said he has never met you before.   ⇒ _____

3 I was so angry because someone has deleted my file.   ⇒ _____

4 She had never seen so many people before she had moved here. ⇒ _____

5 Theo can't drive because he had lost his glasses.   ⇒ _____

6 Lucy has never learned Korean before her family moved to Korea. ⇒ _____

G 우리말과 같은 뜻이 되도록 주어진 동사를 이용하여 문장을 완성하시오.

1 Anna는 남자친구가 문자를 보낼 때까지 줄곧 우울했다. (be, depressed, text)

⇨ Anna _____ until her boyfriend _____ her.

2 전기가 나가기 전까지 그 컴퓨터는 잘 작동되고 있었다. (work, well, go out)

⇨ The computer _____ before the power _____.

3 그는 그 소설을 전에 읽은 적이 있다는 것을 깨달았다. (realize, read)

⇨ He _____ that he _____ the novel before.

4 내가 나의 한국인 남자친구를 만나기 전에는 한국식 고기구이를 먹어본 적이 없었다. (never, try, meet)

⇨ I _____ Korean barbecue before I _____ my Korean boyfriend.

5 Liam은 그 영화를 이미 보았다. 그러나 그는 어젯밤에 그것을 또 보았다. (already, watch, watch)

⇨ Liam _____ the movie. But he _____ it again last night.

H 밑줄 친 부분을 바르게 고쳐 쓰시오. 틀리지 않았다면 ○표 하시오.

1 The thief had left the building when the police arrived. ⇨ _____

2 They will live together for more than ten years next month. ⇨ _____

3 Olivia has been teaching English since two years. ⇨ _____

4 Peter had been working two jobs until the company found out. ⇨ _____

5 Tom has finished his homework before his parents came home from work. ⇨ _____

I 주어진 단어를 이용하여 완료시제 문장으로 완성하시오.

1 be interested in / coding

⇨ Harry _____ in since first grade.

2 will already repair / the car

⇨ The mechanics _____ by the time you leave the hospital.

3 be working on / this project

⇨ My team _____ on this project for three months now.

4 download / the files

⇨ Many internet users _____ for free by the time they catch the hacker.

5 phone / you / several times

⇨ Mr. Ericsson _____ before you came in.

6 never take / the subway

⇨ David _____ to the airport before his last vacation.

Chapter 2   to부정사

A 주어진 동사를 어법에 맞게 바꿔 문장을 완성하시오.

1   We don't deserve _____ champions. (be)

2   Come before lunch if you wish _____ Mr. Sanders. (see)

3   I can't afford _____ another car. (buy)

4   The diner just wanted _____ his meal. (enjoy)

5   The manager asked us _____ the store. (leave)

B 두 문장이 같은 의미가 되도록 it을 이용하여 문장을 다시 쓰시오.

1   To wear a suit is not necessary.

  ⇨ _____

2   To pass Ms. Davidson's history class is easy.

  ⇨ _____

3   To rent electric scooters with this app is possible.

  ⇨ _____

4   To touch this metal without gloves on is dangerous.

  ⇨ _____

C 〈보기〉와 같이 문장을 바꿔 쓰시오.

> They have made a decision. They're going to hire another 1,000 employees.
> ⇨ They have made _____ a decision to hire _____ another 1,000 employees.

1   Aria is a great person. People like to work with her.

  ⇨ Aria _____.

2   I am hungry. I'd like to eat something.

  ⇨ I'd like _____ because I am hungry.

3   He purchased a magazine. He wanted to read it on the subway.

  ⇨ He purchased _____ on the subway.

4   She has to go out. Someone has to look after her daughter.

  ⇨ She should have _____ her daughter.

5   Mr. Carter's legs hurt. He needs to sit on a chair.

  ⇨ Mr. Carter needs _____.

6   Jason paid for his lunch. He used cash.

  ⇨ Jason used _____ for his lunch.

D 밑줄 친 부분을 어법에 맞게 고쳐 쓰시오.

1 그들의 새 앨범은 듣기에 좋은 노래들로 가득해.

⇒ Their new album is full of great songs to listen?   ⇒ _____

2 나는 말할 사람이 없어서 외로워.

⇒ I am lonely because I have no one to talk.   ⇒ _____

3 그녀는 같이 놀 친구들이 많다.

⇒ She has many friends to hang out.   ⇒ _____

E 주어진 문장을 「be+to부정사」를 이용하여 바꿔 쓰시오.

1 You should show up on time.

⇒ _____

2 The two old friends were destined to meet again.

⇒ _____

3 If we intend to make more money, we have to invest more.

⇒ _____

4 She could not be forgiven.

⇒ _____

5 The capital city is going to be locked down due to the virus spread.

⇒ _____

F 〈보기〉와 같이 문장을 바꿔 쓰시오.

🔍 **A friend of mine cheated to pass the math test.**

⇒ _____A friend of mine cheated in order to pass the math test._____

⇒ _____A friend of mine cheated so as to pass the math test._____

1 Jayden will write her a letter to tell her how he feels.

⇒ _____

⇒ _____

2 I took a taxi to the airport not to miss my flight.

⇒ _____

⇒ _____

G 주어진 단어를 이용하여 문장을 완성하시오.

1 Why did you allow her _____ early? (leave)

2 I just heard someone _____ outside. (scream)

3 Let him _____ whatever he wants. (ask)

4 My dad told me _____ straight home after school. (come)

H 두 문장의 의미가 통하도록 문장을 완성하시오.

1 It seemed that someone had already removed the sign.
⇨ Someone seemed _____ .

2 It seemed that nobody was on my side.
⇨ Nobody seemed _____ on my side.

3 It seems that they saw me with my new girlfriend.
⇨ They seem _____ me with my new girlfriend.

4 It seems that Annabelle knows a lot about you.
⇨ Annabelle seems _____ a lot about you.

I 주어진 단어와 「too ~ to」 또는 「enough to」의 구문을 이용하여 문장을 완성하시오.

1 Sarah는 그 대회에 출전할 만큼 충분히 똑똑해. (smart, enter)
⇨ Sarah is _____ the contest.

2 너는 운전해도 되는 나이니? (old, drive)
⇨ Are you _____ ?

3 Hugo는 너무 고집이 세서 내 충고를 듣지 않았다. (stubborn, listen)
⇨ Hugo was _____ to my advice.

4 독서하기에 너무 어두운 것 아니니? (dark, read)
⇨ Isn't it _____ ?

5 Arthur는 창문을 통해 들어오기에 너무 컸다. (big, fit)
⇨ Arthur was _____ through the window.

J 우리말과 같은 뜻이 되도록 주어진 단어를 이용하여 문장을 완성하시오.

1 사실을 말하자면, 나는 지금 현찰이 없어. (the truth)
⇨ _____ , I don't have any cash on me.

2 말할 필요도 없이, 제가 가르치는 한국 학생들은 수학을 참 잘합니다. (needless)
⇨ _____ , my Korean students are excellent in math.

3 우선, 저의 행동에 대한 사과의 말씀을 드리고 싶습니다. (begin)
⇨ _____ , I'd like to apologize for my behavior.

4 요약해서 말하면, 우리는 앞으로 발생할 사고를 예방하기 위해 무언가를 해야 합니다. (sum)
⇨ _____ , we have to do something to prevent further accidents.

5 설상가상으로, 내 전화는 인터넷도 안 됐다. (matters)
⇨ _____ , my phone had no Internet connection.

Chapter 3   동명사

A 주어진 말을 어법에 맞게 바꿔 문장을 완성하시오.

1 I'm sorry for not _____ you completely. (trust)

2 Would you mind _____ the window? (close)

3 _____ a child costs a lot of money. (raise)

4 The bride's father thanked everyone for _____. (come)

5 Don't worry about _____ mistakes. (make)

B 밑줄 친 부분을 바르게 고쳐 쓰시오.

1 Thank you <u>not for interrupting</u> me.   ⇨ _____

2 I remember <u>he</u> helping me the other day.   ⇨ _____

3 Nobody likes <u>treated</u> like a child.   ⇨ _____

4 <u>Walking</u> is a really good exercise.   ⇨ _____

5 Having too many friends <u>are</u> not a good thing.   ⇨ _____

6 I'm sorry for <u>accepting not</u> your offer.   ⇨ _____

7 Many people are afraid of <u>be rejected</u>.   ⇨ _____

8 Suddenly, it started <u>rain</u>.   ⇨ _____

C 두 문장이 같은 의미가 되도록 문장을 완성하시오.

1 He was sad that he was alone.

   ⇨ He was sad about _____.

2 I apologize that I kept you waiting.

   ⇨ I apologize for _____.

3 He was thrilled that he saw a live performance for the first time.

   ⇨ He was thrilled about _____ for the first time.

4 She is sorry that she wasted your time.

   ⇨ She is sorry for _____.

5 Would you mind if I called you 'Jen?'

   ⇨ Would you mind _____ 'Jen?'

D 우리말과 같은 뜻이 되도록 주어진 말을 이용하여 문장을 완성하시오.

1 충분한 휴식을 취하지 않는 것은 당신의 몸을 상하게 할 수 있어요. (not, take, enough, rest)
   ⇨ _____ can harm your body.

2 다른 언어를 말할 수 있는 것은 강한 무기이다. (be able to, speak, different, languages)
   ⇨ _____ is a powerful weapon.

3 내 취미 중 하나는 자연의 사진을 찍는 것이다. (take, photos of, nature)
   ⇨ One of my hobbies is _____ .

4 시장은 그 공원 주변에 펜스를 세울 것을 주장했다. (put, a fence, around, the park)
   ⇨ The mayor insisted on _____ .

5 어떤 사람들은 물이 많이 마시는 것이 피부에 좋다고 말한다. (drink, lots of, water, be, good)
   ⇨ Some say _____ for your skin.

E 두 문장의 의미가 통하도록 that절을 이용한 문장으로 바꿔 쓰시오.

1 The suspect admitted having stolen my bike.
   ⇨ The suspect admitted _____ .

2 I am proud of my son's saving the dog from drowning.
   ⇨ I am proud _____ .

3 The politician denied having lied about his wealth.
   ⇨ The politician denied _____ .

4 She didn't mind having to go through the same process again.
   ⇨ She didn't mind _____ .

F 주어진 단어를 이용하여 문장을 완성하시오.

1 She loves _____ about others. (talk)

2 Mike refused _____ my stuff back to me. (give)

3 My mother quit _____ because she is too old. (work)

4 Can you try _____ the sentence again? I couldn't hear you. (read)

5 They finally decided _____ the prisoners go. (let)

6 She just gave up _____ to understand the movie's message. (try)

7 Noah hid himself so he could avoid _____ to the police. (talk)

8 Do you regret not _____ children? (have)

G 〈보기〉에서 알맞은 단어를 골라 어법에 맞게 바꿔 문장을 완성하시오.

[1~5]

| 🔍 | build | read | persuade | ski | see |

1 We will go _____ when it gets cold enough.

2 On _____ the ghost in the closet, I passed out.

3 The city spent a lot of money _____ new schools.

4 The driver had trouble _____ road signs.

5 It is no use _____ him. He has already made up his mind.

[6~10]

| 🔍 | swim | hear | be | fix | go |

6 How about _____ to the movies?

7 There is no _____ the mistake you made at this point.

8 The new employee is far from _____ diligent.

9 I look forward to _____ from you soon.

10 I feel like _____ at the beach.

H 우리말과 같은 뜻이 되도록 주어진 단어를 배열하시오.

1 그녀는 그의 영국 발음을 이해하는 데 어려움을 겪었다. (understanding, difficulty, had)

   ⇨ She _____ his British accent.

2 우리 엄마는 남동생을 돌보느라 바쁘시다. (after, busy, is, looking)

   ⇨ My mother _____ my baby brother.

3 그 공장 노동자들은 야간 근무하는 것에 익숙해졌다. (used, working, got, to)

   ⇨ The factory workers _____ night shifts.

4 그 새로운 정책은 더 많은 일자리를 창출하는 데 기여했다. (creating, contributed, more, to, jobs)

   ⇨ The new policy _____ .

5 아무도 해결할 수 없는 문제에 대해 걱정해도 소용없다. (worrying about, no, it, use, is)

   ⇨ _____ the problem no one can solve.

6 그 영화가 너무 길었기 때문에 나는 잠들지 않을 수가 없었다. (not, falling, asleep, help, could)

   ⇨ I _____ because the movie was too long.

7 그 작가의 최근 소설은 읽을 가치가 없다. (worth, not, reading, is)

   ⇨ The writer's latest novel _____ .

Chapter 4   분사

A 주어진 단어를 이용하여 문장을 완성하시오.

1 How many official languages are _____ in India? (speak)

2 My father went to the shop to get his car _____. (repair)

3 I am so _____ in you. (disappoint)

4 They took the _____ player to the hospital. (injure)

5 The boy _____ in the sandbox is my cousin. (play)

B 주어진 단어를 문맥에 맞게 현재분사나 과거분사로 바꿔 문장을 완성하시오.

1 (touch)   The movie is just full of _____ scenes.

             Everyone in the audience was _____ by her speech.

2 (excite)   You can enjoy lots of_____ things at the amusement park.

             Are you guys _____ about the concert tomorrow?

3 (interest) I found your report very _____.

             Nancy is quite _____ in Korean culture.

4 (amaze)   It was an _____ experience.

             We were all _____ at his quick reflexes.

C 두 문장을 한 문장으로 만들 때 빈칸에 알맞은 말을 쓰시오.

1 The lady is my English teacher. She is wearing a yellow blouse.

   ⇨ The lady _____ is my English teacher.

2 I have a hamster. He is called Biscuit.

   ⇨ I have a hamster _____.

3 She keeps her diary. It is hidden under the mattress.

   ⇨ She keeps her diary _____.

4 Toby has a smartwatch. It was made in Korea.

   ⇨ Toby has a smartwatch _____.

5 Finn has a sister. She works at the airport.

   ⇨ Finn has a sister _____.

6 I felt something. It was crawling up my leg.

   ⇨ I felt something _____.

D 문장의 의미가 통하도록 분사구문을 이용하여 문장을 완성하시오.

1 While he was listening to the radio, he fell asleep on the couch.

⇒ _____, he fell asleep on the couch.

2 She took a hot bath and drank a glass of wine.

⇒ She took a hot bath, _____.

3 If you are brave enough, you can jump into the water from the cliff.

⇒ _____, you can jump into the water from the cliff.

4 Although she lives alone, she has never felt lonely.

⇒ _____, she has never felt lonely.

5 After I graduated from high school, I started to work at a restaurant.

⇒ _____, I started to work at a restaurant.

E 밑줄 친 분사구문을 어법에 맞게 고쳐 쓰시오.

1 Been sick, Scarlett went to see a doctor. ⇒ _____

2 Distracting by him, she was very upset. ⇒ _____

3 Seeing from above, everything looks tiny. ⇒ _____

4 She kept talking with her arms cross. ⇒ _____

5 He walked up to them a rock with in his hand. ⇒ _____

F 우리말과 같은 뜻이 되도록 주어진 단어를 이용하여 문장을 완성하시오.

1 돈이 없어서 난 버스를 타는 것 대신에 걸어서 출근을 했다. (have, no, money)

⇒ _____, I walked to work instead of taking the bus.

2 그는 그 소설을 읽다가 자신의 어린 시절을 떠올렸다. (read, the novel)

⇒ _____, he thought of his childhood.

3 그녀는 자신의 데이트 상대를 기다리며 다른 커플들이 지나가는 것을 보았다. (wait for, date)

⇒ _____, she watched other couples passing by.

4 그녀는 정말 지루했지만, 즐거운 시간을 보내고 있는 척 했다. (be, really, bored)

⇒ _____, she pretended to be having a good time.

5 최선을 다한다면, 당신의 꿈은 이루어질 것입니다. (do one's best)

⇒ _____, your dream will come true.

6 우리는 점심으로 파스타를 먹고 후식으로 애플파이를 먹었다. (have, apple pie, for dessert)

⇒ We had pasta for lunch, _____.

G 우리말과 같은 뜻이 되도록 주어진 말을 알맞게 배열하시오.

1 집에 도착해서 우리 엄마는 곧바로 화장실로 향하셨다. (headed, home, straight, my mother, arriving)

⇨ _____ to the bathroom.

2 병원으로 옮겨졌지만 그 불쌍한 여자아이는 어떠한 치료도 받을 수 없었다. (receive, taken, the poor girl, to, couldn't, the hospital)

⇨ _____ any medical treatment.

3 길을 따라 걷다가 나는 중학교를 같이 다니던 옛 친구를 우연히 만났다. (I, walking, the street, ran into, down)

⇨ _____ an old friend from middle school.

4 급여를 충분히 받지 못해서 그는 새로운 직장을 찾기로 했다. (decided to, he, not, enough, getting, find, paid)

⇨ _____ a new job.

H 두 문장이 같은 의미가 되도록 「with+명사+분사」 형태를 이용하여 문장을 완성하시오.

1 The suspect started to run, and his hands were tied behind his back.

⇨ The suspect started to run _____ .

2 I was driving my truck, and my arm was hanging out the window.

⇨ I was driving my truck _____ .

3 The girl was listening to the birds singing, and her eyes were closed.

⇨ The girl was listening to the birds singing _____ .

4 Isabelle goes jogging every morning, and her dog follows behind.

⇨ Isabelle goes jogging every morning _____ .

I 우리말과 같은 뜻이 되도록 주어진 단어를 이용하여 분사구문의 문장을 완성하시오.

1 그녀의 목소리로 판단하건대, 그녀는 정말 겁을 많이 먹었었어요. (judge, voice)

⇨ _____ , she was really frightened.

2 부탁을 요청할 때는 공손해야 한다. (when, ask)

⇨ You should be polite _____ for a favor.

3 엄격하게 말해서, 원주율(π)은 정확히 3.14는 아니다. (strictly, speak)

⇨ _____ , π(pi) is not exactly 3.14.

4 날씨가 너무 안 좋아서 우리는 여행을 연기해야 했다. (the weather, awful)

⇨ _____ , we had to postpone the trip.

5 Henderson 선생님 얘기가 나와서 말인데 우리는 그의 체육 수업이 매우 즐거워요. (speak, of)

⇨ _____ , we have so much fun in his phys-ed class.

Chapter 5   조동사

A 빈칸에 can이나 be able to 중 알맞은 것을 써넣으시오. (둘 다 가능하면 can을 쓸 것)

1 I'm in the bathroom. _____ you get the door for me please?

2 Toby might _____ help you if he's not too busy.

3 Grace will _____ join us tonight since she has already finished her report.

4 When _____ babies really start talking?

5 I _____ drive her home because we live in the same neighborhood.

B 우리말과 같은 뜻이 되도록 주어진 단어와 함께 may나 might를 이용하여 문장을 완성하시오.

1 Ryan이 돌아오면 너는 화장실을 가도 돼. (go)
  ⇨ You _____ to the bathroom when Ryan gets back.

2 점심시간이 안 끝났으니까 그녀는 식당에 있을지도 몰라. (be)
  ⇨ Lunch's not over, so she _____ at the cafeteria.

3 안녕하세요. 손님. 주문하시겠습니까? (take)
  ⇨ Hello, Sir. _____ your order?

4 그 가게는 모든 것을 팔아. 그들은 네가 찾고 있는 것을 가지고 있을지도 몰라. (have)
  ⇨ The store sells everything. They _____ what you are looking for.

C 〈보기〉에서 알맞은 말을 골라 should (not) 또는 should (not) have p.p.를 이용하여 대화를 완성하시오.

> take   tell   stay   be   go   talk

1 A Ian doesn't want to see you because he thinks you are a liar.
  B I know. I deserve it. I _____ him the truth.

2 A Dad. I think Liam is stupid. He still can't read the alphabet.
  B That's a terrible thing to say. You _____ about your brother that way.

3 A It's a bad idea to drive during rush hour.
  B You are right. I _____ public transportation.

4 A Something's wrong with me. I feel dizzy, and everything looks blurry.
  B I think you _____ see your doctor as soon as possible.

5 A Ethan. Look what you did. You broke another vase.
  B I am sorry. I _____ more careful, but Max was playing too.

6 A Mom. It's 8:50. Why didn't you wake me up? I am late for school.
  B Don't blame me. You _____ up late playing video games.

D 빈칸에 would 또는 used to를 써넣으시오. (둘 다 가능한 경우 would를 쓸 것)

1 Jason _____ work for me, but now he runs his own company.

2 My father _____ make pancakes for us every Saturday morning.

3 There _____ be a bench under the tree, but now it's gone.

4 We _____ have a minivan, but it got stolen last year.

5 My next-door neighbor _____ wave at me every time I said hello to him.

E 우리말과 같은 뜻이 되도록 주어진 단어를 배열하시오.

1 그들은 그 중고차를 사는 것에 관해 내 말을 들었어야 했는데. (should, me, listened to, they, have)
   ⇨ _____ about buying the used car.

2 난 감기 기운이 있는 것 같아요. 난 그 파티에 안 가는 게 좋겠어요. (not, I, that party, had, go to, better)
   ⇨ I think I'm coming down with a cold. _____

3 사람들은 여름에 날 생선을 먹기를 피해야 한다. (raw fish, should, people, eating, avoid)
   ⇨ _____ in the summer.

4 날이 어두워지네. 우리 이제 길을 나서는 게 좋겠어. (get, we, going, better, had)
   ⇨ It's getting dark. _____.

5 발표하는 동안 어떠한 실수도 하면 안 됩니다. (make, to, any, you, not, mistakes, ought)
   ⇨ _____ during your presentation.

F 두 문장의 의미가 통하도록 문장을 완성하시오. (must, can, may 등의 조동사로 쓸 것)

1 I am sure that Dad forgot my birthday.
   ⇨ Dad _____ my birthday.

2 I am sure that Anna didn't pass the test.
   ⇨ Anna _____ the test.

3 I am sure that I said something silly.
   ⇨ I _____ something silly.

4 I am sure that he didn't see us at the amusement park.
   ⇨ He _____ us at the amusement park.

5 It is possible that she was nervous on the stage.
   ⇨ She _____ nervous on the stage.

6 I am sure that she loves watching Korean dramas.
   ⇨ She _____ watching Korean dramas.

G 밑줄 친 부분에 유의하여 해석을 완성하시오.

1 You <u>must not drive</u> if you are drunk.

⇨ 네가 술을 마셨으면 _____.

2 You <u>don't have to do</u> anything, if you are not feeling well.

⇨ 당신은 몸이 안 좋으면 아무것도 _____.

3 The police have been asking my friends about me. They <u>must have found out</u> what I did.

⇨ 경찰이 내 친구들에게 나에 대한 질문을 해오고 있어. 그들은 내가 한 일을 _____.

4 We <u>must have</u> our seat belts on when the plane takes off.

⇨ 비행기가 이륙할 때 우리는 안전벨트를 _____.

H 〈보기〉에서 알맞은 말을 골라 대화를 완성하시오.

🔍 **need   should   must   cannot   would**

1 I _____ rather do the dishes than babysit my brother.

2 The driver ran over a pedestrian. He _____ have kept his eyes on the road.

3 We now understand why Emma reacted that way. So she _____ not make an apology.

4 Jessica _____ have missed the train since she arrived at the station early in the morning.

5 I just heard something. Someone _____ be in the house.

I 우리말과 같은 뜻이 되도록 주어진 단어를 이용하여 문장을 완성하시오.

1 너의 폰이 그냥 탁자 위에 놓여있었으면 누군가 그것을 가지고 갔을지도 몰라. (may, take, phone)

⇨ Someone _____ if it was just sitting on the table.

2 그녀의 부산 여행은 매우 흥미진진했던 게 틀림없어. (be, very, exciting)

⇨ Her trip to Busan _____.

3 우리는 좀 더 특별한 것을 준비했어야 했는데. (prepare, something, more special)

⇨ We _____.

4 내가 A학점을 받을 수도 있었는데 한두 개의 실수를 범했다. (get, an 'A')

⇨ I _____ but I made a couple of mistakes.

5 그는 그 끔찍한 것들을 말했을 리가 없어. 그는 내가 아는 가장 착한 사람 중 하나야. (say, those, horrible, things)

⇨ He _____. He is one of the nicest guys I have known.

Chapter 6   수동태

A 우리말과 같은 뜻이 되도록 주어진 단어를 이용하여 수동태 문장을 완성하시오

1 그의 진짜 정체가 전국으로 방영되는 TV 방송에서 드러났다. (reveal)

⇨ His true identity _____ on national television.

2 물건들은 컨베이어 벨트 위에서 자동적으로 스캔됩니다. (scan)

⇨ Items _____ automatically on the conveyor belt.

3 그 가수는 어젯밤 3명의 무장 강도에 의해 돈을 빼앗겼다. (rob)

⇨ The singer _____ by three gunmen last night.

4 그 결정은 안전상을 이유로 만들어진 것입니다. (make)

⇨ The decision _____ for safety reasons.

B 능동태 문장을 수동태 문장으로 바꿔 쓰시오. (by+행위자 생략)

1 I was downloading the file at that time.

⇨ The file _____ at that time.

2 You should remove these stickers.

⇨ These stickers _____.

3 The police have not located the stolen vehicle yet.

⇨ The stolen vehicle _____ yet.

4 The machine is washing the dishes.

⇨ The dishes _____.

C 우리말과 같은 뜻이 되도록 〈보기〉에서 알맞은 말을 이용하여 문장을 완성하시오.

🔍 solve   include   take   postpone   build

1 쓰레기는 지금 바로 밖으로 내다 놓아야 해.

⇨ The garbage must _____ out right now.

2 당신들의 이름은 대기자 명단에 포함되어 있지 않습니다.

⇨ Your names _____ on the waiting list.

3 우리 집은 50년 전에 할아버지에 의해서 지어졌다.

⇨ My house _____ by my grandfather 50 years ago.

4 너의 문제는 가족과 나눌 때 해결될 수 있어.

⇨ Your problems can _____ if you share them with your family.

5 그 경기는 악천후로 인해 연기될 것입니다.

⇨ The match will _____ due to bad weather.

D 다음 문장을 수동태 문장으로 바꿔 쓰시오. (by+행위자 생략)

1 They offered him another opportunity.

⇒ Another opportunity _____ .

⇒ He _____ .

2 Professor McMaster teaches freshmen basic chemistry.

⇒ Basic chemistry _____ .

⇒ Freshmen _____ .

3 The company gave Freya a two-story house and a brand new car.

⇒ A two-story house and a brand new car _____ .

⇒ Freya _____ .

E 우리말과 같은 뜻이 되도록 주어진 단어를 이용하여 문장을 완성하시오.

1 그들은 그 난장판을 치우게 되었다. (make, clean up)

⇒ They _____ the mess.

2 아무도 그 구역에 들어가도록 허용되지 않아. (allow, enter)

⇒ No one _____ the area.

3 Reggie가 기타를 연주하는 게 들렸다. (hear, play)

⇒ Reggie _____ the guitar.

4 1990년대 후기에서 2010년대 초기에 태어난 사람들은 Z세대라고 불린다. (call, Generation Z)

⇒ Those born between the late 1990s and early 2010s _____ .

5 그 학생은 교장실에 가라고 명령을 받았다. (tell)

⇒ The student _____ to go to the principal's office.

F 주어진 문장을 수동태 문장으로 바꿔 쓰시오.

1 I took good care of the kitten.

⇒ The kitten _____ .

2 A team of international specialists will carry out the rescue mission.

⇒ The rescue mission _____ .

3 A tow truck should take away the car because it is parked illegally.

⇒ The car _____ because it is parked illegally.

4 They called off the final match because of the typhoon.

⇒ The final match _____ .

5 The driver almost ran over a deer crossing the street.

⇒ A deer crossing the street _____ .

G 〈보기〉에서 알맞은 전치사를 골라 빈칸에 써넣으시오.

🔍   to   in   from   as

[1-4]

1   Why are you interested _____ my hobbies?

2   Who is known _____ the greatest soccer player of all time?

3   Many cardboard boxes are made _____ recycled paper.

4   Nancy is married _____ a handsome young man.

🔍   to   of   at   with

[5-8]

5   Lucy's talent is well known _____ everyone at school.

6   The kid was frightened _____ being left alone.

7   We were all surprised _____ how beautiful she looked in her wedding dress.

8   She was not too pleased _____ what I brought home.

H 우리말과 같은 뜻이 되도록 주어진 단어를 배열하시오.

1   내 방은 봉제 인형으로 가득해. (with, stuffed animals, filled, is)

    ⇨ My room _____ .

2   그 산꼭대기는 항상 눈으로 덮여있다. (covered, always, with, is, snow)

    ⇨ The mountain top _____ .

3   그 팀원들은 결과에 만족하지 않았다. (satisfied, the result, with, were, not)

    ⇨ The team members _____ .

4   그 가수는 허스키한 목소리로 유명하다. (known, her, voice, is, for, husky)

    ⇨ The singer _____ .

I 다음 문장을 수동태 문장으로 바꿔 쓰시오. (by+행위자 생략)

1   People think that Asian students are good at math.

    ⇨ Asians students _____ .

2   People believe that the actor has three children.

    ⇨ It _____ .

3   They say that nothing can travel faster than light.

    ⇨ It _____ .

4   They considered that Mr. Austin was the man responsible for the accident.

    ⇨ Mr. Austin _____ .

Chapter 7 가정법

A 주어진 단어를 이용하여 문장을 완성하시오.

1 If it _____ sunny tomorrow, let's go swimming at the beach. (be)

2 If Mike _____ you with another boy, he would have been disappointed. (see)

3 If she had many friends, we wouldn't _____ so lonely. (feel)

4 If I weren't busy, I _____ to the concert. (will, go)

5 If you _____ me, you would do the same. (be)

B 두 문장이 같은 뜻이 되도록 가정법 문장을 완성하시오.

1 As it is freezing outside, I have to wear my snow boots.

⇨ If it _____ freezing outside, I _____ wear my snow boots.

2 As Leo is not tall enough, he can't ride the roller coaster.

⇨ If Leo _____ tall enough, he _____ the roller coaster.

3 As I don't speak Japanese, I don't know what Haruto really wants.

⇨ If I _____ Japanese, I _____ what Haruto really wants.

4 As you had a big lunch, you can't enjoy this delicious cherry pie now.

⇨ If you _____ a big lunch, you _____ this delicious cherry pie now.

5 As the movie was boring, I fell asleep.

⇨ If the movie _____ boring, I _____ asleep.

C 우리말과 같은 뜻이 되도록 주어진 단어를 배열하시오.

1 Finn이 무엇을 해야 할지 알았더라면, 그는 허둥지둥 대지 않았을 텐데. (what, Finn, do, known, to, had)

⇨ If _____, he wouldn't have panicked.

2 내가 부자라면, 나는 스포츠카를 수집할 텐데. (cars, would, I, collect, sports)

⇨ If I were rich, _____.

3 Aaron이 사과했더라면 우리 부모님은 그렇게 화내지 않았을 텐데. (wouldn't, so, my parents, angry, been have)

⇨ If Aaron had apologized, _____.

4 그녀가 내 옆집에 산다면, 나는 매일 그녀와 함께 걸어서 등교할 텐데. (door, lived, next, she)

⇨ If _____, I would walk to school with her every day.

5 네가 좀 더 사려 깊었다면, 네 여동생은 울지 않았을 텐데. (little, sister, have, your, cried, wouldn't)

⇨ If you had been more considerate, _____.

D 주어진 단어를 이용하여 가정법 문장을 완성하시오.

1 The lady talks as if she _____ my mother. (be)

2 I wish I _____ a suit to the job interview. I was the only one in a T-shirt and blue jeans. (wear)

3 She wishes that she _____ someone to talk to. (have)

4 Without my father, I _____ late for school. Thankfully, he gave me a ride. (be)

5 If it were not for the support from family, it _____ so hard to move towards my goal. (be)

E 주어진 상황에 맞게 I wish 가정법 문장을 완성하시오.

1 I'm sorry I don't live by myself. My parents care about me too much.

⇨ I wish _____. My parents care about me too much.

2 I'm sorry you didn't watch the sunrise with us.

⇨ I wish _____.

3 I'm sorry there are not more books in the library.

⇨ I wish _____.

4 I'm sorry Alex can't come to my birthday party.

⇨ I wish _____.

5 My roommate likes to talk loudly on the phone. I'm sorry she is not quieter.

⇨ My roommate likes to talk loudly on the phone. I wish _____.

F 두 문장의 의미가 통하도록 혼합 가정법 문장을 완성하시오.

1 As I didn't bring my wallet with me, I can't have lunch now.

⇨ _____

2 As Toby went to the bathroom, we can't get on the train now.

⇨ _____

3 As Molly dropped my phone, I am angry with her now.

⇨ _____

4 As you forgot your passport, we are not flying to Hawaii now.

⇨ _____

5 As the driver wasn't careful enough, the passengers are in the hospital now.

⇨ _____

6 As I didn't spend my allowance wisely, I only have $1 in my bank account now.

⇨ _____

G **주어진 문장을 but for, without 가정법 문장으로 바꿔 쓰시오.**

1 If it had not been for his help, we wouldn't have survived.

⇨ _____

⇨ _____

2 If it were not for the police, people wouldn't feel safe.

⇨ _____

⇨ _____

3 If it were not for the moon, it would get so dark at night.

⇨ _____

⇨ _____

4 If it had not been for your advice, I couldn't have expanded my business.

⇨ _____

⇨ _____

H **우리말과 같은 뜻이 되도록 주어진 단어를 배열하시오.**

1 그 젊은 기술자는 마치 자신이 경험이 많은 것처럼 이야기 한다. (he, experience, as, had, though, plenty of)

⇨ The young technician talks _____.

2 이 애플리케이션이 없으면 문자와 사진을 빨리 보내기 어려울 거야. (not, were, application, this, it, for)

⇨ _____, it would be difficult to send texts and photos quickly.

3 그녀의 경고가 없었더라면 우리는 안에 갇혔을 거야. (her, for, it, been warning, had, not)

⇨ _____, we would have been trapped inside.

4 그 의사는 자신이 수천 명의 목숨을 구한 것처럼 행동한다. (had, lives, if, thousands of, saved, as, she)

⇨ The doctor acts _____.

5 내가 충분히 똑똑하다면, 항공 우주 공학을 공부할 텐데. (enough, I, smart, were)

⇨ _____, I would study aerospace engineering.

6 만약 당신이 한국으로 돌아온다 하여도, 나에게 연락하려고 하지 마세요. (to, you, if, back, should, Korea, come)

⇨ _____, do not try to get in touch with me.

7 그가 너의 건강 상태에 대해 알았더라면 그는 너를 도왔을 거야. (your, about, he, health conditions, known, had)

⇨ _____, he would have helped you.

Chapter 8 비교급, 최상급

A 〈보기〉에서 알맞은 것을 골라 as ∼ as를 사용하여 문장을 완성하시오.

🔍 loudly   pretty   often   interesting
    early   expensive   well

1 It's moving day tomorrow. So you need to get up _____ you can.

2 I can't sing _____ my sister does.

3 His new movie isn't _____ the last one.

4 Jayden's backpack is three times _____ mine.

5 They came to see me _____ possible.

6 Nobody in my class is _____ Olivia.

7 The fans shouted out his name _____ they could.

B 두 문장이 의미가 통하도록 주어진 단어를 이용하여 문장을 완성하시오.

1 The cheese burger is $4. The barbeque burger is $5.

⇒ The cheese burger is _____ the barbeque burger. (expensive)

2 The owner made $100, and the part-time worker made $30.

⇒ The owner made _____ the part-time worker. (money)

3 Myles is 16 years old. Emily is 17 years old. Theo is 15 years old.

⇒ Theo is _____ of the three. (young)

4 Lily types 200 words a minute. Jason types 300 words a minute.

⇒ Jason types _____ Lily does. (fast)

C 빈칸에 than과 to 중 알맞은 것을 써넣으시오.

1 Why does your grandma look younger _____ her friends?

2 It's not true that Korean cars are inferior _____ Japanese cars.

3 The situation in Africa is much worse _____ we have imagined.

4 Seth wears expensive clothes because he wants to feel superior _____ his coworkers.

5 Alice, can I have a word with you prior _____ the meeting?

6 The problems are actually more complicated _____ they look.

D 다음 밑줄 친 부분을 바르게 고쳐 쓰시오.

1 The creature looks more like an octopus <u>to</u> a squid.   ⇒ _____

2 <u>More</u> I talk to her, <u>less</u> I want to be with her.   ⇒ _____

3 The blue skirt is the more expensive <u>than</u> the two.   ⇒ _____

4 Your daughter's English is <u>very</u> better than yours.   ⇒ _____

E 우리말과 같은 뜻이 되도록 주어진 단어를 배열하시오.

1 어느 물체가 더 빨리 움직일수록 그것의 에너지는 더 커진다. (becomes, its, the, the, bigger, faster, energy)
   ⇒ _____ an object travels, _____.

2 더 많은 채소를 섭취할수록 당신은 더 건강해집니다. (the, the, healthier, get, more, you, vegetables)
   ⇒ _____ you eat, _____.

3 그가 운동을 하면서 그의 근육은 점점 더 강해졌다. (grew, and, stronger, his muscles, stronger)
   ⇒ As he worked out, _____.

4 네가 어떤 것에 더 많은 노력을 쏟을수록 너는 더 큰 결과를 성취할 수 있다. (the, the, results, effort, greater, more)
   ⇒ _____ you put into something, _____ you can achieve.

F 문장의 의미가 통하도록 문장을 완성하시오.

1 You are not as tall as Jack.
   ⇒ Jack is _____ you.

2 Issac explained his plan to us as clearly as possible.
   ⇒ Issac explained his plan to us _____.

3 The diver tried to hold her breath as long as she could.
   ⇒ The diver tried to hold her breath _____.

4 This carrot cake looks less delicious than the blueberry pie.
   ⇒ This carrot cake doesn't look _____ as the blueberry pie.

5 A mother's love is the greatest thing.
   ⇒ Nothing is _____ as a mother's love.

6 The roller coaster was less exciting than I expected.
   ⇒ The roller coaster was not _____ as I expected.

7 The thieves got out of the building as quietly as possible.
   ⇒ The thieves got out of the building _____.

G 〈보기〉에서 알맞은 것을 골라 최상급으로 바꿔 문장을 완성하시오.

🔍   smart   tall   tough   hot   wonderful

1 It is _____ experience I have ever had.

2 What is _____ subject taught in school?

3 Is Daegu known as _____ city in Korea?

4 He may be _____ man alive.

5 Liam is _____ student in my class.

H 우리말과 같은 뜻이 되도록 주어진 단어를 이용하여 문장을 완성하시오.

1 그의 얼굴은 점점 더 어두워지고 있어. (dark)

   ⇨ His face is getting _____ .

2 집이 더 크면 클수록, 공공요금을 더 많이 낼 것이다. (large, more)

   ⇨ _____ the house, _____ you will pay in utility bills.

3 그 오래된 자동차를 사느니 차라리 새 자전거를 사는 게 낫겠다. (get)

   ⇨ I _____ a brand new bike than buy that old car.

4 가능한 한 빨리 사무실로 돌아와주세요. (soon, possible)

   ⇨ Please come back to the office _____ .

5 그것은 내가 지금까지 본 것 중 가장 이상한 영화다. (strange, movie)

   ⇨ It is _____ I have ever watched.

I 최상급 의미가 되도록 문장을 완성하시오.

1 Lisa is the most intelligent member of the Simpson family.

   ⇨ Lisa is _____ of the Simpson family. (비교급, any other)

   ⇨ _____ member of the Simpson family is _____ Lisa. (no, 비교급)

   ⇨ _____ member of the Simpson family is _____ Lisa. (no, 원급)

2 He is the wealthiest man in the world.

   ⇨ He is _____ in the world. (비교급, any other)

   ⇨ _____ man in the world is _____ him. (no, 비교급)

   ⇨ _____ man in the world is _____ him. (no, 원급)

3 This is the deadliest virus on the planet.

   ⇨ This is _____ any other virus on the planet. (비교급, any other)

   ⇨ _____ virus on the planet is _____ this. (no, 비교급)

   ⇨ _____ virus on the planet is _____ this. (no, 원급)

Answers: p.50

A 밑줄 친 부분을 어법에 맞게 고쳐 쓰시오.

1 The rest of the money <u>were</u> found in the attic. ⇒ _____

2 Most of his income <u>come</u> from his YouTube videos. ⇒ _____

3 It's obvious that the rich <u>is</u> going to get richer. ⇒ _____

4 The Maldives <u>are</u> a beautiful country in the Indian Ocean. ⇒ _____

5 Everything in the boxes <u>are</u> very expensive. ⇒ _____

6 A number of wild animals <u>has</u> died due to drought. ⇒ _____

7 One of the largest lakes in Asia <u>are</u> in Kazakhstan. ⇒ _____

B 우리말과 같은 뜻이 되도록 〈보기〉에서 알맞은 동사를 골라 문장을 완성하시오.

be   seem   increase   cost

1 너의 친구 중 몇몇은 나를 좋아하는 것 같아.
⇒ Some of your friends _____ to like me.

2 각각의 제품은 배송 비용으로 $20가 소요됩니다.
⇒ Each product _____ more $20 for shipping.

3 아침식사를 거르는 학생들의 수가 증가하고 있다.
⇒ The number of students skipping breakfast _____.

4 직원의 반이 회사의 새로운 정책에 반대한다.
⇒ Half of the employees _____ against the company's now policy.

C 주어진 단어를 이용하여 문장을 완성하시오.

1 He said that he _____ glad to see me, but I knew he was lying. (be)

2 I thought she _____ accept my apology, but she didn't. (will)

3 The teacher told us that the crew of Apollo 11 _____ on the moon in 1969. (land)

4 It is true that everyone _____ mistakes sometimes. (make)

5 Mr. Donahue said that it _____ about 365 days for the earth to spin around the sun. (take)

D 주절의 시제를 과거 시제로 바꿔 문장을 완성하시오

1 I think that she likes me.

⇨ I thought that _____ .

2 I think that she is going to pass out.

⇨ I thought that _____ .

3 She wonders how I fixed the door.

⇨ She wondered _____ .

4 He doesn't believe that they can fly.

⇨ He didn't believe that _____ .

E 우리말과 같은 뜻이 되도록 주어진 이용하여 문장을 완성하시오.

1 우리 화학 선생님께서 구리는 약 1085℃에서 녹는다고 말씀하셨어. (tell, melt)

⇨ My chemistry teacher _____ me that copper _____ at around 1085C°.

2 Anna는 자신이 재능 있는 가수라고 믿는다. (believe, be, a talented singer)

⇨ Anna _____ that she _____ .

3 우리는 한국 전쟁이 1950년에 시작됐다는 것을 배웠다. (learn, start, in 1950)

⇨ We _____ that the Korean War _____ .

4 나의 아이들이 숙제를 할 거라고 내게 말했지만, 그들은 하지 않았다. (say, will, do)

⇨ My children _____ to me that they _____ their homework, but they didn't.

5 그녀는 Oscar가 자신에게 펜 하나를 빌려갔다는 사실이 기억났다. (remember, borrow, a pen)

⇨ She _____ that Oscar _____ from her.

F 직접 화법을 간접 화법으로 바꿔 문장을 완성하시오.

1 Roy said to me, "Do you want to go to the movies with me?"

⇨ Roy asked me _____ .

2 My brother said, "Have you seen my baseball cap?"

⇨ My brother asked me _____ .

3 Leah said, "What are you doing tomorrow?"

⇨ Leah asked me _____ .

4 Ethan said to me, "Why did you call me yesterday?"

⇨ Ethan asked me _____ .

5 She said to me, "I have to do the dishes now."

⇨ She told me that _____ .

G 간접 화법을 직접 화법으로 바꿔 문장을 완성하시오.

1 Mom told me not to touch her laptop.

⇨ Mom said, _____

2 The man asked me if I knew when Henry would be back.

⇨ The man said to me, _____

3 Aunt Nancy asked me if I had eaten.

⇨ Aunt Nancy said to me, _____

4 Harry asked me where he could park.

⇨ Harry said to me, _____

5 Bella said that she gets up at 6 every morning.

⇨ Bella said, _____

H 우리말과 같은 뜻이 되도록 주어진 단어를 이용하여 문장을 완성하시오.

1 의사선생님이 우리 아빠에게 금연하라고 충고하셨다. (advise, my dad, quit)

⇨ The doctor _____ smoking.

2 나는 그들에게 빨간 신호등에 건너지 말라고 말했다. (tell, cross)

⇨ I _____ on a red light.

3 우리 엄마는 내가 미술 프로젝트 하는 것을 도와주시겠다고 내게 말씀하셨다. (tell, can, help)

⇨ My mother _____ with the art project.

4 Jessica는 오빠에게 전화기를 어디다가 숨겼는지 물었다. (ask, brother, where, hide)

⇨ Jessica _____ her phone.

5 그 여자는 짧게 통화를 해야겠다고 말했다. (say, have to, make)

⇨ The lady _____ a quick phone call.

I 우리말과 같은 뜻이 되도록 주어진 단어를 배열하시오.

1 구조대원 중 한 명이 우리에게 물에서 나오라고 말했다. (us, of, get out, to, told, the water)

⇨ One of the lifeguards _____.

2 그 경찰관은 내가 수상한 사람을 본 적이 있는지 물었다. (me, seen, asked, had, I, someone, suspicious, if)

⇨ The police officer _____.

3 Mitchell 대령은 자신의 부하들에게 서로 얘기하지 말라고 명령했다. (not, one another, ordered, to, to, his men, speak)

⇨ Captain Mitchell _____.

4 James는 Sienna에게 그녀가 어떻게 자신보다 먼저 도착했는지 물었다. (Sienna, before, arrived, how, she, asked, had, him)

⇨ James _____.

Chapter 10 관계사

A 밑줄 친 부분을 어법에 맞게 고쳐 쓰시오.

1 I need sneakers <u>who</u> can protect my ankles.   ⇨ _____

2 I'd like to date a boy <u>who</u> hobby is reading.   ⇨ _____

3 The guy <u>whose</u> Leo came to the library with is my cousin.   ⇨ _____

4 I'll never forget the things <u>what</u> you told me.   ⇨ _____

5 Did you get <u>that</u> I asked for?   ⇨ _____

B 우리말과 같은 뜻이 되도록 주어진 단어를 이용하여 문장을 완성하시오.

1 그녀는 어젯밤 한 일을 나에게 말해 주었다. (do)

⇨ She told me _____ last night.

2 기차를 기다리고 있던 사람들에게는 무슨 일이 일어났나요? (wait for)

⇨ What happened to the people _____ the train?

3 나는 Ruby가 읽고 있는 소설을 이미 읽었다. (read)

⇨ I have already read the novel _____.

4 Ethan이 쓰고 있었던 그 빨간 펜은 사실 나의 것이다. (write with)

⇨ The red pen _____ is actually mine.

C 생략 가능한 부분을 생략하여 문장을 다시 쓰시오.

1 The movie that I watched yesterday was boring.

⇨ _____

2 Did Rosie see the girl who was sitting by the window?

⇨ _____

3 She is the character whom I love the most in the story.

⇨ _____

4 The man who is walking down the stairs is my father.

⇨ _____

5 The plan that he had come up with seemed brilliant.

⇨ _____

6 I ate the cookie which was on the table.

⇨ _____

D 두 문장의 의미가 통하도록 관계대명사를 이용하여 문장을 완성하시오.

1 Summer is the season. People are most active in summer.

   ⇨ Summer is the season in _____ .

2 That is the hospital. I was born in the hospital.

   ⇨ That is the hospital _____ in.

3 I have a daughter, and she is very wise and polite.

   ⇨ I have a daughter, _____ .

4 My office is in the Nexus Tower, and the building is located at 11th Avenue and Wall Street.

   ⇨ My office is in the Nexus Tower, _____ .

5 We ordered a large pepperoni pizza, and we had it for lunch.

   ⇨ We ordered a large pepperoni pizza, _____ .

6 The bed is smaller than mine. My parents sleep in it.

   ⇨ The bed _____ in is smaller than mine.

E 우리말과 같은 뜻이 되도록 관계부사를 이용하여 문장을 완성하시오.

1 원유로부터 휘발유와 경유를 얻는 방법을 당신은 아시나요?

   ⇨ Do you know _____ we get gasoline and diesel from crude oil?

2 이곳은 그가 자신의 자동차를 만든 차고입니다.

   ⇨ This is the garage _____ he built his own vehicle.

3 나는 네가 처음으로 나에게 미소 지었던 그 순간을 절대 잊지 못할 거야.

   ⇨ I could never forget the moment _____ you smiled at me for the first time.

4 왜 교장선생님이 분노했는지 아무도 이해하지 못하는 것 같았다.

   ⇨ Nobody seemed to understand _____ the principal was furious.

F 우리말과 같은 뜻이 되도록 관계부사와 주어진 단어를 이용하여 문장을 완성하시오.

1 오직 Tommy만이 Grace가 어제 결석한 이유를 알고 있다. (be, absent)

   ⇨ Only Tommy knows the reason _____ yesterday.

2 그 영화는 주인공이 아내의 죽음에 대해 어떻게 복수하는지 보여주지 않는다. (the main character, avenge)

   ⇨ The movie doesn't show _____ his wife's death.

3 그가 거주하곤 했던 그 장소는 여기서 멀지 않아. (used to, live)

   ⇨ The place _____ is not far from here.

4 우리는 그 비극이 그들에게 일어난 날이 여전히 기억나요. (tragedy, happen)

   ⇨ We still remember the day _____ to them.

G 밑줄 친 부분을 어법에 맞게 고쳐 문장을 다시 쓰시오. (that 사용 금지)

1 This is the time of the year <u>why</u> we can enjoy cherry blossoms.

⇒ _____

2 Noah didn't tell us the reason <u>where</u> he showed up late to class.

⇒ _____

3 There are several <u>ways how</u> you can improve your English.

⇒ _____

4 This is the hall <u>how</u> your birthday party will be held.

⇒ _____

5 The coffee shop <u>when</u> we first met is now shut down.

⇒ _____

H 밑줄 친 부분을 한 단어로 바꿔 쓰시오.

1 <u>Every time</u> I try to talk to her, her friends block me.　　　⇒ _____

2 <u>No matter whom</u> you are with, always love yourself more.　　⇒ _____

3 Don't get close to <u>anyone who</u> tries to control you.　　　　⇒ _____

4 My dog eats <u>anything that</u> is left on the plate.　　　　　　⇒ _____

5 <u>No matter how</u> hard you try, you can't beat me.　　　　　　⇒ _____

I 우리말과 같은 뜻이 되도록 주어진 단어를 배열하시오.

1 네가 무엇을 하든 간에 너의 비밀을 아무에게도 말하지 마. (do, you, whatever)

⇒ _____, do not tell your secrets to anyone.

2 우리 엄마는 내가 어딜 가든지 날 따라다니셔. (I, wherever, go)

⇒ My mom follows me _____.

3 그가 아무리 부유하든 상관없이 그는 마음을 가질 수 없어. (rich, is, he, however)

⇒ He can't win my heart _____.

4 그 대회에 참가하고 싶은 자는 누구든지 나이가 18세 이상이어야 합니다. (enter, whoever, to, the contest, wishes)

⇒ _____ must be over 18 years of age.

5 나는 그렇게 까다롭지 아니니까 네가 원하는 아무 영화나 보자. (movie, like, whichever, would, you)

⇒ I am not so picky, so let's watch _____.

6 내가 그와 이야기할 때마다 나는 긴장한다. (talk to, I, whenever, him)

⇒ I get nervous _____.

Chapter 11 접속사, 전치사

A 주어진 동사를 어법에 맞게 바꿔 쓰시오.

1 Not only the students but also the teacher _____ to read comic books. (love)

2 Either Aria or I _____ to pay for the damage. (have)

3 Neither my parents nor my girlfriend _____ a lot about me. (know)

4 Both my sister and I _____ to do the laundry. (need)

B 두 문장의 의미가 통하도록 주어진 상관접속사를 이용하여 문장을 완성하시오.

1 You can choose coffee, or you can choose juice. (either ~ or)

⇒ You can choose _____.

2 Maybe he went to bed early, or he lost his phone. (either ~ or)

⇒ _____

3 This creature can survive under water, and it can survive in the dessert, too. (both ~ and)

⇒ The creature can survive _____.

4 Their language course was expensive, and it was impractical, too. (both ~ and)

⇒ Their language course was _____.

5 My students are intelligent, and they are hardworking, too. (not only ~ but also)

⇒ My students are _____.

6 Emily doesn't like to play mobile games, and her boyfriend doesn't like to, either. (neither ~ nor)

⇒ _____ to play mobile games.

7 My next-door neighbor hasn't seen anything like it, and I haven't, either. (neither ~ nor)

⇒ _____ have seen anything like it.

8 Holly was able to solve the math question, and we were able, too. (not only ~ but also)

⇒ _____ were able to solve the math question.

C 〈보기〉에서 알맞은 접속사를 골라 써넣으시오. (중복 사용 가능)

🔍   that   whether   if

1 _____ they will launch the rocket or not depends on the weather.

2 We all know _____ it's not your fault.

3 What you shouldn't tell them is _____ I am suffering multiple injuries.

4 The fact _____ he has an IQ of 160 surprised all of us.

5 I was wondering _____ you could help me with my math homework.

6 Ryan just realized _____ he has to pick up his little sister from daycare.

7 I have no idea _____ or not they completed the mission successfully.

D 주어진 문장을 unless 또는 if ~ not을 이용하여 바꿔 쓰시오.

1 If the steps are not repaired, someone will get hurt.

    ⇨ _____

2 Unless it is dark and quiet, I can't go to sleep.

    ⇨ _____

3 Unless he calls you, you don't have to come to work tomorrow.

    ⇨ _____

4 If you don't show me yours first, I am not going to show you mine.

    ⇨ _____

5 If she is not ready, she shouldn't lead the marketing department.

    ⇨ _____

6 Unless you have further questions, you may go back to your seat.

    ⇨ _____

E 〈보기〉에서 알맞은 접속사를 골라 써넣으시오.

    🔍   although   while   since   by the time

[1-4]
1 He will do anything for you _____ he is in love with you.

2 The robbers will have gotten away _____ the police show up.

3 _____ my children were cooking dinner for me, I took a shower.

4 _____ he lived in the UK for three years, his English hasn't improved.

    🔍   so that   even if   until   because

[5-8]
5 The meeting continued _____ they came up with better ideas.

6 I wrote her a letter _____ I could express my true feelings for her.

7 Dave won't take the job _____ they offer him a lot of money.

8 Maria was upset _____ we made fun of her.

F 우리말과 같은 뜻이 되도록 주어진 말을 알맞게 배열하시오.

1 세입자들이 제때에 월세를 내기만 하면 그들은 쫓겨나지 않을 것이다. (on time, the tenants, as long as, pay, their rent)

⇨ _____, they won't get kicked out.

2 나는 숫자를 다루는 것을 좋아하는 반면 내 쌍둥이 형은 미술과 음악에 관심이 있다. (my twin brother, art and music, while, interested in, is)

⇨ I like to work with numbers, _____.

3 그 애플파이는 너무 맛있어서 나는 한 조각을 더 먹었다. (delicious, another, that, I, so, piece, had)

⇨ The apple pie was _____.

4 그들이 더 좋은 계획이 있는 게 아니라면 그들은 우리의 제안을 꼭 받아들일 거예요. (plans, unless, have, they, better)

⇨ _____, they will definitely accept our offer.

G 밑줄 친 부분을 어법에 맞게 고쳐 쓰시오.

1 Despite your essay is great, I can't give you an 'A.'   ⇨ _____

2 The lady on black looks so sad.   ⇨ _____

3 We traveled to Busan in bus.   ⇨ _____

4 The patient was in a lot of pain because of the wound was deep.   ⇨ _____

5 Charlie kept biting his fingernails during he was talking on the phone.   ⇨ _____

6 I love action movies, but I am not fond at comedy movies.   ⇨ _____

H 우리말과 같은 뜻이 되도록 주어진 단어를 이용하여 문장을 완성하시오.

1 우리는 거기까지 걸어가는 대신 버스를 타기로 결정했다. (walk, there)

⇨ We decided to take the bus _____.

2 팬데믹에도 불구하고 사업은 줄곧 잘됐어요. (spite, the pandemic)

⇨ Business has been great _____.

3 뉴스보도에 의하면 그 비행기는 짙은 안개로 인해 숲으로 추락했습니다. (news reports)

⇨ _____, the plane crashed into the woods due to heavy fog.

4 우리는 새로운 정책 덕분에 안전한 환경에서 일할 수 있습니다. (the new policy)

⇨ We can work in safe environments _____.

5 연휴 기간 동안 자동차 사고가 많이 발생한다. (the holiday season)

⇨ Many car accidents happen _____.

Chapter 12 특수 구문

A 밑줄 친 부분을 어법에 맞게 고쳐 쓰시오.

1 Julie is not only smart but also beauty. ⇨ _____

2 Either they or me have to give a presentation. ⇨ _____

3 It's not easy to speak smoothly and correct. ⇨ _____

4 She finished reading the book and write an essay. ⇨ _____

B 다음 괄호 안에 주어진 말을 이용하여 주어진 문장을 다시 쓰시오.

1 Sarah loves swimming. She loves rock climbing, too. (not only, but also)
   ⇨ _____

2 Emma is able to speak German. Eva is able to speak German, too. (both, and)
   ⇨ _____

3 Uncle Bill does not like cooking. He does not like drinking, either. (neither, nor)
   ⇨ _____

4 What the journalist said was important. It was shocking, too. (both, and)
   ⇨ _____

5 She listens to music after dinner. Or she watches TV. (either, or)
   ⇨ _____

C 밑줄 친 부분을 강조하는 문장으로 바꿔 쓰시오.

1 You look beautiful in the white dress.
   ⇨ You _____ beautiful in the white dress.

2 She has a point.
   ⇨ She _____ a point.

3 I feel bad for the victims.
   ⇨ I _____ bad for the victims.

4 We remained calm in the dark.
   ⇨ We _____ calm in the dark.

5 They saw me in the hallway.
   ⇨ They _____ me in the hallway.

6 William loves his wife deeply.
   ⇨ William _____ his wife deeply.

D 밑줄 친 부분을 강조하는 「It ~ that」 문장을 완성하시오.

1 The student lost his backpack underline{two weeks ago}.

   ⇨ It was _____ .

2 I watched the basketball game with underline{Elliot}.

   ⇨ It was _____ .

3 My dad wants to avoid underline{taking out the trash}.

   ⇨ It is _____ .

4 My cats were sleeping quietly underline{in the closet}.

   ⇨ It was _____ .

5 underline{Grace} bought me a hat for my birthday.

   ⇨ It was _____ .

6 The delivery man had underline{a cheeseburger} for supper.

   ⇨ It was _____ .

7 The singer is scheduled to start her rehearsal underline{at four}.

   ⇨ It is _____ .

E 우리말과 같은 뜻이 되도록 주어진 단어를 배열하시오.

1 도대체 너는 어디에 있었어? (you, the world, where, have, in, been)

   ⇨ _____

2 아이들이 티파티(다과회)를 벌이고 있는 곳은 바로 뒤뜰에서야. (the kids, it, are, is, having, that, in the backyard)

   ⇨ _____ a tea party.

3 Chloe는 매일 초콜릿 우유를 마셔. 하지만 지금은 뭔가 다른 것을 마시고 있어. (every day, drink, Chloe, chocolate milk, does)

   ⇨ _____ , but she is drinking something else now.

4 너는 도대체 어떻게 그녀에 대해서 알게 된 거야? (on earth, find out, you, how, did)

   ⇨ _____ about her?

5 너의 제안에 반대 투표한 사람은 Gabriel이었다. (Gabriel, against, it, voted, who, was)

   ⇨ _____ your proposal.

6 그가 스트라이커로서 프로 무대에 데뷔한 것은 10년 전이었다. (made, a decade ago, was, when, he, his professional debut, it)

   ⇨ _____ as a striker.

F So 또는 Neither를 이용하여 대화를 완성하시오.

1 **A** I am so angry with Harry.

   B _____ He broke my mechanical pencil.

2 **A** Jason and I were very surprised to see Mr. Nash there.

   B _____ I thought he was still in the hospital.

3 **A** I don't like watching horror movies.

   B _____ I am really scared of ghosts.

4 **A** I couldn't finish the science assignment.

   B _____ Science is so difficult.

G 〈보기〉와 같이 밑줄 친 단어를 강조하는 문장으로 바꿔 쓰시오.

      A candle was on the table.
      ⇨ **On the table** _____ was a candle _____ .

1 They could hardly believe what I had told them.
   ⇨ Hardly _____ .

2 My father's books were on the bottom shelf.
   ⇨ On the bottom shelf _____ .

3 He had never been so embarrassed before.
   ⇨ Never _____ .

4 They seldom have breakfast on school days.
   ⇨ Seldom _____ .

H 우리말과 같은 뜻이 되도록 주어진 단어를 배열하시오.

1 그녀는 지금까지 자신의 업무일정에 관해 불평한 적이 거의 없다. (work schedule, has, about, she, her, complained)
   ⇨ Rarely _____ .

2 금요일이 되어서 James는 자신의 지갑이 없어졌다는 것을 깨달았다. (James, his, did, was missing, realize, wallet)
   ⇨ Not until Friday _____ .

3 그 집 앞에 거대한 떡갈나무가 있었다. (giant, stood, a, oak tree)
   ⇨ In front of the house _____ .

4 우리 집 옆에 캐나다에서 온 젊은 부부가 살았다. (Canada, lived, from, a young couple)
   ⇨ Next to my house _____ .

MEMO

MEMO

MEMO

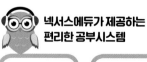

LEVEL CHART

	초1	초2	초3	초4	초5	초6	중1	중2	중3	고1	고2	고3
VOCA	초등필수 영단어 1-2 · 3-4 · 5-6학년용									WORD PASS		
			The VOCA + (플러스) 1~7									
			THIS IS VOCABULARY 입문 · 초급 · 중급					고급 · 어원 · 수능 완성 · 뉴텝스				
				WORD FOCUS 중등 종합 5000 · 고등 필수 5000 · 고등 종합 9500								
Grammar			초등필수 영문법 + 쓰기 1~2										
			OK Grammar 1~4									
			This Is Grammar Starter 1~3									
				This Is Grammar 초급~고급 (각 2권: 총 6권)								
					Grammar 공감 1~3							
					Grammar 101 1~3							
					Grammar Bridge 1~3 (NEW EDITION)							
					The Grammar Starter, 1~3							
						한 권으로 끝내는 필수 구문 1000제						
							구사일생 (구문독해 Basic) 1~2					
								구문독해 204 1~2 (개정판)				
									고난도 구문독해 500			
							그래머 캡처 1~2					
								[특급 단기 특강] 어법어휘 모의고사				

★ NEW EDITION ★

GRAMMAR BRIDGE

넥서스영어교육연구소 · 김경태 지음

Level

3

정답 및 해설

NEXUS Edu

★ NEW EDITION ★

GRAMMAR BRIDGE

넥서스영어교육연구소 · 김경태 지음

Level

3

정답 및 해설

NEXUS Edu

Chapter 1

1-1 현재완료   p.12

Exercise 1

1 have, heard
2 has, become
3 Have, ever, ridden
4 has, never, been
5 have, already, seen
6 have, just, sent

Exercise 2

1 have, visited
2 Have, read
3 has, finished
4 has, lived
5 have, been

Exercise 3

1 has, lost
2 has, gone
3 have, lived
4 has, been
5 has, studied

Exercise 4

1 I have just finished breakfast.
2 The doctor has not arrived yet.
3 He has left his glasses in the library.
4 I have never caught a fish before.
5 I have met the soccer player before.
6 She has taken care of the orphans since 2005.
7 Sally has taught biology for twenty years.
8 He has bought a smartphone for his son.
9 She has gone to the USA to study English.

1-2 현재진행/현재완료진행   p.14

Exercise 1

1 has been
2 are
3 have
4 been reading
5 have been

Exercise 2

1 is listening to
2 is practicing
3 is reading
4 is washing
5 are running

Exercise 3

1 has been taking
2 has been watching
3 have been waiting for
4 have been reading
5 have been fishing

1-3 과거완료/과거완료진행   p.15

Exercise 1

1 had lost
2 has learned
3 had lived
4 had stayed
5 had expected
6 had already left
7 had seen
8 had been
9 has learned
10 had been raining
11 had left
12 had practiced
13 had been walking
14 has been watching
15 had been preparing

Exercise 2

1 had asked for
2 had played[had been playing]
3 had already left
4 had lived[had been living]
5 had watched[had been watching]
6 had left
7 had read[had been reading]
8 had learned

Exercise 3

1 has been going through[has gone through]
2 had already gone
3 has been learning[has learned]
4 had worked
5 had played[had been playing]

Exercise 4

1 he had left his homework at home
2 Peter and Kelly had already known each other
3 she had been reading a magazine for three hours
4 breakfast had already been prepared for me

1-4 미래완료   p.17

Exercise 1

1 will have seen
2 has volunteered
3 will have taken off
4 will have lived
5 will have already finished

Exercise 2

1 they will have lived in Australia for ten years
2 The boat will have already left
3 she will have studied Korean for two years
4 the staff training process will have been completed

01 ④ 02 ② 03 ③ 04 ⑤ 05 ③ 06 ⑤
07 ③ 08 ④ 09 ⑤ 10 ⑤ 11 ① 12 ③
13 ③ 14 ⑤ 15 ③ 16 ④ 17 ⑤ 18 ②
19 ⑤ 20 ③ 21 ③ 22 ② 23 ⑤ 24 ①

25 just, just

26 already, yet

27 already, just

28 has, been, talking, with

29 had, been, reading

30 will, have, studied

31 had, made

32 have, been

33 had met, have visited

01 Tom은 돈을 다 써버려서 책을 살 수 없다. : 과거에 돈을 다 써버린 행동이 현재에 책을 살 수 없게 만들었다. 과거의 행동이 현재까지 영향을 미칠 때는 현재완료 시제를 쓰는 것이 적절하다.

02 Alice는 어제 역으로 가는 길에 차가 막혀서 기차를 놓쳤다. 그녀가 역에 도착했을 때 기차는 이미 떠나고 없었다. : Alice가 역에 도착한 것(과거)보다 기차가 떠난 것이 더 앞서 발생한 일이기 때문에 과거완료 시제를 쓰는 것이 적절하다.

03 나는 아내가 내게 사준 시계를 잃어버렸다. : 내가 시계를 잃어버린 것(과거)보다 아내가 내게 시계를 사준 것이 더 앞서 발생한 일이기 때문에 과거완료 시제를 쓰는 것이 적절하다.

04 그가 내년에 은퇴하면 그는 30년 동안 군 생활을 한 것이 된다. : 미래의 어느 한 시점까지 계속되는 일은 미래완료 시제를 쓰는 것이 적절하다.

05 ③은 과거부터 현재까지 계속되는 상태를 나타내고, 나머지는 모두 경험을 나타낸다.

06 〈보기〉 나는 영어를 2년 동안 공부하고 있다. : 과거부터 현재까지 계속되는 상태를 나타낸다. ①은 결과, ②는 경험, ③, ④는 완료를 나타낸다.

07 〈보기〉 나는 이미 저녁을 먹었다. : 과거에 시작한 일이 현재에 완료됨을 나타낸다. ①, ④는 경험, ②, ⑤는 계속을 나타낸다.

08 ④ when은 특정 시점을 묻는 의문사이기 때문에 현재완료 시제와 함께 쓰지 않는다. 따라서 When did you go to Boston?으로 고쳐야 한다.

09 나는 3년 전에 이 오토바이를 타기 시작했고, 아직도 그 오토바이를 탄다. : 과거에 시작한 일이 현재에도 지속되고 있는 경우는 현재완료 시제를 쓰는 것이 적절하다.

10 나는 6세 때부터 클래식 음악을 듣기 시작했고, 지금도 클래식 음악을 듣고 있다. : 과거에 시작한 일이 현재에도 진행 중인 경우는 현재완료진행 시제를 쓰는 것이 적절하다. 현재완료진행은 「have[has] been+-ing」의 형태로 쓴다.

11 ② 현재완료 시제의 부정은 have[has]에 not을 붙이므로 doesn't를 hasn't로 고쳐야 한다.
③ never를 삭제해서 '나는 그에게 이미 말을 했다.'라는 뜻으로 쓰거나, already를 삭제해서 '나는 그에게 말해 본 적이 없다.'라는 뜻으로 쓸 수 있다.

④ '스위스에 가본 적이 있니?'라고 경험을 나타낼 때에는 have gone to를 쓸 수 없다. have gone to는 '~에 가버렸다 (그래서 지금 여기에 없다)'라는 뜻으로 완료나 결과를 나타낸다. 따라서 gone을 been으로 고쳐야 한다.
⑤ 접속사 since는 '~부터'라는 뜻으로 여자가 선생님이 된 것보다 여자가 대학을 졸업한 것이 더 먼저 일어난 일이므로 graduates를 graduated로 고쳐야 한다.

12 ① 경험을 묻는 질문이므로 Did를 Have로 고쳐서 현재완료 시제로 쓰는 것이 적절하다.
② 현재완료진행 시제는 「have[has] been+-ing」로 쓴다.
④ 현재완료 시제의 의문문은 「Have[has]+주어+p.p. ~?」로 쓴다. 따라서 Do you have를 Have you로 고쳐야 한다.
⑤ 전치사 since는 '~부터'라는 뜻으로 뒤에 특정 시점이 오고, 전치사 for는 '~동안'이라는 뜻으로 뒤에 기간을 나타내는 수치가 온다.

13 ③ last semester는 '지난 학기'라는 뜻으로 정확한 과거시점을 나타내는 부사구이고, 현재완료 시제와 함께 쓰지 않는다. 따라서 has passed를 passed로 고쳐야 한다.

14 ⑤ 우리가 체육관에 도착한 것(과거)보다 결승전이 끝난 것이 더 앞서 발생한 일이기 때문에 과거완료 시제를 쓰는 것이 적절하다. 따라서 has를 had로 고쳐야 한다.

15 〈보기〉 그가 벌써 숙제를 다 했니? : 긍정이면 Yes, 부정이면 No로 대답할 수 있다. 현재완료 시제로 물었으므로 현재완료 시제로 답한 ③이 가장 적절한 대답이다. ④는 No로 답했지만, 뒤에는 긍정의 내용이 오기 때문에 답이 될 수 없다.

16 〈보기〉 나는 열쇠를 잃어버렸다. : 현재완료 시제 중 결과를 의미한다. 과거에 열쇠를 잃어버려서 현재 가지고 있지 않다는 뜻이므로 ④와 그 의미가 같다. ① 나는 열쇠를 잃어버렸다가 찾았다. ② 열쇠가 주머니에 있다. ③ 나는 열쇠를 잃어버렸지만 지금 가지고 있다. ⑤ 나는 처음부터 열쇠를 가지고 있지 않았다.

17 A 당신은 얼마나 오래 회사에서 일하고 있습니까?
B 나는 10년 동안 일하고 있습니다.
과거에서 시작한 일이 현재에도 계속 진행 중인 것은 현재완료진행 시제(have[has] been+-ing)를 쓴다.

18 내가 펜역에 도착했을 때 보스턴행 열차는 이미 떠났다. : 역에 도착한 것보다 열차가 떠난 것(과거완료)이 더 앞서 발생한 일이다. 접속사 when은 특정 시점을 나타내기 때문에 when절에는 과거 시제가 오는 것이 적절하다. 과거완료 시제는 「had+p.p.」로 쓴다.

19 • Lucy는 병원에 입원하기 전에 일주일 동안 아파서 누워 있었다. : 병원에 입원한 것(과거)보다 일주일 동안 아파서 누워 있었던 것이 더 앞서 발생한 일이므로 과거완료 시제를 쓰는 것이 적절하다.
• 나는 지난 토요일 이후로 잠을 자지 못한다. : 과거부터 지금까지 계속되는 일은 현재완료 시제를 쓰는 것이 적절하다.

20 • 그가 아침에 일어날 때 즈음에 비가 이미 그쳤다. : by the time은 접속사로 쓰여서 '~할 때까지', '~할 때 즈음에'라는 뜻이다.
• 우리는 내년이면 25년 동안 결혼생활을 하는 것이 된다. : 전치사 for는 '~ 동안'이라는 뜻이고, 뒤에 기간을 나타내는 수치가 온다.
• 내 여동생은 집에 온 이후로 통화 중이다. : 접속사 since는 '~ 이후로'라는 뜻이고, 뒤에 행동이나 상태의 시작을 나타내는 절이 온다.

21 '네, 그녀는 그곳에 한 번 가본 적이 있습니다.'라고 대답하고 있으므로 '~을 방문해 본 적이 있습니까?'라고 경험을 묻는 현재완료 시제가 쓰인 의문문이 오는 것이 가장 적절하다.

22 ② 이틀 후는 미래이다. 미래의 한 시점까지 계속되는 일은 미래완료 시제로 나타낸다. 따라서 had been을 will have been으로 고쳐야 한다.

23 ⑤ A 오늘 아침에 비가 오기 시작했고 아직도 내리는 중이야. : 오늘 아침부터 비가 내리기 시작해서 지금도 내리고 있으므로 현재완료진행 시제가 오는 것이 적절하다. 따라서 will have been raining을 has been raining으로 고쳐야 한다.

24 ① 그녀는 제주도에 가본 적이 있다. ≠ 그녀는 제주도에 가는 중이다.
② 나는 월요일 이후로 Alex를 보지 못했다. = 월요일이 내가 Alex를 본 마지막 날이다.
③ 한 시간 동안 비가 내리고 있다. = 한 시간 전에 비가 내리기 시작해서 아직도 내리고 있다.
④ Amy와 Bob은 20년 동안 결혼생활을 하는 중이다. = Amy와 Bob은 20년 전에 결혼했고, 아직도 결혼생활 중이다.
⑤ Joe와 Ralph는 1년 동안 함께 살았다. = Joe와 Ralph는 1년 전에 함께 살기 시작해서 아직도 함께 살고 있다.

25 '방금', '막'이라는 뜻의 부사는 just이다. 완료를 나타내는 현재완료 시제와 함께 쓴다.

26 '이미'라는 뜻의 부사는 already이고, 완료를 나타내는 현재완료 시제와 함께 쓴다. yet은 부정문에서는 '아직'이라는 뜻이다.

27 '이미'라는 뜻의 부사는 already이고, '방금'이라는 뜻의 부사는 just이다.

28 두 시간 전에 시작한 대화가 아직 이어지고 있는 것이므로 현재완료진행 시제(has been talking with)로 쓰는 것이 적절하다. 주어 My teacher가 3인칭 단수이므로 has를 쓴다.

29 그가 방에 들어왔을 때(과거) 나는 책을 읽는 중이었으므로 과거완료진행 시제(had been reading)를 쓰는 것이 적절하다.

30 시간을 나타내는 부사절에서는 현재 시제가 미래 시제를 대신한다. 따라서 부모님께서 나를 데리러 오는 것은 미래에 있을 일이므로 이전에 시작한 일이 미래의 어느 한 시점까지 계속되는 것을 의미하는 미래완료 시제(will have studied)를 쓴다.

31 남자의 아들이 대학에 간 것은 과거의 일(went to college)이고, 남자가 아들에게 약속한 것은 더 앞서 발생한 일이므로 과거완료 시제(had made)를 쓰는 것이 적절하다.

32 과거에 시작한 행동이 현재 시점에서 완료된 상태이므로 현재완료 시제(have been)를 쓴다. 부사 just는 현재완료의 완료용법과 함께 쓰여서 '막', '방금'이라는 뜻이다.

33 • 나는 전에 어딘가에서 그 소녀를 만난 적이 있다는 것을 알았다. : 내가 안 것(knew)보다 내가 그 소녀를 만난 것이 더 먼저 일어난 일이므로 과거완료 시제(had met)를 쓰는 것이 적절하다.
• 나는 전에 L.A.에 여러 번 가봤기 때문에 그 도시를 잘 안다. : 과거부터 현재까지 겪은 경험을 나타낼 때는 현재완료 시제(have visited)를 쓴다.

보너스 유형별 문제 p.22

1 had broken
2 has stolen → had stolen
3 The thief has been arrested.
4 ①

[1-3] 휴가를 보내고 지난주에 집으로 돌아왔을 때 나는 매우 화가 났다. 집이 완전히 엉망이었다. 누군가 침입했었음이 명백했다. 나는 도둑이 내 최신형 자전거를 훔쳐 가기 때문에 절망했다. 나는 즉시 경찰에 신고를 했지만 그들은 내 자전거를 되찾기 어려울 것이라고 말했다. 하지만 방금 경찰서에서 전화가 왔다. 도둑이 체포되었다. 아마 내 자전거를 되찾을 수 있을 것 같다.

1 누군가 침입한 것이 명백한 것은 과거이며 침입 행위는 그 이전에 일어난 것이므로 과거완료(had+p.p.)가 적절하다.

2 내가 절망한 것보다 도둑이 자전거를 훔친 것이 더 이전에 발생한 일이므로 과거완료가 적절하다.

3 현재완료의 수동태는 「have been p.p.」로 쓴다.

4 오늘 밤 저는 여동생의 피아노 발표회에 갔습니다. 몇 주 동안 매일 밤 연습을 했음에도 불구하고 동생은 매우 불안해했지요. 저는 동생이 긴장을 풀고 자신을 믿는다면 아주 잘 해낼 수 있을 거라고 확신했어요. 연주할 차례가 되자, 동생은 무대로 올라가 심호흡을 하고 연주를 시작했습니다. 동생은 모든 음을 완벽하게 쳤지요. 연주가 끝나자 관중은 큰 박수갈채를 보냈습니다. 동생은 일어나 고개 숙여 인사하고 관중을 향해 미소를 지었습니다.
과거의 시점을 기준으로 그 이전에 일어난 것에 대해 말하므로 현재완료가 아닌 과거완료를 써야 옳다. 따라서 has는 had로 써야 적절하다.

Chapter 2

2-1 명사적 쓰임 p.24

Exercise 1

1 to read	2 To collect
3 to give up	4 to go
5 To swim	6 to feel
7 to send	8 to watch over

Exercise 2

1 how to drive	2 how to use
3 where to stay	4 what to say

Exercise 3

1 It is very interesting to learn English.
2 It is fun to play volleyball on the beach.
3 It is not possible to read people's minds.
4 It is very difficult to break one's bad habits.
5 It was hard to prepare for the annual festival.
6 It is impossible to complete the project by myself.

Exercise 4

1 to catch the criminals on behalf of the police
2 to send more troops to the conflict area
3 to become a great actor since childhood

4 how to get to City Hall
5 to build the bridge within three months
6 to extend the contract for an additional year

so that I could tell him the result of his exam
6 in order to win a gold medal at the Olympic Games
so that he could win a gold medal at the Olympic Games

2-2 형용사적 쓰임 p.26

Exercise 1

1 to buy　　　　　　2 to take care of
3 to show　　　　　 4 to visit
5 to eat

Exercise 2

1 It's time to go to school.
2 You have to give her paper to write on.
3 I would like to have something to drink.
4 Andrew just transferred to a new school, so he doesn't have many friends to hang out with.

Exercise 3

1 All children are to respect their parents.
2 The document was not to be found again.
3 The World Cup is to be held next year.
4 Aaron was never to see his country again.
5 If you are to pass the exam, you have to study hard.

Exercise 4

1 homework to finish
2 nothing to say
3 a beautiful dress to wear
4 a book to read

Exercise 5

1 was to be a great actor
2 If you are to succeed
3 are to finish writing your essay
4 is to take place at the convention center

2-3 부사적 쓰임 p.28

Exercise 1

1 in order to buy a laptop computer
so that she can buy a laptop computer
2 in order to watch the soccer game
so that they could watch the soccer game
3 in order to play computer games
so that he could play computer games
4 in order to become a diplomat
so that she could become a diplomat
5 in order to tell him the result of his exam

Exercise 2

1 to surf　　　　　　2 to be
3 to go　　　　　　　4 to run across
5 to hear

Exercise 3

1 감정의 원인　　　　2 판단의 근거
3 결과　　　　　　　 4 형용사 수식
5 목적

Exercise 4

1 is easy to assemble
2 grew up to be a famous pianist
3 go to the market to buy
4 are so pleased to invite you to the meeting
5 a genius to develop the theory of relativity

2-4 의미상의 주어 p.30

Exercise 1

1 Tony to help her carry the baggage
2 Mark to repair her computer
3 Carol to clean up her room
4 David to go out and play

Exercise 2

1 for　　　　　　　　2 of
3 of　　　　　　　　 4 of
5 of　　　　　　　　 6 for

Exercise 3

1 to sell　　　　　　2 to take
3 to go　　　　　　　4 to do
5 to understand　　　6 to do
7 to finish　　　　　 8 to share
9 to use　　　　　　10 to call

Exercise 4

1 advised him to stop smoking
2 rude of you to say
3 want me to go to the library
4 allowed me to go
5 expects me to help

Exercise 1

1 not to meet
2 not to fail
3 not to be
4 not to use
5 not to swim
6 not to worry

Exercise 2

1 to not eat → not to eat
2 to not lose → not to lose
3 to not missed → not to miss
4 to not making → not to make
5 not to spent → not to spend
6 to skip not → not to skip

Exercise 3

1 It is useful to read many English books.
2 It is important to do exercise every day.
3 It is not easy for me to speak Chinese fluently.
4 It is hard for me to break the bad habit of nail-biting.
5 It is difficult for amateurs like us to climb up mountains like Everest.

Exercise 4

1 it, to understand
2 it, to take a walk
3 It, to swim
4 it, to go
5 It, to exercise
6 it, to repeat
7 It, to travel

Exercise 1

1 to know
2 to be
3 to devote
4 to have

Exercise 2

1 to have stolen
2 to have broken
3 to have been
4 to have worked

Exercise 3

1 she was aware of the fact
2 to have lost his wallet
3 to win the match
4 she saw [has seen] a ghost in the restroom
5 our soccer team will advance to the finals
6 to have gone to the International Film Festival by himself

Exercise 4

1 Helen seems to be angry at me.
2 He seemed to have been a famous soccer player.
3 Jessy hopes to finish the project in time.
4 It seems that she has worked with Tim before.
5 It seems that she is quite an attractive woman.
6 Eric seemed to have collected many stamps from all over the world.

Exercise 1

1 called
2 know
3 play/playing
4 enter/entering
5 paint
6 clean
7 water
8 solve, to solve

Exercise 2

1 to run → run [running]
2 join → to join
3 waited → wait [waiting]
4 to read → read

Exercise 3

1 cry [crying]
2 watch
3 take
4 fix
5 to study

Exercise 4

1 The red shirt made her look younger.
2 I heard the pianist play the piano.
3 I made him finish his homework by nine.
4 I heard the kids in the cave yelling for help.
5 They watched Eddie play baseball with his friends.
6 Mandy felt something crawling on her head.
7 When the earthquake happened, I felt my house shake.

Exercise 1

1 so tired that I couldn't play basketball anymore
2 so small that it can fit into a box
3 too shy to talk to her
4 energetic enough to run a marathon

Exercise 2

1 too, hot, to, drink
2 old, enough, to, go
3 brave, enough, to, do
4 so, busy, I, couldn't, have

2-9 독립부정사

p.39

Exercise 1

1 Needless to say
2 To be frank with you
3 so to speak
4 Strange to say
5 not to mention

Exercise 2

1 설상가상으로, 그는 또 다른 실수를 했다.
2 요약하면, 당신은 건강을 위해 매일 운동을 해야 한다.
3 솔직히 말해서, 당신의 컴퓨터는 내일까지 수리될 수 없습니다.
4 말할 필요도 없이, 우리는 여름휴가 동안에 해변에 가기를 원한다.

Review Test

p.40

01 ③	02 ①	03 ⑤	04 ②	05 ②	06 ①
07 ①	08 ②	09 ②	10 ④	11 ③	12 ②
13 ②, ③		14 ②	15 ④	16 ①	17 ④
18 ①	19 ④	20 ①	21 ③	22 ⑤	23 ⑤
24 ③	25 ④	26 ③	27 ①	28 ④	29 ③

30 for
31 it[It]
32 His handwriting is too bad to read.
33 Richard was smart enough to solve the puzzle.
34 to understand
35 to have been
36 too, to
37 not to turn up
38 to hold
39 To make matters worse, I was late for school.
40 Strange to say, I don't want to go to university.

01 나는 차를 살 충분한 돈이 없다. : 밑줄 친 to buy는 앞에 있는 명사 money를 수식하는 형용사적 용법으로 쓰였다.
① 형용사 glad를 수식해서 감정의 원인을 나타내는 부사적 용법
② 동사 want의 목적어로 쓰인 명사적 용법
③ 명사 house를 수식하는 형용사적 용법
④ 문장의 주어로 쓰인 명사적 용법
⑤ 목적을 나타내는 부사적 용법

02 나는 미국에 가려고 계획했다. : 밑줄 친 to go는 동사 plan의 목적어로 쓰인 명사적 용법이다.
① 동사 want의 목적어로 쓰인 명사적 용법
② 명사 things를 수식하는 형용사적 용법
③ 대명사 something을 수식하는 형용사적 용법
④ 목적을 나타내는 부사적 용법
⑤ 결과를 나타내는 부사적 용법

03 나는 책을 읽으려고 도서관에 갔다. : 밑줄 친 to read는 목적을 나타내는 부사적 용법이다.
① 동사 want의 목적어로 쓰인 명사적 용법
② 명사 books를 수식하는 형용사적 용법
③ 문장의 주어로 쓰인 명사적 용법
④ 주격보어로 쓰인 명사적 용법
⑤ 목적을 나타내는 부사적 용법

04 회의는 내일 열릴 예정이다. : 밑줄 친 is to be는 예정을 나타내는 「be동사+to부정사」이다.
① 너는 이야기들은 대로 해야 한다.(의무)
② 그는 오늘 밤에 싱가포르를 떠날 것이다.(예정)
③ 길에서 아무도 볼 수 없었다.(가능)
④ 너는 늦어도 10시까지 집에 와야 한다.(의무)
⑤ 만약 친구로 남으려면 너는 솔직해야 한다.(의도)

05 「how+to부정사」는 '어떻게 ~할지', '~하는 방법'이라는 뜻이다. 「의문사+to부정사」는 명사구 역할을 한다.

06 have는 사역동사로, 「have+목적어+동사원형」의 형태로 쓰며, '~에게 …하게 시키다'라는 뜻이다.

07 see는 지각동사로, 「지각동사(see[watch, hear, feel, listen to])+목적어+동사원형/현재분사」의 형태로 쓰이며, '~가 …하는 것을 보다[보다, 듣다, 느끼다, 듣다]'라는 뜻이다.

08 「order+목적어+to부정사」는 '~에게 …하도록 명하다'라는 뜻이다. 이때 목적어가 목적격보어로 쓰인 to부정사의 의미상 주어이다.

09 「ask+목적어+to부정사」는 '~에게 …하도록 부탁하다'라는 뜻이다. 이때 목적어가 목적격보어로 쓰인 to부정사의 의미상 주어이다.

10 ① 그렇게 말하는 것을 보니 그는 바보임이 틀림없다. : 판단의 근거로 쓰인 부사적 용법
② 이 질문은 대답하기 어렵다. : 형용사 hard를 수식하는 부사적 용법
③ 그들은 상을 받기 위해서 최선을 다했다. : 목적을 나타내는 부사적 용법
④ 너는 10시까지 여기에 와야 한다. : 의무를 나타내는 「be동사+to부정사(형용사적 용법)」
⑤ Tom은 커서 영어 선생님이 되었다. : 결과를 나타내는 부사적 용법

11 to부정사의 의미상 주어는 일반적으로 「for+목적격」으로 나타내고, kind, nice, rude, wise처럼 사람의 성격을 나타내는 형용사가 오면 「of+목적격」으로 나타낸다.

12 • 「지각동사(see[watch, hear, feel, listen to])+목적어+동사원형/현재분사」는 '~가 …하는 것을 보다[보다, 듣다, 느끼다, 듣다]'라는 뜻이다.
• 「사역동사(make, have, let)+목적어+동사원형」은 '~에게 …하게 시키다'라는 뜻이다.

13 「사역동사(make, have, let)+목적어+동사원형」은 '~에게 …하게 시키다'라는 뜻이다. 「get/ask/tell+목적어+to부정사」는 '~에게 …하게 시키다/부탁하다/말하다'라는 뜻이다.

14 목적격보어로 to부정사(to pick up)가 쓰였다. want, advise, force, tell은 모두 목적격보어로 to부정사를 취하는 동사이다. 사역동사 let은 목적격보어로 동사원형을 취한다.

15 to부정사의 부정형은 to부정사 앞에 not/never를 붙인다. 「have to+동사원형」은 '~해야 한다'라는 뜻의 조동사로 쓰인다.

16 네가 성공하고자 하면 열심히 일해야 한다. : are to는 의도를 나타내는 「be동사+to부정사」이다. intend to는 '~하고자 하다'라는 뜻이다. ③ have to는 '~해야 한다'라는 뜻으로 의무 ④ can은 '~할 수 있다'는 뜻으로 가능 ⑤ be destined to는 '~할 운명이다'라는 뜻으로 운명을 나타낸다.

7

17 회의는 3시에 열릴 예정이었지만 취소되었다. : 밑줄 친 was to는 예정을 나타낸다. be supposed to는 '~하기로 되어 있다'라는 뜻이다.

18 「형용사+enough+to부정사」는 '~할 만큼 충분히 …한'이라는 뜻이다. enough가 한정사로 쓰이면 명사를 앞에서 수식하고, 부사로 쓰이면 형용사나 부사를 뒤에서 수식한다.
e.g. I have **enough** money to buy a car.
나는 차를 살 정도로 충분한 돈이 있다.
I am <u>rich</u> **enough** to buy a car.
나는 차를 살 정도로 충분히 부자이다.

19 ④ see는 지각동사로, 「지각동사+목적어+동사원형/현재분사」의 형태로 쓰이므로 to dance로 쓸 수 없다.

20 ① 「tell+목적어+to부정사」는 '~에게 …하라고 말하다'라는 뜻으로 stop을 to stop으로 고쳐야 한다.

21 ③ 「have+목적어+동사원형」은 '~에게 …하도록 시키다'라는 뜻으로 to come을 come으로 고쳐야 한다.

22 ⑤ 「watch+목적어+동사원형/현재분사」는 '~가 …하는 것을 보다'라는 뜻으로 to play를 play나 playing으로 고쳐야 한다.

23 to부정사의 의미상 주어 앞에 전치사 of가 오는 경우는 사람의 성격을 나타내는 형용사가 올 때이다. silly(바보 같은), clever(영리한), rude(무례한), wise(지혜로운)는 모두 사람의 성격을 묘사하는 형용사이다.

24 to부정사의 의미상 주어는 사람의 성격을 나타내는 형용사가 올 때를 제외하고 대부분 「for+의미상 주어」의 형태로 쓴다. careless(부주의한)는 사람의 성격을 묘사하는 형용사이다.

25 kind, nice, foolish, careless는 모두 사람의 성격을 묘사하는 형용사이므로 to부정사의 의미상 주어 앞에 전치사 of가 온다. easy는 사람의 성격을 묘사하는 형용사가 아니므로 to부정사의 의미상 주어 앞에 전치사 for가 온다.

26 「advise+목적어+to부정사」는 '~에게 …하라고 조언하다'라는 뜻이다. to부정사의 부정형은 to부정사 앞에 not/never를 쓴다.

27 「have+목적어+동사원형」은 '~에게 …하도록 시키다'라는 뜻이다.

28 동사 make, find, think 등의 목적어가 to부정사일 때 가목적어 it을 사용하고, 진목적어는 문장 뒤로 보낸다. ①, ②, ③ '그것'이라는 뜻의 대명사 it ④ find의 가목적어로 쓰인 it(진목적어는 to study English) ⑤ '만들다'라는 뜻의 동사 make의 목적어로 쓰인 대명사 it

29 • 「too ~ to …」는 '너무 ~해서 …할 수 없다'라는 뜻이다. to부정사의 의미상 주어는 「for+의미상 주어」의 형태로 to부정사 앞에 쓴다.
• 「형용사+enough+to부정사」는 '~할 정도로 충분히 …한'이라는 뜻이다.

30 to부정사의 의미상 주어는 사람의 성격을 나타내는 형용사가 오는 경우를 제외하고는 「for+의미상 주어」의 형태로 쓴다. necessary, important는 사람의 성격을 나타내는 형용사가 아니므로 빈칸에 for가 들어가는 것이 가장 적절하다.

31 • make, find, think 등의 동사가 왔을 때 목적어로 쓰인 to부정사(구)를 문장의 뒤로 보내고 가목적어 it을 to부정사 대신 쓴다.
• 문장의 주어가 to부정사이면서 긴 경우 가주어 it을 주어 자리에 쓰고 to부정사를 문장의 뒤로 보낸다.

32 「too ~ to …」는 '너무 ~해서 …할 수 없다'라는 뜻이다.

33 「형용사+enough+to부정사」는 '~할 정도로 충분히 …한'이라는 뜻이다.

34 그는 너무 바보 같아서 그 의미를 이해할 수 없었다. : 「so ~ that+주어+cannot …」 = 「too ~ to …」는 '너무 ~해서 …할 수 없다'라는 뜻이다.

35 그녀는 건축가였던 것처럼 보인다. : to부정사의 시제가 주절의 시제보다 앞선 경우 「to have p.p.」의 형태로 쓴다.

36 Paul은 너무 배가 불러서 더는 먹을 수가 없었다. : 「so ~ that+주어+cannot …」 = 「too ~ to …」는 '너무 ~해서 …할 수 없다'라는 뜻이다.

37 「ask+목적어+to부정사」는 '~에게 …하라고 부탁하다'라는 뜻이다. to부정사의 부정형은 to부정사 앞에 not/never를 쓴다.

38 「형용사+enough+to부정사」는 '~할 정도로 충분히 …한'이라는 뜻이다.

39 to make matters worse는 '설상가상으로'라는 뜻의 관용적 표현이다.

40 strange to say는 '이상한 말이지만'이라는 뜻의 관용적 표현이다.

보너스 유형별 문제   <small>p.44</small>

1 well enough to do

2 seemed to sing

3 ④

[1-2] A 이봐, Lucas. 너 학교 축제 때 노래 자랑 대회에 참가할 거니?
B 아니, 나는 그럴 만큼 노래를 잘 하지 않아.
A 지난번에 네가 노래하는 것을 들었을 때 너는 노래를 매우 잘 하는 것 같았어.
B 고마워. 하지만 대신 Emmett과 나는 댄스 대회에 참가 신청했어. 우리는 이길수 있도록 매우 열심히 연습하고 있어.

1 '~할 정도로 충분히 …하게'는 「부사+enough+to부정사」로 쓴다.

2 to부정사의 시제가 주절과 같은 경우 「to+동사원형」을 쓰고 과거의 일을 나타내므로 「seemed+to부정사」를 쓴다.

3 고등학생 컴퓨터 해커 세 명이 절도 혐의로 체포되었다. 이 16세 소년들은 복잡한 인터넷 기법을 써서 고가의 컴퓨터 장비를 훔쳤다. 그들은 로컬 인터넷 서버에 침입해 신용 카드 번호를 훔친 후, 온라인으로 물건을 구입했다. 그들은 3천 달러 상당의 컴퓨터 장비를 주문해, 그 지역의 빈집으로 배송시켜 방과 후에 가져갈 수 있게 했다. 이런 수상한 행동에 의심을 품은 이웃 주민들이 경찰에 신고했고, 그들은 즉시 현장에 도착했다. 그들이 그런 일을 꾸민 이유를 묻는 질문에, 소년들은 무언가 흥미진진한 것을 하길 원했다고 말했다.
'~할 정도로 충분히 …하게'는 「부사+enough+to부정사」로 쓴다. 따라서 부사(quickly)와 enough의 위치가 서로 바뀌어야 한다.

Chapter 3

3-1 명사적 쓰임 p.46

Exercise 1

1 taking
2 reading
3 becoming
4 saying
5 winning
6 giving

Exercise 2

1 The most important thing is enjoying your life.
2 She loves reading classic novels.
3 Going shopping is my favorite activity.
4 The instructor started practicing yoga in 2015 and began teaching in 2021.

3-2 동명사의 시제 p.47

Exercise 1

1 being poor
2 being early adopters
3 having won the marathon race
4 having done such a foolish thing

Exercise 2

1 having stepped on your toes
2 having won the marathon
3 sharing clothes with my sister
4 having received an acceptance letter

3-3 의미상의 주어/부정형 p.48

Exercise 1

1 my son's being clever
2 my brother's being rude
3 his being jealous of her
4 their being late for the meeting
5 his cousins' visiting him last week
6 her winning the gold medal this time

Exercise 2

1 그는 자기 아버지가 그곳에 가야 한다고 주장했다.
2 나는 우리 아들이 국가대표로 뽑힌 것이 자랑스러웠다.
3 Wilson은 자기 할아버지가 한국전쟁에 참전했었다는 것을 확신한다.
4 Tom은 자기가 주차할 때 그녀가 건물로 들어가던 것을 기억했다.

Exercise 3

1 not keeping the promise
2 her not telling him
3 not smoking in this building
4 not lending him the book

Exercise 4

1 I am sorry for your failing the test.
2 She was ashamed of his lying.
3 We are looking forward to his visiting Korea.
4 I am worried about kids' bothering the puppy.

3-4 동명사와 to부정사 Ⅰ p.50

Exercise 1

1 to go
2 opening
3 To go/Going
4 writing
5 to listen to/listening to
6 solving
7 doing
8 to receive

Exercise 2

1 accepting → to accept
2 to go → going
3 meeting → to meet
4 renovating → to renovate
5 to talk with → talking with
6 to read → reading

Exercise 3

1 to take turns
2 turning off
3 going
4 to practice
5 holding
6 to meet

Exercise 4

1 give up studying to become
2 avoid making
3 agreed to postpone holding
4 decided to quit learning

3-5 동명사와 to부정사 Ⅱ p.52

Exercise 1

1 yelling
2 seeing
3 to rest
4 watching
5 to turn off
6 eating

Exercise 2

1 reading
2 to study
3 to return
4 drinking, taking

3-6 to+동명사/to+동사원형 {p.53}

Exercise 1

1 riding	2 climb
3 seeing	4 playing
5 resign	6 fall

Exercise 2

1 receiving	2 playing
3 cry	4 wearing

3-7 동명사의 주요 표현 {p.55}

Exercise 1

1 smiling	2 arriving
3 going	4 bringing
5 adjusting	6 watching

Exercise 2

1 How about eating out tonight? [Let's eat out tonight.]
2 made a point of getting up
3 couldn't but laugh at his funny costume
4 It is no use regretting

Exercise 3

1 Did you have difficulty finding my house?
2 It is no use trying to persuade her.
3 She made a point of taking a walk every day.
4 I couldn't look at Jacob without thinking of his brother.

Review Test {p.56}

01 ② 02 ④ 03 ④ 04 ② 05 ② 06 ④
07 ② 08 ⑤ 09 ⑤ 10 ③ 11 ⑤ 12 ①
13 ② 14 ③ 15 ⑤ 16 ② 17 ② 18 ④
19 ③ 20 ⑤ 21 ② 22 ① 23 ② 24 ③
25 ② 26 to 27 making
28 but, laugh, at
29 Eating
30 stop reading
31 keep, solving
32 On leaving
33 her winning
34 being not → not being
35 arrive → arriving
36 to cry → crying
37 I'm busy studying
38 remembered visiting the zoo

01 enjoy는 목적어로 동명사를 취하는 동사이다.

02 mind는 목적어로 동명사를 취하는 동사이다. 「Would you mind ~?」는 '~해주시겠습니까?'라는 뜻으로 정중하게 부탁하거나 허락을 구할 때 하는 말이다.

03 「be good at」은 '~을 잘 하다'라는 뜻으로 전치사 at의 목적어로 명사나 명사 역할을 하는 어구가 와야 한다. 동명사는 동사의 성질을 가지고 있으면서 명사처럼 쓰인다.

04 「have difficulty (in) -ing」는 '~하는 데에 어려움이 있다'라는 뜻이다. finish는 목적어로 동명사를 취하는 동사이다.

05 stop은 목적어로 동명사를 취해서 '~하는 것을 멈추다'라는 뜻으로 쓰인다. stop 뒤에 to부정사가 오면 to부정사는 목적어가 아니라 부사로 쓰여서 '~하기 위해서 (하던 일을) 멈추다'라는 뜻이 된다. '시끄럽게 하는 것을 멈추다'라는 의미가 되어야 하므로 목적어(making)가 와야 한다. try는 목적어로 동명사와 to부정사를 모두 취할 수 있는데, 동명사가 오면 '~을 시험 삼아 해보다'라는 뜻이고, to부정사가 오면 '~하려고 노력하다'라는 뜻이다.

06 「spend+시간+-ing」는 '~을 하느라 시간을 보내다'라는 뜻이다. 따라서 빈칸에는 동명사가 들어가야 한다.

07 give up은 목적어로 동명사를 취하는 동사이다.

08 목적어 자리에 동명사(telling)가 왔으므로 빈칸에 동명사를 목적어로 취하는 동사가 들어가야 한다. avoid, stop은 동명사를 목적어로 취하는 동사이고, start, begin은 동명사와 to부정사를 모두 목적어로 취하면서 의미의 차이가 거의 없는 동사이다. want는 to부정사를 목적어로 취하는 동사이므로 빈칸에 들어갈 수 없다.

09 목적어 자리에 동명사(playing)가 왔으므로 빈칸에 동명사를 목적어로 취하는 동사가 들어가야 한다. enjoy, practice, keep은 동명사를 목적어로 취하는 동사이고, like는 동명사와 to부정사를 모두 목적어로 취하면서 의미의 차이가 거의 없는 동사이다. hope는 to부정사를 목적어로 취하는 동사이므로 빈칸에 들어갈 수 없다.

10 밑줄 친 traveling은 동사 like의 목적어로 쓰인 동명사이다.
① 「hear(지각동사)+목적어+현재분사」의 형태로 목적격보어로 쓰인 현재분사
② '춤추는 인형'이라는 뜻이 되도록 명사 doll을 수식하는 현재분사
③ 동사 enjoy의 목적어로 쓰인 동명사
④ 'Tom과 이야기하는 여자'라는 뜻이 되도록 the woman을 수식하는 현재분사
⑤ 「be동사+-ing」 형태로 진행 시제를 만드는 현재분사

11 ① mind는 목적어로 동명사를 취하는 동사이므로 to smoke가 아니라 smoking이 되어야 한다.
② want는 목적어로 to부정사를 취하는 동사이므로 going이 아니라 to go가 되어야 한다.
③ 「cannot help -ing」는 '~하지 않을 수 없다'라는 뜻의 숙어이므로 take가 아니라 taking이 되어야 한다.
④ 「feel like -ing」는 '~하고 싶다'는 뜻으로 to laugh가 아니라 laughing이 되어야 한다.

12 ① 「be동사+-ing」 형태로 진행 시제를 만드는 현재분사
② 전치사 of의 목적어로 쓰인 동명사
③ 동사 stop의 목적어로 쓰인 동명사
④ 동사 finish의 목적어로 쓰인 동명사
⑤ 동사 enjoy의 목적어로 쓰인 동명사

13　② 「have trouble (in) -ing」는 '~하는 데 어려움을 겪다'라는 뜻이므로 to concentrate는 concentrating이 되어야 한다.

14　③ 「look forward to -ing」는 '~을 학수고대하다'라는 뜻으로 to는 전치사로 쓰였기 때문에 to 뒤에 동사원형이 아니라 동명사가 와야 한다. 따라서 see는 seeing이 되어야 한다.

15　⑤ deny는 목적어로 동명사를 취하는 동사이기 때문에 to know는 knowing이 되어야 한다.

16　밑줄 친 making은 문장에서 주어로 쓰인 동명사이다.
　① 명사 baby를 수식하는 현재분사
　② 전치사 of의 목적어로 쓰인 동명사
　③ 「be동사+-ing」 형태로 진행 시제를 만드는 현재분사
　④ 명사 The boy를 수식하는 현재분사
　⑤ 「be동사+-ing」 형태로 진행 시제를 만드는 현재분사

17　동사 forget은 목적어로 동명사와 to부정사를 모두 취할 수 있고 의미는 다르다. 「forget+동명사」는 '(과거에) ~했던 것을 잊다'라는 뜻이고, 「forget+to부정사」는 '(미래에) ~할 것을 잊다'라는 뜻이다. because they were too busy를 통해서 바빠서 해야 할 일을 하지 못했다는 의미임을 알 수 있다. 따라서 ② writing은 to write가 되어야 한다.

18　나는 그 폴더를 삭제한 것을 기억한다. : remember는 목적어로 동명사와 to부정사를 모두 취할 수 있고 의미는 다르다. 「remember+동명사」는 '(과거에) ~했던 것을 기억하다'라는 뜻이고, 「remember+to부정사」는 '(미래에) ~할 것을 기억하다'라는 뜻이다. ① 나는 그 폴더를 삭제할 것을 기억한다. ② 나는 그 폴더를 삭제하고 있는 것을 기억한다. ③ 나는 그 폴더를 삭제할 것을 기억한다. ④ 나는 그 폴더를 삭제한 것을 기억한다. ⑤ 나는 그 폴더를 삭제해야 한다는 것을 기억한다.

19　일어난 일을 후회해도 소용없다. : 「It is no use -ing」는 '~해도 소용없다'라는 뜻으로 「It is useless to+동사원형」과 같은 뜻이다. ① 일어난 일을 후회하는 것은 유용하다. ② 일어난 일을 후회하는 것은 가치가 있다. ③ 일어난 일을 후회해도 소용없다. ④ 우리에게 일어난 일을 후회하는 것은 유용하다. ⑤ 일어난 일을 후회하는 것은 우리에게 유용하다.

20　「be ashamed of」는 '~한 것이 부끄럽다'라는 뜻이다. 과거에 한 일에 대해서 지금 부끄러워한다는 의미가 되어야 하므로 문장의 시제는 현재형으로, of의 목적어로 쓰이는 동명사는 완료형 동명사(having+p.p.)가 되어야 한다.

21　「can't help -ing」는 '~하지 않을 수 없다'라는 뜻이다.

22　remember는 목적어로 동명사와 to부정사를 모두 취할 수 있고 의미는 다르다. 「remember+동명사」는 '(과거에) ~했던 것을 기억하다'라는 뜻이고, 「remember+to부정사」는 '(미래에) ~할 것을 기억하다'라는 뜻이다. the following month는 미래를 나타내는 부사구이므로 목적어로 to부정사가 와야 한다.

23　• 「far from -ing」는 '~와 거리가 먼', '~이기는커녕'이라는 뜻이다.
　• 「be accustomed to -ing」는 '~에 익숙하다'라는 뜻이다.

24　• '말하는 것을 멈추고 내 말을 들어라.'라는 뜻이 되어야 자연스럽다. '~하는 것을 멈추다'라는 의미가 되려면 stop 뒤에 목적어가 와야 하므로 동명사 talking이 적절하다.
　• Tom은 작별인사도 하지 않고 나갔다. : 전치사 without의 목적어로 명사나 명사 역할을 하는 어구가 와야 하므로 동명사 saying이 적절하다.

25　• keep은 목적어로 동명사를 취하는 동사이다.
　• 「feel like -ing」는 '~하고 싶다'라는 뜻이다.

26　• 「be worth -ing」는 '~할 가치가 있다'라는 뜻이다.
　• want는 목적어로 to부정사를 취하는 동사이다.
　• 동사 forget은 목적어로 동명사와 to부정사를 모두 취할 수 있고 의미는 다르다. 「forget+동명사」는 '(과거에) ~했던 것을 잊다'라는 뜻이고, 「forget+to부정사」는 '(미래에) ~할 것을 잊다'라는 뜻이다. tomorrow는 미래 시제를 나타내는 부사이다.
　• 「look forward to -ing」는 '~을 학수고대하다'라는 뜻이다.

27　Alice는 우리의 비밀을 말하는 실수를 저질렀다. 그녀는 자신이 그 일을 해서 미안하게 느낀다. : regret은 목적어로 동명사와 to부정사를 모두 취하는 동사이다. 「regret+동명사」는 '~한 것을 후회하다'라는 뜻이고, 「regret+to부정사」는 '~하게 되어 유감이다'라는 뜻이다. 따라서 빈칸에는 동명사(making)를 쓰는 것이 적절하다.

28　나는 그의 모습을 보고 웃지 않을 수 없었다. : 「can't help -ing」는 '~하지 않을 수 없다'라는 뜻으로 「cannot but+동사원형」으로 바꿔 쓸 수 있다.

29　단것을 너무 많이 먹는 것은 치아에 좋지 않다. : to부정사가 주어로 쓰였다. 주어로 쓰인 to부정사는 동명사로 바꿔 쓸 수 있다.

30　stop은 목적어로 동명사를 취해서 '~하는 것을 멈추다'라는 뜻으로 쓰인다. stop 뒤에 to부정사가 오면 to부정사는 목적어가 아니라 부사로 쓰여서 '~하기 위해서 (하던 일을) 멈추다'라는 뜻이 된다. '읽는 것을 멈추다'라는 의미가 되어야 하므로 목적어(reading)가 와야 한다.

31　• '모직으로 된 옷은 따뜻함을 유지하기 위해서 사용된다.'라는 뜻이 되는 것이 자연스럽다. 이때 are used는 use의 수동형이고, to keep은 to부정사의 부사적 용법으로 쓰여서 '~하기 위해서'라는 뜻의 목적을 나타낸다.
　• 나는 어려운 수학 문제를 푸는 것이 익숙하다. : 「be used to -ing」는 '~에 익숙하다'라는 뜻이다.

32　그는 학교를 떠나자마자 유럽으로 갔다. : 「as soon as」는 '~하자마자'라는 뜻으로 「on -ing」로 바꿔 쓸 수 있다. 따라서 빈칸에는 On leaving이 들어가야 한다.

33　나는 그녀가 경주에서 이길 거라고 확신한다. : 전치사 of의 목적어로 동명사가 와야 한다. 동명사의 의미상 주어는 동명사 앞에 명사나 대명사의 소유격을 쓴다. winning the race의 의미상 주어가 she이므로 she의 소유격인 her를 쓴다.

34　동명사의 부정형은 동명사 바로 앞에 not/never를 쓴다. 따라서 being not을 not being으로 고쳐야 한다.

35　'~ 하자마자'라는 뜻의 표현은 「on -ing」이다. 따라서 arrive를 arriving으로 고쳐야 한다.

36　'~ 하고 싶다'라는 뜻의 표현은 「feel like -ing」이다. 따라서 to cry를 crying으로 고쳐야 한다.

37　'~ 하느라 바쁘다'라는 뜻의 표현은 「be busy -ing」이다.

38　remember는 목적어로 동명사와 to부정사를 모두 취할 수 있고 의미는 다르다. 「remember+동명사」는 '(과거에) ~했던 것을 기억하다'라는 뜻이고, 「remember+to부정사」는 '(미래에) ~할 것을 기억하다'라는 뜻이다. 동물원에 갔던 것을 기억하는 것이므로 목적어로 visiting이 와야 한다.

1 considering becoming

2 Try to find, like doing[to do]

3 ②

[1-2] A 너는 자라서 축구선수가 되고 싶니? 너는 항상 손흥민에 대해 얘기하 잖아.

    B 나는 내가 어떤 일을 하는 것을 좋아하는지 모르겠어. 너는 어때?

    A 나는 요리사가 되려고 생각 중이야.

    B 저번에 내게 그 맛있는 파스타를 요리해준 게 생각난다.

    A 응. 난 요리하는 거 좋아해. 너에게 목표가 생기길 바랄게. 네가 좋아하 는 일을 찾도록 노력해 봐.

    B 노력할게. 고마워. 네 꿈에 행운을 빌어.

1   consider(~을 고려하다)는 동명사를 목적어로 취하므로 become은 becoming으로 써야 적절하다.

2   '~을 하기 위해 노력하다, 애쓰다'는 「try+to부정사」로 표현하고, like는 목적어로 동명사와 to부정사 둘 다 취하므로 do는 doing 또는 to do 로 쓸 수 있다.

3   Monica와 그녀의 남편은 가족들의 활동과 일정을 기록하기 위한 가족 달력을 만들었다. 세 아이들이 할 일이 많았고 Monica는 모두를 제때에 제대로 된 장소로 데려다 주는 것에 어려움을 느꼈다. Luke는 축구 연습 이 있었고, Amanda는 첼로 수업이, Jessie는 합창단 연습이 있었다. Monica는 부엌 벽에 새로운 달력을 붙여 놓았고, 가족들은 일요일 저녁 마다 가족회의에서 스케줄을 재검토했다. 몇 주 후에 Monica는 훨씬 효 과적으로 가족 모두의 시간을 관리할 수 있음을 느꼈다.

    '~하는 데에 어려움이 있다'는 「have difficulty (in) -ing」를 쓰므로 to get이 getting으로 쓰여야 옳다.

Chapter 4

Exercise 1

1 fallen	2 called
3 called	4 stolen
5 used	6 sitting
7 playing	8 covered
9 playing	

Exercise 2

1 bored, boring

2 pleasing, pleased

3 embarrassing, embarrassed

4 frightened, frightening

Exercise 3

1 standing at the bus stop

2 written by J. K. Rowling

3 located in the center of the city

4 built two years ago by his grandfather

5 wearing the same school uniform as you

Exercise 1

1 Seeing me on the street

2 Hating the project

3 Being sick

4 Solving this problem

5 Waiting for Susie

6 Turning to the right

7 Smiling at them

Exercise 2

1 When I was walking down the street

2 Because[When] I heard the bad news

3 Because[When] he bought a new car

4 Because he was poor

5 Even though he lives near the school

6 When she opened the door

Exercise 3

1 b	2 d
3 e	4 a
5 c	

Exercise 4

1 Waving	2 wounding
3 singing	4 listening to
5 arriving	

Exercise 5

1 entered the house, taking off her hat[taking her hat off]

2 Being interested in paintings

3 Walking along the street, I came across

4 took notes, listening to the biology lecture

5 Feeling dizzy, he wanted to take a break

Exercise 1

1 Looking out of the window

2 Having fixed his car

3 Having completed my project yesterday

4 Having lost her diamond ring
5 Saving enough money
6 Arriving home
7 Having taken the medicine
8 Having lived in Germany when she was young
9 Arriving at the airport

Exercise 2

1 we had finished the race
2 I had read the book
3 I don't have any money
4 he had found the lost wallet
5 I had finished my homework
6 he arrived at home
7 she has watched the movie twice
8 you go straight for two blocks

Exercise 3

1 Having had a big dinner
2 Having met him before
3 Having left my wallet at home
4 Having lost my cell phone
5 Having studied French at university
6 Having had a great time there

4-4 주의해야 할 분사구문 p.69

Exercise 1

1 Not knowing what to say
2 Not having had breakfast
3 Not having any friends
4 Not having slept well
5 Not having done his homework
6 Never having read the book
7 Not wanting to stay home
8 Not having enough money
9 Not having read the novel
10 Not being tall enough

Exercise 2

1 (Being) Impressed by his self-confidence
2 (Being) Pleased with Annie's grade
3 (Being) Compared with Scott
4 (Having been) Painted by Picasso
5 (Having been) Written in Old English
6 (Being) Satisfied with my work

Exercise 3

1 Seen from space
2 Written in easy English

3 Not having gotten enough sleep
4 Not knowing her phone number
5 Being interested in architecture
6 Not having grown up in Seoul
7 Being disappointed with the test result

4-5 with+명사+분사 p.71

Exercise 1

1 with his son left alone
2 with the alarm clock ringing
3 with one of his eyes closed
4 with the dog leading ahead of him

Exercise 2

1 Judging from his name
2 Speaking[Talking] of James
3 Strictly speaking
4 Frankly speaking

Review Test p.72

1 ①	2 ③	3 ②	4 ④	5 ④	6 ④
7 ④	8 ④	9 ①	10 (A) held (B) crying		
11 ③	12 ①	13 ⑤	14 ④	15 ③	16 ②
17 ②	18 ⑤	19 ①	20 ⑤	21 ②	22 ②
23 ③	24 ①	25 ②	26 ①	27 ④	

28 shocking
29 Generally speaking
30 dancing
31 understanding → understood
32 When/As I had dinner
33 (Being) Surprised
34 Having finished my homework
35 Not wanting to talk to him
36 (A) watering (B) written

01 분사가 목적격보어로 쓰이면 분사의 형태는 목적어와 목적격보어의 관계에 따라서 결정된다. 목적어와 목적격보어의 관계가 능동, 진행이면 현재분사를, 수동, 완료이면 과거분사를 쓴다. 부사절에서 '그의 이름이 불리는 것'이라는 뜻으로 his name과 call의 관계가 수동이므로 called가 들어가야 한다.

02 '나를 기다리게 하다'라는 뜻으로 me와 wait for의 관계가 능동이므로 waiting for가 들어가야 한다.

03 '교실에서 쓰이는 언어'라는 뜻으로 language와 speak의 관계가 수동이므로 spoken이 들어가야 한다.

04 • window를 수식해서 '깨진 유리'라는 의미가 되어야 하므로 완료의 의미를 담고 있는 과거분사 broken이 적절하다.

13

- 목적어 him과 talk의 관계는 능동이므로 talking이 적절하다.

05 감정을 나타내는 분사는 '~한 감정을 느끼는'이라는 의미일 때 과거분사를 사용한다. 주어 I가 피곤함을 느끼는 주체이기 때문에 tired가 적절하다. 「keep (on) -ing」는 '계속해서 ~하다'라는 뜻이다.

06 • 감정을 나타내는 분사는 '~한 감정을 느끼는'이라는 의미일 때 과거분사를 사용한다. 주어 I가 놀라는 주체이기 때문에 surprised가 적절하다.
- 감정을 나타내는 분사는 '~한 감정을 느끼게 하는'이라는 의미일 때 현재분사를 사용한다. 명사 news를 수식해서 '놀라운 뉴스'라는 의미가 되어야 하므로 surprising이 적절하다.

07 ④ 「지각동사+목적어+현재분사/과거분사」에서 분사의 형태는 목적어와 목적격보어의 관계에 따라 결정된다. 목적어 window와 break의 관계가 수동이므로 breaking이 아니라 broken이 되어야 한다.

08 ④ 명사 door를 수식하는 분사이다. '잠긴 문'이라는 뜻이 되어야 하므로 locking이 아니라 수동의 의미를 담고 있는 과거분사 locked가 되어야 한다.

09 ① '창문이 닫힌 채로 있었다.'라는 뜻으로 동사 keep은 상태를 의미한다. 분사가 주격보어로 쓰일 때는 주어와의 관계에 따라서 분사의 형태가 결정된다. window와 close의 관계는 수동이므로 closing이 아니라 closed가 되어야 한다.

10 (A) 우리 시립 공원에서 열린 야외 록 콘서트 : concert와 동사 hold(개최하다)의 관계는 수동이므로 과거분사 held를 쓰는 것이 적절하다.
(B) 분사가 목적격보어로 쓰이면 목적어와 목적격보어의 관계에 따라 형태가 결정된다. babies와 cry의 관계는 능동이므로 crying을 쓰는 것이 적절하다.

11 〈보기〉 내 노트북 컴퓨터를 가져오지 않아서 너에게 빌려줄 수 없다. : 밑줄 친 분사구문은 As I didn't bring my laptop으로 고칠 수 있다.
① 배가 고파서(As he felt hungry)
② 바위투성이의 산에 올라서(As she climbed a rugged mountain)
③ 운전을 조심히 한다면(If you drive a car carefully)
④ 네가 날 부르는 걸 듣지 못해서(As I didn't hear you calling me)
⑤ 열심히 공부해서(As he had studied hard)

12 분사구문에서 주어를 생략하는 경우는 주절의 주어와 부사절의 주어가 같을 때이다. 주어 the island와 see의 관계는 수동이므로 Seeing이 아니라 (Being) Seen이 되어야 한다.

13 ① 문장의 주어 she와 know의 관계가 능동이므로 현재분사로 쓰여야 한다. 따라서 Not known이 아니라 Not knowing이 되어야 한다.
② 문장의 주어 he와 drive의 관계가 능동이므로 현재분사로 쓰여야 한다. 따라서 driven이 아니라 driving이 되어야 한다.
③ 「Strictly speaking」은 '엄밀히 말해서'라는 뜻의 비인칭 독립분사구문이다.
④ not이나 never 같은 부정어는 분사 앞에 온다. 따라서 Wanting not이 아니라 Not wanting이 되어야 한다.

14 부사절을 분사구문으로 바꿀 때 접속사를 생략하고, 주절의 주어와 같은 경우에 주어를 생략하고 동사를 현재분사형(-ing)으로 바꾼다. 명령문의 주어는 항상 you이므로 주어를 생략하고 cross를 crossing으로 바꾼다. 분사구문의 뜻을 명확하게 하기 위해서 접속사를 남겨 두기도 한다. 따라서 답은 ④이다.

15 무엇을 해야 할지 몰라서 그녀는 내게 도와달라고 부탁했다. : 주어 she와 know의 관계가 능동이므로 현재분사(knowing)가 와야 한다. not

이나 never 같은 부정어는 분사 앞에 온다.

16 나는 길을 걷다가 그가 서점 옆에 서 있는 것을 보았다. : 주절과 분사구문의 시제가 같으므로 단순형 분사구문(Walking)이 와야 한다.

17 ① 목적격보어로 쓰인 현재분사
② 전치사 for의 목적어로 쓰인 동명사
③ 「be동사+현재분사」의 형태로 진행 시제를 만드는 현재분사
④ 분사구문에 쓰인 현재분사
⑤ The boy를 수식하는 분사구를 이끄는 현재분사

18 부사절을 분사구문으로 만들 때 접속사를 생략하고, 주절의 주어와 부사절의 주어가 같을 경우 주어를 생략한다. 부사절의 주어가 the weather이고 주절의 주어는 we이므로 the weather는 생략할 수 없다. 부사절의 동사 was wonderful은 -ing 형태가 되어서 being wonderful로 쓴다.

19 부사절의 시제가 주절의 시제보다 앞선 경우에는 완료형 분사구문을 쓴다. 따라서 Having been born in France가 된다. 수동 분사구문에서 having been은 생략할 수 있으므로 (Having been) Born in France로 고쳐야 한다.

20 부사절의 시제가 주절의 시제보다 앞선 경우에는 완료형 분사구문을 쓴다. 따라서 Having traveled a lot이 적절하다.

21 접속사와 주어를 생략하고 entered를 현재분사 entering으로 고친다.

22 그는 눈을 감은 채 천천히 걷고 있었다. : 「with+명사+분사」는 '~을 …한 채로'라는 뜻으로 동시동작을 나타낸다. 이때 명사와 분사의 관계가 수동이면 과거분사로, 명사와 분사의 관계가 능동이면 현재분사로 쓴다.

23 부사절을 분사구문으로 바꿀 때 부사절과 주절의 주어가 같은 경우 주어를 생략할 수 있다. 부사절과 주절의 주어가 다르므로 there를 생략하지 않는다. 따라서 There being이 되어야 한다.

24 분사구문이 부정의 의미일 때 부정어 not/never는 분사의 바로 앞에 위치한다. 따라서 Not finishing이 된다.

25 ① 일반적으로 말해서 ② 솔직히 말해서 ③ 표로 판단하건대 ④ 돈 이야기가 나와서 말인데 ⑤ 엄격히 말해서

26 「with+명사+분사」는 '~을 …한 채로'라는 뜻으로 동시동작을 나타낸다. 이때 명사와 분사의 관계가 능동이면 현재분사, 수동이면 과거분사를 쓴다. my fingers와 cross는 수동의 관계이므로 with my fingers crossed가 되어야 한다.

27 주어 I와 like의 관계가 능동이므로 현재분사를 써야 한다. 분사구문이 부정의 의미일 때 부정어 not/never는 분사의 바로 앞에 위치한다. 따라서 Not liking his idea가 된다.

28 감정을 나타내는 분사는 '~한 감정을 느끼게 하는'이라는 의미일 때 현재분사를 사용한다. 명사 accident를 수식해서 '충격적인 사건'이라는 의미가 되어야 하므로 shocking이 적절하다.

29 Generally speaking은 '일반적으로 말해서'라는 뜻이다.

30 저 아이는 내 아들이다. 그는 무대에서 춤을 추고 있다. : 주어 The child와 dance의 관계는 능동이다. 따라서 dancing이 적절하다.

31 목적어와 목적격보어의 관계가 능동이면 현재분사를 쓰고, 수동이면 과거분사를 쓴다. 내가 이해하는 것이 아니라 나를 영어로 (다른 사람들에게) 이해시키는 것이므로 목적어와 목적격보어는 수동 관계이다.

32 식당에서 저녁을 먹다가 친구 한 명을 만났다. : 접속사 when이나 as로 고칠 수 있다. 주어가 생략되었으므로 주절의 주어와 같고 주절의 시제가 과거 시제이므로 having은 had로 고친다. 따라서 When/As I had dinner가 들어가야 한다.

33 그가 그 소식에 놀라 창백해졌다. : 접속사 when과 주어 he를 생략할 수 있다. 수동 분사구문에서 being은 생략할 수 있으므로 (Being) Surprised가 들어가야 한다.

34 숙제를 다 한 것은 과거 시제, 컴퓨터 게임을 할 수 있는 것은 현재 시제이다. 분사구문의 시제가 주절보다 앞선 경우 완료형 분사구문(having p.p.)을 쓴다. 따라서 Having finished my homework가 들어가야 한다.

35 분사구문이 부정의 의미일 때 부정어 not/never가 분사의 바로 앞에 위치한다. 동사 want는 목적어로 to부정사를 취하는 동사이다. 따라서 Not wanting to talk to him이 들어가야 한다.

36 (A) 「be동사+현재분사」는 진행형을 나타낸다. 「be동사+과거분사」는 수동태이다. (B) '미국 소설가에 의해 쓰인'이라는 의미가 되어야 하므로 과거분사 written이 들어가야 한다.

보너스 유형별 문제   p.76

1 While volunteering
2 (B) named (C) shocked
3 ②

[1-2] 지난여름에 아동 병원에서 자원봉사를 하는 동안 Kyle이라는 환자 한 명을 알게 되었다. 그는 내가 만났던 가장 다정한 아이 중 한 명이었다. 그는 자신도 환자였지만 다른 환자들을 도와주고 그들과 이야기 나누는 것을 좋아했다. 곧 우리는 친구가 되었고 나는 그에게 왜 여름에 모자를 쓰고 있는지 물었다. 그는 내 질문에 대답하는 대신 그냥 웃으며 자신의 모자를 벗었다. 놀랍게도 그는 머리카락이 없었다. 그는 암 투병 중이었다. 그는 항상 건강하고 행복해 보였기 때문에 나는 충격을 받았다. 나는 그의 용감함에 매우 감명을 받았다. 그는 내가 아는 가장 용감한 사람이다.

1 '~하는 동안'은 접속사 「while+주어+동사」로 쓸 수 있는데 이를 분사구문으로 「(while)+-ing」로 쓴다.

2 (B) 이름이 지어진 것이므로 과거분사인 named가 적절하다.
(C) 주어가 충격을 주는 것이 아닌 받은 것이므로 과거분사인 shocked가 적절하다.

3 신나는 여름 여행지를 찾지 못했다면, 바로 여기 당신이 찾는 곳이 있습니다. 오전 9시에 Town Park에서 출발하여 White Valley까지 왕복으로 모셔다 드립니다. 캠핑과 래프팅 장비는 걱정하지 마세요. 음식뿐만 아니라 필요한 모든 장비가 포함된 금액입니다. 게다가 전문 가이드들이 계곡 탐험을 도와 드리기 때문에 가장 안전하면서도 즐거운 여행을 하실 수 있습니다.
부대상황을 나타내기 위해 분사구문을 쓸 수 있다. 따라서 동사는 동사원형이 아닌 -ing으로 쓰여야 하므로 leave가 leaving으로 바뀌어야 옳다.

Chapter 5

5-1 can/could   p.78

Exercise 1

1 그 뉴스는 사실일 리가 없다.
2 그것을 다시 한번 말해 주시겠습니까?
3 탁자 위에 있는 피자를 좀 더 먹어도 되나요?
4 나 혼자 집 전체를 청소할 수는 없다.

Exercise 2

1 is able to take off   2 Are you able to pick up
3 am not able to help   4 Is she able to play

5-2 may/might   p.79

Exercise 1

1 성공하기를!
2 확실하지는 않지만, 그는 극장에 있을지도 몰라.
3 나는 회의에 십 분 늦을지도 몰라.
4 우리 아버지가 나에게 친구들과 캠핑을 가도 된다고 하셨다.

Exercise 2

1 may, not, be   2 may, go
3 may, be   4 may, not, smoke
5 may, use

5-3 will/would   p.80

Exercise 1

1 Will   2 would
3 would   4 would
5 Will

Exercise 2

1 물에 빠진 사람은 지푸라기라도 잡기 마련이다[잡을 것이다].
2 그는 그것을 나에게 돌려주겠다고 말했다.
3 저는 회의 전에 커피를 좀 원해요.
4 그녀는 아파서 누워 있기 때문에 회의에 참석하지 않을 것이다.
5 나는 어렸을 때, 아침마다 산책하곤 했다.

5-4 must/have to   p.81

Exercise 1

1 You have to repair   2 Do I have to go

3 You don't have to bring　　4 She has to go

Exercise 2

1 had	2 must
3 must	4 must
5 have	6 must

5-5　shall/should/used to/need　p.82

Exercise 1

1 walk	2 ought
3 are used to	4 need not
5 come	6 used to
7 using	8 should
9 used to	10 has

Exercise 2

1 우리 어디에서 만날까요?

2 그는 우리에게 즉시 그것을 하라고 명령했다.

3 전에는 정원에 큰 단풍나무가 있었다.

4 그들은 초등학교에 다닐 때 함께 자전거를 타곤 했다.

Exercise 3

1 used, to	2 used, to
3 need, not	4 ought, to

Exercise 4

1 that I should stay home

2 You ought not to cheat on exams.

3 Shall we take a walk after dinner?

4 should do your best in everything

5-6　조동사+have+p.p.　p.84

Exercise 1

1 should, have, stayed	2 must, have, passed
3 cannot, have, slept	4 may, have, found

Exercise 2

1 cannot, have, been	2 must, have, eaten
3 may, have, been	4 should, have, seen
5 cannot, have, been	

5-7　조동사의 관용 표현　p.85

Exercise 1

1 You'd better not go fishing in the ocean today.

2 I cannot but wonder how far we have come.

3 Whenever I watch this movie, I cannot help crying.

4 I'd rather go shopping with you than stay here doing nothing.

5 You'd better get up early tomorrow if you don't want to miss the first train.

Exercise 2

1 had better not go out

2 cannot but admire[cannot help admiring]

3 would rather take a nap, drink coffee

4 had better leave

5 would rather live

Review Test　p.86

01 ②	02 ④	03 ⑤	04 ①	05 ②	06 ⑤
07 ③, ④	08 ⑤	09 ①, ②	10 ④		
11 ②	12 ③	13 ③	14 ②	15 ③	16 ③
17 ④	18 ②, ④	19 ③	20 ⑤	21 ①	
22 ②	23 ④	24 ⑤	25 ①, ④	26 ③	

27 You don't have to write the report.

28 I would rather exercise than skip a meal.

29 cannot, help

30 have, to

31 should, not, have, told

32 had, better, not

33 should, be

34 cannot, have, visited

35 You, should, respect, older, people /
He, should, have, joined, the, meeting

01　'어제 파티는 매우 재미있었다.'라는 A의 말과, '미안, 예상치 못한 일이 있었어.'라는 B의 말을 통해서 빈칸에 '네가 왔어야 했다.'라는 의미의 문장이 와야 함을 알 수 있다. 과거의 일에 대한 유감, 후회를 나타내는 표현은 「should have+p.p.」이다.

02　'그 소년은 예전보다 지금 훨씬 더 힘이 세다.'라는 뜻이 되는 것이 자연스럽다. 과거의 습관이나 상태를 나타내는 표현은 「used to+동사원형」이다. 형용사 strong은 상태를 표현한다. 조동사 would는 과거의 습관을 의미하지만 상태를 의미할 수 없으므로 답이 될 수 없다.

03　'소리 지르지 마. Jim이 지금 자고 있어. 너는 조용히 해야 해.'라는 뜻이 되는 것이 자연스럽다. '~해야 한다'는 should, ought to, must, have to 등으로 표현할 수 있다.

04　'Harry가 시험에서 만점을 받았다.'라는 A의 말을 듣고 B가 Harry의 기분을 추측하는 말을 할 수 있다. '~임이 틀림없다'라는 뜻의 강한 추측은 조동사 must를 써서 표현한다.

05　'Mike가 건강이 좋아 보이지 않는다.'라는 A의 말에 B는 '그가 쉬는 것이 나을 것 같아.'라고 말하는 것이 자연스럽다. 「had better+동사원형」은 '~하는 것이 좋겠다'라는 뜻이다.

06　「be able to+동사원형」은 '~할 수 있다'라는 뜻으로 가능을 의미하는

16

조동사 can과 바꿔 쓸 수 있다. 밑줄 친 was not able to에서 was는 과거 시제를 나타내고 not은 부정을 나타내므로 couldn't로 바꿔 쓸 수 있다.

07 '당신은 내 여동생의 깜짝 생일 파티에 올 수 있습니까?'라고 물었으므로 ③ '미안하지만, 안 돼.', ④ '응. 파티에 갈게.'라고 대답할 수 있다.

08 '집 안에서 신발을 벗어야 합니까?'라는 A의 질문에 B가 No로 답했다. 뒤에는 집 안에서 신발을 벗지 않아도 된다는 내용이 나와야 하므로 ⑤가 가장 적절하다. 「don't have to+동사원형」은 '~할 필요 없다'라는 뜻이다.

09 '당신과 일주일 동안 있어도 됩니까?'라는 뜻의 부탁, 요청으로 허락할 때는 yes, 그렇지 않을 때는 no로 답한다. ①의 why not?은 부탁, 요청 등에 동의하여 '좋아.'라는 뜻이다.

10 ④ shall은 제안의 의미로 쓰여서 '내가 언제 너를 방문할까?'라는 뜻이다. I'm sorry I can't.는 상대방의 부탁, 요청을 거절할 때 하는 말이다.

11 〈보기〉 너의 아버지께서는 분명히 너를 자랑스러워하실 거야. : must는 '~임이 틀림없다'라는 뜻으로 추측을 의미한다.
① 나는 지금 가야 한다.(의무)
② 그녀는 분명히 매우 바쁠 것이다.(추측)
③ 너는 안전모를 써야 한다.(의무)
④ 우리는 어질러진 것을 치워야 한다.(의무)
⑤ 너는 네 남동생들을 돌봐야 한다.(의무)

12 〈보기〉 너는 내가 외롭다고 생각할 수도 있다. : may는 '~일지도 모른다'라는 뜻으로 추측을 의미한다.
① 내가 들어가서 기다려도 되나요?(허가)
② 평화가 당신과 함께 하기를!(기원)
③ 그 소식은 사실이 아닐지도 모른다.(추측)
④ 내가 당신의 쿠키를 하나 맛보아도 될까요?(허가)
⑤ 아이들은 어른과 동반하면 입장할 수 있습니다.(허가)

13 • 너는 그것을 봐도 되지만 만져서는 안 된다.
• 너는 원한다면 나가 놀아도 된다.
'~해도 된다'라는 뜻의 허가의 의미를 나타내는 조동사는 can, may이다.

14 「주장, 제안, 명령, 요구의 의미를 가진 동사+that+주어(+should)+동사원형」은 '~하도록 …하다'라는 뜻이다. suggest(제안하다), insist(주장하다), demand(요구하다), propose(제안하다)는 빈칸에 올 수 있지만 refuse(거절하다)는 빈칸에 올 수 없다.

15 「주장, 제안, 명령, 요구의 의미를 가진 동사+that+주어(+should)+동사원형」에서 조동사 should는 생략 가능하다. should가 생략되더라도 동사원형은 그대로 유지되므로 that절의 동사의 형태에 유의한다.

16 ① 너는 쓰레기를 가지고 나가야 한다.
② 그는 잃어버린 서류가방을 찾을 수 있었다.
③ 너는 다시는 그를 만나면 안 된다. ≠ 너는 다시는 그를 만날 필요가 없다.
④ 당신은 멀리 떨어진 별을 볼 수 있습니까?
⑤ 그는 다리가 부러져서 당분간 걸을 수 없다.

17 ① 제가 당신의 휴대 전화를 써도 됩니까?
② 제가 요리하는 것을 도와주시겠습니까?
③ 당신은 자신의 침대를 정리해야 합니다.
④ 나는 영화를 보러 가곤 했다. ≠ 나는 영화를 보러 가는 것이 익숙하다.
⑤ 비행기는 오후 7시에 이륙할 것이다.

18 내가 당신의 컴퓨터를 써도 되나요? : 긍정일 땐 yes, 부정일 땐 no로 대

답한다. ② 아니오, 써도 돼요. ④ 아니오, 나는 안 돼요.

19 ③ 「would rather A than B」는 'B하기 보다 차라리 A하겠다'라는 뜻의 관용표현으로, A와 B 자리에는 동사원형이 와야 한다. 따라서 to eat을 eat으로 고쳐야 한다.

20 ⑤ 어젯밤에 자러 가기 전에 약을 먹어야 했다. : 과거의 일에 대한 유감, 후회를 나타낼 때는 「should have+p.p.」를 쓴다. 따라서 should take를 should have taken으로 고쳐야 한다.

21 ① 나는 저녁 먹으러 나가고 싶다. : 「would like+명사」는 '~을 원하다'라는 뜻이고, 「would like to+동사원형」은 '~하고 싶다'라는 뜻이다. 따라서 go out을 to go out으로 고쳐야 한다.

22 〈보기〉 그녀는 자신의 의견을 잘 표현한다. : 능력/가능을 나타내는 조동사 can을 써서 표현한 ② '그녀는 자신의 의견을 잘 표현할 수 있다.'와 그 의미가 같다.

23 〈보기〉 당신은 놀이공원에 가고 싶습니까? : '~하고 싶다'라는 뜻을 나타내는 동사 want를 써서 표현한 ④ '당신은 놀이공원에 가고 싶습니까?'와 그 의미가 같다.

24 ① 그는 나만큼 높이 뛸 수 있다.(능력/가능)
② 나는 네가 질문에 답하는 것을 도와줄 수 있다.(능력/가능)
③ 우리는 일정대로 프로젝트를 끝낼 수 있다.(능력/가능)
④ 그들은 내 시계를 훔쳐간 소년을 찾을 수 있었다.(능력/가능)
⑤ 그는 대학교에서 역사를 공부했으므로 의사일 리가 없다.(추측)

25 'Mary가 어제 나타나지 않았다. 그녀는 요즘 매우 바빠 보인다.'라는 A의 말을 통해서 B는 Mary가 약속을 잊어버렸다고 추측하거나 단정하는 말을 할 수 있다. 과거에 대한 가능성이 있는 추측은 「may/might have+p.p.」로 '~이었을지도 모른다'라는 뜻이고, 과거에 대한 단정적인 확신은 「must have+p.p.」로 '~이었음이 틀림없다'라는 뜻이다.

26 '~해야 한다'라는 뜻의 조동사는 have to, should, must, ought to 등으로 표현할 수 있다.

27 '~하지 않아도 된다'는 「don't have to+동사원형」으로 표현한다.

28 「would rather A than B」는 'B하기보다 차라리 A하겠다'라는 뜻의 표현으로, A와 B 자리에는 동사원형이 와야 한다.

29 「cannot but+동사원형」은 '~하지 않을 수 없다'라는 뜻으로 「cannot help -ing」로 바꿔 쓸 수 있다.

30 당신은 일출을 보려면 일찍 일어나야 합니다. : '~해야 한다'라는 의미를 나타낼 때 조동사 must는 have to와 바꿔 쓸 수 있다.

31 「should have+p.p.」는 '~했어야 했는데'라는 뜻으로 과거의 일에 대한 유감, 후회를 나타낸다. '~하지 말았어야 했는데'는 「should not have+p.p.」로 표현한다.

32 「had better+동사원형」은 '~하는 것이 좋겠다'라는 뜻이다. 부정형은 「had better not+동사원형」이고 '~하지 않는 것이 좋겠다'라고 해석한다.

33 「주장, 제안, 명령, 요구의 의미를 가진 동사+that+주어(+should)+동사원형」은 '~하도록 …하다'라는 뜻으로, should는 생략 가능하다. '주장하다'라는 뜻의 동사 insist가 쓰였으므로 빈칸에 should be가 들어가야 한다.

34 과거의 일에 대해 단정적으로 부정할 때는 「cannot have+p.p.」를 쓰며 '~했을 리가 없다'라고 해석한다. 따라서 빈칸에 cannot have visited가 들어가야 한다.

35 '~해야 한다'라는 뜻의 조동사는 have to, should, must, ought to

등으로 표현할 수 있다. '~했어야 했다'는 「should have+p.p.」로 표현한다. 따라서 두 문장에 공통으로 들어가야 할 조동사는 should이다.

보너스 유형별 문제   p.90

1 ⓐ was using ⓑ had to ⓒ have been ⓓ will never
2 We used to be good friends
3 ②

[1-2] 지난 월요일에 Chloe는 내 무선 이어폰을 빌렸다. 그녀가 그것을 쓰면서 하나를 떨어뜨렸고 그것을 부수었다. 그녀는 사과도 하지 않고 나에게 그것을 돌려주었다. 나는 그것을 서비스센터에 가져가야 했고 그것을 고치느라 100달러를 썼다. 나는 이것에 대해 그녀에게 말했지만, 그녀는 자신의 잘못이 아니라고 말했다. 그때 이후로 나는 그녀에게 정말 화가 나 있다. 나는 다시는 절대로 그녀와 말을 하고 싶지 않다. 우리는 좋은 친구였지만 지금은 아니다. 나는 그녀를 절대 용서하지 않을 것이다.

1 ⓐ 과거의 한 시점에 진행 중인 일이므로 과거진행시제 was using을 쓴다. ⓑ 의무를 나타내는 must의 과거형은 had to로 쓴다. ⓒ 과거에 일어난 일이 현재까지 영향을 미치고 있으므로 현재완료인 have been을 쓴다. ⓓ never가 있는 will의 부정은 「will never+동사원형」의 순으로 쓴다.

2 과거의 상태를 나타낼 때는 「used to+동사원형」로 쓰며 '~이다'의 be동사를 함께 사용하여 used to be good friends를 써야 옳다.

3 지난주에 나는 화산 폭발에 대한 과학 연구 과제를 끝내려 하고 있었다. 과제의 이미지 부분만 완성하면 되었는데, 막 작업을 시작하려고 할 때 마커와 펜이 없다는 것을 알았다. 분명 전날 그것들을 책상 위에 놓아두었던 것 같은데, 그 자리에 없었다. 부엌, 방, 심지어 욕실까지도 살펴보았지만 어디에서도 찾을 수가 없었다. 도대체 그것들이 어디에 있는지 전혀 모르겠네!
'~해야 한다, ~할 필요가 있다'는 「need to+동사원형」으로 쓰므로 completing은 to complete으로 바꾸어야 한다.

Chapter 6

6-1 수동태의 전환   p.92

Exercise 1

1 is cleaned
2 are caused
3 was found
4 isn't being used
5 elected
6 didn't catch

Exercise 2

1 was translated
2 is made
3 was painted
4 was invented
5 were fixed

Exercise 3

1 The letter wasn't written by her.
2 Hangeul was invented by King Sejong.
3 A fancy car was bought for my wife (by me).
4 Plastic bottles must be recycled (by them).
5 My watch was lost yesterday by my friend.
6 Money should be saved for a rainy day (by us).
7 The pictures on the wall were drawn by some kids.
8 This song was remade by a lot of famous singers.
9 Those cookies and cakes were made by my mom.
10 The room is cleaned every Sunday by my brother.
11 Some candies were given to the children by Johnson.
12 My mother was taken to the hospital yesterday by them.
13 Their summer concert will be performed in June (by them).
14 200 people were employed last year by the electric vehicle manufacturer.
15 The new uniform will be worn in the next game by the soccer player.

6-2 진행형/완료형/의문문/명령문의 수동태   p.94

Exercise 1

1 drawn
2 noticed
3 has been used
4 hit
5 will be delivered
6 has been imported
7 have been invited
8 will be served
9 had been recorded
10 Is your boss respected

Exercise 2

1 By whom was your school founded?
2 Is English spoken in India (by people)?
3 Were the plants on my desk watered by someone?
4 I haven't been informed of the event by my boss.
5 The air is being polluted seriously by exhaust fumes.
6 This building has been built for three years (by people).
7 When I got home, the old couch was being renovated by my father.
8 Many studies on the environment are being carried out around the world (by people).

Exercise 3

1 The government is building a dam.
  A dam is being built by the government.
2 She has written five novels over the last four years.
  Five novels have been written over the last four years by her.
3 Who discovered the American continent?

By whom was the American continent discovered?

4 A lot of teenagers have read the detective novel.
The detective novel has been read by a lot of teenagers.

Exercise 1

1 was bought for me by my husband
2 was cooked for me by my sister
3 was made for my baby sister by my mother
4 was brought to me after school by my grandmother

Exercise 2

1 We were taught American history by Elise.
American history was taught to us by Elise.
2 He was paid five dollars for parking by her.
Five dollars was paid to him for parking by her.
3 Susan was given a bunch of flowers by Tom.
A bunch of flowers were given to Susan by Tom.
4 I was offered a new position by the company.
A new position was offered to me by the company.
5 We were told the theory about the origin of life by my teacher.
The theory about the origin of life was told to us by my teacher.
6 He was asked many questions during class by the students.
Many questions were asked of him during class by the students.

Exercise 3

1 is called
2 were made
3 entering
4 to
5 to participate
6 was asked
7 heard
8 to get off
9 for
10 was told

Exercise 4

1 I was made to come here by her.
2 He was elected president by Americans.
3 He was seen leaving the classroom by them.
4 My daughter is called Cathy by her friends.
5 We were allowed to eat some more cake by my mom.
6 Jenny was heard singing a song in the cafeteria by us.
7 We were told not to run in the classroom by the teacher.
8 I was asked to walk the dog in the morning by my father.
9 She has been named as the new head of department by them.

Exercise 5

1 was, seen, crossing
2 was, asked, to, go, out
3 were, observed, swimming
4 were, made, to, keep, a, diary

Exercise 1

1 with
2 with
3 at
4 of
5 to
6 in
7 with
8 at
9 with
10 to

Exercise 2

1 A drunk driver ran over the dog.
2 The evidence will be made use of by the judge.
3 My sister looked up to the teacher.
4 The children make fun of the new student.
5 Our cat will be taken care of during the holiday by Christina.
6 My dog will be looked after by her while I'm on a business trip.

Exercise 3

1 laughed at by
2 known for
3 looked after by
4 taken care of by

Exercise 4

1 known as
2 pleased with
3 covered with[in/by]
4 satisfied with

Exercise 1

1 It was believed that the Earth was flat.
The Earth was believed to be flat.
2 It was reported that the actor had lung cancer. The actor was reported to have lung cancer.
3 It is considered that Andy Warhol is the Father of Pop Art.
Andy Warhol is considered to be the Father of Pop Art.
4 It is said that he is one of the best singers in the world.
He is said to be one of the best singers in the world.
5 It is said that Mt. Everest is the highest mountain in the world.
Mt. Everest is said to be the highest mountain in the world.

6 It was said that Daniel was the best player of the final game.

Daniel was said to be the best player of the final game.

7 It is thought that taking a walk every day is good for your health.

Taking a walk every day is thought to be good for your health.

Review Test

p.102

01 ①	02 ①	03 ④	04 ⑤	05 ③	06 ⑤
07 ⑤	08 ②	09 ①	10 ④	11 ⑤	12 ①
13 ④	14 ②	15 ④	16 ①	17 ⑤	18 ⑤
19 ③	20 ⑤	21 ②	22 ④	23 ②	24 ④

25 Spanish is spoken in Mexico.

26 Hong Kong is known for its beautiful skyline.

27 was held

28 been cut down

29 (A) sing   (B) have been passed down
(C) were sung

30 has been told to us

31 was seen walking

32 have been recycled

33 was heard singing a song

34 is being used

35 is said, is said to be

01 지금 강 위로 새 다리가 건설 중이다. : 주어가 동작을 당하는 대상이 되는 것을 수동태라고 한다. 다리(bridge)는 지어지는 대상이므로 수동태를 쓴다. 진행형의 수동태는 「be+being+p.p.」의 형태로 쓴다.

02 2002년 월드컵이 한국과 일본에서 개최되었다. : 동사 hold는 '열다', '개최하다'라는 뜻이고, 2002년 월드컵은 과거에 일어난 일이므로 과거형 수동태를 쓴다. 과거형 수동태는 「was/were+p.p.」의 형태로 쓴다.

03 내가 네게 현미경을 사용하는 방법을 가르쳐 줬으니, 이제 네가 들은 대로 현미경을 사용하라. : you는 이야기를 들은 대상이므로 수동태 were told가 들어가야 한다.

04 넬슨 만델라는 남아프리카의 첫 번째 흑인 대통령으로 선출되었다. : 동사 elect는 '선출하다', '뽑다'라는 뜻이다. 주어인 Nelson Mandela가 대통령으로 선출된 것이므로 수동태(was elected)를 쓴다.

05 내가 어렸을 때, 나는 조부모님의 보살핌을 받았다. : take care of는 '~을 돌보다'라는 뜻의 동사구로, 하나의 동사로 취급하기 때문에 수동태로 만들 때 분리하지 않는다. 따라서 was taken care of로 고치고, by 이외의 전치사를 쓰는 동사구가 아니기 때문에 by를 생략하지 않는다.

06 • 이 회사는 1724년에 설립되었다. : '설립하다'라는 뜻의 동사는 found이고, 과거분사형은 founded이므로 was founded로 쓴다. find의 과거분사형 found와 혼동하지 않도록 주의한다.
• 두 남자가 어제 교통사고로 부상을 당했다. : injure는 '다치게 하다'라는 뜻이므로 수동태로 써서 were injured로 쓴다.

07 • 그녀는 자신의 훌륭한 공연에 만족했다. : 「be satisfied with」는 '~

에 만족하다'라는 뜻으로 by 이외의 전치사를 쓰는 수동태이다.
• 그는 우리에게 작가로 알려져 있다. : 「be known to/by/for/as」는 뒤에 오는 전치사에 따라 의미가 조금씩 달라진다. 「be known to」는 '~에게 알려져 있다'라는 뜻으로 by 이외의 전치사를 쓰는 수동태이다.

08 「be filled with」는 '~으로 가득 차다'라는 뜻이고, 「be pleased with」는 '~에 기뻐하다'라는 뜻으로, 둘 다 by가 아니라 with를 쓰는 수동태이다.

09 '~되고 있는 중이다'는 진행형 수동태를 쓴다. 진행형 수동태의 형태는 「be동사+being+p.p.」이다. A National Museum과 The International Arts Festival은 단수이므로 is being이 들어가는 것이 가장 적절하다.

10 ④ 사역동사가 있는 5형식 문장의 수동태는 목적격보어(원형부정사)를 to부정사로 바꿔준다. 따라서 She was made to go into the room.이 되어야 한다.

11 ⑤ 능동태를 수동태로 바꿀 때 능동태의 목적어가 수동태의 주어가 되어야 한다. 목적어가 me이므로 I was introduced to their teacher by them.이 되어야 한다.

12 〈보기〉 그녀가 약속을 지켰다고 여겨졌다. : 문장의 동사가 believe이고 목적어가 절인 문장은 「It is ~ that …」이나, 「that절의 주어+be동사 +p.p.+to+동사원형」 형태의 수동태 문장으로 바꿔 쓸 수 있다. 따라서 She was believed to keep the secret.가 적절하다.

13 〈보기〉 비평가들도 그 책이 재미있다고 느꼈다. : 5형식 문장으로, 목적어 the book을 주어로 하는 수동태로 만들 수 있다. 문장의 시제가 과거 시제이고, find의 과거분사형이 found이므로 The book was found interesting.이 적절하다. founded는 동사 found(설립하다)의 과거분사형이므로 혼동하지 않도록 주의한다.

14 지각동사가 있는 문장의 수동태에서 목적격보어가 분사(crying)인 경우에는 그대로 쓴다. 따라서 ② A baby was heard crying in the bathroom by the police officer.가 적절하다.

15 문장의 동사가 say, believe, think, report 등이고, 목적어가 절인 문장은 「It is ~ that …」이나, 「that절의 주어+be동사+p.p.+to+동사원형」 형태의 수동태 문장으로 바꿔 쓸 수 있다. 따라서 ④ He is said to be a very famous writer in Korea.가 적절하다. 가주어 It을 주어로 하는 수동태 문장으로 바꿔 쓰려면 It is said that he is a very famous writer in Korea.가 되어야 한다.

16 ① resemble은 수동태로 쓰지 않는 동사이다. 그 밖에 수동태로 쓰지 않는 동사로는 appear, become, happen, cost, have 등이 있다.

17 ⑤ 우리의 생활은 기술 발전에 의해 변할 것이다. : our lives가 동작을 당하는 대상이므로 수동태(will be changed)로 써야 한다.

18 ⑤ 4형식 문장을 수동태로 바꿀 때 직접목적어를 주어로 할 때는 간접목적어 앞에 전치사 to, for, of를 쓴다. buy는 전치사 for를 쓴다. 또한 buy, make, cook 등의 동사는 간접목적어를 주어로 한 수동태 문장을 만들지 않는다.

19 '나무는 종이를 만들기 위해서 사용된다.'는 의미가 되어야 하므로 수동태(are used)로 쓰여야 한다. '전 세계적으로 40억 그루의 나무가 매년 종이를 만들기 위해서 잘린다.'라는 뜻이 되어야 하므로 수동태(are cut down)로 쓰여야 한다.

20 그들은 아픈 사람들을 돌보고 있다. : 진행형의 수동태는 「be동사 +being+p.p.」로 쓴다. take care of는 by 이외의 전치사를 쓰는 수

20

동태가 아니므로 「by+행위자」를 써야 한다.

21 그들은 그녀가 프랑스에서 유명한 영화배우라고 생각한다. : 문장의 동사가 say, believe, think, report 등이고, 목적어가 절인 문장은 「It is ~ that …」이나, 「that절의 주어+be동사+p.p.+to+동사원형」 형태의 수동태 문장으로 바꿔 쓸 수 있다. 따라서 It is thought that she is a famous movie star in France.나 ② She is thought to be a famous movie star in France.로 쓸 수 있다.

22 ① 수동태 문장에서 행위자 앞에 전치사 by를 쓴다. run over가 아니라 run over by가 되어야 한다.
    ② 「be filled with」는 '~으로 가득 차다'라는 뜻으로 by 이외의 전치사를 쓰는 수동태이다. was filled of가 아니라 was filled with가 되어야 한다.
    ③ 4형식 문장을 수동태로 바꿀 때 직접목적어를 주어로 할 때는 간접목적어 앞에 전치사 to, for, of를 쓴다. buy는 전치사 for를 쓴다. bought my brother가 아니라 bought for my brother가 되어야 한다.
    ⑤ 지각동사가 있는 문장의 수동태에서 목적보어가 원형부정사인 경우는 to부정사로 바꾸고, 분사인 경우는 그대로 쓴다. play가 아니라 playing이나 to play가 되어야 한다.

23 ① 주어 She가 말한 것이 아니라 유명한 가수라고 불리는 것이므로 수동태로 쓴다. said가 아니라 is said가 되어야 한다.
    ③ 사역동사가 있는 문장의 수동태에서 목적격보어는 to부정사로 바꾼다. clean이 아니라 to clean이 되어야 한다.
    ④ look after는 '돌보다'라는 뜻의 동사구이다. look after는 by 이외의 전치사를 쓰는 수동태가 아니므로 by를 생략하면 안 된다. looked after가 아니라 looked after by가 되어야 한다.
    ⑤ allow는 목적격보어로 to부정사를 취하는 동사이다. watch가 아니라 to watch가 되어야 한다.

24 빈칸을 포함하는 절은 문맥상 '할머니의 질문을 받았을 때'라는 뜻이 되어야 한다. I는 질문을 받는 대상이므로 수동태를 써야 한다. 따라서 ④ I was asked by가 들어가야 한다.

25 수동태의 형태는 「be동사+p.p.」이다. in은 장소 앞에 쓰인 전치사이다.

26 「be known for」는 '~으로 유명하다'라는 뜻으로, by 이외의 전치사를 쓰는 수동태이다.

27 주어 The 2022 World Cup이 동작(watch)의 주체가 아니라 동작을 받는 대상이므로 수동태를 써야 한다.

28 완료형 수동태는 「have+been+p.p.」의 형태로 쓴다.

29 (A) 주어 we가 동작을 하는 주체이므로 능동태 sing이 적절하다.
    (B) 주어 These songs가 사람들 사이에서 전해져 내려오는 것이므로 수동태를 써야 한다. 완료형 수동태는 「have+been+p.p.」이므로 have been passed down이 적절하다.
    (C) 주어 these songs가 불려지는 것이므로 수동태 were sung이 적절하다.

30 완료형 수동태는 「have+been+p.p.」의 형태로 쓴다. 주어가 단수이므로 has를 쓴다.

31 지각동사가 있는 문장의 수동태에서 목적보어가 분사(walking)인 경우는 그대로 쓴다.

32 완료형 수동태는 「have+been+p.p.」의 형태로 쓴다.

33 지각동사가 있는 문장의 수동태에서 목적보어가 분사(singing)인 경우는 그대로 쓴다.

34 진행형 수동태는 「be동사+being+p.p.」의 형태로 쓴다.

35 문장의 동사가 say, believe, think, report 등이고, 목적어가 절인 문장은 「It is ~ that …」이나, 「that절의 주어+be동사+p.p.+to+동사원형」 형태의 수동태 문장으로 바꿔 쓸 수 있다. 따라서 It is said that she is a good singer.나 She is said to be a good singer.로 쓸 수 있다.

보너스 유형별 문제   p.106

1 ⓒ Do → Is

2 Everything is covered with/in snow

3 ②

[1-2] 안녕 탄.
메리 크리스마스!
여기 한국은 화이트 크리스마스야. 밖은 모든 것이 눈으로 덮여 있어. 나는 화이트 크리스마스를 꿈꿨는데, 내 소원이 이루어졌어. 비록 눈 때문에 안에 머물러야 하지만, 나는 정말 행복해. 베트남의 크리스마스는 어떠니? 베트남에서 크리스마스를 기념하니? 12월 25일에 예수가 태어났기 때문에 우리는 크리스마스를 기념해. 우리는 크리스마스트리를 장식하고 캐럴도 불러. 우리는 교회에도 가고 특별한 행사를 열지.
베트남의 크리스마스에 대해 얘기해줘.
수지가.

1 현재시제 수동태 의문문은 「Be동사의 현재형+주어+p.p.(+by 행위자)」의 형태가 되어야 하고 주어(Christmas)는 3인칭 단수이므로 Do가 Is로 쓰여야 옳다.

2 '~로 덮여 있다'는 「be동사+covered with/in」으로 쓰고 주어인 everything이 3인칭 단수이므로 be동사는 is를 쓴다.

3 일찍 등록해 주세요. 등록은 선착순 신청입니다. 수업 정원이 다 차면 학생들은 대기자 명단에 올라갑니다. 지원서는 우편 혹은 직접 제출입니다. 전화, 이메일, 팩스를 통한 지원은 받지 않습니다. 행정 수수료는 과목당 30달러입니다. 지원서에 수표를 동봉해 주십시오. 수수료 납입이 안 된 지원서는 접수되지 않습니다. 별도 통보가 없으면, 지원 학생들은 프로그램 참여가 예정된 것으로 생각하시면 됩니다. 확인 통지는 보내지 않습니다. 학생들이 대기자 명단을 올리는 것이 아니라 명단에 올려지게 되는 것이므로 수동태로 쓰여야 옳다. 조동사(will)와 함께 있으므로 수동태는 「be+p.p」의 형태로 be put이 쓰여야 한다.

Chapter 7

p.108

7-1 가정법 과거

Exercise 1

1 go
2 could lend
3 were
4 would help
5 would like

Exercise 2

1 If I didn't have a class, I could go to the concert.
2 If I were a poet, I could write a beautiful poem.
3 If I had an extra blanket, I could give it to you.
4 If my teacher were here, I could get advice on this topic.
5 If my children didn't make noise, I could concentrate on my work.

7-2 가정법 과거완료

p.109

Exercise 1

1 had gone
2 had come
3 had got(ten) up
4 have lent
5 have finished

Exercise 2

1 If this book had been published in Korea, I could have bought it.
2 If we had made a reservation, we could have got(ten) good seats.
3 If I hadn't had a lecture in the evening, I could have gone to the movies.
4 If they had agreed with my idea, we could have worked together.
5 If she hadn't taken the subway, she couldn't have arrived at home before midnight.

7-3 I wish 가정법

p.110

Exercise 1

1 had gone out
2 had
3 had studied
4 could speak
5 had got(ten) up
6 had saved
7 had passed
8 could stay

Exercise 2

1 I had a laptop computer

2 I had learned how to swim
3 I could meet him here
4 I had participated in the summer camp

Exercise 3

1 I wish I didn't live far from school.
2 I wish I could go hiking with you.
3 I wish he liked Italian food.
4 I wish I didn't have to go to school today.
5 I wish I spoke Korean fluently enough to travel alone.

Exercise 4

1 I wish she had seen my memo earlier.
2 I wish my team had won the final game.
3 I wish you could have cleaned your room before noon.
4 I wish you could have come to the housewarming party.
5 I wish I had informed you about my traveling to Europe.

7-4 혼합가정법

p.112

Exercise 1

1 had eaten, wouldn't be
2 hadn't snowed, wouldn't be
3 hadn't missed, would be
4 had studied, could answer

Exercise 2

1 hadn't stayed up, wouldn't be very tired
2 hadn't lost, could lend
3 hadn't taken, could make a call
4 hadn't bought, would have

7-5 as if[as though] 가정법

p.113

Exercise 1

1 as if he had seen a ghost
2 as if she had stayed home all day
3 as if he had witnessed the accident
4 as if he had met her mother before
5 as if he were an expert on marine mammals
6 as if he had used this lawn mower before
7 as if she were a professional opera singer
8 as if he knew the truth behind the accident

Exercise 2

1 he didn't climb Mt. Everest
2 his major isn't computer science
3 she doesn't work out at the gym every day
4 she didn't make a mistake in the document

5 she didn't cook all the food for the party by herself

6 he didn't interview the actress about the new movie

1 as if he hadn't lied

2 as if he were

3 as if she weren't embarrassed about

4 as if she knew

5 as if she had lived

6 as if he had been

7-6 if 생략
p.115

1 Were I in your position

2 Had I had a car

3 Should you need my help

4 Had he told the truth

1 Were he honest

2 Had I known her address

3 Had I had enough money

4 Had he taken the doctor's advice

7-7 without/but for
p.116

1 Without the computer
  But for the computer
  Were it not for the computer

2 Without his advice
  But for his advice
  Had it not been for his advice

3 Without the homework
  But for the homework
  Were it not for the homework

4 Without the rescue workers
  But for the rescue workers
  Had it not been for the rescue workers

1 Without her help, I couldn't have found the bank.

2 Without water, all animals on Earth would not exist.

3 Without e-mail, we couldn't have conducted a worldwide survey.

4 But for the subway, the traffic would be much worse than it is now.

5 If it had not been for his car, we would have been late for school.

1 If it were not for the map, I would be lost in the middle of the forest.

2 If it were not for the Internet, we could not collect information easily.

3 If it had not been for the rainy season, we would have had a great vacation.

4 If it had not been for your advice, I could not have started my own business.

5 If it had not been for his leadership, they could not have survived the shipwreck.

Review Test
p.118

01 ④	02 ④	03 ⑤	04 ②	05 ③	06 ③
07 ②	08 ③	09 ⑤	10 ④	11 ②	12 ③
13 ⑤	14 ⑤	15 ③	16 ④	17 ④	18 ④
19 ⑤	20 ③	21 ⑤	22 ④	23 ⑤	24 ④

25 If the Sun disappeared

26 If I had lived in the Stone Age

27 it, had, not, been, for

28 wish, were

29 as, if[though]

30 had, looked, for

31 had

32 had, known

33 had, finished, could, go

34 had, not, been, not, have, been

01 내가 너라면 그곳에 혼자 가지 않을 텐데. : 현재 사실에 반대되는 것이나 실현 불가능한 일을 가정하는 가정법을 가정법 과거라고 한다. 가정법 과거는 「If+주어+동사의 과거형, 주어+조동사의 과거형+동사원형」의 형태로 쓴다. 따라서 빈칸에 조동사의 과거형인 would가 들어가야 한다.

02 네가 운동을 더 많이 했더라면 지금 더 건강할 텐데. : 과거에 실현되지 못한 행동이 현재에 영향을 미칠 때 쓰는 가정법을 혼합가정법이라고 한다. 혼합가정법은 「If+주어+had+p.p., 주어+조동사의 과거형+동사원형」의 형태로 쓴다. 따라서 빈칸에 had done이 들어가야 한다.

03 내가 어제 장갑을 잃어버리지 않았다면, 지금 너에게 빌려줄 수 있을 텐데. : 혼합가정법이 쓰인 문장이다. 따라서 빈칸에는 had not lost가 들어가야 한다.

04 시험이 취소된 것을 알았더라면, 어젯밤을 새지는 않았을 텐데. : 과거 사실과 반대되는 일을 가정하는 가정법을 가정법 과거완료라고 한다. 가정법 과거완료는 「If+주어+had+p.p., 주어+조동사의 과거형+have+p.p.」의 형태로 쓴다. 따라서 빈칸에 had known이 들어가야 한다.

05 나에게 귀여운 강아지가 있었으면 좋을 텐데. 나는 어렸을 때 몹시 외로웠다. : 과거에 이루지 못한 일에 대한 소망이나 유감을 나타내는 가정법은 「I wish+주어+had+p.p.」의 형태로 나타낸다. 따라서 빈칸에 had had가 들어가야 한다.

06 그는 마치 전에 나를 본 적이 있는 것처럼 말한다. : '마치 ~였던 것처럼'이라는 뜻으로 과거 사실에 반대되는 일을 나타내는 가정법은 「as if+주어+had+p.p.」의 형태로 나타낸다. 따라서 빈칸에 had met이 들어가야 한다.

07 현재 사실에 대한 소망이나 유감은 「I wish+주어+동사의 과거형」으로 나타낸다. 따라서 빈칸에 were가 들어가야 한다. 가정법 과거의 조건절에서 be동사는 인칭에 관계없이 were를 쓴다.

08 현재 사실에 반대되는 것이나 실현 불가능한 일을 가정하는 가정법을 가정법 과거라고 한다. 가정법 과거는 「If+주어+동사의 과거형, 주어+조동사의 과거형+동사원형」의 형태로 쓴다. 따라서 빈칸에 knew가 들어가야 한다.

09 ①, ②, ③, ④는 모두 '책이 없다면 우리는 지식을 거의 습득하지 못할 것이다.'라는 뜻이다. 현재 있는 것을 없다고 가정할 때는 「If it were not for+명사, 주어+조동사의 과거형+동사원형」, 「Were it not for+명사, 주어+조동사의 과거형+동사원형」, 「Without[but for]+명사, 주어+조동사의 과거형+동사원형」의 형태로 쓸 수 있다. ⑤는 「If it had not been for+명사, 주어+조동사의 과거형+have+p.p.」로 과거에 있었던 것을 없었다고 가정해서 '~가 없었다면'이라는 뜻이다.

10 내가 어제 너를 방문하지 않아서 유감이다. : 과거에 이루지 못한 일에 대한 소망이나 유감을 나타내는 가정법은 「I wish+주어+had+p.p.」의 형태로 나타낸다. 따라서 빈칸에 visited가 들어가야 한다.

11 날씨가 좋지 않아서 우리는 밖에 나가지 않을 것이다. : 현재 사실에 반대되는 것을 가정하는 가정법은 가정법 과거를 쓴다. 가정법 과거는 「If+주어+동사의 과거형, 주어+조동사의 과거형+동사원형」의 형태로 쓴다. 따라서 빈칸에 were, would가 들어가야 한다.

12 그는 차가 없어서 이곳에 오지 못했다. : 과거 사실에 반대되는 것을 가정하는 가정법은 가정법 과거완료이다. 가정법 과거완료는 「If+주어+had+p.p., 주어+조동사의 과거형+have+p.p.」의 형태로 쓴다. 따라서 빈칸에 had had, would have come이 들어가야 한다.

13 네가 상한 음식을 먹어서 지금 배가 아프다. : 과거의 행동이 현재에 영향을 미칠 때 쓰이는 가정법은 혼합가정법이다. 혼합가정법은 「If+주어+had+p.p., 주어+조동사의 과거형+동사원형」의 형태로 쓴다. 따라서 빈칸에 had not eaten이 들어가야 한다.

14 과거 사실에 반대되는 것을 가정하는 가정법은 가정법 과거완료를 쓴다. 가정법 과거완료는 「If+주어+had+p.p., 주어+조동사의 과거형+have+p.p.」의 형태로 쓴다.

15 과거에 실현되지 못한 행동이 현재에 영향을 미칠 때 쓰는 가정법을 혼합가정법이라고 한다. 혼합가정법은 「If+주어+had+p.p., 주어+조동사의 과거형+동사원형」의 형태로 쓴다.

16 과거 사실에 반대되는 것을 가정하는 가정법은 가정법 과거완료를 쓴다. 가정법 과거완료는 「If+주어+had+p.p., 주어+조동사의 과거형+have+p.p.」의 형태로 쓴다.

17 ④ 그가 그렇게 게으르지 않다면 지금 성공해 있을 텐데. : 현재 시제를 나타내는 부사 now를 통해서 혼합가정법이 쓰인 것을 알 수 있다. 따라서 might have been successful을 might be successful로 고쳐야 한다.

18 ④ 가정법 과거완료의 조건절은 「if+주어+had+p.p.」이다. 따라서 didn't work를 hadn't worked로 고쳐야 한다.

19 ⑤ John이 내게 피아노를 쳐주었더라면 나는 훨씬 더 행복했을 텐데. : 가정법 과거완료를 써야 한다. 따라서 played를 had played로 고쳐야

20 네가 더 일찍 출발했더라면 회의에 참석할 수 있었을 텐데. : 가정법 과거완료가 쓰였고 과거 사실과 반대되는 일을 가정한다. ③ 네가 더 일찍 출발하지 않아서 회의에 참석하지 못했다.

21 내가 어제 그 파란색 셔츠를 입었더라면 좋을 텐데. : 과거에 이루지 못한 일에 대한 소망이나 유감을 나타내는 가정법은 「I wish+주어+had+p.p.」의 형태로 나타낸다. ⑤ 나는 어제 그 파란색 셔츠를 입지 않아서 유감이다.

22 ① 내가 부자라면 그 아파트를 살 수 있을 텐데. = 내가 부자가 아니라서 그 아파트를 사지 못한다.
② 그가 열심히 일했다면 실패하지 않았을 텐데. = 그가 열심히 일하지 않아서 실패했다.
③ 네가 더 일찍 도착했다면 그를 만날 수 있었을 텐데. = 네가 일찍 도착하지 않아서 그를 만나지 못했다.
④ 네가 일이 너무 많아서 유감이다. ≠ 네가 일이 많지 않다면 좋을 텐데. : 현재 사실에 대한 소망이나 유감을 나타내는 I wish 가정법은 「I wish+주어+동사의 과거형」으로 나타낸다. hadn't had를 didn't have로 고쳐야 한다.
⑤ 내가 시간이 충분하다면 인도에 갈 수 있을 텐데. = 내가 시간이 충분하지 않아서 인도에 갈 수 없다.

23 ① 나는 가난해서 차를 살 수 없다. = 내가 가난하지 않다면 차를 살 텐데.
② 나는 아파서 그곳에 가지 않았다. = 내가 아프지 않다면 그곳에 갔을 텐데.
③ 내가 너를 도와주지 못해서 유감이다. = 내가 너를 도와줄 수 있으면 좋을 텐데.
④ 사실, 그는 진실을 모른다. = 그는 진실을 알고 있는 것처럼 말한다.
⑤ 내가 돈이 충분하지 않아서 집을 살 수 없었다. ≠ 내가 돈이 충분했다면 집을 살 수 있을 텐데. : 과거 사실에 반대되는 것을 가정하는 가정법은 가정법 과거완료를 쓴다. 가정법 과거완료는 「If+주어+had+p.p., 주어+조동사의 과거형+have+p.p.」의 형태로 쓴다.

24 ① 내가 새라면 너에게 날아갈 수 있을 텐데.
② 내가 젊었을 때 영어를 배웠더라면 좋을 텐데.
= 내가 젊었을 때 영어를 배우지 않아서 유감이다.
③ 내가 가난하지 않았으면 대학을 중퇴하지 않았을 텐데.
④ 눈이 내리지 않았다면 벼룩시장은 일정대로 열렸을 텐데. : 주절의 동사를 통해서 가정법 과거완료가 쓰였다는 것을 알 수 있다. 따라서 조건절은 If it had not been for the snow가 되어야 한다.
⑤ 그녀의 부모님의 반대가 없었다면 그녀는 외국으로 갔을 텐데.

25 태양이 사라진다면 지구상의 모든 생물이 죽을 텐데. : 가정법 과거가 쓰인 문장이다. 가정법 과거의 조건절의 시제는 과거형이므로 If the Sun disappeared로 고쳐야 한다.

26 내가 석기시대에 살았다면 사냥꾼이 되었을 텐데. : 가정법 과거완료가 쓰인 문장이다. 가정법 과거완료의 조건절의 시제는 과거완료이므로 If I had lived in the Stone Age로 고쳐야 한다.

27 '~이 없었더라면'은 「If it had not been for+명사」로 나타낸다.

28 현재 사실에 대한 소망이나 유감은 「I wish+주어+동사의 과거형」으로 나타낸다. 가정법 과거의 조건절에서 be동사는 인칭에 관계없이 were를 쓴다.

29 '마치 ~인 것처럼'이라는 뜻으로 현재 사실에 반대되는 일을 나타내는 가정법은 「as if[though]+주어+동사의 과거형」의 형태로 나타낸다.

30 네가 열쇠를 주의 깊게 찾지 않아서 찾을 수 없었다. : 과거 사실과 반대

되는 일을 가정하는 가정법을 가정법 과거완료라고 한다. 가정법 과거완료는 「If+주어+had+p.p., 주어+조동사의 과거형+have+p.p.」의 형태로 쓴다.

31 사실, 그는 돈이 많지 않다. : '마치 ~인 것처럼'이라는 뜻으로 현재 사실에 반대되는 일을 나타내는 가정법은 「as if+주어+동사의 과거형」의 형태로 나타낸다.

32 나는 그녀를 잘 알지 못했던 것이 유감이다. : 과거에 이루지 못한 일에 대한 소망이나 유감을 나타내는 가정법은 「I wish+주어+had+p.p.」의 형태로 나타낸다.

33 내가 우리 어머니께서 시키신 집안일을 못 끝내서 지금 너와 영화를 보러 갈 수 없어. : 과거에 실현되지 못한 행동이 현재에 영향을 미칠 때 쓰는 가정법을 혼합가정법이라고 한다. 혼합가정법은 「If+주어+had+p.p., 주어+조동사의 과거형+동사원형」의 형태로 쓴다.

34 경제 상황이 나빠서 개막식이 취소되었다. : 과거 사실과 반대되는 일을 가정하는 가정법을 가정법 과거완료라고 한다. 가정법 과거완료는 「If+주어+had+p.p., 주어+조동사의 과거형+have+p.p.」의 형태로 쓴다.

보너스 유형별 문제 p.122

1 If it had not been dry that day, the fire wouldn't have spread quickly.

2 had not been, wouldn't have been destroyed

3 ③

[1-2] 지난 토요일 강원도에서 산불이 발생했다. 그날은 매우 건조했기 때문에 불은 빠르게 퍼졌다. 소방관들은 불을 끄려고 매우 열심히 노력했지만, 화재 이후에 남아있는 것은 아무것도 없었다. 뉴스에서는 그 산불이 담배꽁초에서 비롯되었다고 말한다. 화재 전에는 그 숲은 항상 푸르렀다. 그 아름다운 숲을 다시 볼 수 있으면 좋겠다.

1 주어진 문장은 과거에 발생한 사건을 말하고 있어. 가정법 과거완료인 「If+주어+had+p.p., 주어+조동사의 과거형+have+p.p.」로 표현한다. 의미상 '~하지 않았을 텐데'를 나타내기 위해 조동사 wouldn't를 쓰며 동사 spread의 과거형과 과거분사형은 spread로 원형과 동일하다.

2 글은 담배꽁초로 인해서 산불이 발생한 사건을 말하고 있어 '만약 그 흡연자가 아니었다면 숲은 파괴되지 않았을 것이다.'라는 말을 「If it had not been for ~, 주어+조동사의 과거형+have+p.p.」로 표현한다. 숲이 파괴된다는 수동의 의미를 나타내기 위해 「have+p.p.」를 「have been p.p.」로 써야 한다.

3 내 친구 Lisa와 그녀의 남편은 집에 변화를 약간 주려고 생각하는 중이다. Lisa는 욕실을 하나 더 만들려고 생각하고 있다. 이제 두 아이들도 쑥쑥 자라고 있어서 아이들만의 욕실이 필요하다고 본다. 그녀는 주방도 넓히고 싶어 한다. 기회가 있을 때마다 아이들과 함께 식사를 준비하는데, 세 명에게 주방은 다소 좁게 느껴진다. 하지만 그녀의 남편은 다른 생각을 갖고 있다. 그는 벽난로를 설치하고 싶어 한다. 벽난로가 있으면 가족들이 더 자주 모일 수 있을 거라고 여긴다. 그리고 더 큰 차고도 원한다. 차고에 물건이 너무 많아서 그곳에서 편하게 일을 할 수 없기 때문이다. 가정법 과거는 「If+주어+동사의 과거형, 주어+조동사의 과거형+동사원형」으로 쓰므로 will은 would로 써야 옳다.

Chapter 8

8-1 비교급과 최상급 p.124

Exercise 1

1 better
2 farther
3 last
4 most
5 latest
6 further

Exercise 2

1 longer, longest
2 hotter, hottest
3 more useful, most useful
4 earlier, earliest
5 more, most
6 elder, eldest
7 further, furthest
8 later, latest
9 less, least
10 better, best
11 wider, widest
12 more famous, most famous
13 easier, easiest
14 funnier, funniest
15 wiser, wisest
16 more careful, most careful
17 uglier, ugliest
18 shorter, shortest
19 noisier, noisiest
20 huger, hugest
21 more important, most important
22 sunnier, sunniest
23 more popular, most popular
24 more interesting, most interesting
25 worse, worst
26 latter, last
27 larger, largest
28 farther, farthest
29 bigger, biggest
30 older, oldest

Exercise 3

1 eldest
2 most
3 least
4 older
5 most
6 better
7 last
8 less
9 best
10 higher

8-2 원급/비교급/최상급 p.126

Exercise 1

1 than
2 of
3 hardest
4 in
5 interesting

Exercise 2

1 less heavy
2 heavy
3 heaviest
4 heavier, lighter

Exercise 3

1 braver
2 less populous
3 more comfortable
4 more impressive
5 less effective
6 less popular

Exercise 4

1 as expensive as my car
2 less crowded than the bus
3 as tall as
4 as fluently as
5 the smartest student
6 the oldest building in town

8-3 비교급 강조 p.128

Exercise 1

1 much
2 a lot
3 more
4 very
5 much
6 very

Exercise 2

1 a, lot, heavier, than
2 even, more, intelligent, than
3 much, more, nutritious, than
4 much, more, crowded, than
5 far, more, fantastic, than
6 a, lot, worse, than

8-4 다양한 원급 표현 p.129

Exercise 1

1 as, clearly, as, could
2 as, efficiently, as, possible
3 five, times, as, expensive, as
4 ten, times, larger, than

Exercise 2

1 three times larger than that plastic one
2 four times as old as I am
3 as much as he could
4 people in need as much as possible

8-5 비교급을 이용한 다양한 표현 p.130

Exercise 1

1 colder and colder
2 worse and worse
3 more and more bored
4 better and better
5 louder and louder

Exercise 2

1 the smarter
2 less and less
3 would rather
4 stronger and stronger
5 the more

Exercise 3

1 The older Richard gets, the wiser he becomes.
2 The colder it gets, the more people drink hot coffee.
3 The worse the situation becomes, the calmer I become.
4 The harder you study, the better scores you'll get.
5 The more luxurious the car is, the more expensive it is.
6 The further you throw the ball, the more points you will get.
7 The higher we climb the mountain, the thinner the air will get.
8 The older he becomes, the more he is interested in science.
9 The more heavily it snows, the worse the road condition becomes.
10 The sooner you finish the homework, the sooner you can watch TV.
11 The more severely it rains, the slower the cars on the highway move.
12 The longer she stays abroad, the poorer her native language skills will become.

Exercise 4

1 the, larger
2 the, taller
3 the, more, diligent
4 would, rather, leave, than
5 the, healthier
6 colder, and, colder
7 prettier, and, prettier
8 less, and, less
9 more, and, more, interested
10 more, and, more, popular
11 The, longer, the, better

8-6 기타 비교급
p.133

Exercise 1

1 junior, to
2 senior, to
3 inferior, to
4 superior, to
5 prefer, to
6 inferior, to
7 superior, to
8 prior, to
9 senior, to

8-7 최상급 표현 I
p.134

Exercise 1

1 No other ring in the shop is more expensive than this ring.
No other ring in the shop is as expensive as this ring.
This ring is more expensive than any other ring in the shop.
2 No other boy in his school is smarter than Jonathan.
No other boy in his school is as smart as Jonathan.
Jonathan is smarter than any other boy in his school.
3 No other mountain in the world is higher than Mt. Everest.
No other mountain in the world is as high as Mt. Everest.
Mt. Everest is higher than any other mountain in the world.
4 No other actor in Canada is more handsome than Dennis.
No other actor in Canada is as handsome as Dennis.
Dennis is more handsome than any other actor in Canada.

8-8 최상급 표현 II
p.135

Exercise 1

1 one of the most famous scientists
2 one of the largest cities
3 the smartest student, I've ever taught
4 the thickest book, I've ever read

Exercise 2

1 Roxy Theater is the biggest theater that I've ever seen.
2 The Nile is one of the longest rivers in Africa.
3 This is the most delicious pancake that I've ever tried.
4 Jerry is one of the most talented musicians in the world.

Review Test
p.136

01 ①　02 ④　03 ②　04 ③　05 ①　06 ③
07 ⑤　08 ④　09 ④　10 ②　11 ④　12 ④
13 ③　14 ③　15 ②　16 ③　17 ④　18 ④
19 ②　20 ③　21 ①　22 ③　23 ②　24 ②
25 ②

26 as, strong, as
27 The, higher, the, colder
28 as, expensive, as
29 more, important, than, anything
30 less, than
31 three, times, more, expensive
32 smaller, smaller
33 (A) highest　(B) higher　(C) low　(D) lowest

01 그들은 가능한 한 빨리 걷고 있다. : 「as+원급+as+주어+can」은 '가능한 한 ～하게 …하다'라는 뜻이다.

02 새 체육관은 예전 것보다 훨씬 좋다. : 「much+비교급+than」은 '～보다 훨씬 더 …하다'라는 뜻이다.

03 우리는 집 없는 사람을 가능한 한 많이 돕고 싶다. : 「as+원급+as+주어+can」은 '가능한 한 ～하게 …하다'라는 뜻이다.

04 연습하면 할수록 너의 기술이 좋아질 것이다. : 「the+비교급+주어+동사, the+비교급+주어+동사」는 '～하면 할수록 더욱더 …하다'라는 뜻이다.

05 내 누나가 자신의 반에서 가장 크다. : 「최상급+in+장소, 범위의 단수명사」, 「최상급+of+기간, 비교의 대상이 되는 복수명사」

06 ③ far의 최상급은 most far가 아니라 farthest(거리), furthest(정도)이다.

07 이 화병이 저 화병보다 훨씬 싸다. : very는 비교급을 수식하지 않는다.

08 fast의 비교급은 faster이므로 앞에 more가 붙지 않는다.

09 • 더 자세한 정보를 원하시면, 123-456-7890으로 전화하세요.
• 더 깊이 공부하면 할수록. 더 많이 알게 될 것이다. : far(정도) - further '더 깊이', '더 자세히'

10 • 훌륭한 운동선수가 되려면 가능한 한 많이 운동해라. : 「as+원급+as+주어+can」은 '가능한 한 ～하게 …하다'라는 뜻이다.
• 그의 새 컴퓨터는 내 것보다 훨씬 좋다. : 「much/even/a lot/still/far+비교급」은 비교급을 강조해서 '훨씬 ～한'이라는 뜻이다.

11 음악이 가장 중요하다. : music is the most important
= nothing is as important as music
= nothing is more important than music
= music is more important than anything else

12 ① 시간적으로 더 오래됐음을 의미할 때의 비교급은 elder가 아니라 older로 써야 한다.
② 비교급 앞에는 관용표현을 제외하고는 the가 오지 않으므로 the taller가 아니라 taller가 되어야 한다.
③ 더 가깝다고 했으므로 close가 아니라 비교급 closer가 되어야 한다.
⑤ large의 비교급은 more large가 아니라 larger이다.

27

13 그 살인자에 대한 소문은 훨씬 심해졌다. : 비교급을 강조해서 '훨씬'이라는 뜻이다.
① 그는 심지어 자기 부인이 미쳤다고 말했다.
② Mary는 심지어 어두운 곳에서도 책을 읽을 수 있다.
③ Sunny는 자신의 아버지보다 훨씬 빨리 걷는다.(비교급 강조)
④ 심지어 고대에도 살인은 큰 사회적 문제였다.
⑤ 그녀는 지난달에 200만 달러나 벌었음에도 우리를 위해 많은 돈을 쓰지 않았다.

14 경찰은 도둑을 잡으려고 가능한 한 빨리 달렸다. : 「as+원급+as+주어+can[could]」 = 「as+원급+as+possible」은 '가능한 한 ~하게 …하다'라는 뜻이다.

15 이 에어컨은 저 에어컨만큼 싸지 않다. (이것 〉 저것)
→ 저 에어컨은 이 에어컨보다 싸다. (저것 〈 이것)

16 가격이 더 낮아질수록, 사람들이 더 많이 사게 될 것이다. : 「the+비교급+주어+동사, the+비교급+주어+동사」 '~하면 할수록 더 …하다'

17 ① 모차르트는 역사상 가장 훌륭한 음악가이다.
② 역사상 모차르트만큼 훌륭한 음악가는 없다.
③ 역사상 모차르트보다 훌륭한 음악가는 없다.
④ 모차르트는 역사상 다른 음악가들만큼 훌륭하다.
⑤ 모차르트는 역사상 다른 어떤 음악가보다 훌륭하다.

18 ① 그는 가능한 한 많이 읽으려고 노력했다. : tried가 과거이므로 can이 아니라 could가 되어야 한다.
② 그는 내가 지금까지 본 사람 중에서 가장 크다. : 「the+최상급(+that)+주어+have ever+p.p.」는 '지금까지 ~한 것 중에서 가장 …하다'라는 뜻으로 taller가 아니라 tallest가 되어야 한다.
③ 우리 집은 너의 집의 세 배만큼 크다. : 「as+원급+as」이므로 bigger가 아니라 big이 되어야 한다.
④ 우리 마을에서 우리 학교만큼 큰 학교는 없다.
⑤ 그는 과학클럽의 다른 어떤 학생보다 똑똑하다. : 「비교급+than any other+단수명사」는 '다른 어떤 ~보다 더 …하다'라는 뜻으로 students가 아니라 student가 되어야 한다.

19 ① 우리 엄마는 내 동생보다 크다. : tall의 비교급은 more taller가 아니라 taller이다.
② 어느 치마가 더 길어, 이것이니 아니면 저것이니?
③ 그는 과학에서 이전 어떤 때보다 훨씬 잘하고 있다. : '훨씬 더 잘하고 있다'라는 뜻의 비교급 문장이므로 well이 아니라 better가 와야 한다.
④ 나는 우리 반의 어떤 학생보다 훨씬 빨리 달린다. : much, a lot, even, far, still 등의 부사가 비교급을 수식하므로 many가 아니라 much 등이 되어야 한다.
⑤ 더 많이 벌면 벌수록 책을 사는 데 더 많은 돈을 쓸 수 있다. : 「the+비교급+주어+동사, the+비교급+주어+동사」는 '~하면 할수록 더 …하다'라는 뜻으로 More가 아니라 The more가, more가 아니라 the more가 되어야 한다.

20 ① 일이 점점 더 힘들어지고 있다. : 「비교급+and+비교급」 '점점 더 ~해지다'
② 그의 가방은 그녀의 가방의 세 배만큼 무겁다. : 「A+배수사+times+as+원급+as+B」 'A는 B의 ~배만큼 …하다'
③ 그는 캐나다에서 가장 훌륭한 화가 중 한 명이다. : 「one of the+최상급+복수명사」는 '가장 ~한 … 중 하나'라는 뜻으로 painter가 아니라 painters가 되어야 한다.
④ 나는 영화를 보는 것보다 밖에서 노는 것을 선호한다. : 「prefer A to B」 'B보다 A를 선호하다'
⑤ 그녀는 내가 지금까지 본 사람 중에서 가장 빠른 수영선수이다. :

「the+최상급(+that)+주어+have ever p.p.」 '지금까지 ~한 것 중에서 가장 …하다'

21 ① 두 투수 중에서 누가 더 크니? : 「the+비교급+of the two(+복수명사)」는 '둘 중에서 더 ~한'이라는 뜻으로 taller가 아니라 the taller가 되어야 한다.
② 이 책은 저 책보다 덜 재미있다.
③ Tom은 자신의 학교의 다른 어떤 학생보다 빨리 달린다. (Tom은 자신의 학교에서 가장 빨리 달린다.)
④ 백화점은 어제보다 더 붐빈다.
⑤ 더 많이 연습하면 할수록, 더 완벽해질 것이다. : 「the+비교급+주어+동사, the+비교급+주어+동사」 '~하면 할수록 더 …하다'

22 ① 제주도는 한국에서 가장 큰 섬이다.
② 이것은 우리 가게에서 가장 싼 침대이다.
③ 이것은 나의 정원에서 다른 어떤 나무보다 더 큰 나무이다. : 「비교급+than any other+단수명사」는 '다른 어떤 ~보다 더 …하다(가장 ~하다)'라는 뜻으로 trees가 아니라 tree가 되어야 한다.
④ Diana는 Linda보다 피아노를 잘 친다.
⑤ 더 열심히 훈련하면 할수록 너는 더 강해질 것이다.

23 ① 나는 노란색보다 분홍색을 더 좋아한다.
② 내 딸은 Jenny만큼 똑똑하지 않다. (my daughter 〈 Jenny) ≠ Jenny는 내 딸보다 똑똑하지 않다. (my daughter 〉 Jenny)
③ 우리 팀에서는 모두가 나보다 선임이다. = 우리 팀에서 나보다 후임인 사람은 없다.
④ 도쿄는 일본에서 가장 큰 도시이다. = 일본의 다른 어떤 도시도 도쿄보다 크지 않다.
⑤ 네가 공부를 더하면 더 좋은 점수를 얻게 될 것이다. = 네가 공부를 하면 할수록 더 좋은 점수를 얻게 될 것이다.

24 ① 그 컴퓨터 게임은 내가 생각했던 것만큼 흥미로웠다.
② 그 컴퓨터 게임은 내가 생각했던 것만큼 흥미롭지 않았다.
③ 그 컴퓨터 게임은 내가 생각했던 것보다 훨씬 더 흥미로웠다.
④ 나는 그 컴퓨터 게임이 다른 어떤 것보다 더 흥미롭다고 생각했다.
⑤ 나는 그 컴퓨터 게임이 다른 어떤 것보다 훨씬 더 흥미롭다고 생각했다.

25 ① 건강은 그렇게 중요한 것이 아니다.
② 건강만큼 중요한 것은 없다.
③ 건강은 가장 덜 중요한 것이다.
④ 건강은 다른 어떤 것만큼 중요하지 않다.
⑤ 건강은 다른 어떤 것보다 덜 중요하다.

26 나는 너보다 강하다. → 너는 나만큼 강하지 않다.

27 우리가 더 높이 올라갈수록 더 추워질 것이다. : 「the+비교급+주어+동사, the+비교급+주어+동사」 '~하면 할수록 더 …하다'

28 세상의 다른 어떤 기타도 내 기타보다 더 비싸지 않다. : 「no other+명사+비교급+than A」 = 「no other+명사+as+원급+as A」 'A보다 더 ~한 것은 없다(A가 가장 ~하다)'

29 야구가 내 인생에서 가장 중요하다. : 「nothing+비교급+than A」 = 「A 비교급+than anything else」 'A보다 더 ~한 것은 없다(A가 가장 ~하다)'

30 야구를 하는 것은 내가 생각했던 것만큼 어렵지 않았다. = 야구를 하는 것은 내가 생각했던 것보다 덜 어려웠다.

31 「A+배수사+times+비교급+than B」는 'A는 B보다 ~배 더 …하다'라는 뜻이다.

32 「비교급+and+비교급」은 '점점 더 ~한'이라는 뜻이다.

33 위 표는 다섯 개의 도시에서 잃어버린 지갑이 돌아온 비율을 보여준다. 서울은 모든 도시 중에서 두 번째로 높은 회수율을 보였다. 뉴욕은 다른 어떤 도시보다 높은 회수율을 보였다. 도쿄는 지갑의 회수율이 방콕과 같았다. 홍콩의 회수율은 뉴욕의 회수율보다 세 배 낮았다. 홍콩은 모든 도시 중에서 가장 낮은 회수율을 보여줬다.

보너스 유형별 문제   p.140

1 ⓐ fastest ⓑ faster
2 the fastest animal, faster than any other animal
3 twice as fast as
4 ⑤

[1-3] 육지에서 가장 빠른 동물은 무엇인가요? 치타를 떠올렸다면 맞아요. 육지의 다른 어떤 동물도 치타보다 빠르지 않아요. 치타는 시속 70마일로 달릴 수 있어요. 얼마나 빠른지 상상이 되나요? 고속도로에서 시속 70마일로 달리는 차를 상상해 보세요. 다른 동물은 어떤가요? 사자는 시속 50마일로 달릴 수 있고, 하이에나는 시속 35마일로 달릴 수 있어요. 치타는 사자보다 빨리 달릴 수 있고 하이에나보다 두 배만큼 빨리 달릴 수 있어요.

1 ⓐ '육지에서 가장 빠르다'라는 뜻이므로 fast의 최상급인 fastest가 적절하다.
　ⓑ '사자보다 빨리 달릴 수 있다'라는 뜻이므로 fast의 비교급인 fastest가 적절하다.

2 「No other ~ 비교급 than …」은 '…보다 더 ~한 것은 없다'라는 표현으로 이를 「the 최상급+명사」, 「비교급 than any other+명사」로 바꿔 쓸 수 있다.

3 '~의 몇 배만큼 …한'은 「배수사+as+원급+as」으로 표현한다. '두 배'는 twice로 쓴다.

4 학기가 끝나는 만큼 모두들 수업을 잘 듣고 있기를 바란다. 특히 스트레스가 심한 시기일 수 있지만 멋지게 사이클링 시즌을 마무리할 수 있을 거야. 이번 토요일에 올해 마지막 사이클링 모임이 있어. 모임 장소는 유니언 스퀘어야. 각자 점심 도시락이랑 물병 챙겨 오는 것 잊지 말고, 가능한 많이 왔으면 좋겠다!
'가능한 한 ~하게'는 「as ~ as possible」을 쓰므로 possibly를 possible로 바꿔야 한다.

Chapter 9

9-1   수의 일치 I   p.143

Exercise 1

1 requires	2 is
3 were	4 was
5 were	6 were
7 want	8 has passed
9 is	10 has to
11 helps	12 is

Exercise 2

1 knows	2 consists of
3 is	4 are
5 is	6 is
7 are	8 has
9 is	10 is
11 is	12 has

Exercise 3

1 is → are	2 make → makes
3 is → are	4 is → are
5 are → is	6 wear → wears
7 are → is	8 have → has

Exercise 4

1 Each, country, has
2 The, are, the
3 Five, kilometers, is
4 Collecting, stamps, is
5 The, number, has
6 The, doctor, and, writer, is
7 Economics, is, students, want
8 A, number, people, were

9-2   수의 일치 II   p.145

Exercise 1

1 was	2 was
3 have	4 was
5 are	

Exercise 2

1 has	2 look
3 are	4 have
5 has	

Exercise 3

1 are → is	2 has → have
3 doesn't → don't	4 were → was
5 was → were	6 were → was
7 are → is	

9-3   수의 일치 III   p.146

Exercise 1

1 was	2 gets
3 is	4 needs
5 are	6 am

1 am
2 is
3 are
4 am
5 has to
6 have to

9-4 시제의 일치 p.147

Exercise 1

1 went [had gone]
2 wanted [had wanted]
3 reads
4 took
5 won [had won]
6 had

Exercise 2

1 She couldn't find the place where the book was.
2 She thought that Sally would marry Mr. Kim.
3 Did you see the lion which escaped[had escaped] from the zoo?
4 I asked my son where he had been all day.
5 I believed that you would get a perfect score on the test.

9-5 시제 일치의 예외 p.148

Exercise 1

1 migrate
2 doesn't
3 moves
4 discovered
5 broke out
6 contains

Exercise 2

1 was → is
2 was → is
3 play → plays
4 invades → invaded
5 will be → is
6 declares → declared

9-6 화법 전환 I p.150

Exercise 1

1 He told me (that) he agreed with me.
2 My brother said (that) he lost[had lost] his book the day before[the previous day].
3 She told me (that) she had written that report that day.
4 Brooke said (that) she would study in the library that Saturday.
5 My boss told me (that) I had to come there on time.
6 Edward said (that) his family would move to the urban area.
7 She said (that) she would go to Japan to study Japanese the following week.

Exercise 2

1 My mom said, "It may rain today."
2 Mr. Kim said to us, "I will join the club."
3 She said, "I want to go out for dinner."
4 She said, "I am excited about going to university."
5 Emma said to us, "I will go to the beach next week."
6 Tina said, "My sister went to China to meet her friend yesterday."

9-7 화법 전환 II p.151

Exercise 1

1 He asked me how long I would stay there.
2 She asked me why I looked so sad.
3 The man asked me where the nearest bank was.
4 Bella asked him what he was going to do that weekend.
5 He asked me why I hadn't[didn't] come to the party the previous Friday.
6 She asked me what conclusion I drew[had drawn] from the report.
7 My mother asked my father what he wanted to eat for dinner.
8 Jessica asked me what I had done with my brother the day before[the previous day].

Exercise 2

1 She asked me if[whether] I knew his full name.
2 Jack asked me if[whether] I could lend him some money.
3 Janet asked me if[whether] she could borrow my cell phone.
4 James asked me if[whether] I had been to Switzerland.
5 Mom asked me if[whether] I went[had gone] anywhere interesting.
6 My teacher asked me if[whether] I was[had been] in the class the day before[the previous day].
7 Mary asked me if[whether] I talked[had talked] over my problems with my teacher.

Exercise 3

1 that → if[whether]
2 could I → I could
3 I → he
4 whether when → when
5 he → I
6 did I see → I saw[seen]
7 they → we

Exercise 1

1 to organize the stuff on my desk
2 to keep quiet during the test
3 not to be mean to my little brother
4 not to play soccer in the classroom

Exercise 2

1 told them not to be late for the class
2 advised me not to cross the street
3 not to talk with my mouth full
4 My father asked me to bring his briefcase.

Review Test

p.154

01 ④	02 ②	03 ③	04 ④	05 ③	06 ②
07 ③	08 ⑤	09 ①	10 ④	11 ③	12 ③
13 ③	14 ④	15 ④	16 ④	17 ④	18 ③
19 ④	20 ②	21 ②	22 ①	23 ⑤	

24 have	25 is	26 are

27 I had to get up then

28 why he looked so depressed

29 to drink a lot of water

30 if[whether] I had ever been to France

31 whom I had lent[I lent] my notebooks

32 air is gas

33 haven't made up their minds

01 그는 우리에게 그 전날 그녀를 본 적이 있는지 물었다. : 의문사가 없는 의문문의 간접 화법에서는 접속사 if나 whether를 쓴다.

02 그는 교사이자 시인인 그 사람이 파티에 참여할 거라고 생각했다. : the teacher and poet은 한 사람이고, thought가 과거이므로 would attend가 적절하다.

03 한 학생이 역사 선생님에게 콜럼버스가 언제 미국을 발견했는지 물었다. : 콜럼버스가 미국을 발견한 것은 역사적 사실이므로 과거 시제가 와야 한다.

04 선생님이 나에게 "너 챕터 2를 읽었니?"라고 말했다. → 선생님이 나에게 내가 챕터 2를 읽었는지 물었다. : 의문사가 없는 의문문의 간접 화법은 「if[whether]+주어+동사」로 쓴다. 이때 주어와 동사의 시제를 전달자의 입장에서 적절하게 바꿔야 한다.

05 그는 그녀에게 "너의 도쿄 여행이 어땠니?"라고 물었다. → 그는 그녀에게 그녀의 도쿄 여행이 어땠냐고 물었다. : 의문사가 있는 의문문의 간접 화법은 「의문사+주어+동사」로 쓴다. 이때 주어와 동사의 시제를 전달자의 입장에서 적절하게 바꿔야 한다.

06 그녀가 나에게 "어려운 일을 두려워하지 마."라고 말했다. → 그녀가 나에게 어려운 일을 두려워하지 말라고 말했다. : 부정명령문을 간접 화법으로 바꿀 때는 「not+to+동사원형」을 쓴다.

07 그녀가 나에게 "너 오늘 운전면허 시험을 볼 거니?"라고 물었다. → 그녀가 나에게 그날 운전면허 시험을 볼 거냐고 물었다. : 의문사가 없는 의문문의 간접 화법은 「if[whether]+주어+동사」로 쓴다. 이때 주어와 동사의 시제 및 부사(구)를 전달자의 입장에서 적절하게 바꿔야 한다.

08 아버지가 나에게 "나는 내일 런던으로 떠날 거야."라고 말씀하셨다. → 아버지가 나에게 아버지는 그 다음날 런던으로 떠날 거라고 말씀하셨다.

09 • 신생아의 수가 감소 중이다. : 「the number of+복수명사+단수동사」 '~의 수'
 • 많은 사람이 식사를 즐기고 있다. : 「a number of+복수명사+복수동사」 '(수가) 많은 ~'
 • 나이 든 사람들은 젊은 사람들보다 인내심이 많다. : 「the+형용사+복수명사」 '~한 사람들'

10 • 모든 사람은 자질구레한 일을 하는 자신만의 방식이 있다. : 「everyone+단수동사」
 • 아기들을 돌보는 것은 쉬운 일이 아니다. : 「동명사구 주어+단수동사」
 • 나머지 학생들은 토론에 참여해야 한다. : 「the rest of+복수명사+복수동사」 전체나 부분을 나타내는 수식어구 뒤에 오는 명사에 동사의 수를 일치시킨다.

11 • 승객의 5분의 3이 사고로 부상당했다. : 「분수+복수명사+복수동사」 전체나 부분을 나타내는 수식어구 뒤에 오는 명사에 동사의 수를 일치시킨다.
 • 이야기의 절반은 사실이 아니다. : 「the half+단수명사+단수동사」 전체나 부분을 나타내는 수식어구 뒤에 오는 명사에 동사의 수를 일치시킨다.
 • 이 건물에서는 흡연이나 음주가 허용되지 않습니다. : 「neither A nor B」는 B에 동사의 수를 일치시킨다.

12 • 물리학은 나에게 가장 어려운 과목 중 하나이다. : 학과명은 -s로 끝나더라도 복수가 아니므로 단수동사로 받는다.
 • 그녀뿐만 아니라 너도 요리를 잘한다. : 「not only A but also B」는 B에 동사의 수를 일치시킨다.
 • 100달러는 장갑 한 켤레의 가격으로 너무 비싸다. : 시간, 거리, 가격, 무게 등의 단위는 복수형이더라도 단수동사로 받는다.

13 ① 쥐구멍에도 볕 들 날이 있다. : every는 단수명사를 수식하고 단수동사로 받으므로 have가 아니라 has가 되어야 한다.
 ② 모든 개는 이름이 있다. : all 뒤에는 셀 수 있는 명사의 복수형이 오므로 dog이 아니라 dogs가 되어야 한다.
 ③ 지구의 4분의 3은 물로 덮여 있다.
 ④ 많은 학생이 도서관에서 공부하고 있다. : 「A number of+복수명사+복수동사」는 '(수가) 많은 ~'이라는 뜻으로 is가 아니라 are가 되어야 한다.
 ⑤ 우리 정원에 있는 밤나무들은 나와 나이가 같다. : The chestnut trees가 주어이므로 garden 뒤의 문장의 동사는 is가 아니라 are가 되어야 한다.

14 ① 내일 비가 오면 우리는 집에 머무를 것이다. : 조건의 부사절에서는 현재 시제가 미래 시제를 대신하므로 will rain이 아니라 rains가 되어야 한다.
 ② 그는 그녀가 곧 돌아올 거라고 생각했다. : 주절의 시제가 thought로 과거이므로 will이 아니라 would가 되어야 한다.
 ③ 우리는 학교에서 2 더하기 2는 4라고 배웠다. : 2 더하기 2가 4라는 것은 현재에도 변하지 않는 사실이므로 was가 아니라 is가 되어야 한다.
 ④ 뉴턴이 중력의 법칙을 발견했다고 말해진다.
 ⑤ 코끼리의 수가 지난 십 년 동안 줄어들고 있다. : 「The number of+

31

복수명사+단수동사」는 '~의 수'라는 뜻으로 have가 아니라 has가 되어야 한다.

15 the only one이 선행사이면서 단수이므로 ④의 are는 단수동사 is가 되어야 한다.

16 ① 대상자의 4분의 3이 남자이다.
② 상자 안에 있던 금의 나머지는 어디에 있니?
③ 사진을 찍는 것은 내가 제일 좋아하는 취미 중 하나다.
④ 식당의 모든 테이블이 이미 차 있었다. : All of the tables가 주어이고 전체를 나타내는 수식어구 뒤에 오는 명사에 동사의 수를 일치시키므로 was가 아니라 were가 되어야 한다.
⑤ 그녀에게 100달러는 바지 값으로 지불하기엔 너무 큰돈이다.

17 ① 모든 사람이 책 읽는 것을 좋아한다.
② 나는 그가 정직하다고 생각했다.
③ 나는 아무도 그 강을 건너려고 하지 않을 거라고 네게 말했다.
④ 우리 모두는 학교에서 지구가 둥글다고 배웠다. : 지구가 둥글다는 것은 현재에도 변하지 않는 사실이므로 was가 아니라 is가 되어야 한다.
⑤ 나는 그에게 내일 박물관을 방문하라고 권했다.

18 ① 천천히 꾸준히 하는 자가 경기에서 이긴다.
② 감자의 3분의 2가 썩었다.
③ 정치학은 흥미 있는 연구 분야이다.: 학문명은 -s로 끝나더라도 복수가 아니므로 동사는 are가 아니라 is가 되어야 한다.
④ 버터 바른 빵은 우리가 오늘 아침으로 먹은 것이었다.
⑤ 대부분의 시간을 컴퓨터 게임을 하는 데 썼다.

19 ① 그녀와 나 둘 다 옳지 않다.
② 학생들 각각 책을 다섯 권씩 가지고 있다.
③ 수학은 내가 제일 좋아하는 과목이다.
④ 우리 반의 모든 학생들이 거기에 있었다. : All the students가 주어이고 전체를 나타내는 수식어구 뒤에 오는 명사에 동사의 수를 일치시키므로 was가 아니라 were가 되어야 한다.
⑤ 영화에서 노래하고 있는 소녀들을 봐.

20 ① 그녀는 나에게 즉시 가라고 명령했다. : 명령문의 간접 화법 전환은 to부정사를 사용하므로 that I go가 아니라 to go가 되어야 한다.
② 그는 그녀에게 고양이에게 먹이를 주었는지 물었다.
③ 나는 그들에게 늦지 말라고 말했다. : 부정명령문의 간접 화법 전환은 to부정사의 부정형을 사용하므로 do not이 아니라 not to be가 되어야 한다.
④ 그녀는 자기가 그를 만나기를 원했다고 말했다. : 주어가 she이므로 간접 화법으로 전달되는 문장의 주어는 I가 아니라 she가 되어야 한다.
⑤ 그가 나에게 그 편지를 썼냐고 물었다. : 그가 나에게 묻는 문장이므로 간접 화법에서 전달되는 문장의 주어는 you가 아니라 I가 되어야 하고, 시제는 과거(wrote) 또는 과거완료(had written)가 되어야 한다.

21 ② 그녀는 나에게 독서를 좋아하냐고 물었다. : 의문사가 없는 의문문의 간접 화법에서는 접속사로 if나 whether를 쓰고 주어와 동사의 어순을 평서문과 같이 바꿔 준다. that이 아니라 if[whether]가 되어야 한다.

22 ① 그녀가 나와 함께 쇼핑을 가겠다고 말했다. : 주어가 she이므로 간접 화법에서 전달되는 문장의 주어는 she가 되어야 하고, you는 me가 되어야 한다.

23 ⑤ John이 나에게 자신이 밴드에 참여해도 되냐고 물었다. : 주어가 John이고 간접 화법에서 전달되는 문장의 주어가 he이므로 직접 화법에서 전달되는 문장의 주어는 you가 아니라 I가 되어야 한다.

24 「B as well as A」는 B에 동사의 수를 일치시킨다. The students가

복수이고 '10월 이후로 계속 사용하고 있다'라는 의미이므로 계속을 의미하는 현재완료(have used)가 가장 적절하다.

25 Every animal이 주어이므로 단수동사 is가 와야 한다.

26 「분수+복수명사+복수동사」 전체나 부분을 나타내는 수식어구 뒤에 오는 명사에 동사의 수를 일치시키므로 복수동사 are가 와야 한다.

27 우리 엄마가 나에게 내가 그때 일어나야 한다고 말했다. :
you → I, have to → had to, now → then

28 나는 그에게 왜 그가 그렇게 우울해 보이냐고 물었다. : 의문사가 있는 의문문의 간접 화법은 「의문사+주어+동사」 순으로 쓴다.

29 의사가 나에게 물을 많이 마시라고 말했다. : 명령문의 간접 화법은 「to+동사원형」을 사용한다.

30 그의 어머니가 나에게 프랑스에 가본 적이 있는지 물었다. : 의문사가 없는 의문문의 간접 화법은 「if[whether]+주어+동사」 순으로 쓴다.

31 그녀가 나에게 내 공책을 누구에게 빌려 줬는지 물었다. : 의문사가 있는 의문문의 간접 화법은 「의문사+주어+동사」 순으로 쓴다.

32 '공기는 기체다'라는 말은 과학적 사실을 나타내므로 현재 시제로 써야 한다.

33 「분수+복수명사+복수동사」 전체나 부분을 나타내는 수식어구 뒤에 오는 명사에 동사의 수를 일치시키므로 빈칸에 haven't made up their minds가 들어가야 한다.

보너스 유형별 문제　　p.158

1 (A) was → were
　(B) were → was

2 asked me why I looked so sad

3 said to me, "Do not [Don't] get depressed

4 ③

[1-3] 어제 시험 성적이 나왔다. 결과는 대부분 나쁘지 않았다. 하지만 수학은 끔찍했다. 나는 수학에 많은 노력을 쏟았기 때문에 무척 실망했다. 오늘 저녁을 먹으면서, 아빠가 내게 "왜 그렇게 슬퍼 보이니?"라고 물으셨다. 나는 "열심히 공부했지만 C학점을 받았어요."라고 말했다. 아빠는 내게 우울해하지 말라고 말씀하셨다. 그리고 아빠는 내게 "적어도 이번에는 낙제는 안 했네."라고 말해 주셨다.

1 (A) 부분을 나타내는 표현의 경우 of 뒤에 나오는 명사의 수에 일치시켜야 하므로 was가 아니라 were가 적절하다.
　(B) 학문명은 단수 취급하므로 were가 아닌 was가 적절하다.

2 의문사가 있는 경우, 화법 전환 시 전달동사를 ask로 바꾸고 어순은 「의문사+주어+동사」로 쓴다.

3 문장 형태로 보아 명령문의 간접화법임을 알 수 있다. 직접화법 전환 시 그 당시에 실제 말했던 명령문의 그대로 써야 한다.

4 나는 케이크와 쿠키를 줄이기로 마음먹고, 과일 디저트를 찾고 있었다. 친구들 중 한 명의 저녁 식사에 초대받았는데, 그녀가 너무나도 맛있고 바삭거리는 과일 디저트를 대접했다. 저녁 식사 후에 그녀에게 무슨 요리이며 어떻게 만드는지 묻자, 레시피를 주며 집에서 한번 만들어 보라고 했다. 그 친구가 만든 것과 똑같은 맛이 날지 잘 모르겠지만 만들어 보려고 한다.
의문사가 있는 경우, 화법 전환 시 전달동사를 ask로 바꾸고 어순은 「의문사+주어+동사」로 써야 한다. 따라서 was it을 it was로 바꿔야 옳다.

Chapter 10

10-1 who/which/that
p.160

Exercise 1

1 whom	2 which
3 whose	4 whom
5 which	6 who
7 which	

Exercise 2

1 who(m)[that]	2 which[that]
3 who(m)[that]	4 which[that]
5 whose	6 which[that]
7 whose	8 who(m)[that]
9 which[that]	

Exercise 3

1 that	2 are
3 are	4 whose
5 are	

Exercise 4

1 whose gate	2 which[that]
3 who(m)[that]	4 which[that]
5 who(m)[that]	6 belongs to
7 who[that] are	8 which were
9 which[that]	10 is

Exercise 5

1 who[that] was serving us
2 which[that] goes to City Hall
3 who(m)[that] I want to meet
4 who[that] is in the hospital
5 who[that] designed many beautiful houses and churches
6 who[that] was eating lunch

Exercise 6

1 whose hair is white
2 whom many people like
3 a friend whose father is a doctor
4 which I wanted to have
5 who was wearing a red dress
6 which always make me feel better

10-2 that
p.163

Exercise 1

1 that	2 that
3 that	4 that

Exercise 2

1 anything that I can do to ease my headache
2 the longest movie that I have seen
3 The first student who came to the library
4 the only food that we have in the refrigerator

10-3 what
p.164

Exercise 1

1 what	2 what
3 what	4 what
5 that	

Exercise 2

1 What he did
2 what I asked for
3 what you did last summer
4 What made me happy
5 What I really want to do
6 what we had for dinner last night
7 what I was supposed to do with my brother

10-4 관계대명사의 생략
p.165

Exercise 1

1 X	2 O
3 O	4 X
5 O	6 O
7 O	8 O

Exercise 2

1 The wallet Jeff lost was not found.
2 English is the subject I'm most interested in.
3 The man looking for his lost dog is my friend.
4 The woman I wanted to see was staying in Seoul.
5 Do you know the girl talking to Charles by the window?

10-5 관계대명사의 용법
p.166

Exercise 1

1 who	2 who
3 which	4 who

5 which

Exercise 2

1 that, who
2 that, which
3 who
4 which
5 which

Exercise 3

1 and, it
2 and, it
3 and, they
4 and, she

Exercise 4

1 Jimmy went to the flower shop, which was closed.
2 We stayed at the Hilton Hotel, which a taxi driver recommended to us.
3 Seoul, which is the capital of Korea, is one of the biggest cities in the world.
4 Tom Cruise starred in the film *Top Gun: Maverick,* which was released in 2022.

Exercise 5

1 which was crowded with a lot of people
2 who became lawyers
3 which made him famous
4 which made her teacher upset

10-6 전치사+관계대명사
p.168

Exercise 1

1 George didn't get the job which he applied for.
  George didn't get the job he applied for.
  George didn't get the job for which he applied.
2 We could go to the wedding which we were invited to.
  We could go to the wedding we were invited to.
  We could go to the wedding to which we were invited.
3 This is the house which my grandparents have lived in for 50 years.
  This is the house my grandparents have lived in for 50 years.
  This is the house in which my grandparents have lived for 50 years.
4 This is the tunnel which about thirty thousand cars a day go through to reach the beach.
  This is the tunnel about thirty thousand cars a day go through to reach the beach.
  This is the tunnel through which about thirty thousand cars a day go to reach the beach.

10-7 관계부사
p.169

Exercise 1

1 in which
2 which
3 that
4 in which
5 where
6 when
7 why
8 where
9 when
10 why

Exercise 2

1 where
2 why
3 where
4 where
5 when
6 when
7 why
8 how
9 where
10 where

Exercise 3

1 which 삭제 / in which
2 when
3 how 삭제 / in which
4 which 삭제 / why
5 where
6 where

Exercise 4

1 how, you, fixed
2 where, are, exhibited
3 the, reason, why, is
4 the, year, when, broke, out

Exercise 5

1 This is the village where I was born.
2 We went to the city where my grandparents used to live.
3 This is the hospital where my father works as a janitor.
4 October 15th is the day when World War II ended.
5 He showed me the basement where he had lived during the war.
6 I know the reason why Joanna broke up with her boyfriend.

Exercise 6

1 how I can make the best cookies
2 where we had dinner last night
3 how she could gather the information
4 when Cathy first came to our school
5 why she couldn't catch the first train
6 where they are going to stay during the vacation

10-8 복합관계사
p.172

Exercise 1

1 whatever
2 Whatever
3 Whichever team
4 Whoever

Exercise 2

1 Whatever
2 whomever
3 Whatever
4 whoever

10-9 복합관계부사

p.173

Exercise 1

1 Wherever
2 wherever
3 Whenever
4 However

Exercise 2

1 He went to the beach whenever he felt lonely.
2 Whenever you visit the zoo, you can see the lions.
3 Wherever you go, you can buy our books online.
4 However difficult the project is, we'll finish it as scheduled.

Review Test

p.174

01 ④	02 ③	03 ④	04 ③	05 ②	06 ③
07 ①	08 ②	09 ③	10 ③	11 ①	12 ②
13 ①	14 ③	15 ③	16 ②	17 ⑤	18 ②
19 ①	20 ④	21 ②	22 ③	23 ②	24 ④
25 ③	26 ②	27 ③	28 ②		

29 whoever

30 Whatever

31 what you said

32 Whenever he takes a walk

33 I have two daughters, who are journalists.

34 She is the girl who(m)[that] I asked the way to the hotel this morning.

35 Whatever, you, do

36 However, smart, he, is

01 이 사람이 나에게 우체국으로 가는 길을 알려준 소년이다. : the boy가 선행사이고, showed의 주어가 되는 주격 관계대명사 자리이므로 who가 와야 한다.

02 도쿄는 2022년 올림픽이 개최된 도시이다. : the city가 선행사이고, 빈칸 뒤에 완전한 절(the 2022 Olympics were held)이 왔으므로 관계부사 where가 와야 한다.

03 너는 네가 원하는 사람은 누구든지 파티에 초대할 수 있다. : '~하는 사람은 누구든지'라는 의미를 가진 복합관계사 자리이다. want의 목적어가 되어야 하므로 목적격 복합관계사가 와야 한다.

04 이 기계가 작동하는 방법을 나에게 말해 줄래? : '~하는 방식'이라는 의미의 관계부사 how가 와야 한다.

05 내가 지금 가장 필요로 하는 것은 사랑이다. : 선행사를 포함하면서 주어절을 이끄는 관계대명사 what이 와야 한다.

06 • 이 사람이 뉴욕에서 5년 동안 산 사람이다. : the person이 선행사이고, has been living의 주어가 되는 주격 관계대명사 자리이므로 who나 that이 와야 한다.
• 나는 Tom이 지은 집을 보았다. : the house가 선행사이고, built의 목적어가 되는 목적격 관계대명사 자리이므로 which나 that이 와야 한다.
• 증인이 우리에게 말한 모든 것이 사실이다. : everything이 선행사이고, told의 직접목적어가 되는 목적격 관계대명사 자리이므로 that이 와야 한다.

07 나는 설탕을 더 넣었는데 그것이 커피를 달게 해 주었다. : 앞 문장 전체를 선행사로 받는 계속적 용법의 주격 관계대명사 which이다. 계속적 용법의 관계대명사는 「접속사+대명사」로 바꿔 쓸 수 있다.

08 이것이 내가 찾고 있던 그것이다. : the thing which는 선행사를 포함하는 관계대명사 what으로 바꿔 쓸 수 있다.

09 너는 우리가 처음 만났던 장소를 기억하니? : 장소를 나타내는 '전치사+관계대명사/at which'는 관계부사 where로 바꿔 쓸 수 있다.

10 네가 어디를 가든지 온라인으로 공부할 수 있다. : '어디를 가더라도'라는 의미의 복합관계부사 wherever는 no matter where로 바꿔 쓸 수 있다.

11 너는 네가 원하는 것은 무엇이든지 입을 수 있다. : '~하는 것은 무엇이든지'라는 의미의 복합관계사 whatever는 anything that으로 바꿔 쓸 수 있다.

12 • 우리는 책을 몇 권 샀는데 그것은 매우 재미있다. : some books가 선행사이고 were의 주어가 되는 계속적 용법의 주격 관계대명사 자리이므로 which가 와야 한다.
• 우리 모두 모래로 덮여있는 해변으로 나갔다. : the beach가 선행사이고, was covered의 주어가 되는 주격 관계대명사 자리이므로 which나 that이 와야 한다.
• 이곳이 그들이 휴가 기간 동안 머물렀던 호텔이다. : the hotel이 선행사이고, 전치사 at의 목적어가 되는 목적격 관계대명사 자리이므로 which가 와야 한다. at which는 관계부사 where로 바꿔 쓸 수 있다.

13 • 이것은 내가 찾고 있던 바로 그 책이다. : the very book이 선행사이고, looking for의 목적어가 되는 목적격 관계대명사 자리이므로 that이 가장 적절하다.
• 이것이 내가 지금까지 본 것 중에서 가장 아름다운 강이다. : the most beautiful river가 선행사이고, seen의 목적어가 되는 목적격 관계대명사 자리이므로 that이 가장 적절하다.
• 너에게 나에 대해 물어봤던 사람이 어디 있니? : the person이 선행사이고, asked의 주어가 되는 주격 관계대명사 자리이므로 that이나 who가 와야 한다.

14 ① 그는 내가 그에게 준 가방을 들고 있다. : 목적격 관계대명사는 생략 가능하다.
② Tom은 지금 노래하고 있는 소녀를 좋아한다. 「관계대명사+be동사+분사」의 구문에서 관계대명사와 be동사는 함께 생략 가능하다.
③ 나는 Mary가 태어난 마을을 안다. : 관계대명사가 전치사 바로 뒤에 위치해서 전치사의 목적어로 쓰였을 때는 생략할 수 없다.
④ 그녀가 나에게 자신이 지난달에 만든 드레스를 주었다. : 목적격 관계대명사는 생략할 수 있다.
⑤ 우리가 어제 본 남자는 Tiger Woods이다. : 목적격 관계대명사는 생략할 수 있다.

15 ① 그는 모두가 좋아하는 소년이다. : 목적격 관계대명사는 생략 가능하다.
② 프랑스에서 만든 그 스카프는 그녀의 것이다. : 「관계대명사+be동사+분사」에서 관계대명사와 be동사는 함께 생략 가능하다.

③ 이것이 Sam이 그린 그림이다. : 「관계대명사+be동사+분사」에서 관계대명사만 생략할 수는 없다.

④ 교실에서 공부하고 있는 학생들을 봐라. : 「관계대명사+be동사+분사」에서 관계대명사와 be동사는 함께 생략 가능하다.

⑤ 탁자 위에 있는 책은 매우 재미있다. : 「관계대명사+be동사+부사구」에서 관계대명사와 be동사는 함께 생략 가능하다.

16 ① 사람은 말을 할 수 있는 유일한 동물이다. : the only animal이 선행사이고, 주격 관계대명사 자리이므로 that이 가장 적절하다.

② 나는 두 명의 아들이 있는데 그들은 의사이다. : two sons가 선행사이고, 계속적 용법의 주격 관계대명사 자리이므로 who가 와야 한다.

③ 그녀는 내가 지금까지 본 사람 중에 가장 예쁜 소녀이다. : the prettiest girl이 선행사이고, seen의 목적어가 되는 목적격 관계대명사 자리이므로 that이 가장 적절하다.

④ 거기에서 달리고 있는 소년과 그의 개를 봐라. : the boy and his dog이 선행사이고, are running의 주어가 되는 주격 관계대명사 자리이므로 that이 와야 한다.

⑤ 부상을 입지 않고 탈출한 승객이 거의 없었다. : few passengers가 선행사이고, escaped의 주어가 되는 주격 관계대명사 자리이므로 who나 that이 와야 한다.

17 ① 내가 수영했던 수영장의 이름이 무엇이니? : What's the name of the pool?+I swam in the pool. → What's the name of the pool where[in which] I swam?

② 우리가 머물렀던 호텔은 매우 작았다. : The hotel was very small.+We stayed at the hotel. → The hotel where[at which] we stayed was very small.

③ 나는 오래된 책을 많이 볼 수 있는 장소를 안다. : I know a place.+You can find many old books in the place. → I know a place where[in which] you can find many old books.

④ 저것이 내 고양이와 개가 잠자기 좋아하는 의자이다. : 관계대명사 that은 전치사 바로 뒤에 위치하여 전치사의 목적어로 쓰일 수 없으므로 that이 아니라 which가 되어야 한다.

⑤ 나는 어머니가 한국에서 유명한 가수인 친구가 있다.

18 ① 내가 잊어버린 무언가가 있다.

② 이곳이 우리가 사는 집이다. : This is the house.+We live in the house. → This is the house (which) we live in.

③ 민수는 내가 산 재킷을 입고 있다.

④ 그것이 그들을 만족하게 하는 유일한 가격이다.

⑤ 그는 Joe가 찍은 사진 몇 장을 보고 있다.

19 ① 이것은 내가 찾고 있는 것이 아니다. : looking for의 목적어가 없는 불완전한 문장이 왔으므로 that이 아니라 선행사를 포함하는 관계대명사 what이 되어야 한다.

② 우리는 우리가 필요한 것을 모두 확인했다.

③ 그가 남극에 가장 먼저 도착한 사람이었다.

④ 나는 아버지가 변호사인 친구가 있다.

⑤ 네가 나에게 사준 사과는 모두 썩어 있었다.

20 ① 내가 정말 원하는 것은 너의 도움이다.

② 너는 네가 원하는 것은 무엇이든 선택할 수 있다.

③ 네가 어젯밤에 입은 재킷은 좋았다.

④ 이것은 고흐가 그린 그림이다. : 주격 관계대명사는 생략할 수 없으므로 was가 아니라 which was가 되어야 한다. 또는 「관계대명사+be동사+분사」 구문에서 관계대명사와 be동사는 함께 생략할 수 있으므로 was를 삭제해야 한다.

⑤ 그는 도쿄에 위치한 회사에서 일한다.

21 ① 저곳이 내가 태어난 마을이다. : the town이 선행사이고, 관계부사 자리이므로 where가 와야 한다.

② 저것이 템스 강인데 전에는 오염되어 있었다. : the Thames가 선행사이고, used to be의 주어가 되는 계속적 용법의 주격 관계대명사 자리이므로 which가 와야 한다.

③ 우리가 살았던 도시는 매우 크고 깨끗했다. : The city가 선행사이고, 관계부사 자리이므로 where가 와야 한다.

④ 나는 우리가 텐트를 세울 수 있을 만한 좋은 장소를 안다. : a good place가 선행사이고, 관계부사 자리이므로 where가 와야 한다.

⑤ 나는 공기가 신선한 나라에서 살고 싶다. : a country가 선행사이고 관계부사 자리이므로 where가 와야 한다.

22 ① 나는 Cindy를 보았는데 그녀는 우리 반 친구이다. : Cindy가 선행사이고, is의 주어가 되는 계속적 용법의 주격 관계대명사 자리이므로 who가 와야 한다.

② 나는 어제 예의 없는 소년을 만났다. : a boy가 선행사이고, was의 주어가 되는 주격 관계대명사 자리이므로 who나 that이 와야 한다.

③ 나는 Jones 부인을 만날 예정인데 그녀의 아들은 나의 학생이다. : Ms. Jones가 선행사이고, son을 받는 소유격 관계대명사 자리이므로 whose가 와야 한다.

④ 준호는 항상 제시간에 도착하는데 아직 오지 않았다. : 준호가 선행사이고, arrives의 주어가 되는 계속적 용법의 주격 관계대명사 자리이므로 who가 와야 한다.

⑤ 우리 할아버지는 70세이신데 매주 등산을 하신다. : My grandfather가 선행사이고, is의 주어가 되는 계속적 용법의 주격 관계대명사 자리이므로 who가 와야 한다.

23 ① 나는 아버지가 작가인 친구가 있다. : 소유격 관계대명사는 생략할 수 없다.

② 선반 위에 컵은 내 것이다. : 「관계대명사+be동사+부사구」에서 관계대명사와 be동사는 함께 생략 가능하다.

③ 그들은 그가 일하는 사무실로 들어왔다. : 관계대명사가 전치사 바로 뒤에 위치해서 전치사의 목적어로 쓰였을 때는 생략할 수 없다.

④ 저것은 태국에서 온 코끼리이다. : 주격 관계대명사는 생략할 수 없다.

⑤ 우리는 눈으로 덮인 산을 보았다. : 주격 관계대명사는 생략할 수 없다.

24 앞 문장 전체를 선행사로 받으면서 계속적 용법의 관계대명사로 쓸 수 있는 것은 which이다.

25 '아무리 ~해도'라는 의미의 복합관계부사는 however이다. 「however+형용사+주어+동사」 '아무리 ~해도 …하다'

26 나는 많은 실수를 한 의사들을 믿지 않는다. : doctors를 선행사로 받는 주격 관계대명사

① 지구가 둥글다는 것은 사실이다. : 진주어절을 이끄는 접속사

② 그는 나를 진실로 사랑하는 사람이다. : the man을 선행사로 받는 주격 관계대명사

③ 저 소년이 반에서 키가 가장 크다. : 지시형용사

④ 두 개의 책 중 나는 저것보다 이것이 더 좋다. : 지시대명사

⑤ 김 씨는 너무 바빠서 어젯밤에 낚시하러 가지 않았다. : 「so+형용사+that+주어+동사」는 '너무 ~해서 …하다'라는 뜻의 절을 이끄는 접속사

27 그것이 내가 생각하고 있던 바로 그것이다. : '~한 것'(선행사를 포함하는 관계대명사)

① 네가 가장 좋아하는 노래는 무엇이니? : '무엇'(의문대명사)

② 몇 시에 만날까요? : '몇'(의문형용사)

③ 나는 그가 말한 것을 이해할 수 없었다. : '~한 것'(선행사를 포함하는 관계대명사)

④ 그는 정말 무엇을 해야 할지 모른다. : '무엇'(의문대명사)

⑤ 그럼 네가 무슨 책을 사는지 나에게 말해 봐. : '무슨'(의문형용사)

28 우리 아버지와 나는 붐비지 않는 거리를 걷고 있었다. 우리는 검은 고양이를 쫓고 있는 몇 마리의 개를 보았다. 나는 아버지에게 개들이 검은 고양이를 쫓고 있는 이유를 물었지만, 아버지는 아무 말 없이 계속 걸었다. : (A) the street가 선행사이고, was의 주어가 되는 주격 관계대명사 자리이므로 which가 와야 한다. (B) a few dogs가 선행사이고, were running의 주어가 되는 주격 관계대명사 자리이므로 which가 와야 한다. (C) the reason이 선행사이고, 이유를 나타내는 관계부사 자리이므로 why가 와야 한다.

29 그는 자신의 도움이 필요한 그 누구라도 도와줄 것이다. : anyone who = whoever

30 무슨 일을 하더라도 너는 성공할 수 없을 것이다. : no matter what = whatever

31 「what+주어+동사」 '~하는 것'

32 「whenever+주어+동사」 '~할 때마다'

33 나는 두 명의 딸이 있는데, 그들은 언론인이다. : 계속적 용법의 관계대명사를 사용하여 두 문장을 한 문장으로 전환한다.
I have two daughters.+They are journalists.
→ I have two daughters, who are journalists.

34 그녀는 내가 오늘 아침에 호텔로 가는 길을 물었던 소녀이다. : the girl을 선행사로 받는 목적격 관계대명사 who(m)[that]을 사용하여 두 문장을 한 문장으로 전환한다.
She is the girl.+I asked her the way to the hotel this morning. → She is the girl who(m)[that] I asked the way to the hotel this morning.

35 「whatever+주어+동사」 '~가 무엇을 하든'

36 「however+형용사+주어+동사」 '~가 아무리 …하다 할지라도'

보너스 유형별 문제
p.178

1 that

2 the parking lot where Rafael works

3 ⑤

[1-2] Rafael은 예술가이다. 그는 그림을 매우 잘 그린다. 사람들은 그가 만든 그림을 좋아한다. 하지만 Rafael과 그의 예술에는 뭔가 특별한 것이 있다. 그것은 그가 물감이나 붓을 사용하지 않고 그림을 그린다는 것이다. 사실 그는 자동차 위에 있는 먼지에 그림을 그린다. Rafael은 손가락을 사용하는데 차 위의 먼지 사이로 손가락을 이리저리 움직인다. 그의 손가락은 먼지 속에서 선을 만들고, 아름다운 건물과 새가 차 위에 나타나게 한다. 그 그림들은 너무 멋지게 보인다. 사람들은 먼지투성이 자동차를 Rafael이 작업하는 주차장에 두고 간다. 그들은 Rafael이 자동차 위에 그림을 그려주길 원한다. 저렴한 주차 요금으로 그들은 훌륭한 예술품을 갖게 된다.

1 선행사 the pictures가 오고 뒤에 주어와 동사가 오므로 목적격 관계대명사 which나 that이 옳은데 이 중 글에서 찾을 수 있는 있는 것은 that이다.

2 「선행사(장소)+관계부사 where+주어+동사」의 순으로 배열해야 옳다.

3 최근에 나는 자전거를 배워서, 자전거를 타고 출근하기로 마음먹었다. 출근길에는 멋진 풍경을 볼 수 있다. 먼저, 주말마다 친구들과 시간을 보내는 작은 공원을 따라 달린다. 평일에는 녹색 벤치에 앉아 신문을 읽고 있는 한 노인을 보게 된다. 공원을 지나면 사무실이 있는 거리로 이어지는 작은 다리를 건너야 한다. 그다음 퇴근길에 종종 과일을 사는 가게가 보인다. 두 블록 더 가면 내가 제일 좋아하는 음반 가게가 있다. 직장에서 길고 바쁜 하루를 보낸 후에 이 가게에 들러 여러 음악을 듣는다.
선행사 a fruit store는 장소이므로 when이 아닌 where가 쓰여야 옳다.

Chapter 11

11-1 상관접속사
p.180

Exercise 1

1 but
2 neither
3 and
4 but
5 either

Exercise 2

1 helps
2 are
3 like
4 is
5 sings, writes

Exercise 3

1 as well as
2 Either, or
3 Neither, nor
4 Both, and
5 not, but

Exercise 4

1 are → is
2 has to → have to
3 was → were
4 is → am
5 are → is

Exercise 5

1 He is irresponsible as well as selfish.
2 I have neither a pen nor a pencil.
3 This book is not only useful but also amusing.
4 Both he and she speak English fluently.
5 Neither Amanda nor her best friend came to the party.

11-2 종속접속사 I
p.182

Exercise 1

1 if
2 that
3 that
4 That
5 that
6 whether
7 that
8 whether

Exercise 2

1 whether　　　　2 whether
3 that　　　　　4 whether
5 that　　　　　6 that

Exercise 3

1 It is sad that he had a car accident.
2 It was strange that she was still at home.
3 It is natural that she has no knowledge of American history.
4 It is important that you gather information about the company.
5 It is impossible that he didn't get a wink of sleep for seventy-two hours.

Exercise 4

1 can't, believe, that
2 that, canceled
3 wondered, whether, or, not
4 don't, know, whether[if], or, not
5 isn't, sure, whether, or, not
6 asked, whether, or, not

11-3　종속접속사 Ⅱ　　p.184

Exercise 1

1 While　　　　2 If
3 while　　　　4 As
5 Unless　　　6 as

Exercise 2

1 As　　　　　2 While
3 As　　　　　4 Unless

11-4　종속접속사 Ⅲ　　p.185

Exercise 1

1 until　　　　2 until
3 since　　　　4 until
5 since　　　　6 since

Exercise 2

1 until the war is over
2 I have lived in the apartment since
3 until everyone left the room
4 He has been staying in New York since
5 Since the tickets to the match have been sold out

11-5　종속접속사 Ⅳ　　p.186

Exercise 1

1 despite　　　2 in spite of
3 Even if　　　4 Although
5 Though　　　6 Even though

Exercise 2

1 Although[though], he, is, poor
2 Although[though], I, stayed, up
3 Despite, all, her, efforts
4 Even, though[if], we, win
5 in, spite, of, bad, weather

11-6　기타 주요 접속사　　p.187

Exercise 1

1 no sooner　　2 by the time
3 so that　　　4 don't know, until
5 so, that　　　6 too, to
7 No sooner, than

Exercise 2

1 so, that　　　2 so, that
3 didn't, know, until　4 so, that
5 No, sooner, than　6 so, that, could

Exercise 3

1 so that we can see the picture
2 No sooner had the boy[The boy had no sooner] seen me than
3 It was so hot that I couldn't sleep
4 She was so busy with her businesses
5 Not until he heard my idea did he tell
6 so that she would not be late for the interview
7 They were so poor that they couldn't buy

11-7　전치사 Ⅰ　　p.189

Exercise 1

1 on　　2 as　　3 against
4 as　　5 for

Exercise 2

1 from　　2 in　　3 of[from]
4 in　　5 by, by

1 I'm writing a thesis on English grammar.
2 She has been seriously suffering from stress.
3 He isn't showing enough leadership as a manager.
4 the reason why we have to vote for him
5 looked very manly in his uniform
6 since the book is written in French
7 He is always against my opinion
8 almost sixteen-thousand children die of hunger
9 he went to school by bike
10 is known as an artist

11-8 전치사 II
p.191

Exercise 1

1 Thanks to
2 In addition to
3 despite
4 According to
5 instead of

Exercise 2

1 Despite[In spite of]
2 Instead of
3 Thanks to
4 In addition to
5 According to

11-9 동사, 형용사와 함께 쓰는 전치사
p.192

Exercise 1

1 at
2 of
3 of
4 of
5 to
6 after
7 in
8 to
9 into
10 to
11 for
12 from

11-10 주의해야 할 접속사/전치사
p.193

Exercise 1

1 while
2 because
3 during
4 because of
5 Despite

Exercise 2

1 Though[Although / Even though]
2 despite
3 While
4 because
5 during
6 Because of

Review Test
p.194

01 ④　02 ⑤　03 ①　04 ⑤　05 ②　06 ⑤
07 ④　08 ③　09 ②　10 ⑤　11 ③　12 ④
13 ①　14 ④　15 ②　16 ③　17 ⑤　18 ①
19 ③
20 so, that, couldn't, reach
21 no, sooner
22 as, well, as
23 ②　24 ③　25 ②　26 ③　27 ④　28 ①
29 ④　30 to　31 for　32 of
33 after, while, as
34 Even, though, he, had, enough, money
35 No, sooner, had
36 consists, of, ten, chapters

01 너와 그녀 둘 중 한 명은 방을 청소해야 한다. : 「either A or B」는 'A와 B 둘 중 하나'라는 뜻이다.

02 나는 여기에 온 이후로 한국 역사를 배우고 있다. : since는 '~한 이후로'라는 뜻이다.

03 그들은 공적이고 사적인 투자 둘 다 필요하다. : 「both A and B」는 'A와 B 둘 다'라는 뜻이다.

04 그는 어린데도 불구하고 복잡한 문제들을 풀 수 있다. : even though는 '~에도 불구하고'라는 뜻이다.

05 그들은 같은 디자인과 색깔의 옷을 입는 것이 싫증이 났다. : 「be tired of」는 '~에 싫증이 나다'라는 뜻이다.

06 • 그는 Eric과 Tony 둘 다를 자신의 생일 파티에 초대했다. : 「both A and B」는 'A와 B 둘 다'라는 뜻이다.
　• 그녀와 나 둘 다 그 영화를 좋아하지 않았다. : 「neither A nor B」는 'A와 B 둘 다 아닌'이라는 뜻이다.
　• 나는 중국어와 일본어 중 하나를 배우기를 원한다. : 「either A or B」는 'A와 B 둘 중 하나'라는 뜻이다.

07 • 나는 그 영화가 너무 지루해서 잠이 들었다. : 「so+형용사+that+주어+동사」는 '너무 ~ 해서 …하다'라는 뜻이다.
　• 햇볕이 있을 동안에 건초를 만들어라. : while은 '~동안에'라는 뜻이다.

08 • 네가 소녀들에게 관심을 갖는 것은 자연스러운 일이다. : 「be interested in」은 '~에 관심이 있다'라는 뜻이다.
　• 나는 내 연구에 집중을 할 수 없다. : 「concentrate on」은 '~에 집중하다'라는 뜻이다.

09 • 중국어로 쓰인 그 책은 너무 어려워서 이해할 수 없다. : 「in+언어」는 '~으로'라는 뜻이다.
　• 네 건강을 위해 콜라 대신에 주스를 마셔야 한다. : 「instead of」는 '~ 대신에'라는 뜻이다.

10 「not only A but also B」는 'A뿐만 아니라 B도'라는 뜻으로 B에 동사의 수를 일치시킨다.

11 「despite+명사(구)」, 「even though[though/although]+주어+동사」는 '~에도 불구하고'라는 뜻이다.

12 어두웠기 때문에 거리에서 아무도 볼 수 없었다. : since는 '~ 때문에'라

는 뜻으로 as로 바꿔 쓸 수 있다.

13 우리는 그녀가 돌아올 것인지 아닌지 확신하지 못한다. : whether는 '~ 인지 아닌지'라는 뜻으로 if로 바꿔 쓸 수 있다.

14 〈보기〉 비가 많이 와서 교통 체증이 매우 심했다. : 접속사(~ 때문에)
① 나는 네가 가지고 있는 것과 같은 가방을 가지고 있다. : 접속사(~와 같은, ~ 처럼)
② 우리는 세 배만큼 지불할 것이다. : 부사(꼭 그 만큼)
③ 그녀는 한국에서 가수로 매우 유명하다. : 전치사(~로)
④ 그들은 텔레비전을 보기를 원했기 때문에 거실로 나갔다. : 접속사(~ 때문에)
⑤ 내가 방에 들어갔을 때, 나는 엄마가 방을 청소하고 있는 것을 보았다. : 접속사(~ 할 때)

15 〈보기〉 나는 뉴욕으로 이사한 이후로 그녀를 본 적이 없다. : 접속사(~이 후로)
① 나는 유치원때부터 프랑스어를 배우고 있다. : 전치사(~이후로)
② 나는 여기에 온 이후로 그를 알고 지낸다. : 접속사(~이후로)
③ 나는 그의 주소가 없어서 그에게 편지를 쓸 수가 없다. : 접속사(~ 때문에)
④ 그들은 지난 주말 이후로 아무것도 먹지 않았다. : 전치사(~이후로)
⑤ 그는 배가 고팠기 때문에, 무엇인가 먹을 것을 원했다. : 접속사(~ 때문에)

16 〈보기〉 그가 살아있다는 것은 믿기 어려운 일이다. : 진주어절을 이끄는 접속사
① 이것과 저것 중에 어느 것을 선호하십니까? : '저것'이라는 의미의 지시대명사
② 그것이 그녀가 나를 보러 온 이유이다. : '그것'이라는 의미의 (지시)대명사
③ 내 방이 매우 지저분해서 부끄럽다. : 진주어절을 이끄는 접속사
④ 이것은 내가 어제 산 것과 같은 카메라이다. : 목적격 관계대명사
⑤ 나는 어젯밤에 화산이 폭발했다는 소식을 들었다. : the news의 동격절을 이끄는 접속사

17 「thanks to+명사(구)」는 '~ 덕분에'라는 뜻이다.

18 「according to+명사(구)」는 '~에 따르면'이라는 뜻이다.

19 「in spite of+명사(구)」는 '~에도 불구하고'라는 뜻이다.

20 소년은 너무 작아서 꼭대기 선반에 닿을 수가 없었다. : 「too+형용사+to+동사원형」=「so+형용사+that+주어+cannot+동사원형」은 '너무 ~해서 …할 수 없다'라는 뜻이다.

21 그녀는 집에 오자마자 요리를 하기 시작했다. : 「as soon as+주어+동사」, 「주어+had+no sooner+p.p.」, 「No sooner+had+주어+p.p.」는 '~하자마자 …했다'라는 뜻이다.

22 우리는 그들에게 약간의 돈뿐만 아니라 약간의 음식도 보냈다. : 「not only A but also B」=「B as well as A」는 'A뿐만 아니라 B도'라는 뜻이다.

23 • 그 영화는 그의 소설을 토대로 했다. : 「be based on ~」은 '~을 근거로 하다', '~을 토대로 하다'라는 뜻이다.
• 외교 문제에 관련된 그 책은 매우 유용하다. : on은 '~에 관한', '~에 관련된'이라는 뜻이다.

24 • 우리는 우리의 전통의상이 자랑스럽다. : 「be proud of」는 '~이 자랑스럽다'라는 뜻이다.
• 그들은 비웃음을 당하는 것이 두렵다. : 「be afraid of」는 '~이 두렵

25 만약 네가 학생이 아니라면 할인을 받을 수 없다. : unless(= if ~ not)는 '만약 ~이 아니라면'이라는 뜻이다.

26 그녀의 많은 단점에도 불구하고 우리 반 학생들은 모두 그녀를 많이 좋아한다. : 「in spite of+명사(구)」는 '~에도 불구하고'라는 뜻이다.

27 ① 서두르면, 버스를 잡을 수 있을 것이다.
② 내가 요리를 하는 동안 그는 통화를 했다.
③ 그는 작년부터 런던에 살았다.
④ 그는 목이 말랐기 때문에 마실 것을 원했다. : '목이 말랐음에도 불구하고 마실 것을 원했다.'라는 의미가 성립되지 않으므로 Though가 아니라 이유, 원인을 나타내는 Because, As 등이 되어야 한다.
⑤ 그녀는 열심히 연습해서 오디션에 통과할 수 있었다.

28 ① 우리는 생선회를 먹는 것에 익숙하다. : 「be used to+-ing」는 '~하는 데 익숙하다'라는 뜻으로 eat이 아니라 eating이 되어야 한다.
② 그녀는 나보다 영어를 잘한다.
③ 어젯밤에 강도들이 보석가게에 침입했다.
④ 그 덕분에 나는 사고를 피할 수 있었다.
⑤ 많은 학생들이 새로운 학교 정책에 반대하고 있다.

29 ① 그 소설은 흥미 있을 뿐만 아니라 감동적이었다.
② 그녀가 결혼식에 참석할 것은 확실하다.
③ 나는 그녀가 우리가 찾고 있는 소녀인지 아닌지 모른다.
④ 만약 내일 바쁘지 않으면 해변에 가자. : '만약 내일 바쁘면 해변에 가자.'는 의미상 어색하기 때문에 if가 아니라 unless가 되어야 한다.
⑤ 우리 형은 너무 늦게 일어나서 학교에 늦었다.

30 이 노트북 컴퓨터는 누구의 것입니까? : 「belong to」는 '~에 속하다'라는 뜻이다.

31 나는 여기서 거의 두 시간 동안 너를 기다리고 있었다. : 「wait for」는 '~를 기다리다'라는 뜻이다.

32 James는 낚시를 매우 좋아해서 일주일에 한 번씩 낚시하러 간다. : 「be fond of」는 '~을 좋아하다'라는 뜻이다.

33 그녀는 병원에서 간호사로 근무하는 동안 자신의 아이를 돌봐 줄 사람이 필요하다. : 「look after」는 '~을 돌보다', while은 '~동안', as는 '~로서'라는 뜻이다.

34 「even though+주어+동사」는 '~임에도 불구하고'라는 뜻이다. 「enough+명사」는 '충분한 ~'라는 뜻이다.

35 「no sooner had+주어+p.p.」는 '~하자마자 …했다'라는 뜻이다.

36 「consist of」는 '~으로 구성되다'라는 뜻이다.

보너스 유형별 문제 p.198

1 Maybe you texted me while I was cooking.

2 If[whether]

3 by

4 ③

[1-3] A 내가 한 시간 전에 문자 보냈는데, 못 받았어?
B 정말? 아마도 내가 요리하고 있을 때 네가 문자를 했나 봐. 무슨 일이야?
A 내가 케이팝 메가 콘서트 표가 2장 있거든. 네가 나랑 같이 가고 싶은지 궁금해.

B 좋지! 그게 언제니?
A 내일 저녁 8시야. 올림픽 경기장에서 열려.
B 공연 전에 저녁을 먹는 게 좋겠다. 우리 언제 만날까?
A 우리는 7시 반까지 경기장 안에 들어가야 하니까 그 햄버거 가게에서 6시에 만나자.

1 접속사 while(~하는 동안)을 이용하여 두 절(you texted ~ / I was cooking)을 연결해야 적절하다.

2 문맥상 '~인지 아닌지'라는 의미로 접속사 if나 whether가 빈칸에 적절하다.

3 7시 30분까지 경기장 안에 들어가야 한다는 내용에서 들어가는 동작이 계속되는 것이 아니라 그 상태가 완료되는 시점까지만 들어가면 되는 것이기에 전치사 by가 적절하다.

4 5년 또는 10년 전까지만 해도 대학 졸업생들은 직장을 찾아서 좋은 경력을 쌓을 수 있을 것이라는 자신감을 가지고 학교를 마칠 수 있었다. 그러나 요즘은 상황이 매우 다르다. 어려운 경제로 인해 졸업 후 곧바로 취업하는 졸업생들은 거의 없다. 기업도 경제적 여유가 없기 때문에 신입 사원을 거의 고용하지 않고 있다. 대신에 많은 졸업생들이 돈을 아끼기 위해 부모님 집에서 함께 살려 하고, 직장 경험을 얻으려고 무보수의 인턴직을 기꺼이 받아들이고 있다.
'because of' 뒤에는 단어나 구가 뒤따라야 하는데 글에서는 절(they simply can't ~)이 뒤따르므로 접속사 because가 쓰여야 옳다.

Chapter 12

12-1 병렬구조
p.200

Exercise 1

1 I	2 playing
3 French	4 on the table
5 withdrew	

Exercise 2

1 not a singer but a dancer
2 and bought a watermelon
3 either call or e-mail him
4 neither in your bag nor on your desk
5 is talented in not only singing but also dancing

12-2 병렬구조의 형태
p.201

Exercise 1

1 kind	2 built
3 in	4 for his mother

Exercise 2

1 I have done this not for me but for you.

2 Neither Eric nor his wife is interested in home decoration.
3 You should either tell him the whole thing or keep it to yourself.
4 Both collecting old coins and making miniatures are my hobbies.
5 I was home yesterday not because I had nothing to do, but because I was sick.

12-3 동격
p.202

Exercise 1

1 The fact that Jerry left Bonnie doesn't surprise me.
2 Tommy, one of my classmates, helped me find the key.
3 The idea of living in the countryside sounds appealing to me.
4 I can't believe the news that the Raiders won the championship.
5 My plan of losing weight and getting into better shape in three months has failed.

Exercise 2

1 Your hobby of collecting
2 The fact that I wasn't on the guest list
3 Timothy, your best friend
4 Your idea of using bacon as bait
5 Tokyo, the capital of Japan

12-4 강조
p.203

Exercise 1

1 My dad repaired his car himself.
2 What on earth did you do there?
3 I did have a good time with them.
4 Who in the world told you to do that?
5 You are the very woman I want to see.
6 Dogs can run much faster than humans.
7 This is the very ring that I was looking for.
8 My daughter herself solved the difficult problem.
9 You should have been more careful. I did warn you.
10 This sofa is even more comfortable than I expected.
11 Emily does look pale. I think she should go to see a doctor.
12 Ms. Charlton did drop by his office, but she couldn't meet him.

Exercise 2

1 myself	2 does
3 by far	4 on earth

5 the very   6 at all

Exercise 3

1 himself, painted
2 does, look, exhausted
3 far, better, than
4 doesn't, help, at, all
5 the, very, man, who
6 Why, on, earth, does, he, bother

12-5 「It is[was] ~ that …」 강조 구문   p.205

Exercise 1

1 who   2 where
3 when   4 which

Exercise 2

1 It was on the bed that[where] I found the necklace.
2 It was three years ago that[when] I graduated from Yale.
3 It was in 1492 that[when] Columbus discovered America.
4 It was Gary that[whom] I ran into on my way from school.
5 It was five dollars that[which] I borrowed from Mary yesterday.
6 It was Rachel that[who] majored in English Literature at Oxford University.

12-6 도치   p.206

Exercise 1

1 Down came the rain.
2 In the restroom was your wristwatch.
3 Right on his desk was the document.
4 Behind the door are steps leading downstairs.
5 On the desk were the books written by Hemingway.
6 In front of the building is the statue of Don Quixote.
7 At the corner of James and Victoria Streets stands a children's hospital.

Exercise 2

1 Little do I know about him.
2 Rarely does it snow in Busan.
3 Hardly can I believe what he said.
4 Never have I seen such a beautiful sight.

Exercise 3

1 So am I.   2 Neither could I.
3 Neither do I.   4 So did I.

Exercise 4

1 On the top of the hill stands a tall tree.
2 On the floor were pieces of broken glass.
3 Never have I heard of the theory.
4 Hardly could I breathe at the moment.

12-7 생략   p.208

Exercise 1

1 What an awful day it is!
2 He said that he would be back by seven.
3 The Sun rises in the east and it sets in the west.
4 Have you read the book that I recommended to you?
5 She had a simple breakfast and she ran to school.
6 Do you know the old man who is sitting over there?
7 I could finish the work, but he couldn't finish the work.
8 Have you ever seen the woman who is standing in front of the bank?
9 When he was working as a part-time waiter, he saved some money.
10 The novels which were written by Rowling are very popular all around the world.
11 He wanted to play soccer after school, but I didn't want to play soccer after school.

Exercise 2

1 they were   2 that
3 who[that] is   4 have a lot of homework
5 that   6 will be served
7 we were

Exercise 3

1 Look at the tree. What a tall tree it is!
2 I tried to talk to her, but I couldn't talk to her.
3 Do you know the girl who[that] is talking to Sam?
4 My younger brother is even taller than Paul is.
5 Ted got up and he went to the gym right away.
6 Some went there by subway, and others went there by bus.
7 These are the books which[that] you were looking for yesterday.
8 Lisa asked me to stand in for her, but I didn't want to stand in for her.
9 Everyone knows that Jeff is the smartest boy in our school.
10 When we were in elementary school, we used to play hide-and-seek.

01 ③　02 ①　03 ③　04 ③　05 ④　06 ④
07 ⑧　08 ③　09 ⑤　10 ①　11 ②　12 ⑤
13 ①　14 ④　15 ③　16 ⑤　17 ①　18 ④
19 ③, ④　　20 ②, ③　　　21 the very
22 in the world　23 much 24 ⑤　25 ③　26 ②
27 ④　28 ③　29 neither, do, I
30 neither, can, Jimmy
31 very　　　32 himself
33 am I　　　34 Neither
35 have I heard of such an amazing story
36 did she know how much I loved her
37 comes the doctor
38 have I been sick since I became a vegetarian
39 Ava is bright and diligent.
40 He can sing and play the piano at the same time.
41 We did have a good time.
42 was at the park that[where] John lost his dog yesterday
43 How did you know this is the very thing I wanted to have?
44 myself helped him overcome the difficulties he was facing
45 I am examining a sculpture discovered at the ancient historic site.

01　나는 우리가 경기에 졌다는 사실을 믿을 수 없다. : 빈칸 뒤에 주어, 동사, 목적어가 다 있는 완전한 절이 왔으므로 빈칸에는 the fact의 동격절을 이끄는 접속사 that이 와야 한다.

02　도대체 누가 그런 이상한 이야기를 믿겠어? : 의문사를 강조할 때는 on earth나 in the world를 쓴다.

03　그는 나를 전혀 이해하지 못한다. : 부정문을 강조할 때는 'not ~ at all' 구문을 쓴다.

04　그는 단연 가장 빨리 달리는 사람이다. : 최상급을 강조할 때 by far를 쓴다.

05　내 직장상사는 내가 자신과 함께 뉴욕에 가기를 정말 원했다. : 과거 시제의 일반동사를 강조할 때는 「did+동사원형」을 쓴다.

06　〈보기〉 그들은 네가 시험에 통과하기를 정말 바란다. : hope를 강조하는 do이다.
　　① 연필을 가지고 있니? : 일반동사의 의문문을 만드는 do
　　② 나는 항상 최선을 다할 것이다. : '최선을 다하다'라는 뜻의 do one's best에 쓰인 본동사 do
　　③ 너는 어제 무엇을 했니? : '~을 하다'라는 의미의 본동사 do
　　④ 나는 영혼의 존재를 정말 믿는다. : believe를 강조하는 do
　　⑤ 그는 영어를 나보다 더 유창하게 한다. : speak을 대신하는 대동사 do

07　③ 부사를 강조할 때는 강조하는 단어를 문장의 앞으로 보내고 주어, 동사의 어순을 바꿔 준다. 주어와 동사의 어순을 바꿀 때 일반동사는 일반동사가 직접 주어 앞으로 나가지 않고 do동사가 대신 나간다. 이때 do

동사는 시제와 인칭에 맞게 바꾸고 뒤에 남아있는 일반동사는 동사원형으로 쓴다.

08　③ 동사를 강조하는 did가 쓰였으므로 did 뒤에는 taught가 아니라 동사원형인 teach가 와야 한다.

09　⑤ the very는 최상급 형용사를 강조하는 것이므로 taller라는 비교급 형용사를 강조하기 위해서는 much, far, even, still, a lot 등을 쓴다.

10　① 부정문을 만드는 do는 생략할 수 없다.
　　② 감탄문의 「주어+동사」는 생략 가능하다.
　　③ 「관계대명사+be동사」 뒤에 분사가 오는 경우, 「관계대명사+be동사」는 생략 가능하다.
　　④ when(ever), while, if 등의 부사절에서 「주어+be동사」는 생략 가능하다.
　　⑤ when(ever), while, if 등의 부사절에서 「주어+be동사」는 생략 가능하다.

11　① 소유격 관계대명사는 생략할 수 없다.
　　② 목적격 관계대명사는 생략 가능하다.
　　③ 「관계대명사+be동사」 뒤에 분사가 오는 경우, 「관계대명사+be동사」는 생략 가능하지만, 관계대명사만은 생략할 수 없다.
　　④ 주격 관계대명사는 생략할 수 없다.
　　⑤ 주격 관계대명사는 생략할 수 없다.

12　① I met your mom.이라는 문장을 목적어인 your mom을 강조한 문장으로 바꿔 쓴 것이므로, 「It ~ that」 강조 구문의 that이다.
　　② I lost my wallet in the mall.이라는 문장을 in the mall을 강조한 문장으로 바꿔 쓴 것이므로, 「It ~ that」 강조 구문의 that이다.
　　③ John sent me some presents yesterday.라는 문장을 yesterday를 강조한 문장으로 바꿔 쓴 것이므로, 「It ~ that」 강조 구문의 that이다.
　　④ A Korean musician performed at the Carnegie Hall.이라는 문장을 A Korean musician을 강조한 문장으로 바꿔 쓴 것이므로 「It ~ that」 강조 구문의 that이다.
　　⑤ a fact의 동격절을 이끄는 접속사 that이다.

13　very는 원급을 강조하는 부사로 비교급을 강조하지 않는다.

14　the plan(계획)과 make a biking trail in our neighborhood(우리 동네에 자전거 길을 만들자)가 동격이므로 이 둘을 동격의 of로 연결한 문장인 ④ He came up with the plan of making a biking trail in our neighborhood.가 가장 바르게 영작된 문장이다. 전치사 of 뒤에는 명사 상당어구가 와야 하므로 make를 making으로 바꿔 준 것이다.

15　③ 감탄문의 주어와 동사는 생략 가능하다.

16　⑤ 반복되는 어구는 생략 가능하다.

17　① 목적어 절을 이끄는 접속사는 생략 가능하다.

18　yesterday(어제)를 강조하는 문장이 되어야 하므로 「It ~ that」 강조 구문을 사용한 ④ It was yesterday that I met Tony.가 정답이다.

19　on my birthday를 강조한 구문으로 빈칸에는 that이 와야 하고, 강조하는 구문이 시간 부사인 경우, that 대신 when을 쓸 수 있으므로 빈칸에 들어갈 수 있는 것은 that과 when이다.

20　Jeff를 강조한 구문으로 빈칸에는 that이 와야 하고, 강조하는 말이 사람이고 주격인 경우, that 대신 who를 쓸 수 있으므로 빈칸에 들어갈 수 있는 것은 that과 who이다.

21　이것이 내가 받기를 원하는 바로 그 선물이다. : 명사를 강조할 때는 the very를 쓴다.

43

22 도대체 네 친구와 무엇을 할 거니? : 의문사를 강조할 때는 in the world를 쓴다.

23 그는 자신의 모든 학급 친구들보다 훨씬 키가 크다. : 비교급을 강조할 때는 much를 쓴다.

24 ① 나는 그것을 매우 사랑했다.
② Jones 씨는 매우 친절한 여성이다.
③ 그 영화는 매우 재미있다.
④ 나는 네가 올 수 있어서 매우 기쁘다.
⑤ 그가 내가 파티에서 만난 바로 그 남자이다.

25 ① 내 컴퓨터를 고쳐준 사람은 바로 Tom이었다. : Tom을 강조한 「It ~ that」 구문의 that이다.
② 내가 정말로 읽기를 원하는 바로 그 책이다. : the book을 강조한 「It ~ that」 구문의 that이다.
③ 그녀가 시험에 합격할 것은 분명했다. : 진주어절을 이끄는 접속사 that이다.
④ 우리가 함께 배드민턴을 친 날은 바로 어제였다. : yesterday를 강조한 「It ~ that」 구문의 that이다.
⑤ 내가 어제 Sally를 만났던 곳은 바로 이탈리아 식당이었다. : in the Italian restaurant를 강조한 「It ~ that」 구문의 that이다.

26 Hardly가 강조되어 문장 앞으로 나왔으므로 주어와 동사의 어순이 바뀌어 ② I have가 아니라 have I가 되어야 한다.

27 나는 다리가 부러졌다. 나는 낚시를 가지 않고 집에 머물렀다. : didn't go와 staying이 병렬 구조를 이루므로 ④ staying이 아니라 stayed 가 되어야 한다.

28 토요일과 일요일 둘 다 안 돼. 나는 그 이틀은 한가하지 않을 거야. : Saturday와 on Sunday가 병렬 구조를 이루므로 ③ on Sunday가 아니라 Sunday가 되어야 한다.

29 그녀는 모험을 좋아하지 않는다. 그리고 나도 모험을 좋아하지 않는다. : 일반동사의 부정에 대한 동의를 나타낼 때는 「neither+do동사+주어」를 쓴다.

30 Joe는 피아노를 칠 줄 모른다. 그리고 Jimmy도 피아노를 칠 줄 모른다. : 조동사의 부정에 대한 동의를 나타낼 때는 「neither+조동사+주어」를 쓴다.

31 이것은 내가 정말로 보고 싶은 바로 그 영화다. : 명사를 강조할 때는 the very를 쓴다.

32 Tony는 그 스스로 부서진 라디오를 고쳤다. : 주어를 강조할 때 재귀대명사를 쓴다. Tony는 3인칭 단수(남성)이므로 himself가 적절하다.

33 '그는 특히 노인을 돕는 자원봉사에 관심이 있다.'라는 말에 '나도 그래.'라는 긍정의 동의를 표현할 때는 「so+조동사[be동사/do동사]+주어」를 쓴다.

34 '나는 그가 오는 것을 보지 못했다.'라는 말에 '나도 못 봤어.'라는 부정의 동의를 표현할 때는 「neither+조동사[be동사/do동사]+주어」를 쓴다.

35 나는 한 번도 그렇게 놀라운 이야기를 들어 본 적이 없다. : never가 강조되어 문장의 앞에 나왔으므로 주어와 동사의 어순이 바뀐다. 완료시제의 경우 have동사가 주어 앞으로 온다.

36 내가 그녀를 얼마나 많이 사랑했는지 그녀는 거의 알지 못했다. : little이 강조되어 문장의 앞에 나왔으므로 주어와 동사의 어순이 바뀐다. 일반동사의 경우 일반동사가 직접 주어 앞으로 나가지 않고 do동사가 대신 나간다. 이때 do동사는 시제와 인칭에 맞게 바꿔야 하고 뒤에 남아있는 일

반동사는 동사원형으로 쓴다.

37 여기 의사선생님이 오신다. : here, there가 도치되어 문장의 앞으로 나갔더라도 주어가 인칭대명사(I, you, he, she 등)이면 주어와 동사는 도치되지 않는다.

38 나는 채식주의자가 된 이후로 거의 아파 본 적이 없다. : rarely가 강조되어 문장의 앞으로 나갔으므로 주어와 동사의 어순이 바뀐다. 완료 시제는 have동사가 주어 앞으로 온다.

39 Ava는 영리하고 부지런하다. : bright와 diligence가 병렬 구조를 이루므로 diligence가 아니라 형용사 diligent가 되어야 한다.

40 그는 노래를 부르면서 동시에 피아노를 칠 수 있다. : sing과 plays가 can에 연결된 병렬 구조이므로 plays가 아니라 play가 되어야 한다.

41 동사를 강조할 때는 do동사를 본동사 앞에 인칭과 시제에 맞게 써 주고, 본동사는 동사원형으로 쓴다.

42 부사구를 강조할 때는 「It ~ that」 강조 구문을 이용하거나, 부사구를 문장의 맨 앞으로 보내고 주어와 동사를 도치시킬 수 있는데 여기서는 앞에 It이 나왔으므로 It과 that 사이에 강조하는 단어나 구를 쓴다.

43 명사를 강조할 때는 명사 앞에 the very를 쓴다.

44 인칭대명사를 강조할 때는 재귀대명사를 쓴다.

45 「관계대명사+be동사」 뒤에 분사가 오면 「관계대명사+be동사」는 생략 가능하다.

보너스 유형별 문제   p.214

1 playing
2 much[even, still, far, a lot]
3 neither had my parents
4 ③

[1-3] 나는 탁구를 정말 좋아한다. 나는 보는 것뿐만 아니라 직접 하는 것도 즐긴다. 우리 학교는 탁구 동아리가 있어서 가입하기를 원했다. 하지만 그 동아리는 가입하고 싶은 모든 사람들을 받아들이지 않는다. 사람들은 그 동아리에 가입하기 위해서 시험을 통과해야 한다. 불행하게도, 나보다 훨씬 잘 하는 사람들이 많아서 나는 시험에서 떨어졌다. 나는 내가 떨어질 것이라고 절대 예상하지 않았고 나의 부모님도 그랬다.

1 'not only A but also B(A뿐만 아니라 B도)'에서 A와 B의 형태는 같아야 하므로 동명사인 watching에 따라 play를 playing으로 써야 적절하다.

2 비교급(better)을 수식하는 표현으로 by far가 아닌 much, even, still, far, a lot을 쓴다.

3 'I had never thought ~'는 부정문이므로 이에 동의하기 위해 so가 아닌 neither가 쓰이고 조동사 had가 그대로 쓰인 'Neither had my parents.'가 적절하다.

4 스마트폰과 컴퓨터가 점점 대중화됨에 따라, 이제 대부분의 사람들은 자기 기계로 게임을 합니다. 하지만 불과 20년 전만 해도, 미국의 가장 인기 있는 게임은 알록달록한 말판과 직접 움직여야 하는 말이 들어 있는 상자였습니다. Monopoly, RISK, Sorry! 같은 게임들은 이제는 역사 속으로 사라지고 있습니다. 장난감 가게에서는 더 이상 많은 보드게임을 취급하지 않는데다가, 탁자에 둘러 앉아 친구들과 게임을 하는 것이 어떤 것인지 아는 아이들은 점점 없습니다.
주어가 you이므로 이에 맞는 재귀대명사 yourself를 써야 옳다.

Workbook

Chapter 1
p.218-220

A
1 has lost
2 has taught
3 has gone
4 have worked
5 has had
6 has remained

B
1 I have been to France once.
2 Jeremy hasn't read my text messages yet.
3 The janitor mopped the floor yesterday.
4 We have known each other for ten years.

C
1 have been sick since last week
2 has passed since you left Korea
3 have never seen anything like it.
4 has been preparing for this event for two months
5 have never been happier

D
1 have been
2 have changed
3 has been waiting
4 has stolen
5 has been playing

E
1 has been dealing
2 When did they discover
3 have you traveled to so far
4 have I been lying
5 has moved

F
1 had already left
2 had never met
3 had deleted
4 moved
5 couldn't drive
6 had never learned

G
1 had been depressed, texted
2 had been working well, went out
3 realized, had read
4 had never tried, met
5 had already watched, watched

H
1 ○
2 will have lived
3 for
4 ○
5 had finished

I
1 has been interested in coding
2 will have already repaired the car
3 has been working
4 will have downloaded the files
5 had phoned you several times
6 had never taken the subway

Chapter 2
p.221-223

A
1 to be
2 to see
3 to buy
4 to enjoy
5 to leave

B
1 It is not necessary to wear a suit.
2 It is easy to pass Ms. Davidson's history class.
3 It is possible to rent electric scooters with this app.
4 It is dangerous to touch this metal without gloves on.

C
1 is a great person to work with
2 something to eat
3 a magazine to read
4 someone to look after
5 a chair to sit on
6 cash to pay

D
1 great songs to listen to
2 no one to talk to[with]
3 many friends to hang out with

E

1 You are to show up on time.

2 The two old friends were to meet again.

3 If we are to make more money, we have to invest more.

4 She was not to be forgiven.

5 The capital city is to be locked down due to the virus spread.

F

1 Jayden will write her a letter in order to tell her how he feels.

Jayden will write her a letter so as to tell her how he feels.

2 I took a taxi to the airport in order not to miss my flight.

I took a taxi to the airport so as not to miss my flight.

G

1 to leave

2 scream(ing)

3 ask

4 to come

H

1 to have already moved the sign

2 to be

3 to have seen

4 to know

I

1 smart enough to enter

2 old enough to drive

3 too stubborn to listen

4 too dark to read

5 too big to fit

J

1 To tell the truth

2 Needless to say

3 To begin with

4 To sum up

5 To make matters worse

Chapter **3** p.224-226

A

1 trusting

2 closing

3 Raising[To raise]

4 coming

5 making

B

1 for not interrupting

2 his[him]

3 being[to be] treated

4 Walking[To walk]

5 is

6 not accepting

7 being rejected

8 raining[to rain]

C

1 being alone

2 having kept you waiting

3 seeing a live performance

4 having wasted your time

5 my[me] calling you

D

1 Not taking enough rest

2 Being able to speak different languages

3 taking photos of nature

4 putting a fence around the park

5 drinking lots of water is good

E

1 that he/she had stolen my bike

2 that my son saved the dog from drowning

3 that he had lied his wealth

4 that she had to go through the same process again

F

1 to talk[talking]

2 to give

3 working

4 reading

5 to let

6 trying

7 talking

8 having

G

1 skiing

2 seeing

3 building

4 reading

5 persuading

6 going

7 fixing

8 being

9 hearing

10 swimming

H

1 had difficulty understanding
2 is busy looking after
3 got used to working
4 contributed to creating more jobs
5 It is no use worrying about
6 could not help falling asleep
7 is not worth reading

Chapter 4

p.227-229

A

1 spoken
2 repaired
3 disappointed
4 injured
5 playing

B

1 touching / touched
2 exciting / excited
3 interesting / interested
4 amazing / amazed

C

1 wearing a yellow blouse
2 called Biscuit
3 hidden under the mattress
4 made in Korea
5 working at the airport
6 crawling up my leg

D

1 Listening to the radio
2 drinking a glass of wine
3 Being brave enough
4 Living alone
5 Graduating from high school

E

1 Being sick
2 (Being) Distracted by him
3 (Being) Seen from above
4 with her arms crossed
5 with a rock in his hand

F

1 Having no money
2 Reading the novel
3 Waiting for her date
4 Being really bored

5 Doing your best
6 having apple pie for dessert

G

1 Arriving home, my mother headed straight
2 Taken to the hospital, the poor girl couldn't receive
3 Walking down the street, I ran into
4 Not getting paid enough, he decided to find

H

1 with his hands tied behind his back
2 with my arm hanging out the window
3 with her eyes closed
4 with her dog following behind

I

1 Judging from her voice
2 when asking
3 Strictly speaking
4 The weather being awful
5 Speaking of Mr. Henderson

Chapter 5

p.230-232

A

1 Can
2 be able to
3 be able to
4 can
5 can

B

1 may go
2 may[might] be
3 May I take
4 may[might] have

C

1 should have told
2 shouldn't talk
3 should take
4 should go
5 should have been
6 shouldn't have stayed

D

1 used to
2 would
3 used to
4 used to
5 would

E

1 They should have listened to me
2 I had better not go to that party.
3 People should avoid eating raw fish
4 We had better get going
5 You ought not to make any mistakes

F

1 must have forgotten
2 can't[cannot] have passed
3 must have said
4 can't[cannot] have seen
5 may[might] have been
6 must love

G

1 운전을 하면 안 된다
2 안 해도 돼
3 알아낸 것이 틀림없다
4 하고 있어야 한다

H

1 would
2 should
3 need
4 cannot
5 must

I

1 may have taken your phone
2 must have been very exciting
3 should have prepared something more special
4 could have gotten an 'A,'
5 cannot have said those horrible things

Chapter 6 p.233-235

A

1 was revealed
2 are scanned
3 was robbed
4 was made

B

1 was being downloaded
2 should be removed
3 has not been located
4 are being washed

C

1 be taken

2 are not included
3 was built
4 be solved
5 be postponed

D

1 was offered to him
  was offered another opportunity
2 is taught to freshmen
  are taught basic chemistry
3 were given to Freya
  was given a two-story house and a brand new car

E

1 were made to clean up
2 is allowed to enter
3 was heard playing
4 are called Generation Z.
5 was told

F

1 was taken good care of by me
2 will be carried out by a team of international specialists
3 should be taken away by a tow truck
4 was called off because of the typhoon (by them)
5 was almost run over by the driver

G

1 in
2 as
3 from
4 to
5 to
6 of
7 at
8 with

H

1 is filled with stuffed animals
2 is always covered with snow
3 were not satisfied with the result
4 is known for her husky voice

I

1 are thought to be good at math
2 is believed that the actor has three children
3 is said that nothing can travel faster than light
4 was considered to be the man responsible for the accident

Chapter 7

p.236-238

A

1 is
2 had seen
3 feel
4 would go
5 were

B

1 weren't / wouldn't have to
2 were / could ride
3 spoke / would know
4 hadn't had / could enjoy
5 hadn't been / wouldn't have fallen

C

1 Finn had known what to do
2 I would collect sports cars
3 my parents wouldn't have been so angry
4 she lived next door
5 your little sister wouldn't have cried

D

1 were
2 had worn
3 would have
4 would have been
5 would be

E

1 I lived by myself
2 you had watched the sunrise with us
3 there were more books in the library
4 Alex could come to my birthday party
5 she were quieter

F

1 If I had brought my wallet with me, I could have lunch now.
2 If Toby hadn't gone to the bathroom, we could get on the train now.
3 If Molly hadn't dropped my phone, I wouldn't be angry with her now.
4 If you hadn't forgotten your passport, we would be flying to Hawaii now.
5 If the driver had been careful enough, the passengers wouldn't be in the hospital now.
6 If I had spent my allowance wisely, I wouldn't only have $1 in my bank account now.

G

1 But for his help, we wouldn't have survived.
  Without his help, we wouldn't have survived.
2 But for the police, people wouldn't feel safe.
  Without the police, people wouldn't feel safe.
3 But for the moon, it would get so dark at night.
  Without the moon, it would get so dark at night.
4 But for your advice, I couldn't have expanded my business.
  Without your advice, I couldn't have expanded my business.

H

1 as though he had plenty of experience
2 Were it not for this application
3 Had it not been for her warning
4 as if she had saved thousands of lives
5 Were I smart enough
6 If you should come back to Korea
7 Had he known about your health conditions

Chapter 8

p.239-241

A

1 as early as
2 as well as
3 as interesting as
4 as expensive as
5 as often as
6 as pretty as
7 as loudly as

B

1 not as expensive as
2 more money than
3 the youngest
4 faster than

C

1 than
2 to
3 than
4 to
5 to
6 than

D

1 than
2 the more, the less
3 of
4 even, much, far, still, a lot 등

E

1 The faster / the bigger its energy becomes
2 The more vegetables / the healthier you get
3 his muscles grew stronger and stronger
4 The more effort / the greater results

F

1 taller than
2 as clearly as he could
3 as long as possible
4 as delicious
5 as great
6 as exciting
7 as quietly as they could

G

1 the most wonderful
2 the toughest
3 the hottest
4 the smartest
5 the tallest

H

1 darker and darker
2 The larger / the more
3 would rather get
4 as soon as possible
5 the strangest movie

I

1 more intelligent than any other member
  No other / more intelligent than
  No other / as intelligent as
2 wealthier than any other man
  No other / wealthier than
  No other / as wealthy as
3 deadlier/more deadly than
  No other / deadlier/more deadly than
  No other / as deadly as

Chapter **9**   p.242-244

A

1 was
2 comes
3 are
4 is
5 is
6 have
7 is

B

1 seem
2 costs
3 is increasing
4 are

C

1 was
2 would
3 landed
4 makes
5 takes

D

1 she liked me
2 she was going to pass out
3 how I had fixed the door
4 they could fly

E

1 told / melts
2 believes / is a talented singer
3 learned / started in 1950
4 said / would do
5 remembered / had borrowed a pen

F

1 if[whether] I wanted to go to the movies with him
2 if[whether] I had seen his baseball cap
3 what I was doing the next day
4 why I called[had called] him the previous day[the day before]
5 she had to do the dishes then

G

1 "Don't[Do not] touch my laptop."
2 "Do you know when Henry will be back?"
3 "Have you eaten?"
4 "Where can I park?"
5 "I get up at 6 every morning."

H

1 advised my dad to quit
2 told them not to cross
3 told me she could help me
4 asked her brother where he had hid
5 said she had to make

I

1 told us to get out of the water
2 asked me if I had seen someone suspicious
3 ordered his men not to speak to one another
4 asked Sienna how she had arrived before him

Chapter 10

p.245-247

A

1 which[that]
2 whose
3 that[who(m)]
4 that[which]
5 what

B

1 what she did
2 who[that] were waiting for
3 which[that] Ruby is reading
4 which[that] Ethan was writing with

C

1 The movie I watched yesterday was boring.
2 Did Rosie see the girl sitting by the window?
3 She is the character I love the most in the story.
4 The man walking down the stairs is my father.
5 The plan he had come up with seemed brilliant.
6 I ate the cookie on the table.

D

1 which people are most active
2 which[that] I was born
3 who is very wise and polite
4 which is located at 11th Avenue and Wall Street
5 which we had for lunch
6 which[that] my parents sleep

E

1 how
2 where
3 when
4 why

F

1 why Grace was absent
2 how the main character avenges
3 where he used to live
4 when the tragedy happened

G

1 This is the time of the year when[at which] we can enjoy cherry blossoms.
2 Noah didn't tell us the reason why[for which] he showed up late to class.
3 There are several ways (in which) you can improve your English.
4 This is the hall where[in which] your birthday party will be held.
5 The coffee shop where[in which] we first met is now shut down.

H

1 Whenever
2 Who(m)ever
3 whoever
4 whatever
5 However

I

1 Whatever you do
2 wherever I go
3 however rich he is
4 Whoever wishes to enter the contest
5 whichever movie you would like
6 whenever I talk to him

Chapter 11

p.248-250

A

1 loves
2 have
3 knows
4 need

B

1 either coffee or juice
2 Either he went to bed early or he lost his phone.
3 both under water and in the dessert
4 both expensive and impractical
5 not only intelligent but also hardworking
6 Neither Emily nor her boyfriend likes
7 Neither my next-door neighbor nor I
8 Not only Holly but also we

C

1 Whether
2 that
3 that
4 that
5 whether[if]
6 that
7 whether

D

1 Unless the steps are repaired, someone will get hurt.
2 If it is not dark and quiet, I can't go to sleep.
3 If he doesn't call you, you don't have to come to work tomorrow.

4 Unless you show me yours first, I am not going to show you mine.
5 Unless she is ready, she shouldn't lead the marketing department.
6 If you don't have further questions, you may go back to your seat.

E

1 since
2 by the time
3 While
4 Although
5 until
6 so that
7 even if
8 because

F

1 As long as the tenants pay their rent on time
2 while my twin brother is interested in art and music
3 so delicious that I had another piece
4 Unless they have better plans

G

1 Although[Even though / Though]
2 in
3 by
4 because
5 while
6 of

H

1 instead of walking there
2 in spite of the pandemic
3 According to news reports
4 thanks to the new policy
5 during the holiday season

Chapter **12**	p.251-253

A

1 beautiful
2 they or I
3 correctly
4 writing an essay

B

1 Sarah loves not only swimming but also rock climbing.
2 Both Emma and Eva are able to speak German.
3 Uncle Bill likes neither cooking nor drinking.
4 What the journalist said was both important and

shocking.
5 She either listens to music or watches TV after dinner.

C

1 do look
2 does have
3 do feel
4 did remain
5 did see
6 does love

D

1 two weeks ago that the student lost his backpack
2 Elliot that I watched the basketball game with
3 taking out the trash that my dad wants to avoid
4 in the closet that my cats were sleeping quietly
5 Grace that bought me a hat for my birthday
6 a cheeseburger that the delivery man had for supper
7 at four that the singer is scheduled to start her rehearsal

E

1 Where in the world have you been?
2 It is in the backyard that the kids are having
3 Chloe does drink chocolate milk every day
4 How on earth did you find out
5 It was Gabriel who voted against
6 It was a decade ago when he made his professional debut

F

1 So am I.
2 So was I.
3 Neither do I.
4 Neither could I.

G

1 could they believe what I had told them
2 were my father's books
3 had he been so embarrassed before
4 do they have breakfast on school days

H

1 has she complained about her work schedule
2 did James realize his wallet was missing
3 stood a giant oak tree
4 lived a young couple from Canada

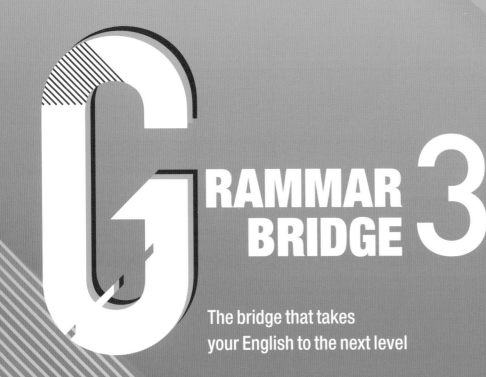

GRAMMAR BRIDGE 3

The bridge that takes
your English to the next level

This 3-level grammar series for basic learners of English

- covers the middle school grammar curriculum
- provides complete and simple explanations
- helps learners to compose sentences properly
- includes a workbook section with extra exercises

	초1	초2	초3	초4	초5	초6	중1	중2	중3	고1	고2	고3

Writing

- 공감 영문법+쓰기 1~2
- 도전만점 중등내신 서술형 1~4
- 영어일기 영작패턴 1-A, B · 2-A, B
- Smart Writing 1~2

Reading

- Reading 101 1~3
- Reading 공감 1~3
- This Is Reading Starter 1~3
- This Is Reading 전면 개정판 1~4
- 원서 술술 읽는 Smart Reading Basic 1~2
- 원서 술술 읽는 Smart Reading 1~2
- [특급 단기 특강] 구문독해 · 독해유형
- [앱솔루트 수능대비 영어독해 기출분석] 2019~2021학년도

Listening

- Listening 공감 1~3
- The Listening 1~4
- 넥서스 중학 영어듣기 모의고사 25회 1~3
- 도전! 만점 중학 영어듣기 모의고사 1~3
- 만점 적중 수능 듣기 모의고사 20회 · 35회

TEPS

- NEW TEPS 입문편 실전 250⁺ 청해 · 문법 · 독해
- NEW TEPS 기본편 실전 300⁺ 청해 · 문법 · 독해
- NEW TEPS 실력편 실전 400⁺ 청해 · 문법 · 독해
- NEW TEPS 마스터편 실전 500⁺ 청해 · 문법 · 독해